Cecilia Goodenough.

9 . 9 . 38 .

Cecilia Green.

LOGIC FOR USE

BY THE SAME AUTHOR

RIDDLES OF THE SPHINX. Revised Edition, Macmillan, 1910. (*Out of print.*)

HUMANISM. Second edition, Macmillan, 1912.

STUDIES IN HUMANISM. Second edition, Macmillan, 1912.

FORMAL LOGIC. Macmillan, 1912.

AXIOMS AS POSTULATES—in PERSONAL IDEALISM. Macmillan, 1902. (*Out of print.*)

PLATO OR PROTAGORAS? Blackwell, Oxford, 1908.

SCIENTIFIC DISCOVERY & LOGICAL PROOF—in Singer's STUDIES IN THE HISTORY AND METHODS OF SCIENCE, vol. i., Clarendon Press, 1917.

HYPOTHESIS—in the same, vol. ii., 1921.

WHY HUMANISM?—in CONTEMPORARY BRITISH PHILOSOPHY, vol. i., George Allen & Unwin, 1924.

PROBLEMS OF BELIEF. Hodder & Stoughton, 1924. Second edition.

PSYCHOLOGY AND LOGIC—in PSYCHOLOGY AND THE SCIENCES, edited by Dr. W. Brown. A. & C. Black, 1924.

TANTALUS OR THE FUTURE OF MAN. Kegan Paul, 1924. Second edition.

EUGENICS AND POLITICS. Archibald Constable, 1926.

CASSANDRA OR THE FUTURE OF THE BRITISH EMPIRE. Second edition, Kegan Paul, 1928.

SOME LOGICAL ASPECTS OF PSYCHICAL RESEARCH—in THE CASE FOR AND AGAINST PSYCHICAL BELIEF, edited by Carl Murchison. Clark University Press and Oxford University Press, 1927.

LOGIC FOR USE

An Introduction
To the Voluntarist Theory
of Knowledge

By

FERDINAND CANNING SCOTT SCHILLER
M.A., D.Sc.

Fellow and late Tutor of Corpus Christi College,
Oxford ; Fellow of the British Academy ;
Professor of Philosophy in the
University of Southern
California

LONDON
G. BELL & SONS LTD
1929

Printed in Great Britain by
NEILL & CO., LTD., EDINBURGH.

PREFACE

In my *Formal Logic* I undertook a radical criticism of the traditional logic by challenging the fundamental abstraction on which it is built, the abstraction from Meaning. I showed, in full detail, how all the troubles of logic arose out of this unavowed abstraction, and tried simultaneously to make this systematic exposure useful as a really intelligible textbook of the 'examinable nonsense' called logic. In this I do not appear to have altogether failed; for my friend, Professor R. T. Flewelling, assured me that he had used *Formal Logic* with success for the instruction of a class of oil engineers in Los Angeles. California is a wonderful country; in England it hardly sounds credible that any sort of engineer or scientist should want to study any sort of logic!

To the destructive criticism of *Formal Logic* this book is intended to be the constructive sequel. Its appearance has been delayed by that tragedy of academic organisation which renders it impracticable for an academic teacher to publish his thoughts while he is still actively teaching; actually most of it was delivered as a course of 'Special Lectures' in the University of California at Los Angeles and at Berkeley, in the first part of 1929. At Oxford, where free inquiry is stifled, and education is enslaved to an essentially unprogressive and practically rigid examination system, this course could never have been given: it would not have been considered 'good for the Schools.' Nevertheless, such of my former pupils as do me the honour of reading it will recognise many of the doctrines which figured for many years in my Logic Lectures for the School of *Lit. Hum.*

The title, perhaps, demands a few words of explanation. To call a book a *Logic for Use* is not to claim that its perusal will turn a bad reasoner into a good one; nor is it to deny that Logic is a *theory* of reasoning. But it is a protest against the subterfuge that a theory is none the worse for being useless, and against the absolute and absurd divorce between 'theory' and 'practice' by which Intellectualism endeavours to conceal

v

its intellectual bankruptcy. It is also to imply that Logic should be *a theory of actual reasoning*, and that a logical theory which cannot conceivably be applied to life and used in scientific inquiry cannot possibly be right: it is not a true 'ideal' of thought, but a false theory of Logic.

'Voluntarism' has been substituted for 'Humanism' in order to sharpen the antithesis to the old Logics, and to bring out wherein they have all failed for the past 2300 years. They have all been based on *intellectualist* assumptions, which they have never examined, and which when examined turn out to be nothing but uncritically accepted conventions of language. In their flight from Psychology they fell a prey to verbiage. Their chief weakness was that they utterly ignored the actual character of human knowing and its relation to the problems of human life. Working on these assumptions, the devoted labours of seventy generations of logicians have reduced the science to a sort of order—as 'examinable nonsense'; but the assumptions themselves are arbitrary and unnecessary. For, as Professor Santayana has profoundly said, "Reason is free to change its logic, as language to change its grammar." It seemed worth while therefore to give some reasons for changing the old logic (which *is* grammar), and to show that Logic *can* dispense with intellectualism. It need not, after all, abstract from meaning, and from the actual procedures of human knowers, nor idolise the immutability of words; and it may be all the better for changes in these customs.

On the other hand I would willingly admit that the Logic of Voluntarism is still in its infancy, and that nothing which is written on it at present can claim to be more than an 'introduction.' But I am buoyed up with the hope that if philosophers will only steel themselves to tolerate the thought that their subject *ought* to be progressive, like the sciences, voluntarist logic may be adorned with technicalities and difficulties enough to be recognised as 'examinable' and 'good mental training,' *without* lapsing into nonsense, in *much less* than two thousand years. As yet, no doubt, it can hardly hope to impress the sort of professional who despises what he can understand even more than what he cannot, and loves technicality, not merely for its own sake, but because it makes him feel superior and 'scientific.' I have not pandered to his tastes, and am aware that I am courting martyrdom at his hands by what he is sure to resent as the culpable simplicity and contemptible easiness of this book. But it was written to interest students, and particularly students of the sciences, in the cognitive operations of their minds; so I may perhaps be forgiven for the offence of writing a Logic that can be read without a professorial commentary.

For the same reason I have refrained as much as possible from foot-notes, references, and controversy: I felt also that I had in my day done enough academic controverting to allow myself, at last, the luxury of straightforward exposition.

I am greatly indebted to my friends, Alfred Sidgwick and Howard V. Knox, who have read the book in typescript and made many helpful suggestions. The latter has also helped me by reading the proofs.

F. C. S. SCHILLER

Los Angeles, *June* 1929

CONTENTS

CHAPTER   PAGE

I. The Uses of Logic 1

II. The Definition of Logic 19

III. Logical Values 36

IV. Meaning 49

V. Relevance 75

VI. Truth 95

VII. The Theories of Truth 116

VIII. The Humanist Theory of Truth . . 145

IX. Error 175

X. The Biologic of Judgment . . . 193

XI. The Formal Theories of Judgment . . 208

XII. From Judgment to Inference . . . 238

XIII. Inference in General 247

XIV. Syllogistic Reasoning 269

XV. The Theory of Proof 287

XVI. Valuable Reasoning 320

XVII. Scientific Method 353

XVIII. Scientific Method—continued . . . 385

XIX. The Casuistry of Knowing . . . 416

XX. Conclusion 440

Index 457

CHAPTER I

THE USES OF LOGIC

1. On understanding ; 2. Is logic useless ? ; 3. Logic as reflection on actual thinking ; 4. Logic as examinable nonsense ; 5. Logic as a bugbear ; 6. Logic as the great word-game ; 7. The inadequacy of verbal meaning ; 8. Greek verbalism : (1) Plato ; 9. (2) Aristotle's verbalism ; 10. Why not convey personal meaning with verbal ? ; 11. Is personal meaning merely psychological ? ; 12. Logics as word-games ; 13. Logic as the handmaid of metaphysics ; 14. Logic's flight to the Absolute ; 15. Is Absolutism logically sound ? ; 16. The autonomy of logic.

§ 1. On Understanding.

The human mind is filled with a longing to understand all things, even itself. But as it does not understand itself sufficiently, neither does it understand 'understanding.' Especially, it does not understand that in understanding it is always *assimilating to itself.* It makes itself at home in the world by interpreting world-processes on the analogy of its own proceedings: yet when it has succeeded in so doing it often disowns its procedure. It claims to have done nothing to bring about the result, and to have merely watched, in pure passivity, the 'independent' development of the objects it 'knows.' This is a great delusion; but it is taken as a guarantee of integrity and good faith.

Were we not so anxious to deceive ourselves we should be willing to accept the limitations of our nature and the method to which they doom us. We should make a virtue of necessity. We should admit that to understand is to interpret in human *and congenial* terms, and should cease to be ashamed of this. We should boldly ask the questions to which we naturally wish to get the answers, and rejoice when they revealed a nature consonant with our own.

In particular, we should no longer be ashamed to ask *What is the use?* of the various things we do. For the human mind is *purposive*, and naturally seeks to justify its various activities by discovering, and approving of, their uses, though it is all too prone to be distracted from them and to be led astray into

1

self-frustrating follies. For all human institutions have a way of growing into perversions of their original purpose that block its attainment. Into the why of this we need not enter here, beyond remarking that those who run the institutions are allowed to acquire interests that conflict with the professed purpose of the institutions they serve;[1] but the remark holds true of our sciences, and especially of Logic. Logic has aimed to be (in some sense) the science of thought; but who in these days would have the audacity to search a logical treatise for light upon the nature of his thinking? He is far more likely to take to Yoga, or to submit himself to psycho-analysis. Yet every one is naturally interested in his thinking, and no one is fully educated until he can understand it. Unfortunately their technical interests have prompted logicians so completely to depersonalise Logic that, in its actual condition, it can yield him no help. So he naturally asks *What is the use of Logic?*, and hardly expects to get an intelligible answer.

§ 2. Is Logic Useless?

Indeed to the man in the street it seems too plain for words that Logic has *no* use, and is consequently hardly worth a thought. He listens therefore to all logical doctrines and disputes with the same stolid indifference or contempt. It is unfortunate, moreover, that he should find so many logicians to agree with him about the uses of Logic: only they draw from his premisses the more flattering conclusion that, since Logic is useless, it must be a high-class theoretic science.

Those on the other hand who have seen that the only way of dealing with impudent and frivolous allegations is to subject them to the pragmatic test of truth, will find it impossible to believe that Logic should have no use: for, were this so, it would follow that it also had no truth, and, in the last resort, no meaning. And though it may in fact be the innermost meaning of the traditional logic that it is a strictly meaningless science, i.e. a game with verbal counters which rests on an

[1] Cp. *Tantalus*, p. 28 f.

abstraction from meaning,[1] it is clear that it would never do to publish this fact at the outset: it could be revealed, if at all, only to experienced adepts who were irrevocably pledged, by years of professorial training and their whole manner of life, not to give away their secret and their livelihood. Moreover, if this should prove to be the real kernel of Logic, it would prove, not that Logic was useless, but that it served as an essential element in the air of mystery which screens the academic life from the gaze of the profane.

Thus closer attention to the matter soon reveals that it is nonsense to deny a use to Logic. The truth is rather that Logic has *many* uses, and that the uses for which it is intended really decide what shall pass for Logic, and determine a 'logic's' character completely. Hence there is no quicker way of penetrating to the core of Logic than to investigate the uses to which Logic is actually put; and we may most fitly begin with a preliminary sketch of the worthiest and most proper use of Logic, though it is, as yet, the rarest.

§ 3. Logic as Reflection on Actual Thinking.

Thinking actually occurs only when an intelligent being capable of thought finds that he has to think; that is, finds himself in a situation where his habits and impulses no longer seem to suffice to guide his actions. He has then *to stop to think* (Chap. X, § 6). Thought arises, therefore, in a quandary, when he no longer seems to himself to know what to do, or is in doubt as to what he had *better* do. The primary purpose of his thinking is thus determined by its origin. It is, to get over his difficulty, to solve his problem, to learn what to do. Thinking is thus a definite stage in a process of knowing, and the knowing has for its origin the stoppage, and for its aim the guidance, of action.

Now it is obvious that all these relations can be investigated, and studied scientifically. It is hardly less obvious that such reflective study may be beneficial, if it *improves* our thinking,

---

[1] For the detailed proof of this suggestion see *Formal Logic*, throughout.

knowing, and acting. If it does not, it is simply a waste of time, and no study for those who have not time to waste. In point of fact, it is usually found that scientific study *is* beneficial: it does improve the processes it studies, by revealing avoidable sources of deficiency and failure which had been overlooked. If this holds true of logic also, we may fairly expect our logical reflections upon thought to issue in suggestions for the improvement of our actual thinking, and such improvement will be the first use of Logic.

But the *ought* of such suggestions will be based strictly on the 'is' of actual practice; Logic will not attempt to lay down the law to thought before there has been any thinking which it has observed. Logical rules will rest on observation of psychical facts, and will not be prior to them as 'laws' which can dictate to fact. It is the purpose of this work to exhibit the possibility, importance, and value of this conception of the use of Logic. It has, however, little vogue among logicians, who (for reasons of their own) mostly prefer to conceive

§ 4. Logic as Examinable Nonsense.

By far the most important and lucrative of the uses of Logic in the academic world and training is to provide a fertile field of examinable nonsense, by cultivating which professors can make a living. It has fulfilled this function ever since Aristotle invented the syllogism, and indeed for a generation or two before him. Only before Aristotle Logic was *debatable nonsense*, the field of 'dialectics,' and the playground on which the Sophists and Socrates could exercise their pupils. Thus, under one name or other, it has figured as an essential ingredient in higher education throughout the world. It might have been supposed, therefore, that in the course of nearly 2500 years its *technique* would have reached such perfection, its rules such refinement, its principles such precision, that by this time no question remained to be asked, with the consequence, of course, that Logic would have ceased to be examinable. This suggestion argues unfamiliarity with the arts of the examiner. No examination ever dies a natural death from sheer exhaustion: even the

Chinese Civil Service Examination, after dominating China for some 3000 years, had to be suppressed by revolutionary violence. So it was easy enough from time to time to inject into the 'logic' of the schools reference enough to the real problems of thinking that were troubling mankind to replenish the supply of examination questions. The rules and presuppositions of the industry could always be trusted to bring it about that by the time a question had been put into 'logical form' it had become examinable nonsense. Subconsciously logicians have long known that their 'science' is nonsense, though it is only in rare moments of precious candour that they are found to confess, with Mrs Ladd-Franklin, "Of course, nonsense propositions are far better for practising logic on than propositions that make sense." [1] She then goes on to ask her colleagues what her "propositions" mean!

Fortunately we need not here linger over this use of Logic: its nature, methods, and results have been so fully studied in *Formal Logic*, that we may refer to it for the hideous details.

§ 5. Logic as a Bugbear.

Nor need much be said about Logic as a bugbear to frighten women withal, and to intimidate the practical man. This is merely a literary or journalistic use, which is not even quite sincere. Satirical references to 'feminine Logic' are simply part of the regular masculine denigration of the feminine intellect, and do not really mean that men are conspicuously more apt than women to listen to logic and to reason. When it looks likely to thwart their passions, they do not yield to logic, but lose their temper and damn logic, like President Wilson on a famous occasion.[2] Again, when the practical man is alleged to defy Logic and to get on with 'practical makeshifts,' there is usually an insinuation that he does well not to trouble about so pedantic a superfluity. We may approve of the sentiment,

---

[1] *Journal of Philosophy*, vol. xxv, p. 700.
[2] "Logic! Logic!" exclaimed the President, "I don't care a damn for logic. I am going to include pensions."—J. M. Keynes, *A Revision of the Treaty*, p. 151.

though not of the reason given for it, namely, that the practical man can always be trusted to muddle through by common sense, 'intuition,' and rule of thumb. This last is also the reason why even our most patriotic journalists (and Sir Austen Chamberlain) never shrink from confessing that other people are more 'logical,' to wit the Latins, and especially the French. On this foible Mr Bertrand Russell's comment cannot be bettered.[1] "What is meant is that, when they accept a premiss, they accept also everything that a person totally destitute of logical subtlety would erroneously suppose to follow from the premiss. This is a most undesirable quality." He himself concludes that "Logic was formerly the art of drawing inferences: it has now become the art of abstaining from inferences, since it has appeared that the inferences we feel naturally inclined to make are hardly ever valid. I conclude therefore that Logic ought to be taught in schools with a view to teaching people not to reason. For if they reason, they will almost certainly reason wrongly." If this is all Logic is good for, no wonder John Bull and the practical man generally are so willing to admit that they are not 'logical.' Such admissions are tinctured with a feeling that in the affairs of life logicality is a trifle absurd, and cost them little; for they are under no illusions as to the value of 'Logic.' Nor are they very far wrong in point of fact, though they are not aware of the reason why. Men of affairs do not use logic, because *no one uses, or can use, the traditional logic*, either for practical or for scientific guidance! Logicians themselves, in moments of candour, admit as much. Mr F. H. Bradley quite agrees about this with Mr Russell. At the end of a long life devoted to logical contemplation, he confessed, "In my actual reasonings, I myself certainly have never troubled myself about any logic."[2]

Possibly, however, these confessions only mean that the traditional 'logic' is not constructed to deal with 'actual reasonings,' and that it would be better, alike for Frenchmen, Britishers, and logicians, if some one undertook to construct a

---

[1] In the *Century Magazine* for December 1926.
[2] *Principles of Logic*,[2] p. 621 ; cp. p. 534.

logic that *was* fit to use and that did not disdain to consider actual reasonings. After all Logic might set itself the ideal, not of 'proving' but of *improving* our knowledge, and certainly a logic that really described the processes of actual thinking in attaining truth might do something to improve them; it would never play the bugbear, and could not safely be ignored or defied by anyone.

§ 6. Logic as the Great Word-Game.

Of course Logic was not originally conceived as a bugbear, nor as the systematic nonsense which results from the abstraction from real meaning. It was born innocent, with the noblest, if somewhat quixotic, ambitions. It did not become examinable nonsense until it had been adapted to the convenience and needs of the professorial caste which made its living by teaching it. Its original aspirations were far loftier. By Aristotle Logic was meant to be the analysis of thought, the method of scientific knowing, the formally valid procedure of logical proof, the guarantor of absolute certainty, and the final classification of ultimate reality. Of these functions the first two would now be regarded as essentially psychological, the next two as logical, while the last would be consigned to metaphysics. It must be admitted, therefore, that the founder of Logic set before his new science a sufficiently comprehensive ideal of work.

Unfortunately Aristotle skipped a preliminary which has proved to be essential. He failed to institute an adequate examination of the structure of Language, and of its functions as the vehicle of meaning; and this was a serious omission. For Language is the instrument by which we normally express our thought, and seek to convey it to others.[1] Language is much the most important, because the most *convenient* way of communicating with others; it is, in consequence, in practically complete control of the passes in intersubjective intercourse: by

---

[1] In academic intercourse the use of other symbols or modes of expression is negligible. For the *argumentum baculinum*, though it has not infrequently been used in the Schools, has always been felt to be logically inelegant, and classed as a ' fallacy.'

using words alone do we obtain access to any thought or any
fact which does not fall within our immediate ken. But words
can also *block* access to whatever they refuse to recognise, and
can distort what they fail to apprehend aright; while, conversely,
whatever has obtained verbal recognition has the support of an
impressive organisation, and is unquestionably real for some
purposes at least. It is tempting, therefore, to take it as real for
other purposes as well, and difficult to treat it as a mere phantom
of linguistic mythology.

§ 7. The Inadequacy of Verbal Meaning.

Nevertheless, a really thorough analysis of thought can never
stop short at words. Words are essentially representative
symbols and vehicles of meaning. So meaning is the ultimate
court to which there should always be an appeal from verbal
technicalities, and the meaning to be apprehended is that of
the man who has used words to convey *his* meaning. There is
always in the last resort a question what his meaning *was*, and
whether he *succeeded* in conveying it. Both these questions,
moreover, are questions of fact, of psychic fact, and history;
and no assumptions, either of 'logic' or of language, should
be allowed to overrule them. The meaning of every judgment,
the only real meaning it has, or can have, is the meaning it *had*,
and was *meant* to have, in the context in which it was made.
All the rest is *ex post facto* speculation about words—and endless and fruitless at that. For the words in which the meaning
was conveyed can, nay must, be used again in various contexts
to convey further meanings. The number of these is not limited,
like that of the words even of the most copious language. So
every word has to express a number of meanings. Hence *in
principle* all words, and all the 'propositions' in which they
can be combined, have an indefinite *plurality* of meanings. In
the misleading phraseology of traditional logic they are all
'*ambiguous*' (Chap. IV, § 7). But it is futile to study their ambiguity as if it could be catalogued in advance of their use, and
fatal to confuse it with the potential plurality of meanings on
which the usefulness of words depends. For, on the one hand,

it is in principle absurd to seek to determine all possible meanings in advance of their occurrence, *a priori*. No one can foresee how a word's meaning will be perverted or extended. And even if he could, he would only render the word *pro tanto* useless. For it could not henceforth be used to convey *new* meanings. On the other hand, the potential plurality of meanings which is inherent in the proper use of words need not involve any *real ambiguity*.[1]

This latter should be said to occur only when a form of words actually conveys different meanings to different persons, or perhaps when it is *intended* so to do. *Verbal* ambiguity, or better *plurality of senses*, which is universal, harmless, and useful, should be sharply distinguished from *real* ambiguity which is tricky and comparatively rare.

§ 8. Greek Verbalism: (1) Plato.

Now the Greek thinkers did not in general know any language but their own, and so problems of translation never forced them to realise the variability of the verbal equivalents [2] of things and ideas, and to separate the thing and their idea of it from their word for it. Their naïve failure to discriminate these three things comes out most conspicuously in a favourite word like λόγος. Here one and the same word has to do duty alike for the *word*, the *notion*, and the essential definition of the thing. So the Greeks never fully grasped the trickiness of language, though they devised many of its finest examples. They were, therefore, far more at the mercy of words than we have any excuse for being.

Plato, for example, unhesitatingly accepts the claim of language, embodied in the form of predication, to express stable being and to guarantee absolute reality. When we say of a flying arrow 'Lo, now it is at A,' the 'is' means a rest which arrests the arrow's motion, and stultifies the evidence of our senses. Thus in a sense his whole Ideal Theory is evolved out of the

---

[1] See further, Chap. IV, §§ 6, 7, 10, and *Formal Logic*, chap. ii, § 8.
[2] It is on this that the educational value of translation largely depends.

verbal implications of the word ' *is*,' which still haunt modern logic with the unsolved problem of ' the existential import of the copula.' That which can be predicated, i.e. stated intelligibly, alone *is*, and conversely whatever *is* can alone be stated intelligibly, while whatever *changes* both is and is not, and so flounders unintelligibly between being and not-being. When our senses, therefore, present us with a flow of changes they discredit themselves. The real cannot change, as the sensible seems to do. This appearance cannot be reality. *That which is* is to be grasped by reason alone, and the changeless alone is real. What a weird phantasmagoria the Platonic metaphysician conjures up out of the little word ' is ' !

§ 9. (2) Aristotle's Verbalism.

Aristotle accepts the philosophic testimony of the facts of language almost as uncritically. His Categories were intended to be a classification of ultimate realities, of ' kinds of being '; it did not strike him nor perturb him that actually they were a rough classification of the principal parts of speech. Throughout his logical researches he never doubts the adequacy of the verbal expression of a thought to express that thought; he never goes behind it to the mind of its thinker. So he innocently set the fatal fashion of accepting the form of words called the 'proposition' as representative of the actual meaning expressed in a judgment. This assumption has dominated Logic ever since, and ruined it. For by a single blow it rules out all the psychological antecedents of the 'judgment,' all inquiry into the motives, aims, and meaning of its maker, into his means of conveying it to others, into the establishing of meaning, into the formation and growth of verbal meaning—in short, into everything that lies beyond the two ends ('terms') of the 'proposition.'

§ 10. Why not Convey Personal Meaning with Verbal?

Nor has there been, at any time since Aristotle, any systematic inquiry into meaning and the possibilities of communicating it, into the relation of the word-symbol to the objects it was used to symbolise, or into the adequacy of verbal meaning to represent actual meaning. If at any time a logician grew weary of teaching his examinable nonsense, or conceived the nobler ambition of achieving something scientifically useful, he at once took up with the idea of a logic that could make a direct attack upon the *thing*, the object thought about, and could thereby *grow* into a valid ontology. Or else he set himself to put an end to the slipperiness of words, to arrest their variations, to catalogue their meanings exhaustively, and to distinguish them more sharply, and to fix them for good and all by precise definition. The really fundamental questions were never raised, nay, their existence was hardly suspected. It never occurred to him to inquire into the function of words as vehicles of meaning, or to question the assumption by which 'logic' was restricted to the meanings of words, or to go behind them to the meaning of the person who was using the words to express *his* meaning.

§ 11. Is Personal Meaning merely Psychological ?

The technical obstacle to raising the really vital questions consisted in the assumption that they did not belong to logic, but to another science. What anyone meant when he used a form of words was 'merely a matter of psychology,' and logically irrelevant; so, too, what anyone else *understood* (or misunderstood) did not affect *the* meaning of the words. Logic was bound to abstract from these complications, and could not be expected to trouble about the indefinite ramifications of individual psychology. The Logician could refuse to recognise 'designation,' i.e. the meaning words were intended to convey in an actual context, and could proudly retort upon the heretic labouring to say what he meant, "You are once and for all and for ever condemned to mean what you *say*.[1] . . . When, for example, you say 'this,' the question is not as to what you are sure is your meaning if only you could utter it. The question is as to what you have got, or can get, in an ideal form into your judgment [i.e. proposition]. And when you revolt against the conclusion that 'this' appears to be a mere unspecified universal, when you

---

[1] Italics mine.

insist that you know very well what this *meant*, and protest that your object was something other than such illogical [i.e. *verbal*] trifling and child's play, . . . what are you doing, we ask, with us here on this road? . . . Our whole way doubtless may be a delusion, but, if you choose to take this way, your judgment means what ideally [i.e. *verbally*] it contains," etc.[1]

So the logician continued contentedly to contemplate his abstract terms and 'propositions' and the 'valid forms' of their connexion. The harder he contemplated the more stable they seemed. So it was natural enough to assume that, ideally if not actually, they could, and should, be fixed. By this assumption he seemed to himself to set beyond the range of doubt the claim of Logic to rank among the 'exact' sciences. If all ambiguous terms could be banished from its vocabulary, if all its technical terms could be defined exactly, the logical calculus would be inexpugnable and its conclusions absolutely true. And incidentally the logician would be enabled to lord it over the sciences, to lay down the law to them, and to decide how nearly they approached to his logical 'ideal.'

§ 12. Logics as Word-Games.

Actually this calculation proved to be erroneous. Although theoretically an infinite number of formal 'logics' could be constructed in this way, according as one term or another was taken as fundamental and indefinable,[2] there could be no guarantee in

---

[1] F. H. Bradley, *Essays on Truth and Reality*, p. 234. The whole passage shows how incapable even so eminent a critic of Formal Logic in its narrower sense was to emancipate himself from its fundamental assumptions, and will justify the comparative scantiness of references to the doctrines of his school. The truth is that 'Idealist' logic, while just as essentially formal as other forms of Formal Logic, is more obscure and less consistent, and even more secretive about the assumptions on which it rests. These qualities have naturally recommended it to academic philosophers who conceive their subject as an exercise in mystification with a flavour of edification.

[2] It is, of course, impossible to define *all* terms ; for the first term to be defined must be defined in terms which are not yet defined, and if these are subsequently defined in terms to the definition of which they have contributed, the definition argues in a circle, a heinous 'fallacy' in formal Logic. For the validity of attempts to turn the 'circle' into a 'system,' see Chap. XV, §§ 8–16.

advance that any of them would be more than a word-game in the end, of which the assumptions would prove to be unrelated to the behaviour of the real, and of which the rules would have little or no bearing on the methods which had to be used in order to know the real successfully. The traditional Formal Logic, which professes to rest on the so-called 'Laws of Thought,' was merely the simplest of these word-games, but neither the most ingenious, nor the most consistent, nor the most completely analysed : it owes its premier position mostly to its convenience for examination purposes.

§ 13. Logic as the Handmaid of Metaphysics.

Philosophers in their inquiries are not often animated, even in their own minds, by the 'disinterested' love of truth they advocate. Far more commonly they are trying to prove some pet theory of their own, in a more or less surreptitious manner. Formerly such 'proofs' used to take the form of proving the existence of God, *a priori*, and without appeal to experience, by some ingenious (or puerile) juggling with words. Hence philosophy seemed content to be a 'handmaid of theology,' *ancilla theologiæ*. The real reason for this subservience was, of course, that it was only on condition of such menial service that these philosophers were allowed to lead the contemplative life they preferred.

After that came a period, heralded by Bacon, when attempts were made to turn philosophy into a handmaid of science, and to conceive 'Logic' in particular as an apparatus which anyone could set in motion for fabricating machine-made truths. But the apparatus would not work, and philosophic pride soon revolted against so subsidiary a function, while the scientists found their work growing too engrossing to have time for logical subtleties : so little came of these efforts, and both sides have now tacitly dropped them.

Philosophy has achieved its independence and is no longer willing to go out into service. Its adepts have emancipated themselves alike from orthodox theology and from scientific control. Every philosopher is now free to construct a metaphysic of his own, with himself as centre and ideal, and to make the rest of his philosophising minister to this ambition. So he elaborates arguments purporting to show that things are not what they seem, and that his thought also is not the petty personal thing it seems, but something far greater and more glorious, and, in truth, divine.

Logic is, of course, pressed into the service of such attempts, and has suffered grievously. It has become a handmaid of metaphysics and been systematically confused therewith. This confusion was rendered easy by the abstraction from the individual knower and the substitution of verbal for personal meaning (Chap. IV). This substitution assigned to Logic the study, not of any actual human intelligences, but of 'intelligence as such.' This can thereupon easily be magnified into something superhuman, because it is not bound by the limitations of any actual mind. We may see the process beginning in Kant and flourishing in Hegel, powerfully aided by the convenient vagueness of the German article.[1] But it is only in the British Hegelians that it is exaggerated into flat contradiction of the actual procedure of human minds and ends in an overt and complete repudiation of human knowing.

§ 14. Logic's Flight to the Absolute.

The most audacious of these attempts to exploit Logic in the interests of metaphysics is that which was advocated by the English 'idealists,' F. H. Bradley and B. Bosanquet. It appeals strongly to the craving for certainty and the willingness to be satisfied with a purely verbal validity, and purports to show that the search for truth, and the demand for valid proof, inevitably conduct the logician straight into the bosom of the Absolute. Its contention is that every judgment and every demonstration are potentially false, because liable to be upset by unforeseen facts and conditions which were not taken into account when they were propounded. It is not possible, therefore, to say how far they are infected with error. Their truth remains essentially

---

[1] It is never possible to tell in Hegel whether *der Geist* means the individual or the universal ' spirit.'

precarious, until they have somehow eradicated or transcended this possibility of error.

But how is this to be achieved? There is only one way. To become really safe and valid every judgment and every proof must obtain a guarantee from the supreme authority, the totality of reality. After that nothing can upset, or even assail, a judgment or a proof thus sanctified. For every consideration that could affect, and detract from, its absolute truth must *ex hyp.* have been included in the all-including whole and rendered incapable of harm. Thus the fangs of every objection are drawn *in advance*, and the Absolute's guarantee once granted is absolute protection against error.

It follows as a corollary that every judgment, no matter what it professes to be about, fails to state the meaning it aims at (its *own* meaning) fully. Failing to state all the conditions which may affect its truth, it means perforce more than it says; and when it tries to make explicit what it means, it has to expand and to include more and more, until it realises that it must take all things into account and cannot stop short of the Absolute. Thus the ultimate object of every judgment must be the totality of reality.

Similarly, proof in ultimate analysis means inclusion in an all-inclusive system. For only such a system yields full assurance; it protects all its contents by the threat 'that or nothing,' whenever any part is questioned; that is, it claims to be so systematic, so perfectly coherent, that nothing can be subtracted from it, or altered in it, without entailing the total ruin of the whole. Now this, it is argued, no objector can conceivably contemplate. It would mean total scepticism, and this is unthinkable. For it could nowhere find standing ground from which to overthrow the cosmos.

§ 15. Is Absolutism Logically Sound?

Is this argument logically sound? It is at any rate specious and impressive. Nor is it a wonder that the contemplation of the contrast, between the wretched insecurity of our truths while they are bandied about in the mouths of men and their ineffable immutability once they are safely lodged in the bosom of the Absolute, should fill absolutist logicians with pseudo-religious ecstasy.

Nevertheless, the bargain that logic strikes with metaphysics is not quite one-sided. The support of logic may be worth more to Absolutism than is openly admitted. And the terrifying threat of scepticism may be intended as an effective way of intimidating logic and of producing an emotional atmosphere in which logic can be driven into scientific suicide.

At any rate, if we can steel ourselves to discount its emotional appeal the absolutist argument will be found to be very vulnerable. This is not the place to display its flaws, and we must be content here to anticipate in brief what will be shown hereafter in full (Chap. XV, §§ 8–16); but neither (1) its metaphysical assumptions, nor (2) its logical contentions, nor (3) the value of its conclusions need be conceded without question.

(1) Metaphysically the existence of the Absolute is left quite unproved. Indeed the Real appears to be such that it can hardly form a totality of the sort required or even a totality at all.

(2) Any recognition of the conceptions of Relevance and Selection, and of the distinction between the judgment and the proposition seems to prove logically fatal to the claims of Absolutism. For all intelligent judgment is based upon selection, and concerns parts only of a whole. No sane man imagines that he can blurt out the whole truth about reality in a single judgment; nor does he want to. But his concentration upon the relevant part does not *vitiate* his judgment; it only omits what is irrelevant and misleading. Thus, if I am asked the time and answer 'It is close upon two,' my answer is not falsified by the facts that time is local, and that, according to Einstein, it is even personal, and that no absolute time can exist at all. If it answers the question in the sense in which the questioner wanted to know the time, it is a *true* judgment and the *right* answer.

(3) Nor do the subsequent developments of knowledge or of reality, after the judgment is made, have power to falsify it. No doubt 'it is two o'clock' grows false, *as a proposition*, the

moment after it was uttered; but it has then done its work, and the original *judgment*, which answered an inquiry about the time, is *not* falsified. If it was true (or true enough) at the time, it continues to work as a truth in the inquirer's scheme of purposes; what grows 'false' is the proposition. The metaphysical logicians ought not to fall into this confusion of judgment and proposition. Propositions, moreover, ought not, as such, to be deemed either true or false. They are only verbal formulas used to convey meaning; if used appropriately to the occasion they fill their place, become judgments, and are true *in their contexts*; if otherwise, they suffer rejection, as no longer 'true' but false. No proposition is universally true, i.e. true on all occasions for all purposes, and in all contexts, not even this one.[1] Hence the whole fuss about the unstated and unknown conditions which vitiate our judgments rests entirely on the substitution of the proposition for the judgment, in the manner so incisively advocated by Bradley in the passages quoted in § 11. If this substitution is disallowed, no paradoxes can be hatched out of this mare's nest.

(4) It is pretty evident that as a way of vindicating human truth the absolutist argument is futile. For if a truth can become absolute only by expressing the whole of truth, it is clear not only that no actual truth fulfils this condition, but that no human truth will ever be in a position to avail itself of the Absolute's guarantee. Indeed, Bradley himself is candid enough to point out that not even the Absolute's judgment about itself could conceivably satisfy his conditions; for being relational it implies a *difference* between its subject and its predicate, which could not exist in the Absolute Reality. So judgment is debarred by its very form from describing the real as it is, and condemned to falsity. The final outcome of the theory, therefore, as its more candid advocates hardly affect to conceal, is complete scepticism.

(5) The Absolute guarantees validity as little as it does truth. For it will be shown in Chap. XV that the contention that

---

[1] For, of course, for the ordinary purposes of life it is a philosophic subtlety which may safely be ignored.

inclusion in the all-inclusive system is perfect proof is a tissue of fallacies and contradictions. The notion of system is really incompatible with that of the Absolute and convicts it of being merely a chaos.

§ 16. The Autonomy of Logic.

It would seem, then, that the double-faced attempt to absorb logic in metaphysics proves a failure. It is made in the interest of a 'metaphysic,' which is a pseudo-science having no means of reaching ultimate reality and is nothing but a wholly verbal analysis of conventional meanings; but it is not in the interest of the more legitimate senses of metaphysic, as either the *locus* of ultimate *problems*, or as a philosopher's conjectural and intensely personal attempt to put together all his *data* (his own idiosyncrasies included!) into a picture that affords him at least æsthetic satisfaction. Nor is it in the interest of Logic that logical discussion should be cut short by the superior might of metaphysics. Logic should preserve its autonomy, and the study of the procedures of human thinking should form an autonomous science, entitled, like the other sciences, to make, in due course, its distinctive contribution to the final synthesis, which is the aspiration of metaphysics. The craving for metaphysics is doubtless strong in certain minds; but it should be schooled to patience and not indulged in prematurely. Nor should it be allowed to corrupt the sciences from which metaphysicians should obtain the materials with which they can build their castles in the air.

CHAPTER II

THE DEFINITION OF LOGIC

1. Definition relative to purpose ; 2. Defining the 'essence'; 3. The meaning of 'essence' in actual use ; 4. No finality in definitions ; 5. Provisional definitions required ; 6. Is the function of definition merely psychological ? ; 7. Four issues for a definition of logic to decide ; 8. Logic as evaluation of actual knowing ; 9. The error of divorcing logic from psychology ; 10. The need for co-operating with psychology ; 11. The abstractions of Formal Logic false ; 12. Because inapplicable ; 13. And concealed ; 14. Formal Logic's actual assumptions ; 15. The Formal assumptions fictions ; 16. The confusion of formal with absolute truth ; 17. The fatal abstractions of Formal Logic ; 18. Need for describing actual knowing ; 19. Why the logician should describe actual knowing.

§ 1. **Definition Relative to Purpose.**

It is only when we have determined the use of Logic that we can define it—that is, *select* a definition suitable for our purpose, i.e. for the use we intend to make of it. In itself, however, this remark tells us little about the actual definition we need: it is merely a way of denying two obsolete but lingering ideas, viz. (1) that definition has the function of stating the 'essence' of a subject, and (2) that there can be an absolute and final definition, either of Logic or of anything else. A little reflection will show that neither of these beliefs is tenable.

§ 2. **Defining the 'Essence.'**

That definition has the duty of revealing the essence of the thing defined is, of course, a venerable doctrine descended from Aristotle, or even from Socrates. It has some curious implications, which should not be slurred over, as they commonly are. It presupposes both that the thing has an 'essence' and that *we* can formulate it. The essence is defined as that in it which makes it what it is, to lose which would spell its annihilation.[1]

---

[1] Whence it easily follows that, as 'life' is of the 'essence' of 'soul,' the soul is immortal. But this *a priori* 'proof' (of Plato's) really rests on the verbal fact that in Greek ψυχή meant *both* 'life' *and* 'soul,' being originally the *breath*.

This 'essence' is conceived as wholly *objective*, as an indwelling force or power which we find, and do not feign. It is never, however, the *whole* of the thing: if a thing is such that no part of it seems more essential and indispensable than any other, it is (paradoxically) said to have *no* 'essence.' Hence no individual man has an essence, though man in general, being a 'rational animal,' has.

In other ways also this weird doctrine seems questionable. What proof can ever be given that anything has an essence? We can neither instil an essence into it, and then watch it grow into the thing it is, nor strip it of its essence and watch it collapse into nonentity. The doctrine of essence seems an unverifiable dogma, a dodge for dealing with the observable changes in the qualities of things, designed to comfort us with an assurance that, despite their changes, they have a core that changes not. But it would be more consistent to infer from the situation that *any* change must affect the essence, and that nothing can remain what it is if stripped of *any* of its qualities, and to reprobate our (undeniable) practice of disregarding unimportant changes as purely empirical and practical, and as giving us no right at all to make *any selection* of 'essential' qualities. It could, then, be pointed out that the idea of selection belongs to a wholly alien type of logic, which allows and even encourages thought to tamper with its objects, and inevitably introduces arbitrariness and subjectivity into whatever is selected. Pure logical theory, therefore, should eschew selection; it should take *all* the qualities of a thing as alike essential, and the essence as the *whole*. Whereby the concrete individual, so far from being essenceless, would be revealed as a 'concrete universal,' and a model for more abstract 'essences.' Unfortunately, this expansion of the essence into the whole ruins the whole doctrine. By raising the 'particular' to the rank of a 'concrete universal' it cancels the distinction between it and the universal. By including all the qualities of a thing in its 'essence,' it precludes all use of its 'definition' as a clue to its qualities. By postulating complete knowledge as a condition of definition, it destroys definition as an instrument of knowledge.

The very philosophers, moreover, who are loudest in professing belief in (partial) essences will be most embarrassed by this plea for consistency; for they are usually most clamorous that a reference to the whole is requisite to determine the place of anything in the universe.

§ 3. The Meaning of 'Essence' in Actual Use.

But what is still more humorous is that neither do they nor does anyone else, in point of fact, use 'essence' in the sense prescribed by this theory of definition. In actual use the essence is not one but many, not objective but subjective, not certain but debatable, not fixed but variable, not absolute but relative. Nor is it ever the whole of the thing; it is whatever aspect of it is most important for the purpose in hand. As Alfred Sidgwick says,[1] it means that "we have mentally divided the concrete thing or event into two parts—its 'essence' and its 'accidents' (or circumstances)—and have selected the 'A' part of it as being its essence. Our certainty that we have made our selection rightly is always open to an opponent's challenge; for it would never do to lay down the rule that every fact is rightly conceived by everybody." The essence being in actual fact a selected *part*, it is obvious that for different purposes different selections will be suitable: 'the' essence will always be the essence-for-a-purpose, whether the purpose is stated or only implied, and the definition will vary similarly. It, too, will have to be selected for a purpose, and for its prospective usefulness. Accordingly, the 'essence' has come to mean the part or aspect of any subject which is important or relevant for any purpose, while, curiously enough, in 'essential propositions' there still lingers a reference to definitions which, having become purely nominal, are merely declaratory of the meanings of words.

§ 4. No Finality in Definitions.

If the 'essence' is thus variable, it follows that no absolute or final definition can be made. Nor, if it could be made, would it be of use. A good definition is always *ad hoc*, for a purpose

[1] *The Application of Logic*, p. 108.

and a use. But being thus relative to its use, it stands to reason that it cannot be absolute. Nor can it be final, if its subject is still alive and growing. Every development of our knowledge must *in fact* affect the definition of the object we know. It need not always affect the *terms* of the definition, because the meaning of words is (happily) elastic, and it is often more convenient to read the new meaning into the old definitions than to devise a new definition in new terms. Thus we continue to speak of 'atoms,' though they no longer mean anything 'indivisible' nor even 'ultimate constituents of matter'; and (in certain contexts) man is still a 'rational animal,' though he is found to be the progeny of apes and full of 'complexes.' In principle, however, it must be denied that growing knowledge can be cooped up in a rigid definition.

§ 5. Provisional Definitions Required.

Thus no science can start with an absolutely final definition of its subject. Indeed, if a definition could claim finality, it could not, strictly, perform the primary function of a definition. It would not be intelligible and would not properly be a definition at all. For to render its subject more familiar is the first business of a definition. Hence a *nominal* definition may be a good definition, if, in order to know what we are talking about, we need to be told the meaning of a word, and a *provisional* definition may be useful if it attaches itself to knowledge we already have; but a definition which presupposes complete knowledge of a subject is unlikely to be intelligible to those whose knowledge is incomplete. And if we do not know what we are talking about what is the use of discussion?

§ 6. Is the Function of Definition merely Psychological?

This may seem to some a proposal to renounce the metaphysical function of definition and a lapse into 'mere psychology.' It may be so without being a mistake. Meanwhile, the facts that 'essential' definitions (in the old sense) have become merely 'nominal,' because the only 'essences' of which a knowledge could be taken for granted were just the meanings of words, while 'nominal' definitions are assuredly 'essential' (in the sense of 'indispensable'), and every definition, to be useful, must at least explain the meaning of a word and enable us to understand what is meant, show that there is something seriously wrong with the traditional doctrine. And we should recognise as soon as possible that a Logic which repudiates psychology repudiates meaning, and lapses into nonsense.

Let us admit then that, to be useful and really instructive, a definition should tell us how to find our way about a subject, and help us to take up a position towards its disputed questions and on its debatable ground. It should be intended to affirm one view, and to rule out others.

§ 7. Four Issues for a Definition of Logic to Decide.

At present there may be said to exist in Logic four great issues on which we commit ourselves by choosing a definition. Is Logic to deal (1) with real thinking or only with forms of thought? (2) with real meaning or only with the meaning of words, or, more technically, with real judgments or mere propositions? (3) with real truth or merely formal truth-claim? (4) with truth for man, which all may get, or with an ideal and absolute truth which no man can attain? It is evident that according as we choose among these alternatives we shall get different logics, which will have little but the name in common.

§ 8. Logic as Evaluation of Actual Knowing.

If throughout we choose the former alternative we can define our Logic as *the systematic evaluation of actual knowing*; but the real significance of this definition lies in the *errors* it is meant to exclude. The following can be enumerated: (1) The idea that Logic can relegate to Psychology the actual processes of thinking, and be content to be merely a juggle with the forms of words which thought has taken; (2) the idea that, as it confines itself to the meaning of words and the formal validity of thoughts in the abstract, it can abstract from the makers of the thoughts and the meaning-in-use which they actually sought to convey; (3) the idea that what concerns logic is not real truth but merely formal

validity and verbal consistency; (4) the idea that as real truths
have not to be established there is no need to avoid *errors*; (5)
the idea that the logician need not trouble about the actual
methods of the sciences, but is entitled to construct an ideal of
knowledge which need have no relation to human science and
to any actual human knowing.

§ 9. The Error of Divorcing Logic from Psychology.

At bottom all these errors arise from a single source. It is
assumed that Logic and Psychology are separate sciences, which
have nothing to do with each other. This assumption is never
argued, and rests in the end on nothing more respectable than
man's natural laziness, to which it seems an abhorrent prospect
to be liable to be involved in the infinite complications of contexts and personalities before one can say what a proposition
means, and to have to distinguish between what it meant (to its
maker), means (to its hearers), and may mean (to posterity) hereafter. This *a priori* conviction of the impossibility of taking into
account the psychological facts of context and personality has,
of course, overlooked the possibilities that their potential relevance need not become actual, and that to leave them out of
account may in fact *create* far more ambiguities and complications than it removes.

§ 10. The Need for Co-operating with Psychology.

At any rate a logic of real thinking will resolutely question the
assumptions, both that the actual process of thought is too complicated to be capable of logical investigation, and that psychological fact can have no lesson for logical theory. It will maintain instead that Logic and Psychology *can* co-operate, if they
are suitably conceived, and indeed that they must do so, if
Logic is to be more than a game with abstractions, and if psychological descriptions are to have more than an æsthetic purpose
and value. It will contend that the opposite policy, of what may
fitly be called Formal Logic (in the widest sense), is a fatal error,
and produces all the difficulty and the difficulties of Logic, and
has, in fact, reduced it to a position of undignified futility and

frivolity, ignored and derided by all who are concerned with the advancement of knowledge. For a conception that renders Logic indifferent to meaning and truth and error, and our human difficulties in discovering them, does not really render it sublime, it only makes it ridiculous.

§ 11. The Abstractions of Formal Logic False

The simple truth, to which logicians seek to blind themselves and their readers by all the arts of their traditional *technique*, is that Formal Logic *has made the wrong abstractions*. They are not to be blamed for basing their science upon abstractions; for every science makes abstractions. It makes them simply because it cannot help it. For no science can deal with everything. It must *select* its subject from a larger whole; and it *does* select, even when it professes, verbally, to deal with the whole. Hence some things are considered irrelevant, even to metaphysics; e.g. that an irritable metaphysician was impelled to swear by a gnat's bite, just as he had completed his proof of the perfection of the Absolute.[1]

§ 12. Because Inapplicable

Once it is admitted that Logic must select the abstractions it rests on, the question arises how it may best do so. This question it is usually attempted to answer by searching for some self-evident and *a priori* principle on which to build a demonstrated superstructure. It is, however, clear that such a method will afford no guarantee that a Logic so deduced will be *applicable* to the actual problems of human knowing. We have to find out empirically and by experiment what abstractions will answer

[1] One feature of the whole reality which the ordinary metaphysics all think fit to abstract from is its ' particularity,' meaning thereby its place, time, and individuality, and reducing the real to what is neither spatial, nor temporal, nor individual. In consequence of this abstraction monistic metaphysics become so highly selective that they have nothing to say about anything, save that it won't do, because it is not the Whole. But the Whole-as-such, to which they restrict themselves, thereby becomes indistinguishable from nothing, as Hegel naïvely confessed. Thus the ' all-inclusive whole ' reveals itself as all-exclusive and nugatory.

and what principles will work. There is no way of establishing
the 'validity' (value) of logical principles, except by showing
that they yield a good and useful science. And 2000 years of
wasted acumen and continuous failure should suffice to show
that the basis on which the traditional logic has tried to operate
is *not* 'valid.'

§ 13. And Concealed.

It is, moreover, a legitimate demand to make upon any logic,
as an indispensable guarantee of good faith, that it should, openly
and frankly, *state* the initial assumptions and abstractions from
which it proceeds. But Formal Logic refuses to satisfy this
demand. It makes a parade indeed of enumerating a (varying)
number of 'Laws of Thought,' which it declares to be self-
evident and indisputable: but they pass as self-evident only
because they are ambiguous and may be taken as truisms, and
are indisputable only because no one can ascertain what they
mean, and all inquiry into their meaning is artfully evaded.[1]

What is still worse is the omission to state the (very different)
assumptions on which Formal Logic really rests. For if they
were stated, it would be impossible to be deceived about the
artificial and essentially verbal character of its doctrine, and it
would at once become clear that it was only in so far as it was
possible to argue from words to things that its doctrines could
be true; thus the reasoner would be warned that he must make
sure of this coincidence of words and things in each case, and
would no longer supinely accept a merely verbal guarantee.

§ 14. Formal Logic's Actual Assumptions.

Actually the whole imposing edifice of Formal Logic may be
shown to rest on the assumptions implied in the statement that
Logic deals with the relations of terms in propositions. For by
'terms' are meant (1) the *meanings of words*, which (2) are
supposed to be *known*, and (3) *fixed*. Grant these assumptions
and a conception of *formal validity* can be formed, on which a

---

[1] Cp. H. V. Knox, *The Will to be Free*, pt. v–vi, and *Formal Logic*,
chap. x.

self-contained and self-sufficient science (or game) can be
erected that considers nothing else in the world, and automatically excludes all inquiry into real meaning, actual thinking,
real truth, real error, the processes of discriminating between
them, and so the process of real knowing. But in order to escape
detection it astutely provides formal substitutes for all these
realities in *verbal* meaning, thought in general (which is no one's
thought), formal truth (which is not distinguishable from
'error'), formal fallacy (which is compatible with valuable
truth), formal 'validity' (which guarantees no real truth), and a
formal 'ideal' of knowledge (which can never be realised). Not
content with these abstractions, Formal Logic indulges further
in a conception of truth which is *essentially ambiguous*. On the
basis of a consistent verbalism all that 'truth' *should* mean for
it is the *formal truth-claim* which is (verbally) implied in all
assertion (however false); but because in false and dubious
truth-claims their real grounds and limitations do not find
(verbal) expression, they may be surreptitiously taken to attest a
truth which is 'absolute' and free from doubt and restrictions.
Thus 'truth' in Formal Logic becomes a perpetual juggle between absolute truth and formal truth-claim, in which each is
used to rescue the other from discredit.

§ 15. The Formal Assumptions Fictions.

Now all these assumptions, when questioned, prove to be
strictly *false*. Whence it follows that, if they are to continue to
figure in Logic, it can only be as *useful fictions*, and that Formal
Logic can at best be a game with such fictions, which may
nevertheless be relevant to the procedures of actual knowing,
and facilitate their analysis. And, of course, even this modest
claim will have to be discussed.

The falsity of the assumption that the meanings of words
are necessarily identical with the meanings of those who use
them, follows at once from the fact that words are instruments
for *expressing* meaning. Naturally, therefore, they will most
easily express and convey meanings which already inhere in
the words, because the words have been used to convey them

before; for they may then be presumed to be *known* to both parties. But what if the situation is sufficiently *novel* to require a meaning, or shade of meaning, never yet expressed, and a usage not yet recognised, and catalogued in a dictionary? Clearly in such a case the *old* meanings of the words will not suffice, and the meaning of the man who uses them must so select and mould them that they will, for the nonce and in that context, express *his* meaning. If he succeeds in conveying it, he will thereby extend and develop the meaning of the words he has used, and *create* new meanings or shades of meaning. But he should recognise that in such a case—(1) his meaning is changing and developing language; (2) that he must not assume that his meaning will be understood, or presuppose that the meaning of his terms is *known*; (3) that his procedure is possible only because (luckily for him) the meaning of terms is *not* completely *fixed*, and language is elastic and capable of perpetual growth. Thus he is forced to realise that the three first assumptions of Formal Logic are strictly false, and that in applying them to the analysis of his thinking he must make allowance for their falsity. The real facts are that personal meaning is primary and verbal meaning secondary, that real meaning cannot be assumed to be known and that there is always a problem of communication, that all terms are elastic and plastic, and that in the transfer from one context to another their meaning may always undergo a change which may vitiate an argument based on their verbal identity.

§ 16. The Confusion of Formal with Absolute Truth.

That the formal truth-claim, which alone a Formal Logic can recognise, is not real truth, and still less absolute truth, becomes evident at once the moment the word 'error' is mentioned. For real truth is truth which excludes error, and formal truth-claim does not. Its 'truth' is *inclusive* of error. It recognises no distinction between the truth-claim of an error and of a real truth. As both claim truth, both are (formally) 'true.' This incapacity, or rather refusal, to distinguish between formal truth-claim and real truth, with a consequent

incapacity to discriminate truth from error, forms the best test
of logical Formalism. Any logic and any theory of truth in
which this incapacity is found thereby betrays its Formal
character.[1]

But Formal Logic not only confuses formal with real truth,
but also with 'absolute' truth. The formal truth-claim no
more expresses any restriction to the 'truth' it claims than it
owns to error. Hence it is easy to interpret the truth claimed as
'absolute.' And if this meant nothing more than just this
absence of express conditions and limitations, formal truth
would, of course, be 'absolute.' But if 'absolute' is supposed
to guarantee exemption from error, from correction, from conditions, and from grounds of doubt, the claim is ludicrously
false.

Formal Logic, moreover, quite fails to observe that the facts
on which it bases itself are, in both cases, merely verbal. It is
a fact that every proposition, formally and as such, lays claim
to truth. None confesses to its own falsity, even though it must
obviously be apprehended as a lie or a joke. Even 'I lie' makes
this formal truth-claim. It is the nearest it is possible to get to
an exemplification of the notion of formal self-contradiction,
for the form here comes into violent conflict with the matter
asserted. The matter is alleged to be false, and yet truth is
simultaneously claimed for this very falsity, in virtue of its form.
The result, however, is neither truth nor falsity. The proposition, as it stands, is *meaningless*. It can acquire a meaning only
by being used in a context which removes its verbal paradox,
e.g. if 'I lie' is referred not to the proposition itself but to
what has just been said.

Similarly, a truth-claim may appear to be absolute merely
because it does not express the doubts, conditions, and reservations in the mind of its maker. Yet they may in fact exist in
infinite variety, and may be readily understood in an actual
context. 'I think so' may express every degree of certainty;

[1] Judged by this vital test nearly all the extant logics and theories
of knowledge are Formal, in the reprehensible sense, and the differences
between them are nugatory.

but, unless the actual context is known, it may be impossible to determine the exact degree. But is it not childish to ignore these obvious facts and to insist on calling it 'absolute' merely because the actual limitations of the formal truth-claim do not find verbal expression?

The simple truth is that such things are not *logical problems*, but *linguistic tricks*. They are, moreover, easily seen through, and a logic of real thinking is not puzzled by them.

§ 17. The Fatal Abstractions of Formal Logic.

Formal Logic not only omits to state and justify the abstractions it employs, it is also reticent about their consequences. It says nothing about the features of real thinking from which it has to abstract in order to use its own abstractions. Yet these are far-reaching and of the utmost importance.

Thus (1) it is never stated honestly, at the outset, that the conception of logical 'form' and the concentration upon 'formal validity' involve total abstraction from 'material truth,' and that under this name are included *all* the processes whereby the sciences establish and test the actual truth of their assertions. This abstraction therefore means a refusal of Formal Logic to concern itself with actual knowledge and to attempt a theory thereof.

Yet (2) by this very attitude it reveals that there *must* be another science which undertakes the task it renounces. For there actually is such an operation or process as knowing, and it can be studied scientifically.

Moreover (3) the science which does this must be a 'presupposition' of Formal Logic, and will reduce it to a condition of dependence. For it alone can supply material truth and declare the purport and actual value of the formal relations between propositions to which Formal Logic restricts itself. In default of a properly guaranteed supply of material truths, these relations are about nothing: Formal Logic remains entirely in the air, and its hypothetical deductions have no application to our actual thinking and reasoning. It ought, therefore, to begin by explaining how and whence it can obtain material truths in the sense it requires.

(4) Actually, however, it merely *postulates* material truth, and postulates it as 'absolute' whenever it chooses, without inquiring whether the actual operations of our knowing are capable of yielding the sort of truth demanded. But actual truths are never absolute. They depend on *data*, premises, probabilities, verifications, which are never absolute certainties, are always more or less incomplete, and may always prove more or less defective. No doubt they are indefinitely improvable, and may be conceived as approximating asymptotically to absolute certainty; but their mobility and progressiveness are far more characteristic of them than their relation to a static 'ideal.' Hence the demand of Formal Logic for a supply of absolutely certain material truths is never met. Formal Logic fails to notice this, because of its own oscillation between absolute and formal truth (§ 16); it ignores also the possibility (exemplified in its own case) that a formal science may remain purely hypothetical, and be actually inapplicable. It is essentially an abstract theory about the formal relations of imaginary objects called absolute truths; it becomes a pseudo-science the moment it tries to be relevant to actual knowledge.

For (5) it has abstracted from all the essential features of actual knowledge, and from the whole context of reasoning. It ignores that every act of thought is performed by some one, at some time, in some place, from some motive, for some end. These circumstances form the context of every thought, and the ground in which it is rooted. But from all this Formal Logic recklessly severs it. It abstracts (*a*) from the *maker* of the thought, alleging that his motives in making it are questions only of his personal psychology. It abstracts (*b*) from the occasion of its making, because the only thought it deigns to contemplate is such as is true always and everywhere, or, in other words, 'eternal and universal.' What is to be made of truths that are good only for the occasion and the purpose in hand it does not stoop to consider, any more than whether the eternal and universal truths it has postulated or fabricated by its abstractions are actually to the point. For it has not realised that in its application to a particular case a general truth, however

'universal' and 'eternal' it may be in the abstract, always remains precarious. Truth in general is no guarantee of truth in a
particular case. The 'eternal truth' of man's rationality is no
security that the next man we meet will not be a lunatic, and
any general rule may be defeated when it is applied to a special
case which, though antecedently it looked like a case of the
rule, yet does not in fact behave like one (Chap. XIV, § 4;
XV, § 4).

Thus (*c*) Formal Logic abstracts from the whole problem of
application or use which, in actual thinking, throws so much
light on the value of a truth-claim. Nothing that happens to a
truth after its formulation is taken to have any logical bearing
or value. Our growing confidence in it, if it works well, our
growing distrust, if it works badly, are equally irrelevant. Thus
(*d*) the value of a truth is abstracted from: it is sacrificed to the
notion of *formal validity*. Now this, on the face of it, is a serious
falsification; for actually all truths are values, or, if by 'truth'
we mean truth-claim, value-claims. They are truths only in
relation to the mind which values them as true, and chooses
them in preference to the truth-claims it rejects.

'Formal validity,' on the other hand, is a wholly verbal
affair. It may be possessed by forms of thought which no one
ever thinks in because they are wholly inapplicable to any
subject of inquiry, and by syllogisms with premisses that are
false or meaningless: it is lacking to the verificatory reasoning by which our hypothetical conclusions grow into truths as
their probability accumulates. And, even verbally, no proof of
'validity' can ever be trusted: for a possibility of 'ambiguity,'
being a condition of the use of language, lurks in all linguistic
expression, and when this affects the middle term of a syllogism it may always vitiate a conclusion that seems otherwise
'formally valid' (Chap. XIV, § 4; XV, § 4).

§ 18. The Need for Describing Actual Knowing.

The above considerations may perhaps suffice to justify, provisionally, our preference for a definition of Logic which decides *against* its Formal conception; but our formula (§ 8) still

requires a little more preliminary explanation. When 'actual thinking' is described as the subject-matter which Logic should evaluate, and as precisely that which Logic is forbidden to consider by the initial abstractions of Formalism, it should be added that it includes all the processes whereby we arrive at the conviction that we know and possess truth, alike in ordinary life and in the sciences, which only refine upon the methods of ordinary life. Actual thinking, no doubt, conducts only to practical, not to absolute, certainty (whatever that may mean); but it is enough to live by, and is what we all do live by, whether or not we acknowledge it to be 'theoretically adequate.'

It is very important, therefore, that it should be properly described. It should be described as it actually occurs, without the suppression of any 'illogicalities' it may seem to exhibit, without any falsifications designed to reduce it to 'logical form,' and without any omissions of what is assumed to have 'merely psychological' interest. Only when he has honestly faced the facts of actual thinking, complete and uncontaminated, should the logician proceed to 'evaluate' them.

§ 19. Why the Logician should Describe Actual Knowing.

If now the question is raised, as it must be, who is to undertake this description of actual thinking, it is clear that the necessary task should naturally fall to the psychologist. For psychology is admittedly a descriptive science which has the aim of describing *all* psychic facts and processes. Strictly speaking, therefore, the psychologist should supply the logician with a serviceable account of actual thinking. As things stand at present, however, he either cannot or will not do so. Intimidated by the seniority and arrogance of the old Logic, psychologists mostly shrink from the thorny subject of the 'higher mental processes,' such as thinking. And they themselves continue to be divided into sects which proceed to the description of psychological facts with different premises and in different terms, and without regard to any ulterior use to which their descriptions may be put. The result is that the various systems of

3

'psychology' have at best æsthetic value, and cannot be trusted to be of service to Logic.

The logician, therefore, who wishes to evaluate actual thinking will have, in the main, to do his own describing. This, however, will have some advantages. Thus he will take good care that his psychological descriptions are in terms which are serviceable to *his* purpose and are relevant to Logic, even though they may not coincide with those which are most favoured by the reigning fashions in psychology.

Moreover, he will thereby be enabled to show that descriptions are just as much relative to purposes as definitions. The purposive character of the human mind reveals itself also in this that it simply *cannot* describe at random. The purpose which animates a description may be trivial or unworthy, its presuppositions may be fantastic or false, but a mind *never* functions with the unintelligent indifference to values of a photographic plate. The logician, therefore, need not hesitate to confess that his description of actual thinking is intended to be serviceable to its evaluation, and that he conceives Logic and Psychology as sciences which can, and should, co-operate.

In order that their co-operation may be fruitful two conditions will have to be fulfilled. The logician must not assume that the facts brought out by psychological descriptions are *eo ipso* to be dismissed as merely irrelevant. Neither must the psychologist assume that differences in the logical value of alternative descriptions are to carry no weight in determining his choice of a description because 'values' are no concern of his. For it does not follow from the fact that, in the scientific division of labour, his *rôle* is description rather than evaluation that he may not mention values. If values exist, if valuations occur—and the facts of language are ample evidence of both— they must be recorded and described. For after all there can be no logical evaluation, unless the values evaluated are psychical facts, and they need evaluation, precisely because as psychical facts they are neither systematic nor concordant. They are *value-claims* and *attempts* at valuation, and the normative sciences—logic, ethics, and æsthetics—find herein their justification and their *raison d'être*. For the conflicting chaos of values and valuations must be reduced to some sort of order somehow. How? is the question the various systems of logic, ethics, and æsthetics try to answer. They answer imperfectly enough, but the duty of evaluation remains. And this is why the function of Logic may fitly be defined as the evaluation of actual thinking.

CHAPTER III

LOGICAL VALUES

1. Logic a normative science ; 2. The vocabulary of values ; 3. ' Fact ' also a value ; 4. Valuation an act and an attitude ; 5. The genesis of intrinsic objective value ; 6. Conflicts of values imply psychological commensurability; 7. The social side to values ; 8. Normative science a social need ; 9. Logic should evaluate truth-claims ; 10. But not lay down the law *a priori* ; 11. Should study actual knowing first ; 12. The ' valid ' and the ' valuable ' ; 13. ' Validity ' merely verbal ; 14. Risk unavoidable in real reasoning.

§ 1. Logic a Normative Science.

The meaning of the definition of Logic adopted in the last chapter might also have been expressed, in vaguer terms, by declaring that Logic was the normative science concerned with cognitive values. Though vaguer, this would have had some advantages. It would have brought out the value-aspect of Logic, and so would have explicitly connected it with the other normative sciences, ethics, æsthetics, and grammar, which are involved in much the same confusion and disputes as to their relation to psychology. For in each of these cases it would appear that there is a problem of correlating a description with an evaluation, of recognising and harmonising *de facto* valuations, of adjudicating between rival claims and of deciding which of them were really right. And after treating the various valuations together and in analogous fashion, we should have found it easier to understand the problem of values and the nature of normative science as a whole. We should thus have realised that the case of Logic was by no means unique and anomalous, and that the claim of Logic to control the sciences, like the claim of ethics to control action and the claim of æsthetics to control taste, was only expressive of the inevitable domination of 'value' over 'fact.' But it is not too late to bring out this neglected side of Logic.

§ 2. The Vocabulary of Values.

Values have in general received much clearer recognition in the facts of language than in the philosophic sciences. Most languages possess a pretty adequate vocabulary for the expression of valuation-attitudes, though one has sometimes to notice curious and significant *lacunæ*,[1] and though a language is often more complete in the adjectives than in the corresponding substantives. The attributions 'true' and 'false,' 'real' and 'unreal,' 'good' and 'bad,' 'good' and 'evil,' 'right' and 'wrong,' 'correct' and 'incorrect,' 'pleasant' and 'painful,' 'beautiful' and 'ugly,' 'noble' and 'low,' 'becoming' and 'unbecoming,' etc., are expressions of valuation-attitudes and the true sources of the normative sciences. Unfortunately these adjectives are not all equipped with equally antithetical substantives. Thus, though 'error,' 'falsity,' and 'falsehood' are all (in various contexts) antithetical to 'truth,' 'goodness' has to serve as the ambiguous antithesis both to 'badness' and to 'evil,' while there is no proper antithesis to 'fact' at all in English. Hence, though 'fact' can stand as the substantive corresponding to the 'real,' there is nothing to perform this service for the 'unreal.'

§ 3. 'Fact' also a Value.

So we naturally fail to recognise 'fact' as a term of valuation at all. It requires some perspicacity to perceive that the fact which 'is really fact' is *always a value,* and the refined end-product of a continual valuation-process which goes on without ending, and has to discard great masses of 'facts' which are alleged, but prove to be unreal, erroneous, and illusory. The consequences have been far-reaching. Logicians have persisted in treating the notion of fact as simple and absolute, and as fit to serve as a firm basis for a theory of knowledge, or at least of 'induction,' without further analysis; while philosophers in general have not ceased from attempts to take it as their starting-point, instead of as their goal and the terminus of a *successful* expedition. In consequence the philosophic systems built upon 'facts' have hardly been more solid than those which have been floated on *a priori* speculation.

[1] Classical Greek, for example, has no words for 'right' and 'wrong,' nor for 'duty' and 'will.' Neither has French words for the first antithesis. The result of such gaps in the vocabulary is that other terms are used as functional equivalents of the missing words, and have to be overworked, like καλὸν-αἰσχρὸν in Greek, or ' *la justice* ' in French.

But this procedure takes for granted, and thereby excludes from logical treatment, the most important and difficult portion of scientific knowing, viz. the ascertaining of the real facts, or otherwise, the *extraction* of scientific fact from *data* which appear to be fact, or are alleged to be so; it thus assumes that done which the sciences are never absolutely sure they have accomplished or satisfied that they have ascertained with absolute completeness. For, actually, whatever is taken as fact can be so only relatively to the state of knowledge at the time, and to the position and purposes of the particular inquiry; hence it is out of the question to take any 'fact' as absolute, and it is often difficult to decide which among the rival 'facts' it is *best* to take as fact. It is from differences of opinion as to what it is best to do in such cases that different schools of thought arise in philosophy and science; and it is clear that unless such problems are frankly faced, and freely discussed, the valuation-aspect of our cognitive procedure will be fatally obscured. Hence the seemingly accidental absence of a negative correlative to 'fact' has sufficed to lead inquiry astray, and shows that we cannot trust language alone to reveal the full scope of our valuations.

§ 4. Valuation an Act and an Attitude.

To appreciate the *rôle* of valuation we must have recourse, in the first instance, to a psychological description of the valuation-process, and, to get an adequate description, we shall have to be careful in the choice of our psychology. It will have to be a *voluntarist* or *activist* psychology, for a valuation can hardly be recognised and described save as an *activity*, and *act*, and a *choice*, which implicates the whole of the valuer's personality. It would be vain to represent it as a 'simple' mental process or as a combination of such processes (or, if verbally possible, so complicated as not to be worth while), seeing that no factor in the infinite complexity of the total personality can be *presumed* to be irrelevant to the outcome of a valuation-process: still less could it be described in terms of a behaviourism which sets itself to ignore the conscious side of intelligent action. But, even when we have equipped ourselves with a psychology willing to recognise the fact of valuation, it is by no means easy to find a suitable term under which to classify it. Of the psychological terms in use 'attitude' is probably the best, or rather the least inadequate; for it implies, even though it does not explicitly state, an active taking up of a position, a weighing of considerations *pro* and *con*, and a manipulation of the given. This valuation-attitude in its turn is a form of the mind's reaction upon external circumstances, and as such is always a *subjective addition* to the 'facts of the case.' The addition always makes a difference, and may entirely transform them—as we may convince ourselves by comparing a pessimist's with an optimist's valuation of the same facts. Their facts have always to be valued, and 'the facts as they really are' emerge from a valuation. It is this process which transforms them from initial and tentative *data* into the real facts upon which we take our stand. Thus our 'facts' in ultimate analysis depend upon our valuations, and a valuation may be described as our operation performed upon *data* or upon a given situation, as the result of which it is approved or disapproved, accepted or rejected. It should be noted further that the various valuations express their approval or disapproval in different terms, and may be classified accordingly.

§ 5. The Genesis of Intrinsic Objective Value.

As a result of an act of valuation value is attributed to the situation or object valued. It becomes '*a value*,' positive or negative, at least for the time being and the purpose in hand. If it, or its like, is sufficiently permanent to be valued frequently in similar situations, and if its valuers agree in a general way about the value they attribute to it, its value will come to seem *intrinsic* and independent of the valuers. They will be thought to recognise an objective value inherent in the object. Thus, gold is judged to be intrinsically a 'precious' metal; because (under normal conditions) there exists an unlimited demand for it, and it is always accepted in payment of a debt.[1]

---

[1] Nevertheless, during the War, Sweden found that it got too much of this good thing, and at one time had to prohibit the importation of gold, whereas other countries prohibited its export.

That, however, the value of an object is intrinsic only in appearance, and really remains relative to the uses to which the object is put, is revealed by the conflicts, variations, and fluctuations of values. As the ancients justly observed, an ass would prefer hay to gold, and even King Midas found that gold could have negative value when everything he touched turned into gold. The same discovery may be made by anyone who is murdered for his possessions. In economics the variations in the values of the objects valued can be expressed in definitely quantitative terms, and the changes in the current market prices of goods are regularly quoted in the newspapers; in the normative sciences quantitative precision is more difficult, and quotations for the various values they deal with are not easy to obtain. The seekers after truth, for example, among whom the professors of logic would presumably enrol themselves *ex officio*, are not sufficiently organised to recognise each new truth as it is discovered at its true value; it has, almost always, to be rediscovered some dozens of times, like America, and so wins the title of truth only by sacrificing its claim to novelty.

§ 6. Conflicts of Values imply Psychological Commensurability.

What is even worse is that they are not agreed about the nature of the truth they seek, and that the *meaning* of '*truth*' is a difficult and contentious matter. Similar disputes exist as to the meaning and nature of good, while the beautiful is so much a matter of individual taste that the normative side of æsthetics is more honoured in the breach than in the observance. So it need hardly occasion surprise that when it comes to comparing values of one kind with those of another we should encounter chaos, and a babel of discordant voices. It is possible, no doubt, to find a common measure of the various values in economic value by inquiring what people would give in cold cash to obtain the several values. The results might be startling, but they would be more expressive of the average man's valuation of them than of the expert's; and one would be sorry to think that the pecuniary remuneration of the producers of the

higher values were a measure of their true value, or even expressed the considered judgment of mankind upon the value of
their services.

Nevertheless, there is no getting away from the generic
similarity of all the values. They are all positive or negative, and,
as negative values may be set off against positive, they all admit
of (more or less accurate) quantitative treatment. Thus they
are always comparable in principle. Language recognises this
by equipping them all with a comparative and a superlative. It
speaks freely of *true—truer—truest*, as of *good—better—best*, and
of *pleasant—pleasanter—pleasantest*, and thereby indicates that
the True, the Good, and the Beautiful must not hastily be taken
as absolute, even where no comparison is expressed. For, when
we go into the circumstances of the case, a judgment about the
true is always found to mean that it is, for reasons that may be
given if demanded, *truer than* a number of alternatives which are
either false outright, or at any rate misleading or of inferior
value.

Moreover, despite their specific differences, all the values are
comparable with each other. Not only can we decide what
pleasures are worth what pains, but we can make up our minds
to sacrifice so much beauty to so much truth, or *vice versa*.
Such decisions, doubtless, hardly claim to be absolute and
objective, irreversible and indisputable. They would not be so
poignant and interesting if they were. They are personal and
'subjective,' and relative to the circumstances of the case.
But they are adequate to these and serve their purpose, and may
continue to be approved as the right or the best decision to have
taken. The comparison and evaluation of values, therefore, is
plainly a psychological fact.

§ 7. The Social Side to Values.

This is also a sociological fact, which may be observed and
studied. By careful observation of the opinions and actions of
men and of the changes which occur in them, by a systematic
comparison of the value-judgments which they pass at different
times, in different places, and under different circumstances, it is

possible to obtain a fairly adequate idea of human valuations and to draw some conclusions. It soon becomes obvious that some values are genuine and others bogus, some important and others trivial. Some are ephemeral, others enduring: some are general and almost 'universal,' others little more than idiosyncrasies and hobbies. Some are believed and acted on, but not (usually) professed. Others are professed, but not (usually) acted on. Some are kept for home consumption, others are good for export and propaganda, and are recommended to others because we have no further use for them. There are, moreover, great differences in the valuations of different individuals and societies and in the same individuals at different times. There are also considerable oscillations in the relative rank of the different values, though these are more marked in some parts of the value-scale than in others which are stabler and are upheld by a more general consensus. But absolute fixity and universal agreement are nowhere to be found.

§ 8. Normative Science a Social Need.

However, all these variations, all these disputes affecting the values actually in being, though they may shock our credulity, only strengthen the case for the normative sciences which set themselves to describe and evaluate the values current. Logic, therefore, like ethics, like æsthetics, like grammar, may claim to be a social necessity, and a science which must continue to be demanded in principle, however pitiably it may chance to fail in fact. For it is an indisputable social fact that our knowledge is built up by valuations, that cognitive values are predicated, that 'truths' are valued and 'errors' avoided, that there are demands for trustworthy *criteria* to distinguish the true from the false, and for explanations of what is meant by 'truth' and 'knowledge' and the processes of acquiring them. Hence Logic exists *in posse* as the science which *should* answer these questions; if actual logics fail to answer them they are simply *failures*, however great the ingenuity that has gone to their construction, however great the formal perfection and verbal consistency they may have attained.

§ 9. Logic should Evaluate Truth-Claims.

It should be clear from what has been said that the raw material of Logic is composed of the cognitive valuations of men and the cognitive values which are recognised: it should be equally clear that this raw material must be treated critically. Hence all these values and valuations must be conceived by logic as *value-claims* to be inquired into and tested; they cannot be accepted forthwith as established and authenticated facts. For their character is plainly not such as to admit of indiscriminate acceptance. The various truths that are alleged, the various bits of knowledge that various persons believe themselves to possess, the various processes by which they acquire their convictions, cannot possibly all be true and sound together. They are infinitely different and incompatible, and contradict each other freely. And even if what is believed to be truth and knowledge were not rent by such internal conflicts and dissensions, and if it could be maintained that all opinions were in some sense and degree true, it would still be necessary to evaluate the *amount* of truth they severally contained, and to distinguish between the more and the less true, and the true for some purposes and for many. This process, therefore, would involve a critical evaluation and scientific re-arrangement of the actual truth-claims, and in performing this function Logic would display its normative competence.

§ 10. But not Lay Down the Law *a priori*.

At the same time too much must not be expected from the normative side of Logic—certainly nothing like so much as Formal Logic has led men to expect, in vain. A Logic that studies cognitive values as they occur in human life, and tries merely to co-ordinate and improve them, is not at all likely to attempt to lay down the law to the human intelligence which has developed in an unceasing struggle with the hard facts of life and grown into so potent a means of human survival. It will wisely renounce attempts to formulate rigid canons of proof or truth, warranted to be verbally invulnerable and fool-proof, and to discover an apparatus of forms which will mechanically turn

out new knowledge, and thereby supersede the use of intelligence in cognitive operations. These were the obstinate illusions
which inspired the old Formal Logic; it conceived logic as a
substitute for intelligence, and set itself the impossible task of
controlling all knowledge by imposing on it its own standard
of formal validity. It appeared to succeed, merely because it
was not noticed that no *valuable* argument is really 'valid,'
because it was not understood that no proof of validity is ever
more than verbal, and that validity is no guarantee of real value
but only the Formal substitute for it.

§ 11. Should Study Actual Knowing First.

A real Logic of the processes by which we do *in fact* test
'truths' and acquire knowledge will begin by a careful study of
these processes. It will study them in their actual complexity,
with all their roots and ramifications in human personality,
without disdaining to notice processes which a hasty psychology
has classified as 'non-cognitive,' and erroneously judged to be
irrelevant, and without attempting the illusory simplifications,
futile fictions, and unworkable abstractions which seem so inseparable from Formal Logic. In other words, it will not start
with any *a priori* prejudice in favour of any arbitrary and artificial logical 'ideal' of 'validity,' and try to force our actual
procedures into subjection and into conformity with this, but
will set out from the actual, from the proved value of methods of
knowing which have approved themselves in human experience.
These natural methods are practised not only in ordinary life
but also in the sciences, which refine and specialise them for
their purposes. They should not be ignored, and cannot be set
aside, but it may be useful to reflect on them. For reflection may
deepen our appreciation of their scope and suggest improvements in their conduct. This function may fitly be assigned to
Logic. At present it is no one's business to study the theory
of actual knowing, to compare and correlate its methods, to
discuss which of them are worth trying in what subjects and
capable of transfer from one subject to another. For ordinary
life such questions are too theoretical, while scientists are usually

too busy with their actual work to reflect upon their methods. So there is room here for the services of the logician who makes a special study of the ways in which knowledge is acquired. Attentive observation of the natural processes of knowing may reveal to him facts which would otherwise escape notice, and enable him to represent knowing as a much more systematic and rational thing than it would otherwise appear to be; it may even enable him to make suggestions to the scientist, and to draw his attention to logical possibilities and alternatives which exist, though no one has as yet conceived the idea of exploring them. But he will not presume to *dictate* to the sciences, any more than he will dream of holding up to their admiration unattainable ideals of a 'validity' he has concocted for his own delectation. The suggestions he makes and the questions he raises will be of the nature of *advice*. And he will not dare even to advise, until he feels that he has at least a general grasp of the problems and issues concerned.

§ 12. The 'Valid' and the 'Valuable.'

Thus Logic will be a comprehensive study of actual values, and will not be restricted to a bare ideal of logical 'validity.' In fact its attitude to this ideal will be severely critical, not to say hostile. For it will recognise that though the *valuable* is often loosely called *valid*, and though the conceptions of value and validity are frequently confused, they are really quite distinct, and even antagonistic. Cognitive processes which are valuable are familiar and common enough; their value admits of more and less, and often of quantitative expression, as when we can calculate the probability that a probable truth will apply to a particular case in which we are interested. But where and when do we come across processes of which we can confidently predicate 'validity'? Validity claims to mean something more than value, and perhaps, in the end, means something less. Etymologically it only meant 'strength,' and so, like value, it should admit of more and less. But its meaning has been specialised by Formal Logic into something absolute. To Formal Logic an argument is either 'valid,' or not. If it is not 'valid' it matters not, to Formal Logic, how *probable* it may be in point of fact. Its 'material truth' is logically irrelevant. It becomes logically negligible, and at best is handed over to mathematics, which makes a gallant attempt to deal with probable reasoning by its calculus of probabilities, but fails to make good its claim to express all practical probability in mathematical terms, and to reduce 'the guide of life' to a mathematical formula.[1] To Formal Logic, if an argument is valid, it is *ipso facto* raised above further criticism. The suggestion that validity may be too rare to be of much importance practically, nay, that it may not actually occur at all but may turn out to be an 'ideal' never realised in fact, and indeed not realisable even in conception, is scouted as the impious impertinence of a sceptic.

Yet it should be obvious that if it is too much to expect of any actual reasoning, whether 'deductive' ('apodictic') or 'inductive' ('epagogic'), that it should be 'valid,' two questions arise about the 'ideal' of validity. In the first place, what becomes of the value of an ideal which cannot be exemplified in fact? Does it not cease to stimulate the actual? Does it not serve merely to discredit it, and possibly itself? Secondly, what is to become of the actual reasonings which sink beneath the notice of a Logic that will recognise nothing short of validity? Are they to be left to their own devices as unfit for scientific study? Or is there to be created a sort of secondary and inferior *pseudo-logic* to attend to defective and invalid reasoning and to assess its merits? In either case (Formal) Logic will have nothing to say to actual reasoning, except to condemn it as invalid. It will occupy a position too exalted to trouble about the difficulties of actual knowing.

§ 13. 'Validity' merely Verbal.

And yet its position is by no means as secure as it fancies. It really rests upon an entirely *verbal* foundation, which crumbles the moment the adequacy of verbal proof is questioned. If a

---

[1] As Mr J. M. Keynes has so brilliantly shown. Cp. Chap. XVI, § 8.

question is raised as to what the reason is for believing that an
argument which seems valid really is valid, all the evidence that
this 'Logic' can adduce is seen to be merely verbal. It all presupposes that the presence of the same *word* in two contexts
is a complete *guarantee* of identity of meaning. All *M is P*, all
S is M, therefore all *S is P*, is the type of a 'valid' argument;
because (and if) M in the two premisses firmly links together
S and P. But when questions arise whether *what is called* 'M'
in the two contexts is really the same thing, and whether what
functioned as 'M' in relation to P will also function as M
when it enters into relation with S, it becomes evident that the
'valid form' simply begs the question of the *real value* of the
reasoning. What alone we can be sure remains the same is just
the word 'M': for the rest, two different things may have been
wrongly called the same, and the application of 'M' to the
two situations may be a mistake. In general it cannot be seriously concluded that two things or situations are the same merely
because some one chooses to call them by the same name, or
even that, because they may be identical for some purposes,
they must necessarily be so for all. If, then, this merely verbal
guarantee is not accepted, and inquiry is made into the rights
of the case and the question whether the two M's are effectively
identical, the emptiness of the conception of validity appears at
once, and with it the utter impotence of Formal Logic to secure
real truth and certainty (Chap. XIII, §§ 3, 5; XIV, §§ 2, 4;
XV, § 2; XVI, § 13 ; XVII, § 13).

§ 14. Risk Unavoidable in Real Reasoning.

Thus, to identify terms that occur twice in the same reasoning,
and to trust to their verbal identity to carry thought on from
one point to another, always involves a *risk*, the risk that *verbal*
is no guarantee of *real* identity. But avoidance of risk has always
been one of the major aims of Formal Logic; it has always tried
to represent its procedure as certain and necessary. It cannot,
therefore, confess to taking a risk in the very core of formal inference, without repudiating the ideal of logical necessity which
it takes to be the only motive force worthy of the dignity of

'valid inference.' But if risks *may* be taken, and indeed *are* taken, even in formal reasoning, is not the absolute distinction between 'valid' reasoning, which is secure and necessary, and 'invalid' reasoning, which recklessly runs appalling risks even though it attains to truth, utterly upset? Will it not become impossible to deny to reasoners the right to *choose* the risks they think worth taking? Will there not be an end to the whole show of formal validity, logical compulsion, and impersonal necessity with which Logic has made such play? Human thought will emancipate itself from the shackles of Formal Logic. It will affirm its nature as essentially a *free* activity. Men will claim the right to think in whatever ways they find most serviceable and most conducive to the attainment of their purposes. A reasoning will be 'good,' not because it observes certain arbitrary conventions of verbal manipulation, but because it leads to the end it was aimed at.

Incidentally, it will no longer be possible to assume that Logic postulates determinism, that logical necessity must prevail over human freedom, that the *best* thought must be 'valid,' and that personality and genius can contribute nothing to the *value* of a thought. Instead of being a dull rehearsal of barren and worthless technicalities, Logic will become a fascinating and progressive study of the *values* which are *created* by adventurous truth-seekers in the achievement of their purpose.

CHAPTER IV

MEANING

1. The lacunæ of Formal Logic ; 2. The omission of meaning ; 3. The biological function of meaning ; 4. The substitution of verbal meaning ; 5. The genesis of verbal meaning ; 6. The antinomy of meaning ; 7. The plasticity of meaning ; 8. How verbal meaning is communicated ; 9. Verbal meaning as raw material for personal ; 10. The ambiguity of verbal meaning ; 11. The description of personal meaning ; 12. Meaning and expression ; 13. Meaning a selection claiming value ; 14. Universality of meaning assumed ; 15. Universals=meanings conceived as ' things ' ; 16. Errors of the doctrine of Universals ; 17. Universals and particulars ; 18. Meaning and context ; 19. Conclusion.

§ 1. The Lacunæ of Formal Logic.

If we make up our minds to study our cognitive operations and activities in the empirical open-minded manner advocated in the preceding chapters, even at the cost of breaking completely with all that has traditionally passed as Logic, and if we consent to abjure the prejudices and to scrap the abstractions of Formal Logic wherever they would blind us to the facts of actual knowing, we shall at once be struck by the existence of a number of *lacunæ* in the old logics. There are many topics upon which nothing is said, or which receive at most perfunctory mention. Yet these topics are very fundamental and most important. They include such matters as Meaning, and its communication—Understanding, Context, Truth, Error, Relevance, Selection, Risk, Interest, and Purpose; and their mere recital suffices to show that without an adequate treatment of them nothing like a logic of real knowing is conceivable. Why, then, are these chapters missing?

The general answer is, because, if they were supplied they would prove incongruous with the edifice of Formal Logic, and would sweep away its foundations. The self-preserving instinct of Formal Logic may therefore be credited with suspecting this, and with omitting them on purpose. But whether this suspicion be well grounded or not, it is for us only an additional reason for making good these omissions of Formal Logic.

4

§ 2. The Omission of Meaning.

The first of these omissions, which determines all the rest and is fraught with the most serious consequences, is the omission of Meaning. It appears, moreover, to be clearly intentional and premeditated. For, as has already been hinted more than once (Chap. I, § 6; Chap. II, §§ 14, 15) and was fully shown in *Formal Logic*, the abstraction from meaning was the essential trick of Formal Logic. In essence and intention Formal Logic is a *meaningless science*—that is, a science which has made abstraction from the great and all-pervasive fact of meaning as it is harboured in human minds.

By making this abstraction Formal Logic covertly declares war upon actual thinking, and repudiates its most essential function, the ascription of Meaning.

§ 3. The Biological Function of Meaning.

It is a psychological fact that ordinarily we not only cherish meanings ourselves, but ascribe them to everybody and everything else. We all suppose all events and all experiences to 'have a meaning'; this is the great animistic postulate that stirs us up to 'understand' the world. A purely 'theoretic' philosophy may find it hard to justify this postulate, but it can hardly deny that it is fundamental and in universal use. We are always trying to find out '*what* others mean' and '*what* things mean.' When our original animism is qualified by experience these two phrases come to diverge somewhat in meaning; the meaning of things is no longer assimilated to our own, though to 'understand what they mean' still means mainly to foresee what they will do, in the case of persons and things alike.

Still it is clear that personally we habitually assume the meaning-attitude, and that it is incidental to this to ascribe meaning to the 'objects' to which we attend. The exceptions to this statement are practically negligible. In some dream-states perhaps we become uncritical enough to let the phantasmagoria glide past without an effort to arrest it with the question —What does this mean?—but such states are rare, and the popularity of dream-books, down to the latest lucubrations of the psycho-analysts, sufficiently attests the reluctance of mankind to believe that even dreams are meaningless. With these doubtful exceptions, the meaning attitude is dominant. Everything 'has a meaning,' because everything is *taken* to have a meaning.

But what precisely is meant by having a meaning? To answer, we should raise the prior question of why we think at all. Thinking at first sight seems a thoroughly uncongenial activity, which does violence to our natural impulses. Man is by nature constructed (like the other animals) to *act*—that is, to react promptly, and without thinking, upon every stimulation: he is equipped, moreover, with an abundance of impulses to do so. Originally, normally, and habitually he does *not* think, but acts 'without reflection' (Chap. X). Thus thinking is an acquisition, and one, moreover, acquired with difficulty, and not free from drawbacks.

For it means an enormous complication of life. It means in the first place a checking of impulse, an inhibition of action. 'Stopping to think' before we act means an *arrest* of action, which at least entails a *delay* of action. Having curbed our impulse, we can proceed to 'reflect,' to think about the situation, to consider how we *ought* to act and whether it would not be *better* to modify our impulsive reaction. Now 'thinking about' the situation means considering *both* how it resembles and differs from past situations which seem to us to be relevant to our case, i.e. *comparing* the present with the past, *and also* guessing at its 'meaning,' i.e. estimating the future to which it points, and anticipating what it leads to. The present 'means' something in the light of the past and with a view to the future. Its 'meaning,' therefore, is both retrospective and prospective; it knits together past and future, and carries our action from the one on to the other.

The biological importance of the whole procedure is obvious. Stopping to think and the control of impulse is a habit which has (to some extent) developed in man in response to the requirements of his life. For man has put his trust in the development of intelligence, and this means that he no longer guides his acts

by quasi-mechanical habits, but has taken to appreciating each
situation on its merits and to modifying his reaction accordingly.
Thinking about his situation is what enables him to do this. It
is of value if, and when, it enables him to change his impulsive
response *for the better*. His reflective response, moreover, must
not only be better, but so much better as to outweigh the loss of
the time spent in 'reflection.' If this were not so, thinking would
be a pernicious habit which natural selection would not allow
to grow up, or would eradicate. Actually, thinking is often
valuable, because it breaks down the uniformity of habitual reaction and initiates new and more various responses which are
improvements on the old, and mediate closer adjustments to the
peculiarities of each case. Every 'case' is, of course, different
from every other in some respects, and it is advantageous
to adjust oneself to a variety of cases; but if it were merely
different we could not argue from it, and it would afford no
guidance. We take it, therefore, *as a 'case,'* i.e. as a variation
upon some general theme, a 'law' or 'universal.' By this
latter we mean a formula to be exemplified also in future cases,
which also will have (irrelevant) differences. But we must show
our judgment in selecting a suitable 'law,' for which the differences between the cases argued from, and to, will *really* be
irrelevant: for otherwise the law will not lead us to the right
anticipations. Thus the test of the right selection, alike of the
'case' we extracted from our situation, and of the 'law' it exemplified, is *successful prediction* and anticipation. Successful
prediction is the *aim* of the thinking that is valuable ('good' and
'true'), and also its *justification*.

For the biological value of successful prediction is beyond dispute. If we can foresee what is coming, we are no longer the
sport of circumstance. We need no longer stumble blindly into
pitfalls. We can to a large extent control our future We can
prepare for events, and avoid them, or alter them. No wonder,
therefore, that prediction and control are eagerly desired, that
we have become creatures that 'look before and after,' and do
both in order that we may survive. Prediction and control are
rightly deemed the very essence of science, and the most con-

vincing attestations of our attainment of truth. And the ascription of meaning is the first and most indispensable step in a scientific procedure which is hallowed by biological need and vindicated by success. It is the first and most fundamental of the great postulates of knowledge which have been so long disguised and distorted as '*a priori* necessities of thought.' They are not necessities (i.e. needs) of thought, but of *life*, and their function is *biological*. That *events shall mean* is, both logically and chronologically, prior to the problem of *what* they mean. Compared with this primary act of faith in our ability to understand our life, our other cognitive assumptions are derivative. Compared with it the 'law of causation,' which has been the subject of so much philosophic wrangling, is a subordinate and dubious consequence. Compared with it even the analysis of a situation as a 'case' of a 'law' ('universal'), though it is the most *successful* (not initially the most promising) of the many modes of divination human ingenuity has devised, is quite secondary. The ascription of Meaning is by far the most fundamental of the 'presuppositions' of the theory of knowledge.

§ 4. The Substitution of Verbal Meaning.

How can Logic, then, dare to ignore it? Certainly to abstract from it seems a stupendous undertaking. Yet Formal Logic has done the trick for ages without being caught out. Naturally it was not an easy thing to carry through, but Formal Logic has been astute enough to see that it could hardly hope to escape detection without proffering a substitute for what it had ruled out. So it has very plausibly substituted *verbal* meaning, the 'dictionary meaning' of words, for *real meaning*, which is the only meaning that has importance for life and science. The latter always arises in a particular situation, and it is always *personal*; i.e. it is what men mean when they *use* words to express and convey *their* meaning.

By this substitution Formal Logic scores doubly. It gets rid at a blow not only of real meaning but also of real use, and this is a very convenient simplification. For it enables Formal Logic to dispense, in principle, with the examination of the actual uses of thoughts and words in the sciences, and so renders 'logical criticism' self-sufficient and unassailable. Equipped with a knowledge of 'the' meaning of words, the logician can, unchallenged, substitute 'propositions' for judgments, 'validity' for truth, 'fallacy' for error, logical 'necessity' for intelligent purpose; he can create a realm of technical abstractions of which he is the undisputed master and to which no one else has the key. Here he can safely lay down the (logical) law, and live unassailed ever afterwards in a Cloud-Cuckootown of his own imagining, while claiming eminent domain over all other regions of knowledge. It is no wonder that suggestions that meaning depends upon use, must be observed in the living thought, and cannot be determined by 'reflection' upon words, are felt to be disturbing; and it becomes possible to understand how any reference to the problems and procedures of actual knowing jars upon the logician, and to appreciate the animosity excited in his breast by any mention of use and usefulness.

§ 5. The Genesis of Verbal Meaning.

The substitution, moreover, of verbal for personal meaning has been an amazing success. Not undeservedly; for it was really a very adroit piece of prestidigitation. Verbal meaning is not merely a very familiar fact, especially to the literary classes from which logicians were recruited, but also a very colourable imitation of real meaning. Moreover, it is undeniably related to it, and interacts with it in sundry subtle ways. These relations will become plainer if we inquire (1) how words acquire meaning, (2) how the antinomy of meaning may be overcome, and (3) how words may be utilised to convey meaning.

(1) Initially words are nothing but noises, i.e. more or less articulate sounds. Hence any meaning they are said to 'have' must plainly be *acquired*. It is clear also that words can acquire meaning only in, and by, use. When they are used to express meaning and succeed in conveying it, the memory of this occurrence may remain. It will prompt one who has successfully expressed annoyance before by crying *pish !* to say *pish !* again

the next time he is annoyed. If he said *pish* impressively enough, and was effectively understood, what was originally *his* meaning becomes 'common'; it comes to be associated with the sound for others also: 'annoyance' then becomes '*the*' meaning of the word '*pish*.' Thereupon the word will suggest 'annoyance' to anyone who hears it, and knows the language to which it belongs. Thus words acquire a power of arousing mental activity, and can throw us into attitudes of expectancy of meanings similar to those which they have conveyed before.

§ 6. (2) The Antinomy of Meaning.

But this is not to say that every word *must* always mean what it meant before, and *can* mean nothing else; nor even that it *should* mean nothing else. Words should exhibit both stability and flexibility of meaning to be really useful, and neither should be overdone.

Bearing this in mind we can easily dispose of what may be called 'the Antinomy of Meaning.' This is at first sight a very pretty paradox, an analogue and foretaste of the puzzle about novelty in reasoning which has baffled logicians for so many centuries (Chap. XIV, § 7).

It may be stated thus: (*a*) Any meaning which is worth conveying must be in a manner *new*. For we neither think nor formulate meaning, unless we find ourselves in a situation which stimulates us in some way to modify our habitual reactions and to change them for something *better*: nor do we desire to convey our meaning to others, unless we think we have news to impart. Bores alone communicate meanings which are already known, and even they may be charitably supposed to believe that they are imparting news.

On the other hand (*b*) it would seem that any meaning we *can* convey must be *old*. For the apparatus by which we seek to convey our novel meaning is of necessity traditional and conventional. It consists of words and gestures with a familiar meaning which is supposed to be known, and must resist any attempt to change it. If, therefore, we try to mean something new with it we shall not be understood. The meanings of words, then, are *fixed*, and cannot be changed at will. And it follows that no new meaning can ever be conveyed, because it is necessarily unintelligible.

This conclusion, however, is obviously absurd. If it is possible to mean and to convey meaning, it must be possible to convey new meaning, expressive of all the new situations in which we find ourselves. And words must be capable of ministering to our needs. Our problem, therefore, is merely that of showing *how* they do so ; any theory which forbids them to do so must be wrong.

Now it is clear that a successful transfer of meaning has to satisfy two conditions. (1) It has to presuppose and respect old meanings and to employ old truths ; but it has also (2) so to arrange them in their contexts as to develop new meanings out of them, in order to express new truths. Thus its business is to pour new wine into old bottles—an achievement which has ceased to be the proverbial impossibility it was with the substitution of glass for goatskins—or otherwise, to bring about in the old meanings the modifications required to adapt them to the new situation.

From this it follows that the meanings of words *must* be plastic, and that their fixity cannot be absolute. The fixity of meaning is in fact a *fiction*, with at most a limited use. If any logic insists on taking it literally, it thereby confesses that it conceives itself merely as a word-game with fictitious counters, which could have no serious use.

For if a word had a *perfectly* fixed meaning it could be used only once, and never again; it could be applied only to the situation which originally called for it, and which it uniquely fitted. If, the next time it was used, it retained its original meaning it could not designate the actual situation but would still hark back to its past use, and this would disqualify it for all future use. Thus, if the meaning of 'Nero' had been tied down to a certain historical Roman Emperor, I could not call my dog 'Nero.' And this would not only be inconvenient but in the end absurd. It would point to the 'ideal' of a language in which all the words had always to be changed every time they were used. It is evident that the intellectual strain of continuously inventing new words would be intolerable, and that the chances of being understood would be very small. Thus the price of fixity would be unintelligibility. The impracticability of such a language might not perhaps be regarded as its 'theoretic' refutation; but after all languages are meant to be used, and human intelligence at any rate could make no use of it.

Accordingly human languages are not so absurd. All their words are capable of repeated use in different situations and with different meanings. They are all 'ambiguous'—potentially—for they are far fewer in number than meanings, and each, therefore, has to express a plurality of meanings. They are all 'universals,' applicable to an indefinite number of particular cases, with infinite shades of meaning. For when the same word is used in two cases it has never quite the same meaning. 'Nero I' may be an infamous emperor. 'Nero II' a good dog, 'Nero III' an indifferent. And let it not be objected that this doctrine holds but of proper names. If I had called the two canine Neros both 'dogs,' I should not have meant 'dog' in quite the same way; though by using the general term I may have implied that for my actual purpose the differences between 'Nero II' and 'Nero III' were irrelevant, and that both were 'dogs' (see further, § 16).

§ 7. The Plasticity of Meaning.

It should be clear, then, that the plasticity of meaning is quite as important as its stability; while its alleged 'fixity' is an illusion. It is, of course, generally desirable that most words should have fairly determinate and approximately recurrent meanings, seeing that these greatly facilitate understanding of 'their' sense (which is properly the sense of those who use them!) on the particular occasions when they are used; and it would never do if any word might mean anything, and so past uses afforded no clue or guidance to future use. But it cannot be too strongly emphasised that every actual meaning is *new*, and that its understanding is a distinct achievement, even where the most commonplace meanings are conveyed in the most ordinary ways. Moreover, besides words with definite and stable meanings, most languages have a stock of expletives, which have no cognitive value and are merely expressions of feeling, and find a use for vague and indeterminate words like 'thingumabob' and 'gadget' which have very little meaning of their own, and, for this very reason, seem applicable to a great variety of situations. For practical purposes, indeed, and in ordinary life, it seems that our most useful words, or at any rate those which are most often used, are somewhat vague and decidedly elastic in their meaning. Logicians are wont to decry them as 'ambiguous,' because they still cherish the 'ideal' of fixity of meaning, and do not distinguish between real ambiguity in actual use and the potential ambiguity or 'plurality of senses' of elastic and useful words.[1] But it ill becomes philosophers to complain of the useful elasticity of ordinary speech, for they are not noted for the precision and asceticism of their own terminology. Indeed, it is one of the chief sources of the difficulty of philosophy that no philosophic term ever retains any technical meaning, because no sooner does one philosopher try to assign a fairly definite meaning to it than another comes and uses it in a different sense, merely because he likes the term.[2]

Now definiteness of meaning, though it is not often possessed by ordinary language, is the virtue of technical terminology.

[1] For this distinction, see *Formal Logic*, chap. ii, § 8.

[2] Almost every philosopher has claimed the right of inventing a technical terminology of his own. This means that to understand him we have, as it were, to learn a new language. But, as to understand anyone we have *in any case* to learn *his* use of words, this claim may be allowed. But he should feel that to appropriate the technical language of another without due notice is both wrong and foolish; foolish because he makes himself so much harder to understand, and wrong because he spoils *good* technical terms. He should feel, therefore, that his privilege of making technical terminology carries with it two duties—that of using his own consistently, and that of respecting that of others. It is because philosophers have never scrupled to set themselves above these duties that philosophic language is such a chaos. This is why e.g. 'idea' and 'cause' have meant such various things, why 'subject' and 'object' have exchanged mean-

It is a valuable property in a term, because it facilitates under-standing by restricting the range of probable variations in use. But it should not be mistaken for fixity. However carefully we define a term, however conscientiously we distinguish and tabulate all its recognised and prescribed uses recorded in a standard dictionary, we cannot tie its *future* uses down to them. We cannot stop all subsequent developments of its meaning. We cannot prevent the next user of the word from using it in a slightly different sense, because he finds himself involved in a slightly different situation. Strictly, indeed, this is what *always* happens, seeing that all events are unique, and that nothing is ever repeated absolutely. Nor can he be prevented from per-verting an established meaning by sarcastic, jocose, meta-phorical, or merely ignorant, usage.

In principle, therefore, the attempt to arrest the growth of meaning is wrong and foolish. If it were possible, it would deprive language of its plasticity and words of their usefulness. For, just in proportion as their meanings had been fixed, they would cease to be transferable to new situations. So to deal with these, masses of new words would perpetually have to be coined, while the old ones, being inseparably attached to past conditions, would rapidly become obsolete, with the resulting inconvenience that even though the words themselves did not change their meanings, the language to which they belonged would be continually changing its words and scrapping its former vocabulary. It is, therefore, preferable to preserve the continuity of a language by allowing it to extend the meaning of its words. It is only thus that we are enabled to 'ride' a bicycle or to 'drive' a motor-car or a train.

ings, and why ' idealism ' and ' realism ' have been so misused that by now either or both may be applied to any philosophy. These strictures, I may add, are partly prompted by my own experience. When I tried to make ' humanism ' a technical term in philosophy in order to describe the attitude which makes man's standpoint central and is antithetical to Absolutism and Naturalism alike, the first thing that Professor J. S. Mackenzie did was to give the title *Lectures on Humanism* to his own version of Absolutism, and since then others have used the term in antithesis to theism.

§ 8. (3) How Verbal Meaning is Communicated.

Meanings would have to be plastic, even if they were strictly personal and used words solely for the purpose of ordering experiences. But the most obvious use of speech is to convey personal meaning to other persons. The meaning of words then becomes *social*,[1] without ceasing to be personal. If we then consider the case of the man who wishes to make use of words to express a meaning he has to convey we reach similar conclusions. Assuming him to know what he means, he has in his mind an entirely definite and specific meaning, bearing on his actual situation, which he burns to communicate. His meaning is an indisputable psychic fact of which he is immediately aware. It is entirely personal, so far, but, if we suppose it to be important enough, it may entirely engross his soul, and absorb all that, for the moment, he actually *is*.

Now how is he to set about it to convey this meaning to others? There are, of course, various modes of expression which, upon occasion, may be more efficacious and eloquent than words, but we will suppose that he decides upon the use of significant sounds, i.e. words. The question then arises *what* words he is to use. He has all the words of the language to choose from, or at any rate all he knows. His first problem, therefore, is a problem of *suitable selection*. He must pick out the words which will *best* convey his meaning. For not all are capable of conveying it, nor will all do so equally well. It may well be, e.g. if he is using a foreign language, that he has not sufficient command of words to express his meaning at all. Or it may be so unique and unprecedented, so wondrous a discovery, as to transcend the existing resources of language or to be ineffable altogether. The mystics, when they attempt to report their revelations, are apt to encounter this difficulty.

So, even when the best words available have been selected, the problem of conveying his meaning with them remains. For though all words are plastic, they are not indefinitely so.

[1] For an excellent account of the social side of language, see *Speech*, by Professor G. A. de Laguna (Yale University Press, 1927).

Socially they have established meanings, which must be more or less respected, and he cannot in general make them mean what he wills. Even Humpty Dumpty, who so masterfully overworked his words, found that it was not enough to say "impenetrability" to Alice, but that he had to explain also what he meant by it. Philosophers frequently neglect to take this precaution when they use technical terms. So there is need of skill in the use of words and of diplomatic manipulation. They may have to be coaxed, and stretched, and transfigured, in order to be adapted to the particular situation. A skilful manipulator may so master language as to mould it into an expression of novel meanings and unheard-of thoughts. But it is also possible to fail, and indeed more usual. This is why even slightly new ideas are always misunderstood at first.

But in all cases we have really the same problem—that of so utilising the meanings words have, or can be made to take on, as to convey the personal meaning one desires to impart. This problem would be insoluble, if language were not plastic and if words could not change their meaning so as to accommodate it to the varying requirements of various situations.

§ 9. Verbal Meaning as Raw Material for Personal.

It is clear then that, alike in origin and importance, personal meaning is primary and verbal meaning secondary. The latter is the raw material 'personal' meaning uses for its communications, the instrument for its expression. So verbal meaning is potential; what it actually means has to be determined on each occasion when it is used, and it is always a problem whether the transition from the meaning of the words to the meaning of the man who uses them has been correctly effected.

This difficulty is perhaps best revealed by considering the problem of *translation*. Here the translator sets himself to reproduce a personal meaning which was in the mind of the writer of his text; but he has direct access only to the words of the latter. These words have (more or less inexact) equivalents in the language he is translating into, and if he does not know their (verbal) meanings he can look them up in the dictionary.

The meanings there recorded, therefore, form the raw material of his version: he has so to select and combine them as to make sense, and the *right* sense, i.e. that which was *intended* by his author. If he is unskilful he will select wrongly and mis-translate, even into nonsense. And if he is also obstinate, as some schoolboys are, or Formalist enough to be content with verbal meaning, he may try to justify his mistranslation by saying, "But, sir, I found these meanings in the dictionary." Whereupon the wise schoolmaster should reply, "But don't you see that they won't do *here*? They make nonsense of this passage, and the author cannot possibly have meant them in these senses. It is no use your saying that you found them in your dictionary. In other contexts they would be right because they would make sense. But they are wrong here. And *your* business was to make out *this* passage. So you should have used your dictionary to select meanings that would make sense here: even if the sense was rare and peculiar, and not in the dictionary, you should have tried to derive from the senses recorded one that would suit your passage."

Thus it is clear that the dictionary meanings only offer advice to the user of a word, and are not *the real and actual meaning* which we attempt to express and to understand, with the aid of verbal meaning, even though the misleading associations of the words we have to employ may often defeat us. Verbal meaning, on the other hand, is only *potential*, and grows actual only when some one can be found to use a form of words as a fit formula wherewith to express *his* meaning. Consequently, it is to sacrifice the substance to the shadow to substitute verbal for personal meaning and to exclude the latter from Logic.

In repudiating this practice we cannot assert too emphatically or too often that meaning depends upon use, and that *no form of words has any actual meaning until it is used*, and that what it means *then* is not a question which can be decided in advance by dictionaries, by speculation, or by any reflection, however prolonged, on the meaning of the words. All this is only a rough guide to their probable use, and cannot overrule the meaning of the man who uses them.[1] It is a question of fact which depends on the *context* in which the words are used, and on the *intention* of their user. It has to be ascertained then and there, or not at all.

§ 10. The 'Ambiguity' of Verbal Meaning.

We arrive, moreover, at the same conclusion by considering the 'ambiguity' of words. According to the reckoning of Formal Logic every word, or form of words, is infinitely 'ambiguous'; for every word or form of words has an indefinite plurality of meanings which vary according to the occasions of its use. Its past uses can (theoretically) be recorded in an exhaustive dictionary, but its future uses can no more be predicted than its future pronunciation.

But this sort of 'ambiguity' does not really matter; it is only another name for the 'plasticity' of language. And it is something wholly different from the *real* ambiguity which occurs when a word or a phrase conveys *several* meanings to those who hear it used *in its actual context*, and leaves them in doubt as to *which* of these was intended, and whether the ambiguity was intentional. In such cases it is useless to appeal to the dictionary and to enumerate and discuss the possible meanings. Our business is to ascertain the actual meaning. There is nothing for it but to *ask* those who have *used* those ambiguities what they *meant*, and to ask them to remove them so that we may reach understanding.

No doubt this simple procedure would strike the logician as crude and unprofessional, much as it would shock a lawyer to plead the intentions of a testator against the wording of his will. For it would instantly dissolve a number of hoary puzzles which have formed part of his stock-in-trade for centuries; but real knowing would be a gainer by the disappearance of a mass of pseudo-problems. Thus, when Epimenides the Cretan said (if

---

[1] Even if he *misuses* them, it cannot be maintained that he did not mean what he meant because his words meant something else. The penalty he incurs by using words wrongly is misunderstanding, and if and when this is cleared up, it is *his* meaning which is recognised, though his actual words may have been discarded as 'incorrect.'

he ever said it !) that all Cretans were liars, the proper way with his assertion was to ask him what he meant, instead of treating it as an all but insoluble paradox capable of determining a whole logical theory. He probably meant 'all the *other* Cretans'; and certainly he could not have meant that no liar ever spoke the truth, which is the interpretation required for the further development of the *Liar* 'fallacy.' Similarly, the way to find out what is meant by ' I lie,' or ' I am dead,' or 'asleep,' is to *ask* those who make such remarks, and so to discover that they are insane, or jesting, or ignorant of English, or speaking in a context which dissipates the verbal paradox.

It follows, therefore, as a corollary from the recognition that real meaning is personal, that it may always be inquired into. When there is any doubt or dispute as to what any doctrine means, the personal meaning always *must* be inquired into. The right thing to do is to ask those who hold the doctrine what they mean by it. Where this cannot be done, because they have been allowed to die before they were questioned, it is usually futile to debate the logical possibilities of its meaning, which will only be verbal and cannot be securely attached to the real meaning; the right moral to draw is that in future the mistake of failing to record historical evidence while it was available should not be repeated.

§ 11. The Description of Personal Meaning.

To say that real meaning is personal is to imply that it has a psychological side and demands psychological description. But such description is not easy to get. For the description of personality and of everything connected therewith is notoriously one of the sorest points of psychology, even though psychology cannot shirk it, like Formal Logic, by abstracting from it altogether. The psychologist may recognise that the subject of meaning has great logical importance, but this is more likely to intimidate than to encourage him, and he will probably fight shy of it. No wonder the descriptions of meaning as a psychical process are left in a thoroughly unsatisfactory condition.

We must begin, therefore, by rejecting certain inadequate

accounts. Initially meaning is nothing 'objective,' though it comes to be ascribed to 'objects'; it is neither a *thing* nor a *relation* between things. It is nothing that the world can be conceived as continuing to possess, if all minds had been eliminated from it. It is, therefore, in this sense, and so far, 'subjective.' It is also plainly an experience. Yet it is not well described as a 'mental process.' For it is not merely a happening in the mind, but rather a reaction of the mind upon the course of events, and an attitude taken up towards potential objects of thought, which are transfigured when meaning is *attributed* to them. As such a flash of intellectual activity meaning is unique and irreducible; there is no substitute for it, and nothing else like it, and nothing that can explain it away.

§ 12. Meaning and Expression.

Nor is it to be identified with any of its forms of expression: it lies much deeper. It springs from the depths of the soul, and no words can exhaust it. So it is essentially independent of what we *say*. A look, a nod, a wink, a sigh, a start, will often reveal meaning better than a rigmarole of words. What we *say* may be restricted by our limited command of language and the recalcitrance of words; it has often to be withdrawn or corrected, as not being what we *meant*. Yet our meaning may be perfectly clear all the time, not only to ourselves but also to others, who recognise that we are not saying what we mean. Thus when a man, eating apple-tart at dinner, asks his neighbour to pass him the pepper, the latter will probably reply, "You mean the sugar." Is it not ludicrous, then, that Formal Logic should put forward the pretension of overruling what is meant by what is said? An honest man will always try to say what he means, and, if he is also *intelligent*, he will succeed in saying it: but, according to Bradley, the logician, being bound to *mean* what he *says*, does the very opposite. This is really a slur upon Logic (Chap. I, § 11).

It is these failures of expression which bring out most clearly both the difference between what is said and what is meant, and

5

also the distinctive character of the meaning-experience. For, as is so often the case with our mental processes, we are most intensely conscious of our meaning-experience when its expression is *obstructed*. When all goes well we hardly attend to it, but when we fail to express our meaning we realise that the meaning-experience may be clear and intense without any utterance at all. Who has not failed to remember a name he meant, though it was 'on the tip of his tongue,' and he was sure he could pick it out of a thousand, if only he heard it? Most of us are familiar also with the agonies of expressing a clearly conceived meaning in a foreign tongue where the words fail us. Nor are conditions of 'aphasia' altogether rare, in which, though meaning persists unimpaired, utterance is inhibited wholly or in part, or the words 'come out wrong'; we are subject also to 'slips of the tongue,' 'spoonerisms,' and other accidents which put us into the position of saying what we do not mean. Clearly, then, the meaning-experience is one thing and its expression is another.

§ 13. Meaning a Selection claiming Value.

It should be noted further that, even when meaning is successfully expressed, there is usually far more meaning felt than finds expression. As a rule the meaning we express is only a selected part of the meaning we experience, to wit the part we judge to be *worth communicating*. It follows that every utterance is the victor in a struggle for existence, and *ipso facto* has prevailed over every alternative that was not uttered. The very fact that it *was* uttered proves that it was judged a *good* thing to say, and worth making, and *better* than any alternative or than preserving an injudicious silence. Thus every assertion actually made in real life, as opposed to paper 'propositions' of 'logic,' must *have been* judged good and useful by its maker in order to come into being at all. The fact that subsequently this judgment may be revoked, and repudiated as wrong, does not alter the psychological situation. But it is important to realise already in describing meaning how completely all our cognitive activities are pervaded by value-judgments and selections.

§ 14. Universality of Meaning Assumed.

Speaking objectively, Meaning is a universal fact. As was shown in § 3, everything has a meaning, or is at least suspected of having one, and the hope of its discovery, if we will but look for it, forms a vital factor in scientific research. We saw also that though Meaning refers to the past it points to the future, and that without this universal assumption of Meaning we should have no means of intelligently anticipating the future. Our assumption, however, is so spontaneous, unconscious, and deep-seated that it does not figure among the *a priori* 'presuppositions' of thought in the logic-books.

Moreover, though the meaning we ascribe claims to be 'objective,' its source remains 'subjective.' That events and things 'have meaning' is an animistic and anthropomorphic postulate and the beginning of all teleology. We *take* all our experiences to have a meaning, because we habitually assume the meaning-attitude ourselves. It is continuous and all-pervasive and colours all our life. It is rare for this attitude to be relaxed, and for the mind to sink into a condition of (approximately) 'pure contemplation.'

Normally, however, Meaning forms a natural postulate both of life and of intelligibility. Without assuming that the course of events has meaning and points to the future, we could do nothing to adjust ourselves to it. Nor could we 'understand' it, i.e. interpret the present and the future in the light of the past. Yet abstractly and 'theoretically' no cogent reason can be given for our assumption. Why should reality oblige us by harbouring a meaning, and not be merely such as it is, with no *arrière pensée* or significance behind it? Or even if it *has* meaning, why should its meaning be comprehensible *to us*? Our assumption is plainly dictated by our interests, and that the world has meaning is a postulate which springs from our needs, and no 'necessity of thought.'

§ 15. 'Universals'=Meanings Conceived as 'Things.'

Finally, there should be mentioned an important development of verbal meaning which has enabled it to play a leading *rôle* in philosophic history. By their use as vehicles of meaning words not only acquire what seems an inherent meaning of their own, but also generate the mysterious entities variously called Ideas, Concepts, or Universals. These entities have been one of the chief topics of philosophy, and have given rise to endless and fruitless disputes among philosophers from Plato's day to ours; but they are nothing really but meanings embodied in words and conceived as *things*, instead of as *attitudes*. The process of thought which ends in this conclusion may be represented as follows.

We have seen that meaning is primarily personal, and the reaction of an agent on a particular situation in which he finds himself. But this involves real meaning in a peculiar disability. Must it not be as *fleeting* as the situation which evokes it, and to which it refers? If it is acted on, it becomes, no doubt, a real factor in the development of the situation and contributes to the making of reality. But the moment its work is done it is superseded and swept into the past. Other meanings take its place, equally active and ephemeral. Meaning thus seems to dissolve into a succession or flow of momentary meanings.

Nevertheless two things endure, the *mind* which engendered the meaning and continues to recognise former meanings and to attribute fresh meanings to further events, and the *words* in which the meaning was expressed. If, thereupon, we yield to the natural objectivist bias of primitive thought and disregard the mind, attention is concentrated on the function of words as conservers of meaning. These can be used again and again (whenever a mind recognises a *similar* situation) without undergoing any visible change. Thus the meanings of words seem stable. They come to seem fixed points amid the flow of phenomena. Men may come and men may go, but 'man' is predicated of them all. 'Man,' therefore, is one and the same, in all cases and for all time. It is 'eternal' and 'universal.' It is the one in the many, the unity which pervades and sustains them.

And then we can begin to perplex ourselves. What is this wondrous and mysterious unity? Surely it is more than a mere word! Rather it is the *essence* of things, and all their varying

qualities are 'accidents.' The Universal is the core of their
being, the 'Man' in all 'men.'

And not only does all being depend upon the presence of such
Universals, but so also does all knowledge. In all knowing we
predicate Universals, and nothing but Universals. The particular as such is indescribable and unutterable. It is not a subject
of science.[1] It is an illusion of our senses, the unreal and unstable product of the intelligible machinery that lurks behind
the scene. The real effective structure of science, as of reality,
is a system of combined and connected Universals; and blessed
alone is the philosopher who recognises this!

After this fashion most philosophers have reasoned, ever since
Plato discovered this way of soaring from the sensible world of
change and decay into an intelligible world of immutable
Truth and imperishable Being, by dint of pure reflection. It
seemed an easy and attractive way of rising above the vulgar
herd and of establishing oneself in a better world.

§ 16. Errors of the Doctrine of Universals.

Unfortunately it was not noticed that, even on its own presuppositions, the doctrine of Universals is not, on a vital point,
a correct transcription of the facts it undertakes to interpret.
Is it true that when we predicate the same 'Universal' of two
cases of 'the same,' the Universal, i.e. meaning, is absolutely
identical, and that the difference between the two cases becomes
totally irrelevant and 'accidental'? When a particular 'Smith'
and a particular 'Jones' are both called 'men,' it is probably
in a context and with a purpose which renders irrelevant their
respective idiosyncrasies and the differences between them, such
as that of establishing their common mortality; but this does not
mean that no differences exist, nor even that we have failed to
observe them. They do not cease to exist because we have
chosen to abstract from them, rightly or wrongly. And for some
purposes the differences between 'Smith' and 'Jones' may become relevant, and even vital. For example, we could hardly

[1] This has hardly been questioned since Plato inferred it
(*Theætetus*, 209).

infer that because 'man loves woman,' a particular man loves a particular woman—say that 'Smith' loves 'Jemima,' or 'Jones' 'Belinda': both may love the same woman, or neither. To argue this would be fully as absurd as to insist that all the many 'Smiths' must have a common quality of essential 'Smithness' in virtue of the Universal 'Smith' which pervades and unites them—a logical implication of its doctrine which even Formal Logic repudiates.

The truth is that when we predicate the same 'universal' of two cases it is always on the supposition that the differences between the cases are irrelevant for the purpose of our argument. The descriptive term which we apply is always applied to a particular case, and is not strictly true unless it *means* that case in its full particularity. *As applied*, therefore, it is particularised, and ceases to be universal, except in so far as we admit that for some purpose, *not ours*,[1] its particularity may be abstracted from. Thus, when I call a man 'Smith,' I mean that particular 'Smith,' and no *other*; when I call a cat 'Puss,' I mean that particular 'puss.' There is not really any difference between common terms and proper names in this respect. When both are *used*, and not merely talked about by philosophers, both refer to particular cases, and aid us, in different ways, to deal with them; abstractly, both *may* apply to an unspecified and indefinite plurality of cases. So, in use, the qualities of the other 'Smiths' and the other 'pusses' are irrelevant *when, and because, they are not meant*, just as the differences become irrelevant when we are interested only in their common aspects.

But whoever predicates 'universals' always *takes a risk*. The connexions we establish between events by means of universals are all tentative and precarious. We have always a *choice* of universals, and it is never absolutely certain that the 'universals' we have chosen to predicate will apply to our case. It is never absolutely certain that the differences between two cases to which the same term is applied will prove irrelevant. The event alone can assure us that we were right, and did well to take our risk. Thus real logic pledges itself to a very radical

[1] For that *ex hypothesi* is to know the particular case.

empiricism and in no wise endorses the Formal view that 'valid reasoning' demands an avoidance of risk.

§ 17. Universals and Particulars.

Thus it is utterly misleading to say that particulars are indescribable, and that knowledge is not concerned with them. Knowledge is concerned with 'particulars' just as much as with 'universals.' And for the simple reason that they are correlative abstractions, both extracted by our act from the flow of events which we must analyse in order to control. That they are correlative appears from the fact that no one can ever say what a 'universal' is except by reference to 'particulars,' or what a 'particular' is except by reference to 'universals,' or what an 'individual' is except some sort of union of universal and particular. It is, moreover, profoundly untrue that some universals are 'concrete,' while others are 'abstract.' All alike are 'abstract' in the sense that they are extracts from our *data*; all alike are 'concrete' *in their use*, while all alike sink into words with merely potential meaning and application when not in use.

When in use they are really describing 'particulars' all the time. For we use them to describe the 'particular cases' we are engaged upon, and we value general principles, 'laws,' and 'universals' only as *instruments* for dealing with a particular case or problem which we *mean* to attack. Thus their real and essential reference is always to such a case or problem.

So much is really implied in the very notion of a 'particular case.' This is not that incredible philosophic myth, a 'mere particular'; it means in the first place a particular *selection* concentrated upon, and in the second an *intention* to treat it, not as something unique and intractable, but as a 'case' *of* a universal, to be correlated with others of the same 'kind.' Our problem, then, is to *find* the kind appropriate to the particular situation.

There is never, therefore, a question whether universals will apply to a particular case. *That* question is always begged—for methodological reasons. The question is always *which* is the *right* universal to apply. And, to answer this, no particularity of the case can be excluded *a priori*; anyone, however latent and inconspicuous, *may* prove relevant and affect the working of the universal we select. We have, therefore, to *experiment* with universals, and to try a number in succession. Probably each one will carry us part of the way, and indeed none can carry us to the very end. For in the end there always remains something unique and novel about every situation, simply because life is too original ever quite to repeat itself.

Universals, therefore, are in no wise higher beings that must be adored. They are verbal meanings which must be used, and they function as instruments. They are no solution of any problem of knowing; and their general usefulness in no wise helps in the actual selection of the right universals for the purposes of any inquiry. In their actual use some are right and others wrong, some are true and others false, and all knowing revolves around the difficulty of selecting the right ones.

§ 18. Meaning and Context.

The nearest approach in traditional logic to a recognition of personal meaning is to be found in the recent, but growing, admission that meaning depends upon *context*. But its recognition of context is hardly more than nominal, and it is very far from apprehending its scope. It hardly realises that context is a substitute for some of its most cherished notions; that a train of thought, for example, is far more completely accounted for by the context in which it arises than by the logical concatenation of the 'propositions' which it formulates. No doubt there are logical considerations which influence the course even of the most 'illogical' thinking, but these are effective only in so far as they enter into it as psychic facts, and even then they never explain everything.

Thus a logical 'contradiction,' involved in the terms a thinker uses, explains nothing *as such* about the course of his thought: so long as he does not feel it, it will make no difference. It begins to make a difference only when it is realised; but what that difference will be cannot be determined until we know the circumstances of an actual case. For what difference a perceived 'contradiction' will make will depend on how clearly it is recognised, on the character and texture of the mind that realises it, on the subject it is about, on how much is at stake, on how important is the aim of the thought it defeats, on a host of accidental secondary circumstances, which may direct or divert a train of thought. Of all these psychological factors Formal Logic takes no cognisance; it is no wonder, therefore, that purely logical considerations will explain so very little about the actual course of events. It is a reasonably safe prediction that the only 'logical' inference from the situation will not occur; there will not be the complete arrest of thought which should result from a logical *impasse*. But we cannot foresee which of the many possible expedients open to him the self-contradicting thinker will actually adopt. He may, conceivably, do what is practically the best thing to do—he may abandon one of his self-contradictory terms or arguments, or both, and endeavour to substitute better ones. But he is much more likely to do something else. He may grow sceptical; he may get angry; he may despair. Or he may 'look the contradiction boldly in the face and pass on,' as if nothing had occurred. Or again he may accept the Law of Contradiction in the abstract and yet refuse to let it apply to his concrete case, and plead that the contradiction is verbal while his meaning remains sound. Where the 'contradiction' has not been discovered by himself and is only alleged against him by others, the possibilities are immensely enlarged: he can always start a dispute, and it is only in the rarest cases that a charge of self-contradiction is ever admitted and carries conviction. So that Formal Logic is really pretty helpless to exercise the coercion which it professes to regard as the ideal of argument.

§ 19. Conclusion.

These considerations seem to show that Formal Logic has erred in regarding self-contradiction as an infallible criterion of truth and the supreme offence against Logic. Self-contradiction may be merely verbal, and may indicate only lack of care in making meaning explicit; at worst it may mean a confusion of thought in which no meaning has found expression. But lack of meaning is the really fatal defect; for it cuts the ground from beneath Logic, and no superstructure can be built upon it once this fundamental conception is removed. It is, therefore, in the interest of Logic itself that we must renew our protest against the Formalist abstraction from Meaning: it may make an easier nonsense-game, but it is death to the science of Logic.

CHAPTER V

RELEVANCE

1. Relevance a practical need ; 2. Positive implications of relevance : (1) Subjectivity ; 3. (2) Is selection of the relevant part ; 4. (3) Is risky ; 5. (4) Is disputable ; 6. Negative implications of relevance ; 7. The vain search for safety ; 8. How the relevant is selected ; 9. The fatal omission of relevance by inductive logic ; 10. Conclusion.

§ 1. Relevance a Practical Need.

If logicians had been able to start with a clean slate, instead of puzzling over the palimpsests of 2000 years, they could hardly have failed to recognise the existence and importance of Relevance much sooner and more explicitly than they have done. As it was, they never discovered it, and the central doctrine of the most prevalent logic still consists of a flat denial of Relevance and of all the ideas associated with it. For it represents knowledge as based upon, and aiming at, all-inclusiveness instead of at selection of the relevant.

But, of course, the blindness of logicians did not prevent the practical man from needing the notion of Relevance. It was left to the lawyers to evolve the conception and its vocabulary. They had, of course, a pressing professional need for the notion. For when a judge has to try a case, or an advocate to state it, he has first of all to outline it, i.e. to determine its limits. He cannot follow all its conceivable ramifications into the infinite. He must draw the line between the circumstances which he considers *relevant*, that is *helpful*, to his purpose and those which are not. He must make up his mind about the facts, the pleadings, and the evidence which have a bearing on the case and may be admitted, and those which are irrelevant and must be excluded. Otherwise he cannot finish his case within a reasonable time, nor arrive at the truth about it: for if everything that is, however remotely, to be connected with the case is allowed to be dragged in, the *good* evidence, which might lead to the discovery of the truth, will be stifled by masses of bad evidence, leading nowhere, or in the wrong direction. He shows

75

the goodness of his judgment, therefore, in making his selection. He excludes the irrelevant and unimportant, and concentrates on the really vital and 'essential' points: the more he can do so, the more expeditiously can the case be decided and better will the decision be. And, of course, good judges and good lawyers were bound to find this out.[1]

Thus Relevance is a shining example, not only of the imperious way in which practical need acts as a stimulus to theoretic progress, but also of the slowness of theorists to learn from experience. For its theory is still rudimentary, though practically the conception is too valuable not to be in constant use under a variety of names, English being the only language equipped with a complete and adequate vocabulary for it. Although it has not yet found its way into the dictionaries of philosophy,[2] even logicians find themselves constrained to use it, in a covert and confused way, though they are still far from recognising it as one of the primary notions in our actual reasoning, and from being willing to discard the traditional theories which conflict with it.

§ 2. Positive Implications of Relevance: (1) Subjectivity.

The logical implications of Relevance may be grouped under the four heads of (1) *subjectivity*, (2) *selectiveness*, (3) *honesty*, and (4) *disputableness*. All of these are *positive* qualities of the relevant, though they lead to negations of widespread logical superstitions.

(1) The relevant clearly views the relations between the

---

[1] The amazing thing is how long it took them to do so. For, as a matter of historical fact, it is only in the Scotch law of the sixteenth century that the proper vocabulary of Relevance begins to appear. According to *The Oxford English Dictionary* ' relevant ' dates from 1560, ' relevancy ' and ' relevantly ' from 1561, while ' irrelevant ' is not quoted till 1786 (Burke) and ' irrelevancy ' till 1802 (Bentham). In other countries not only is this terminology missing, but the actual procedure seems to overlook even the practical need for it. Hence the law seems to us to be extremely lax in admitting masses of irrelevance, and its decisions often seem a travesty of justice.

[2] It is not listed even in the ' corrected ' edition of Baldwin's *Dictionary* (1920).

thinker and his object from the *subjective* side. This does not mean that the relevant is an arbitrary creation of the individual thinker, which pays no regard to any sort of fact. On the contrary it contains an implicit reference to a given *problem*, i.e. to an objective 'given,' out of which the relevant part has to be extracted, while an argument which ignores facts to affirm personal preferences and prejudices will usually be charged with appealing to the irrelevant. To say that relevance means subjectivity merely means that it is conceived not as a quality residing in the thing thought of *per se* but only in its relation to us; *it lies in its value for us and in our attitude towards it*. It implies a relation to a human purpose by its very etymology. The 'relevant' is that which *helps* by affording us *relief*. It confesses this openly, and makes no pretence of turning the usefulness of things for our purposes into an attribute of the things themselves.

Now by avowing this we escape from the naïve objectivism of primitive thought, and the confusions to which it leads, which in this case are very easy to detect. For the original terminology, which that of relevance has superseded, was decidedly *objectivist*. It tried to project into things the values which they have for our varying purposes, and got entangled in hopeless puzzles as to how the same quality could be now 'essential' and now not. The truth was that the 'essential' was sometimes an objectivist term referring to a hypothetical 'essence' supposed to be indispensable to the existence of each thing and to render it what it was (Chap. II, § 2), and sometimes a misnomer for the 'relevant' and akin to other attempts to describe the relevant as inhering in the object. Phrases like οὐδὲν πρὸς τὸ χρῆμα, *nihil ad rem, unwesentlich, sans importance, senza concludenza, it is immaterial, it does not matter, it is not to the point*, are all objectivist descriptions of what is simply the *irrelevant*; but they do not mean anything different from *mal à propos* and *not to the purpose*, which are subjectivist phrases. But *relevant* is superior even to the latter, because it brings out not only *relation* to purpose but also *value for a purpose*. Now purposes clearly imply an act of will, and so the relevant clearly announces itself as belonging to a logic of values which acknowledges the purposiveness of our thought, and does not attempt to abstract from it. It is an integral part of a humanist and voluntarist logic; it can have no meaning for an intellectualism which disdains to notice anything less than the impersonal whole, from which nevertheless it inconsistently excludes the personal as wholly irrelevant (Chap. I, §§ 11, 15).

§ 3. (2) Relevance is Selection of the Relevant Part.

(2) The *relevant* is plainly a *part*, and an *extract*, and *not* the whole of any matter. It is a very important part, for it includes the true and the false, i.e. the whole area of inquiry in which truth is sought and discriminated from error. This area is *never* the whole, and so for intellectualism the relevant is only part of the Truth, which must include all that has been or can be judged true, as well as what is relevant to the particular inquiry. Thus for any human purpose we consider only part of the total truth, of the thinkable logical whole, nay, even of what is before the mind, the *psychological* whole, viz. the part which seems to us likely to further our inquiry and to solve our problem. Nevertheless, at the outset the relevant area is relatively large. It *contains* the truth we seek; but we do not yet know whereabouts, and it is our business to find out. If we fail to get to this point we fall into 'error'; and all the errors which arise in real inquiry fall within the region of the relevant, and consist in not 'getting to the point' (which is the 'truth' desired) and getting to the 'wrong' point instead. But in a *successful* inquiry we progressively narrow down the sphere of the relevant and contract it to 'the point,' as we leave aside one by one the erroneous possibilities which seemed relevant at first. Thus, though at the outset the relevant includes *both* the true and the false, in the end the true alone is relevant. It also follows that, the better the reasoning, the more rapidly will it contract the relevant, and the straighter will it go to the point. As for the irrelevant, it will mean that portion of the total truth which lies outside the sphere of relevance: and it is plain that any influence it exercises will be pernicious; it will only side-track and thwart

the inquiry. Hence successful thinking implies the rule: 'Never consider the whole but only the relevant part' (Chap. I, §§ 11, 17).

How is this part to be extracted? Clearly by discriminating between the true and relevant and the true but irrelevant, *selecting* the former and neglecting the latter. Such selection, of course, means *preference* and *choice* and *rejection* of the irrelevant. Have we the right to make such selections? Assuredly, if we have the right to believe in the value of our thinking; for all our thinking does in fact select. Assuredly, if we have the right to rid ourselves of the rubbish that blocks our path, the right to select the *humanly valuable* part, the right to desist from vain attempts to include everything in a whole which could only be a chaos. Such selection, therefore, is not a sheer bit of human favouritism which logic cannot countenance; it is the condition of all effective thinking—indispensable, characteristic, and 'essential.' At any rate, whoever says 'relevant' means '*partial*,' in both senses of the word, and defies condemnation for it. He should not plead guilty to any *intellectual* shortcoming by way of inattention or omission or failure to include all he might have done, but should justify his selection by ascribing it to conscious, willed, purposive, and rational *concentration* upon *the point*.

§ 4. (3) Relevance is Risky.

(3) Hence the peculiar *honesty* and straightforwardness of the appeal to Relevance, which involves no sailing under false colours. It lays no claim to 'cogency' or 'formal validity' any more than to exhaustiveness. It does not play for safety first, but avows that it takes a *risk*. It does not try to cover up the fact which damns it in the eyes of every formal logic, viz. that a selection of the relevant must always be a risky affair. For it may select too little or too much; and, if it does either, it may fail. If it selects too little, it may leave out the point and miss the truth it aims at; if it selects too much, it may find it has too much on its hands, and may get lost on the way to the truth.

It is by admitting these possibilities of error and failure that the notion of Relevance startles Formal Logic, and shows its superior honesty. Its functional equivalents in language all equivocate, and try to disavow them by pretending to derive guarantees for the selection out of the nature of the whole. But it is not literally true that the *irrelevant* is 'irrelative,' as the seventeenth century tried to maintain, nor that it is '*nihil pertinet ad rem*' and is 'immaterial,' nor that it is '*beziehungslos*' or '*belanglos*.' Irrelevant facts are *just as much facts* as relevant— though they do not lend themselves to our purposes in knowing. Nor have we a right to call them 'unessential'; for we have no right to postulate an objective ground for our selections in an 'essence' which 'makes a thing what it is,' and enables it to dispense with its 'accidents.' We neither know whether there are such 'essences,' nor, if there are, how much belongs to them. It may well be that nothing has any 'essence' in the objective sense at all; or again, that nothing would remain what it is if it were stripped of its merest 'accidents.' The 'essences' we actually allege are always relative and relevant to a purpose, flexible and variable, not permanent and immutable. The metaphysical 'essence' of a thing, however, being 'objective' and *inherent in the thing*, cannot vary, like a chameleon, according to the purpose with which it is regarded; yet this is just what we require of the 'essences' we wish to talk about in logic. They are nothing but such aspects of things as are selected as important and helpful for our various purposes; and 'relevance' is the honest name for the 'essential' quality they must display.

For 'relevance' does not take in vain the name of the immutable 'essences' (if such things there be), and *avows* its dependence on the purpose and needs of the moment. We are encouraged, therefore, to confess that the least change in the circumstances of the situation, in our interests, in our knowledge of the facts, may render relevant what was irrelevant before, and irrelevant what seemed most relevant. For example, if the headless flayed corpse of a female child, which can be medically shown to have breathed, is found in a field, the notion of a 'crime' will obviously suggest itself as relevant to the situation, and the police will search for the 'criminal' who put it there;

but the suspect could at once render irrelevant all these indications of a horrible 'murder' by admitting that he threw away
the remains, and exculpate himself by explaining that the supposed 'child' was the carcase of a young chimpanzee he had
been given to stuff. The relevant evidence then became the
skin of the corpse, which, in the case referred to, was produced,
and easily seen to be that of an 'ape' and not of a 'girl.' Yet
it can hardly be said that, objectively and *per se*, the skin was
'essential,' or more essential to the ape than to the girl.

In general, what is relevant to an inquiry is variable, and
varies as the inquiry proceeds. The discovery of any truth is
always a process which *moves away from* the *data* it started with,
and transforms, corrects, and revalues them. Our 'facts,' our
'truths,' our selections of the relevant, all develop in the course
of the process, and in the end need not exhibit any verbal
identity (or even similarity) with the *data* we started from; for
their continuity is only *genetic*.

§ 5. (4) Relevance is Disputable.

(4) By its honest disclaimer of formal validity the notion
of Relevance admits that it is always *disputable*. For once we
abandon the assumption that aspiration to the totality of truth is
an infallible guarantee, and rest our title to truth on a selection
of the relevant part, we admit that the *value* of any selection may
be questioned. Selections other than those we prefer are thinkable, and others may prefer them. They will differ, therefore,
from us in drawing the line between the relevant and the irrelevant, and in accepting what is to be accounted 'truth.' And it
is possible that they are right. Initially, at any rate, no one can
be sure he is right. No allegation or truth-claim, therefore, can
have a *formal* right to be accepted as indisputable. The merits
of every claim must be investigated, compared with the alternatives and evaluated, and good sense and good judgment must
be brought to their evaluation. Thus Relevance is *never a
matter of verbal form*, and of the implication of words, but always
a question of the comparative values of conflicting truth-claims.
To one who does not know the circumstances of the actual case

an irrelevant argument *looks* just as good and valid as a relevant one; and the worthlessness of a general formula is not revealed until it fails to apply to the case.

To say that Relevance is not a matter of form and not a quality inhering in the nature of things *per se*, is to say that it belongs inalienably to the logic of personality and real knowing (§ 2). It is no accident, then, that Formal Logic has omitted a notion utterly fatal to its pretensions. Its self-preserving instinct has instinctively felt that if ever the world became alive to the importance of Relevance its reign would be over, and it would sink into a sterile and trifling game with the meanings of words. This destructive or iconoclastic side of the conception of Relevance must next be considered.

§ 6. Negative Implications of Relevance.

As has already been hinted (§ 5) these positive characteristics of Relevance have negative implications. They entirely repudiate and exclude three sorts of Formal Logic. By its selectiveness the relevant negates the ideal of the all-inclusive whole, on which the *metaphysical* variety of Formalism bases its case (Chap. I, §§ 13–16), by its arbitrariness—the ideal of formal validity so tenaciously pursued by *deductive* logic—by its riskiness—the ideal of complete enumeration of fact—the will-o'-the-wisp which fascinates *inductive* logic. In each case a clear antagonism appears.

Thus (1) if we aim at selection of the relevant, we cannot so much as *desire* to include everything: conversely, if we endeavour to be all-inclusive, we can in no wise sanction any preferences or rejections. (2) If we aim at universally cogent demonstration possessed of formal validity and refuse to proceed with any train of thought which is not driven by necessity, we cannot allow any alternatives or freedom of choice; nor can we content ourselves with probabilities and *de facto* success. And if (3) we wish to go *safely* in arguing from 'facts,' we must make sure that we have assembled all the facts before we begin to argue. Conversely, if we think it more desirable to attract than to *compel*, we can prefer the *valuable* to the *valid*, and can progress better with growing probabilities than with immovable necessities. And, if we are willing to take risks, we can start at once; we can repudiate 'perfect induction' and begin to reason long before the 'facts' we use as premises approach exhaustiveness. Even verbally, this procedure may be justified by insisting that 'premises' are starting-points and not stopping-places, things 'sent on in advance' for an adventurous thought to go upon, and not fixed foundations for a petrified thought to 'rest' upon.

In short we have here a systematic conflict between two incompatible conceptions of Logic, and the fact that both are coherent makes their encounter all the more instructive. It is a conflict ultimately between the spirit of adventure and the craving for security, and as it springs from a divergence of tastes, aims, and valuations there does not seem to be any 'cogent' way of resolving it. One can, however, understand the motives of both sides and trace them to the needs for which they cater. The logic of adventure is fed throughout the ages by the growth of knowledge, and draws its justification from the need of understanding it. But until recently it played a very minor part, and has not left much mark upon the 'logic' of tradition. The latter sprang from the need of laying down rules for dialectical debate, and for deciding who had won; but this practical aim was soon overshadowed by the desire for formal validity and inerrant truth. Hence the whole history of Formal Logic is best interpreted as an obstinate (though futile) search for an absolutely *safe* road to truth.

§ 7. The Vain Search for Safety.

Safety was first sought in *syllogistic deduction* from true premises, which was supposed to leave no opening for the intrusion of error. But it was an error to suppose that a perfectly valid form of syllogistic reasoning could not go wrong in its use (Chap. XV, § 3).

Also this theory of demonstration presupposed a large supply of unquestionable truths to serve as premises, and required an account of the 'inductive' process which was to put them at the mind's disposal. It soon became clear that to be 'valid' general propositions of the kind required must either be based on exhaustive enumeration or else be self-evident and self-proving. Then it appeared that the former were impracticable and unattainable, while the latter were uncritical and incapable of differentiating themselves from prejudices and delusions. So, as a last resort, a desperate logic threw itself into the arms of a siren metaphysic, and listened to the specious plea that if only it could get a guarantee from the *whole* of truth it would be inexpugnable and safe, and that thus *alone* could any truth be truly true. About the existence of such a whole of truth no doubt was entertained. For, even though it was not strictly proved, it was taken to be undeniable and a necessity of thought. For to deny it would mean to deny that the Universe was a universe. Thus a veil of metaphysical mystery was flung over the logical *lacunæ* in this argument.

For a long time this expedient seemed to suffice. It was a waste of breath to expose the fallacies of this metaphysical logic, the mockery of promising our thought safety and irrefragable validity at the price of absorption in the Absolute when the conditions laid down for the attainment of safety stipulated that no *human* thought could conceivably attain it, the subtle cynicism of labelling a hardly veiled triumph of scepticism a guarantee of absolute truth, the bold impudence of assuming the validity of the 'ontological proof' from the existence of a human idea to that of a reality to correspond, and the naïve verbalism of taking the real as forming a real totality simply because of the verbal custom of calling it a 'whole,' or a 'world,' or a 'universe,' despite the fact that in many ways the real by no means comported itself as a 'whole.' To all such scruples there was one reply: Logic, a partial science, could be relieved of its defects only by merging itself in metaphysics, the science of the Whole.

But it is gradually becoming clear that the self-sacrifice thus demanded of Logic is vain. The metaphysical Absolute is the annihilation of Logic in an abyss of scepticism; but it is neither a guarantee of safety nor a successful exemplar of all-inclusiveness. It cannot be all-inclusive unless it can be conceived as including, not only the totality of truth and reality but also the totality of errors and illusions existing in those whose position in the Whole renders them subject to ignorance, error, and illusion. For every illusion and every error, however easily omniscience may trace it to the ignorance conditioned by every partial standpoint, just because it is relative to a partial standpoint, must after all count as a real ingredient in the total real. The universe does really contain error and evil and ignorance, even though they are said to be 'only appearances.' They, too, are 'necessary,' being the appearances which *must* occur in certain places in the Whole. They, too, therefore must be included in the Absolute, however confident we may feel that they are included only to be transmuted and transcended in the blaze of its glory.

They must be included, moreover, *as they are*, in their unmitigated poignancy. For unless the Absolute could itself feel the agonies of ignorance, uncertainty, error, pain, and defeat, *as we do*, it could not understand these experiences, and would not include them; they would be recalcitrant alike to its power and to its knowledge. It might, privately, assign them to a very low level of reality (or 'appearance'), and regard them as detracting not one whit from the total goodness of its cosmos. But none the less the Absolute is officially bound to do justice to every standpoint possible within it—to that of its deriders as to that of its adorers, to that of the worm with a turn for criticism as to that of the god, to that of the devil as to that of the angel. Unless it does, it fails to be all-inclusive, and so to be absolute —i.e. to be itself. It must, therefore, include, and render compatible, all the most contradictory attributes. And, as everything is such that some one does not know it and cannot do it, the Absolute has somehow to be simultaneously omniscient and omninescient, omnipotent and omni-impotent; so far, therefore, from being that in which no contradictions can exist and from being incapable of contradicting itself, self-contradiction is its normal condition; it is nothing but the *locus* and meeting-place of all contradictions.

But, however capable the Absolute may be of accommodating

all its contents, no *theory* of the Absolute could content itself with such a rag-bag. Even though it despairs of understanding *how* the Absolute transcends and harmonises its appearances, it must at least endeavour to appear as an orderly system itself. So it will have to *select* from the contents of the Whole such items as it deems capable and worthy of fitting into its system. The rest it must treat as irrelevant and leave out of account. This explains why *theories* of the all-inclusive Whole are never themselves all-inclusive, but are forced to omit a great deal. They are in fact quite as selective as the other products of human thought.

But if they are selective, they are also, in principle, as *plural* and *risky* as any other sort of theories. Once selecting is permitted, out of the same mass of *data* an indefinite number of selections may be taken, each with a claim to be the theory of the Whole. This explains the multitude of metaphysics. But, just because there are so many, none of them can claim to be inevitable, cogent, and free from risk. Consequently, we cannot, by adopting the first one of them we encounter, escape the risk of error and obtain a guarantee of absolute truth and infallibility, even in idea. Formal 'safety' is as far off as ever.

§ 8. How the Relevant is Selected.

Thus the pursuit of 'safety' has forced Formal Logic to the brink of a metaphysical abyss into which it is invited to jettison itself and its problems. But to do so, though it may dissolve logic, is not to solve its problems. Even if Formal Logic becomes *felo de se*, the actual nature of our thinking remains, our search for relevance remains, and the problem of its selection remains; and these all remain to be described and appreciated. If, moreover, they are properly described, there will be little difficulty in appreciating their function as integral parts of a logic of adventure which does not need an assurance of absolute safety before it will budge an inch; it is anxious to get on, but it looks before it leaps, and justifies its procedures by their conduciveness to the progress of thought.

Now every act of thought comes into being in an individual

mind which has been stimulated to perform it by its total equipment and history, because it found itself in a situation that seemed to it to demand 'reflection'; i.e. an arrest of action and an analysis of the situation for the sake of determining what it had '*better*' do. In other words, it is a necessary presupposition of any act of thought that the situation should appear *problematic*, and that it should be designed to cope with it: unless it does, habit and impulse would suffice, without thought, to determine the way the situation is met, and would be preferable, as economising both time and trouble. We think, then, only when we are in a difficulty and can think of nothing better to do (Chap. X, §§ 5–7).

If this be so, and it is a psychological fact even the most inexpert observer can easily verify in himself, it stands to reason that the thinker's 'situation' *never* embraces the totality of reality (if such a thing there be); it is always conditioned by the limitations of his knowledge and his personality. Indeed but for this there could be no thinking: for if the totality of reality were present to the mind, it would either form so overwhelming a problem as to paralyse thought, or, if the mind were that of one of those fortunate metaphysicians who flatter themselves that they know it all, there would seem to be no problem at all, and thus no need for thought. Thus all the problems we think about are problems about points and parts, presented to a mind which does not take in the whole of reality, and by its very nature cannot but select a part, and aims at nothing more.

It does not follow, however, that the solution of our problems must be partial also, and cannot be complete; and still less that it must be false and infected with error. For the parts of the whole which are omitted, or ignored, may be *irrelevant* to our purpose; if so, they will not enter into the constitution of *our* problem, nor detract from our complete satisfaction with its solution. So the doctrine that partial truths must be partly false is really a denial of the existence of irrelevance: as a logical doctrine it is quite gratuitous, a mere deduction from a false metaphysic, and unwarranted in fact (Chap. I, § 15).

It should further be noted that not only do our problems not concern the whole of reality, but that they never concern the whole of what is before the mind. The mind always contains much that is felt and judged to be irrelevant, and is therefore neglected by our thought. About the irrelevance of any of these contents it is of course possible to be in doubt and in error; but about the practice of ignoring them there can be no doubt, and the assumption (never justified) that it must always be an error stultifies all actual thinking. Actually, most minds are apt to *include* too much, and to clog themselves with much that is irrelevant: logical theory, on the other hand, even while professing all-inclusiveness as its ideal, has tended to *exclude* too much. For it has shut its eyes to the part of personal idiosyncrasy in determining the course of thought, and, somewhat recklessly, treated as irrelevant and unworthy of consideration the influence of desire, bias, purpose, context, and the like. It has thereby created an artificial chasm between the theory of thought and actual thinking, and needlessly destroyed the relevance of each to the other.

However, there is no doubt that the 'truths' selected for utterance as bearing on a situation are always *thought* to be relevant when they are propounded. Whether we are right or wrong we always endeavour to state a relevant truth. We try to select such portions of the truth that is within our ken as we judge to be relevant, and neither to assert all we know nor to blurt out the total truth about the whole universe in a single gasp.

This goes far to explain a number of facts to which the attention of logicians should be called. It explains why we do not go about asserting things merely because they are true. The truths worth asserting, and asserted, are not the indisputable truths of the first water, but those struggling into being, which others do not as yet see or recognise. To go about declaiming irrelevant truths, reciting platitudes and selections from the Multiplication Table, therefore, would be a sure way of getting oneself execrated as an intolerable bore, while to offer its unchallenged truths in lieu of something relevant, though disputable, would be positively dangerous. A man who always remarked that $2 + 2 = 4$

when asked for the time would probably get himself locked up as a lunatic; for a truth which is not to the purpose is a slur on one's rationality.[1] It explains also why relevance takes precedence over truth, and truth is no excuse for irrelevance. It is rather an aggravation; for an irrelevant answer to a question, which is true, is more irritating and more troublesome than one which is plainly false. For, just because relevance is not a formal quality, the irrelevance of an answer which is in general 'true,' and might be relevant to a different purpose, is always a question of degree and may always be disputed; thus the decision of a question of relevance is commonly harder than that of a question of truth, and Formal Logic naturally shrinks from it.

It explains further why a knowledge of the 'universe of diction' is so necessary to mutual understanding; we must know the range of subjects which are taken as relevant to the inquiry before we can take in the meaning of any discussion. Accordingly, the first thing to be done in every science is to arrive at some delimitation of the 'facts' (real *and* supposed) which may be taken as relevant to its interest. Nor is this initial difficulty easy to overcome. Many sciences struggle with it for centuries. At the outset the really relevant *data* are rarely on the surface, while for various reasons much that is irrelevant is impressive and insistent and attractive, or seems akin in nature to what is highly relevant. It is much easier to deride the errors of early science than to show how they could have been avoided. How, e.g., was a primitive astronomer to realise the enormous differences in the pragmatic value of the heavenly bodies he was so tempted to adore? How was he to find out that while the stars were so distant that they seemed 'fixed' and had no appreciable influence on the solar system, and while the gyrations of the 'planets' had no effect upon the destinies of man, and even the portents of irrupting 'comets' were no heralds of

---

[1] This truth, which has escaped the profoundest logicians, has been grasped by quite low comedy journalists. Thus *The Bystander* for 18th April 1928 had the following dialogue:—" *First Luny* : ' Well, who is going to win the Derby? ' *Second Luny* : ' I can only say that if you drink *crème de menthe* with oysters there is bound to be trouble with the miners.' "

'disaster,' it was yet true that the moon controlled the tides (but not the weather!), and the sun the seasons, and ultimately every movement of terrestrial life? The pseudo-science of the astrologers was a direct consequence of their taking too generous a view of what might be included in the relevant, and in general the infant footsteps of every science and every inquiry are clogged with masses of irrelevance.

§ 9. The Fatal Omission of Relevance by Inductive Logic.

The selection of the relevant, therefore, is not a thing logic can take for granted, if it wishes its procedure to have any likeness or relevance to the processes of actual reasoning and inquiry. It is one of the major achievements of knowing, and prior to the discovery of truth both in time and in urgency. For it is only when we have settled what our subject of inquiry is to mean, and decided, more or less provisionally at first but with growing accuracy, what is relevant to it, that we can begin to discuss the value of the alternatives, which all lay claim to truth, and ultimately make up our minds which of them is the *best*, and so the *truest*.

The theory of induction in particular has suffered much from the slurring over of the conception of Relevance, even as that of deduction has suffered from the omission of a study of Meaning. For so long as it was tacitly taken for granted that the 'facts' from which induction argued were relevant, and that no inquiry need be undertaken to discover how a reasoner came by them, inductive reasoning could be made to appear a quite contemptibly easy job, which demanded little intelligence and no vigilance or alertness of mind but only mechanical accuracy. All an inductive reasoner had to do was to observe the 'facts' which were objectively 'given' him without effort or activity on his part. Having observed them all, or so many as would suffice mechanically to 'validate' his inference, he had merely to recognise the universal principles or laws into which they spontaneously condensed themselves. There was no need, therefore, according to this account, of any special ingenuity or mental activity, either in observing the 'facts' or in formulating the 'laws.' Indeed the process seemed so mechanical that Bacon could conceive the ambition of teaching the meanest intelligence the art of scientific discovery, and other inductive logicians even imagined machines for making inductions; while all believed that inductive reasoning could attain as much 'validity' as deductive. This claim no doubt was rejected by their deductive opponents, who insisted that inductive reasoning could never be formally valid, and inferred that it must be of inferior value. It never occurred to either party to notice that no forms are universally valid, that valid forms are no guarantee of real value, and that real reasoning does not require valid forms (Chap. XIII, § 6).

Nor did either party notice how the notion of Relevance entered into inductive reasoning at every step, and was needed to make sense of their theories.

Thus (1) it is requisite that the 'facts' argued from must be relevant to the subject of inquiry.

(2) They cannot, therefore, be merely 'given,' but must be selected from a much larger mass of irrelevant, alleged, and illusory 'facts,' as *facts-for-the-purpose-in-hand*. This process will involve acts of choice, preference, and valuation.

(3) It is quite clear that the vaunted 'Canons of Induction' would be utterly paralysed, helpless, and invalid, unless the relevance of the 'facts' they operated on were presupposed. How else could the Methods of Agreement and Difference conceivably comply with their own requirements? How could they find two cases in which *only one* circumstance was common or *only one* was changed? This is difficult enough if the circumstance is assumed to be relevant; it becomes frankly absurd if the Method of Agreement is allowed to postulate an all but total change, and the Method of Difference an all but total immutability, in the flux of events.[1]

(4) There is a covert appeal to relevance involved in the very notion of two 'cases' of the same 'law' or 'cause.' For the actual course of events never repeats itself exactly; hence the identical 'cases' are always artificial, and have to be extracted by selection.

[1] Cp. *Formal Logic*, chap. xix, § 7.

Their actual circumstances always differ, but these differences are taken to make no difference, i.e. to be irrelevant. Only so can they figure as cases a^1, a^2 of the law 'A.' But the bare 'law' is never a fact, while the 'case' is merely a fragment of the 'facts,' which always contain much more than what qualifies it to stand as a case of the law. It should always be symbolised not as a, or even as a^1, but as $a^1 + [b^1, c^1 \ldots x]$, and its excess of meaning over the mere 'case' a always affords ground for its interpretation as a 'case' of *other* laws. There is always a logical possibility therefore that other parties to the inquiry may prefer an alternative interpretation, and so turn our case 'a^1' of law 'A' into case 'b' of law 'B.'

(5) Similarly, the 'law,' which our case is taken to exemplify, is also a product of our choice. It has always to be fitted on to the actual observations, the crude 'facts.' These, however, may fit as well, or nearly as well, into a number of other formulas, so that as far as the 'facts' go they might be taken as cases b^1, b^2 of law 'B' as easily as cases a^1, a^2 of law 'A.' It is the relevance of the *data* to a suggested law that enables us to verify the law; but the possibility of their relevance to several 'laws' should not be ignored. Whenever he encounters this situation the inquirer must choose his law, and it is generally its superior relevance to the aim of the inquiry which determines his preference among the rival laws. Thus it is quite false that inductive reasoning is a mechanical process into which our estimates, our aims, our choices do not enter. On the contrary, it is our interventions that initiate it and determine its course.

(6) It is clear that the actual conditions of inductive reasoning nowhere require, or even admit of, formal validity. A selection of 'facts' cannot claim to be a formally cogent totality: a selected 'law' cannot pretend to be the only one. The truth is that in our inductive reasoning validity is everywhere sacrificed to relevance. And rightly, because relevance is a far more valuable notion, and is incompatible with validity. For decisions about the relevant can never be formal: they must be tentative and experimental, and presuppose 'material' knowledge of the actual circumstances of each case. Its strength (or weakness) is

betrayed by no *formal* sign; verbally, an irrelevant argument may exhibit as much formal validity as a relevant.

Nor is dependence on relevance inherent in inductive reasoning alone. It is found in all reasoning. It was shown in the last chapter (§§ 13–14) that the meaning and use of universals involved a double use of the notion of relevance. In the first place, universals can be extracted from their particular exemplifications only by treating the latter as 'cases' of the 'same' universal, and by treating the differences between these cases as *irrelevant*. And, secondly, universals can be *applied* to the interpretation of events only by treating as irrelevant all the contents of phenomena over and above the universal we are seeking to apply to them, and by assuming that though they appear to *be* much more than bare universals they *mean* nothing more.

This twofold limitation imposed on the use of the universal has puzzled Platonising logic from the first: it could never understand why phenomena only exhibited universals obscured and entangled in 'matter,' and would not let themselves be reduced to 'pure' universals or complexes of such; it had desperately to infer that, therefore, phenomena could not be true reality, and that everything sensible must be contaminated with unreality. Nor could it explain why to the same phenomenon a number of *alternative* universals could be applied, and how questions could arise as to which was the *right* one. The notion of relevance relieves universals of these embarrassments; if they are selections of relevant aspects, fashioned as instruments for operating on the flux of happenings, and taken out of larger wholes for our various purposes, our selections will naturally vary with the purposes they serve. And if we are entitled to ignore whatever contents of the real are irrelevant to our purpose, it is no longer unintelligible that it should always contain far more than concerns us at any particular time, and should be all the more valuable on this account.

§ 10. Conclusion.

Relevance, then, is a conception utterly alien to Formalism. The intellectualist logic, therefore, which never looks beyond the forms of propositions and never seeks to penetrate to the meaning of those who use them, and so is nourished on a diet of mere words, finds it quite unpalatable and indigestible. It belongs inalienably to a humanist logic which conceives thoughts as personal acts, demands activity and allows selection, and consequently speaks throughout the language of voluntarism rather than of intellectualism. Such a logic will value Relevance as one of the great pivotal notions on which real reasoning hinges, and will cherish it as one of the best ways it has of expressing the crucial contrast between the voluntarist and the intellectualist treatment of thinking. And it will take special pleasure in showing that no intellectualist account can attain to consistency until it has wholly purged itself of every vestige of Relevance.

CHAPTER VI

TRUTH

1. Truth primarily a practical question ; 2. Truth as the value referring to prediction ; 3. ' True ' and ' false ' as logical values ; 4. Can the logician describe values ? ; 5. Value-claims not values ; 6. The variety of values ; 7. Values initially just psychic facts ; 8. The species of value and their genus ; 9. Truth and truth-claim ; 10. Value and purpose ; 11. Truths and problems ; 12. A theory of truth indispensable ; 13. Is a criterion of truth possible ?

§ 1. Truth Primarily a Practical Question.

There is no reason to suppose that when Pontius Pilate, speaking not in jest but as the much-harassed Procurator of Judæa, inquired *What is Truth ?* he was troubled with any theoretic interest, or had any intention of throwing an apple of discord into the ranks of the theoretical philosophers who have wrangled about this question ever since. It is much more likely that his interest was wholly practical. Himself an occidental, sitting in judgment over an oriental people, he was merely giving vent to a despondent, but very natural, reflection on the quality of the evidence daily brought before his judgment seat, and his question must since have reverberated thousands of times in the hearts of British judges in the East.

However this may be, the question of Truth is primarily a practical one. It is of the utmost vital importance to every one who engages in the strenuous job of keeping alive, with a minimum of distress and disaster, that he should be able to 'discover the truth' about the complicated and deceptive world in which his lot is cast. In other words, he has to find out where and how he can trust himself to be a match for the world—that is, trust his instincts, his impulses, his perceptions, his thoughts, if he means to make a success of his life. And it is, of course, enormously important that he should learn how to *anticipate* the course of events in order that he may be prepared for what is coming. The power of prediction, therefore, is eagerly desired, and human ingenuity exhausts itself in devising the most various and fantastic modes of divination. Among these,

95

however, only one has had any large measure of success. This is the assumption that the variegated flux of happenings can be analysed at will according to our various purposes, and that there can be extracted from it sundry invariant formulas, the blanks in which have merely to be filled up with suitable 'variables' to enable us to forecast the future with more or less exactness. Such is the origin and function of the 'law of nature,' which started as one of the least likely of our modes of divination, and even now can be explained only as meaning that all things have *habits* and that the stupider they are the less apt are they to change them. This, however, is a very wholesale way of reading human nature into nature, and it is safer and sufficient to take the assumption of 'law' merely as a methodological device which has 'worked.'

Prediction, moreover, means, to a large extent, *control*. It enables us to evade what is coming, or to prepare for it a warm reception. For it is only in fable that the practical value of the gift of prophecy is so perversely frustrated, as was Cassandra's by a god's ordaining that no truth foreseen should be believed and acted on, and so no disaster averted. In real life predictions are not merely theoretical but are meant to be used; and even Cassandra, under the conditions imposed on her, might not have found it very hard to defeat Apollo's malice by acting on her predictions, and then explaining that she did not believe in them but was only acting *as if* she did.[1]

§ 2. Truth as the Value referring to Prediction.

It is clear, then, that science has a practical origin. It is derived from prescience, or rather from the need for it, and it remains rooted in that need, however high it may spread its branches into the æther of pure thought.

Two important consequences follow. In the first place, the 'truths' of the sciences are *tested* by this power to predict the course of events, and their claims to be true by their *success* in doing so. Secondly, all the sciences must *distinguish* between a

[1] For a further discussion of the problem of Cassandra, see *Mind*, No. 105 (Jan. 1918).

prediction which comes true and one which fails to do so. They cannot treat them as of equal value, nor look only to the formal validity of a deduction and profess indifference to the question of its application to the real. In other words, if the sciences are essentially methods of predicting and controlling the course of events, they cannot identify 'truth' with '*truth-claim*,' which continues to claim whether it is true or false. 'True' for science must be *exclusive* of 'false'; it must be the term for the *positive* value of successful prediction opposed to 'falsity'—the *negative* value of a failure to predict.

Now this means that the sciences cannot possibly content themselves with the formal truth-claim to which Formal Logic restricts itself, and which it habitually confuses with absolute truth. This formal truth-claim is not in any important sense truth at all; it is a mere matter of verbal form; it is made by every proposition whether it is true or false, whether it is asserted confidently or hesitantly, seriously or in jest, in good faith or in bad. Of all these alternatives the formal truth-claim takes no account and conveys no hint. It is a mere linguistic fact that every proposition lays claim to truth; even in cases, like '*I lie*,' where the content of the proposition contradicts its form. But it is an egregious blunder to infer from this anything as to its real value. It does not follow that it is really true, true as *opposed* to false. And it is a still greater blunder to imagine that, because the form does not overtly announce any limitations or conditions, its 'truth' must therefore be 'absolute,' i.e. unconditional and immutable. 'Truth' is for Formal Logic a formal property of *all* propositions, simply because it has abstracted from their use, and so has rendered irrelevant the question whether they are in fact true *or* false: this, however, is not a question the sciences can abstract from, because it is the very question they are all trying to answer. They cannot, therefore, lump together under a common form of words a false proposition which defeats their purposes and a true one which satisfies them: they must take 'true' in a sense which *excludes* 'false.' For the value of 'truth' is positive, that of 'falsity' negative.

§ 3. 'True' and 'False' as Logical Values.

A Logic, therefore, which is observant of scientific usage must treat 'true' and 'false' as terms of valuation. This treatment has many advantages. It at once assimilates logical values to those of ethics and æsthetics, and brings out the identity of character and procedure in all the 'normative' sciences. All these sciences aim at discovering, not what *is*, but what *ought* to be, what we ought to think, to do, and to admire. Yet a little reflection will show that none of these sciences can get to work upon its problem forthwith. They all have a basis of fact and are conditioned thereby. They all presuppose that we *do* think, act, and admire in certain ways—as is indeed an observable fact —and that the ways we *ought* to think, act, and admire are definitely related to these. It seems merely a matter of common sense that a normative science should not attempt to lay down the 'law,' 'ideal,' or 'norm' before acquainting itself with the facts concerning its subject. For if it enacted norms without regard to the capacities of our nature, it would run the risk of demanding impossibilities, and of being dismissed as mere foolishness, seeing that *ultra posse nemo obligatur*, and there can be no duty to achieve the impossible.

§ 4. Can the Logician describe Values?

But on the question *whose* business it should be to observe our actual valuations opinions may diverge. At first sight it might seem to be the duty of psychology to describe and record impartially all the manifestations of mind, and among them judgments and values of all kinds, as conscientiously as perceptions. Actually, however, psychologists are by no means anxious to volunteer for this arduous duty. They usually prefer to accept from the philosophers a rigid distinction between 'fact' and 'value,' and to consign all questions concerning values to the philosophic sciences. They turn a deaf ear to the simplest demonstrations that the antithesis between 'fact' and 'value' cannot be made absolute and breaks down in the end, because all values are obviously facts, and all facts are covertly values, seeing that they have won their title only by being judged *better* than rival claimants to the status of fact. The truth is that most psychologists shrink from encountering the philosophers, and find it more congenial to cultivate such fields of inquiry as are least exposed to philosophic raiders. So long as they persist in this attitude logicians, moralists, and art critics will have, more or less reluctantly, to do their own describing of the psychical facts relevant to their purpose of evaluation as best they can.

Nor is it impossible, perhaps, that they should do so sufficiently if only they will observe a few cautions.

§ 5. Value-Claims not Values.

(1) They should not hasten to accept uncritically whatever they describe. They should distinguish between *value-claims* and *acknowledged* values. Value-claims are easy to make; they are put forward by all sorts of people on all sorts of occasions, but nothing is true or good or right or beautiful merely because it has occurred to some one to assert it. They should realise, therefore, that all claims should be *tested* before they are approved and passed as 'valid,' and the real value of value-claims depends on the amount and adequacy of the testing they have undergone.

§ 6. The Variety of Values.

(2) They should be prepared also to find a great range and variety in their 'facts.' The most striking thing about all human values at first sight is the way they differ; these differences, moreover, seem to be ultimate and irreconcilable. 'One man's meat is another man's poison' seems to be the only universal law in this region. It is vain to dispute about tastes; and yet the more one studies the differences of opinion that prevail among men, the more one inclines to the conviction that in ultimate analysis all the so-called differences of opinion are reducible to differences of taste. Only a bigoted dogmatist who resolutely shuts his eyes to the facts, therefore, will have the face to start his arguments from the assumption that all men feel, perceive, and think alike. An open-minded observer of the

ways of men will hardly find initial agreement a good working assumption; he will speedily realise that agreement is never a presupposition but always an achievement.

All the sciences concerned with values tell more or less the same tale. The furthest from 'objectivity' and agreement is, of course, æsthetics, in which variety of taste is almost canonical, and agreement hardly anywhere goes further than a common impulse to follow the fashions whithersoever they may lead. Ethics, though it is practically more important, is hardly better off than æsthetics. The biological necessities of life do indeed compel all human societies to organise themselves in what are *practically* equivalent and very similar ways; but superficially at least social customs differ widely, and the utmost variation reigns in the *theoretic* reasons alleged in different societies for doing the same things. The same sort of conduct is variously recommended as 'good,' as 'right,' as 'beautiful' or proper, as pleasurable, as pleasing to the gods; or again, as just customary and what 'every one does.' One may reasonably suspect that it is simply conduct which, in its own interest, every society has somehow to get its members to perform. Besides such conduct, every moral code enjoins great masses of conventions which may vary without limits because they are not vital, or because—though they look different—they express functionally equivalent modes of catering for the same social needs.

Of all the normative sciences Logic seems to come nearest to universal agreement. It looks at first as though all (except a few philosophers!) were willing to accept the laws of thought and rules of logic, and agreed in pursuing truth and execrating error. It is very surprising, thereupon, to find how violently, in spite of their abstract agreement, men continue to differ about what is true and false in the concrete. The reason appears to be that their agreement is only verbal and their acceptance of the logical conventions only nominal: it merely means that they have *not* understood the laws of thought and the rules of logic. It is just as well that they have not; for in the traditional 'logic' the 'laws' are so senseless and the rules so perverse that they would only paralyse any thought that tried to comply with them. Fortunately, however, no one actually thinks according to these 'laws' or troubles about these rules, even among logicians.[1] Every one thinks as it is congenial with his nature to think, and the grounds of his conclusions are immanent in his personal psychology. Nor can he reasonably be expected to think otherwise, or to submit to a logical 'cogency' which is not apparent to him. This means that he thinks with his whole heart and personality, that his feelings enter constantly and copiously into his reasonings, that his nature selects the objects of his thought, and determines his aims and his motives and his methods and the values he assigns to his objects, while his education and history determine the meanings and associations of the instruments of his thinking, viz. the words he uses. In theory at least, therefore, it ought to be possible to account completely for his actual proceedings *on psychological principles alone* ; so it would seem that *logical* explanation must be vain repetition, superfluous where it approves, impotent where it condemns, trains of thought which are coupled together by indwelling psychic forces and pursue their self-directing course under the motive power of essentially personal urges. All thinking, and with it all truth-seeking and knowing, as they occur in fact, then, are really personal proceedings, and the attempts to abstract from this personal side, so far from raising thought to the empyrean, merely plunge it into the abysses of nonsense and drive it into suicide.

From these considerations it follows that the variety of opinions in the fields which are supposed to be the domain of Logic is actually to the full as great as in ethics and æsthetics, and that in those portions of it where its practical bearing is least direct, and where there is least check upon the vagaries of the *intellectus sibi permissus*, such as metaphysics, every philosopher compiles his own 'system,' and there is no 'objective' truth at all.

The individuality of values, then, is an outstanding fact, and

[1] For a handsome confession to this effect by F. H. Bradley, see Chap. I, § 5.

it is imperative to reckon with it in all questions into which values enter. Nothing is gained in such questions by ignoring individual tastes and differences and postulating an unreal and fictitious agreement; on the contrary, this fiction becomes an insuperable obstacle to the attainment of real agreement. The logician, therefore (like the moralist), should beware of prematurely assuming that all men feel, think, and judge alike if he really wishes to improve their ways of thinking. In view of their actual thinking he must reserve the right of correcting it, and of showing how defective and fatuous it often is. Above all, he should wholly eradicate from his soul the lingering superstition that what is called 'true,' and has long been believed true, must be true. Let him observe, as keenly and carefully as he can, how the epithets 'true' and 'false' are bestowed; but let him remember that such observations yield him nothing in the first instance but psychic facts about human nature, and leave entirely open the question of how real truth may be established and welded into a harmonious whole.

§ 7. Values Initially just Psychic Facts.

The practice, then, of valuing beliefs as *true-false* must, like the practice of valuing acts as *good-evil* and objects as *beautiful-ugly*, be regarded as an entirely natural fact. It is, in the first instance, merely a case of the human practice of valuation; and valuation, though it is a characteristically human attitude and may turn out to have much ulterior significance, is just psychic fact to begin with. 'True' and 'false' are terms to indicate a certain species of value—to express our human appreciation of it. This value is the one properly awarded to cognitive operations—though it may be, metaphorically, transferred to ethical and æsthetical subjects—as when a friend or form of art is called 'true,' or again 'false.' It is a sufficient justification of this practice that all the values are species of the same genus and have much in common. Values can nowhere be conceived as wholly 'objective.' They are nothing which we can ascribe to objects *per se* and in the absence of a valuing intelligence. Valuation is a human activity, an attitude we assume towards the

objects we esteem; their 'value' is a reaction which they provoke and a relation to us which we confer on them.

§ 8. The Species of Value and their Genus.

As, moreover, we can either approve or condemn objects on
account of the values imputed to them, all values are positive or
negative, and approval or condemnation is the common meaning
of all our valuations. Yet they naturally fall into species, because
of the diversity of our activities and of our spheres of interest;
so there is little difficulty in recognising their appropriate
domains. 'True' and 'false' are the valuations belonging to our
cognitive enterprises; 'good' and 'evil' and (in a few languages)
'right' and 'wrong,' those applicable to our acts; 'beautiful' and
'ugly,' those indicative of æsthetic appreciation. Furthermore,
all these activities are purposive; so we should expect to find
also terms of valuation which are general and imply merely
adaptation to purpose of whatever sort. Such, accordingly,
would appear to be the proper meaning of 'good' and 'bad,'
which apply to any means in relation to any end, while the end is
also significantly called the 'good.' In English, no doubt, a certain confusion is sometimes engendered by the double sense of
'good,' as the opposite of 'evil' as well as of 'bad'; nevertheless,
it is not difficult to distinguish the specific moral 'good' from
the generic teleological 'good,' of which all the values are species.
The moral 'good' is relative to the end of conduct, or rather to
that portion of conduct which is normally included in the sphere
of the moral judgment, and not many would suppose that in 'a
good man' and 'a good knife' 'good' has precisely the same sense.

Once the teleological 'good' is recognised it is easy to see
that the 'true' is the 'good' of knowing, and the 'false' its
'bad': the one means success, the other 'failure' in a cognitive
undertaking.[1] It is also easy to understand why the various
terms are so readily transferred within the genus value, and

---

[1] Aristotle saw this when he declared, " as for the intellect which
is theoretic and not practical nor productive, its ' well ' and ' ill ' are
truth and falsity (truth being the work of everything intellectual);
while of that which is practical *and* intellectual it is truth in agreement
with right desire."—*Eth. Nic.*, vi, 2, 3.

how the practice may be justified. It is not only natural to fuse
the various sorts of value and to estimate the total value of a
theory by adding in its moral value and its æsthetic (or
'poetic') value to its strictly cognitive or truth-value, but it is
arguable that this procedure is not only universal but also legitimate; since, after all, our whole personality is always implicated
in the choice of our beliefs and may be more capable of attaining
truth than a purely passionless intelligence, which might be
insufficient for this purpose, even if it were not a figment. The
real difficulties which arise from a clash between various sorts
of value are due to the fact that into our total attitude towards
any belief a variety of considerations always enters. The belief
always seems to possess several sorts of value, positive or negative, and these attract and repel different persons in various
degrees.[1] It is no wonder, therefore, that very great differences
of opinion prevail: they could be made to disappear only by
completely standardising human nature.

There is, however, no reason to treat these differences of
opinion differently in the different realms of value. Alike in
logic, in ethics, and in æsthetics the variety of valuations is the
raw material out of which each science has to construct its
edifice. The actual valuations are themselves *data* to be evaluated, and their evaluation has to be critical.

§ 9. Truth and Truth-Claim.

The very first point to be observed in such a critical evaluation of truth-values is that the 'truths' alleged cannot all be
true. For they are often incompatible with each other, and many
of them must be false. It becomes imperative, therefore, to
distinguish between those which are 'really true' and those
which only claim to be so, and to refrain from accepting as true
every allegation which claims to be true. We not only may, but
must, distinguish 'truth-claims' from truths.

Yet in practice this distinction is by no means easy to draw.
It is hard to determine when we are confronted with a real truth
and when with a false truth-claim. For the linguistic form

---

[1] Cp. *Problems of Belief*, pp. 170–175.

affords no help, and we may not have knowledge enough to judge the case on its merits. As a matter of linguistic form our distinction does not exist. Every judgment, good or bad, true or false, made confidently or hesitantly, in good faith or bad, seems to make the same claim. It claims truth, and none ever confesses to falsity. Hence, if we endeavour to go by the form alone, all judgments alike are 'true' and none is false. But their 'truth' is only truth-claim, and, if this sense of 'truth' is adopted, one can only say that such formal 'truth' is not exclusive of falsity, and so is scientifically worthless. Nevertheless it is in this sense that truth has to be taken by the Formal logics, because they do not wish to have to wait to consider the circumstances of actual cases but desire to lay down logical 'laws' *a priori*. This involves them in terrible contradiction, because they *also* need a sense of 'truth' in which it excludes falsity, and because they frequently confuse this formal 'truth' with absolute; but they prefer to wallow in these confusions to renouncing the ambition to dictate to the sciences.[1]

For all other purposes but those of Formal Logic, however, we cannot take 'truth' in this formal way. We *must* mean by it something opposed to falsity and exclusive of it; we cannot equate what furthers with what defeats a cognitive purpose and lump together positive and negative values under the same name. Any account, therefore, of actual thinking must set aside the Formal 'truth,' which is shared by all assertions in judgment-form and is inclusive of falsity.

In actual thinking it is vital to conceive 'true' and 'false' as antagonistic terms. We desire the true, we try to avoid the false. When speaking in good faith we always believe our assertions to be true—'to the best of our knowledge and belief.' But we have mostly had enough experience of the errors we ourselves and others have committed to be wary of accepting all the 'truths' we hear enunciated without further inquiry. So we distinguish between the mere putting forward of a claim and the 'verification,' 'validation,' or 'confirmation' which it has to undergo before winning social recognition, between a truth-

[1] Cp. *Formal Logic*, chap. i, §§ 4–6.

claim and an established truth. This distinction is of the greatest practical importance, and common sense effectively recognises it.

Important, however, as the distinction is, it is not absolute. It is a matter of degree. There is no definite point, to be determined in advance, at which a truth-claim passes into a verified truth. The truth-claim character persists into the 'truth'; our truths remain truth-claims, and remain open to question should the occasion arise. A verified truth may always be improved and revised by further verification, and no amount of verification ever renders it *absolutely* true. Its truth always remains relative to the evidence which has prompted us to value it, and to raise it to the rank of 'truth.'

Nor, on the other hand, are any truth-claims *mere* claims, and quite devoid of a rational basis. They always rest on grounds, good or bad, which seem good to those who set out their claims, and the verifications they receive only corroborate virtues they already possess. The development of a truth-claim into a truth may therefore be represented somewhat as follows.

To begin with, a truth-claim has to be made; in other words, it has to find a maker. A truth-claim is a claim to value, but the value of all truth-claims is not the same. Though they all formally claim the value 'truth,' yet some are better than others. A truth-claim's real value depends in the first instance on the quality of its maker's mind. The better the mind, the better is likely to be the truth it produces. A good mind, capable of pondering comprehensively on a situation and of penetrating to the core of a question before launching a judgment, is likely to enunciate something that both is valuable and is also well-equipped to withstand attacks when it has been launched. In other words, it both makes good truth-claims and verifies them in thought, to some extent, before they are propounded. A careless thinker, on the other hand, may utter the first thing that comes into his head, and may have to withdraw his judgment almost as soon as it is made.

So the amount of verification a 'truth' requires and receives is indeterminate and may vary enormously. The only things to be said universally about the making of a 'truth' is that it always claims to be the *best* or most valuable judgment possible under the circumstances of its making, and that its maker must have preferred it to all the alternatives within his ken. This is true even if he did not, as a matter of psychical fact, himself think of any alternative judgment. For he has at least the alternative of refraining from judgment, and preserving a (golden or injudicious) silence. Moreover, so soon as he has said *S is P* it may be pointed out to him that S^1 *is* P^1 was better, and this may be so obvious that he himself at once adopts the emendation. In such a case we may say that S^1 *is* P^1 was an alternative to *S is P*, even though it was not actually thought of. It was a 'logical,' though not a psychological, alternative, and logical reflection must always reckon with the possibility of such alternatives. It follows that, for logic, there always are alternatives, and that every actual judgment emerges from a mass of possible judgments. Hence any 'truth' actually enunciated should be conceived as the *best* (i.e. most valuable) alternative its asserter could think of. That is the logical claim with which it enters the world, and which is tested by its subsequent career. But, secondly, this claim may clearly be disputed; indeed it usually is. If so, our truth-claim will call for *verification*. This process, again, is to be understood as relative, and not absolute. The amount of verification a truth-claim needs will depend partly on its intrinsic character (e.g. how great is its antecedent improbability), partly on the purpose for which it is needed (e.g. how important accuracy would be), partly on the character of those concerned with it (e.g. how critical or credulous they are): it is not a fixed amount, nor has it to be attained in any definite period. Theoretically, indeed, verification can go on for ever, both because science is capable of infinite progress and because the process is never 'valid,' and no amount of verification can ever make a 'truth' absolute, while any further verification may yet appreciably enhance its value. Consequently, verification is always a matter of degree, as language frankly recognises. Though we never find ourselves possessed of 'absolute' truth, we can always distinguish between greater and less degrees of truth-value, between a more and a less true, a truer and a falser belief; and there is always a relatively *truest*, by comparison with which any inferior values can be decried as 'false,' though they may be 'true enough' for other purposes. Practically, therefore, a limited and usually quite moderate amount of verification is enough to dispel the doubts which actually beset any ordinary truth-claim, even though some minds are harder to convince than others. Alike whether scepticism or credulity has been carried too far, however, nothing irreparable has occurred; for we cannot have too much verification, and can always trust further experience to bring any further verification that may be required.

§ 10. Value and Purpose.

Having made it clear that the amount of verification required to raise a truth-claim to the rank of a 'truth' is nothing fixed and determinate, but varies according to the purpose in hand, we may lay it down that in general logical value is relative to purpose. No judgment, and *a fortiori* no proposition, is true or false in itself; its value is always dependent on its use in the context in which it becomes a vehicle of meaning. Thus no proposition is absolutely true, because it may always be misused, i.e. applied to a situation in which it incites to the wrong reaction; nor is any absolutely false, because there may always arise circumstances under which it would become appropriate. The most that can be claimed for a proposition is that it is true in general, but this does not guarantee its truth in every application: even '2+2=4' will fail us if we are rash enough to apply it to the behaviour of drops of water or of mercury; and if in reliance on the properties of the Euclidean straight line we go straight on on the surface of the earth, we shall presently find ourselves returning to our starting-point.

In the case of real judgments it stands to reason that our reasoning will be good or bad according as it is 'to the point' and calculated to achieve the end in view, or not. But this is not enough; we must not only achieve our end, but achieve it in the best possible way. Moreover, we shall always find that we have a choice of propositions wherewith to express our actual meaning, and so there devolves upon us the duty of discovering the *best* means to each end, and of expressing it in the most suitable terms. In comparison with these all inferior means and expressions may have to be condemned as 'false.' Nor can it any longer be taken for granted that such a thing as economy of effort is irrelevant to logical value: excess of exertion may become as reprehensible as careless negligence. Accordingly the amount of accuracy required will be variable, and will have to be specified in each case.

Absolute accuracy is not possible, if only because no human instrument and no human sense can measure it. But neither is it needed: what is needed is accuracy sufficient for the purpose in hand. If no one wishes to measure the height of a mountain in millimetres, or to evaluate π to 10,000 places of decimals for any rational purpose, it follows that such excessive accuracy is not only needless but also wrong. It is a waste of time and an obstacle in the way of the end desired.

It will follow further that different answers to the same question may be simultaneously 'true.' For example, *Who is the most charming woman in the world?* is a question all lovers will answer differently (unless they happen to be in love with the same woman), and it is, of course, socially desirable that they should *not* agree upon the answer to this question. So common sense finds no paradox here. It simply recognises that A is the 'most charming woman' to B, C to D, and so on. Different answers to the same question, which are simultaneously true, are the commonest thing in the world. Nothing more is needed to make them true than a number of persons considering a question with different interests, however slight the difference in interest and standpoint. Thus for a tourist it may be sufficient, and therefore true enough, to know that a mountain is 10,000 feet high, even though a geographer may need to state it as $10,000 \pm 10$ feet.

Of course it may be objected that when the 'same' question is considered with different purposes it is not strictly the same question, and ought not to be called so; but this will only bring out the cognate fact that, still more strictly, the least change in the persons, interests, times, places, and contexts of a question may imperil its identity. For it may constitute a difference relevant to the purpose in hand. Thus any assertion of 'sameness' is always a (disputable) claim that certain differences may be neglected. As identity never occurs as a 'fact,' and has always to be extracted from the differences in which it is immersed, it is always an *identity-for-a-purpose*, and a hypothesis to be verified. The value, therefore, of a truth-claim can never be completely determined in advance of its use: it always remains dependent on experience of its working. A claim that works well, and is confirmed by the tests to which it is subjected, is acknowledged to be 'true'; it ceases to be in dispute though it does not become indisputable. Conversely, a claim that fails and disappoints us when it is tested is convicted of falsity and error. But it, too, may be revived if circumstances that favour it should arise. There is no 'theoretic' finality about our judgments of truth and falsity simply because there is no end to the knowable; but practically we mostly have only too little difficulty in making up our minds about what is true and false. It is clear, then, that 'true' and 'false' are just expressions for the value of a truth-claim in relation to a purpose.

§ 11. Truths and Problems.

'Truths' being valuable and helpful, and 'errors' dangerous and harmful, it is once more clear that we cannot, humanly speaking, disregard the difference between them. The more so that both originate in the course of the same inquiries. Our cognitive endeavours are furthered by 'truths' and thwarted by 'errors.' The natural stimulus to cognitive endeavour, and so to the discovery, alike of what is 'true' and of what is 'false,' comes from our consciousness of some *problem* which demands solution. Whether the problem is 'theoretic' or 'practical' is secondary and unimportant; for *any* problem that seems urgent and of which we desire a solution is able to start an inquiry. On the other hand, a mind that was incapable of feeling problems, either because it was omniscient or because it was content merely to 'contemplate,' would be incapable of what *we* call 'knowing.'

To common sense it has merely to be stated that truth-seeking arises out of consciousness of a problem. It is familiar with the idea that judgments are made to answer questions, and that the right question is our best starting-point to the right answer. For human thinking does not occur *in vacuo* without provocation. It is when we feel that we do not 'know,' when experience comes in a questionable shape, when our situation seems doubtful and presents alternatives, that we stop to think and begin to deliberate about what we had better do. Thus we realise that truth-finding in general presupposes truth-seeking, truth-seeking means the solving of questions—from questions all inquiries start; in questions (other than rhetorical) ignorance of their answers is always implied, and, if they are not idle, a hope of answering them. Hence we may conclude that willingness to raise and to entertain questions is the first requisite in truth-seeking, and that no logic that seeks to deal with actual thinking should consider 'judgments' in abstraction from the questions they answer and decide.

§ 12. A Theory of Truth Indispensable.

If we have sufficiently made clear the vital importance of truth, and the practical impossibility of ignoring it by accepting formal truth-claim as a substitute for real truth, we have made out a cogent case for demanding from every philosophy and every logic *an adequate theory of truth*. Now, no theory of truth will be adequate unless it succeeds in distinguishing truth from error (in conception at least) and can suggest a way of testing truth-claims. We are entitled, therefore, to declare that a philosophy which has no theory of truth is bankrupt, and that a logic which treats as irrelevant the difference between the true and the false is a silly game.

Of course this demand will not be admitted by the current philosophies and logics. For they all *are* bankrupt on this very point, and know it, though they endeavour to conceal it. So they either deny the possibility of a general theory of truth, or propound as theories of truth doctrines which are palpably inadequate, and which they themselves admit to be beset with 'difficulties.' In the former case they appeal to the impossibility of a general criterion of truth they suppose to have been established by Kant, and as this appeal has a certain speciousness it will be well to examine it next.

§ 13. Is à Criterion of Truth Possible?

It is commonly argued that no general criterion of truth is thinkable because none could carry with it conviction of its own finality. For whatever criterion were alleged, it would either have to guarantee itself, e.g. by claiming intuitive self-evidence, or it would have to be itself guaranteed by a further criterion.

In the former case it would raise all the difficulties involved in making an essentially psychological fact, viz. an intuition of self-evidence, into a logical principle, and would break down over the proved fallaciousness of self-evidence, the impossibility of reaching agreement about what *was* self-evident, and the impossibility of separating logical from psychological self-evidence. Moreover, even if all these difficulties could be overcome, we should reach nothing more logically valuable than a self-validating principle, which would merely be arguing in a circle, because it would have no credentials to offer beyond its own truth-claim. Thus no general criterion of truth could guarantee itself.

In the latter case we should be committing ourselves to an infinite regress of criteria. For once it is admitted that our first criterion may require a second to guarantee it, the same question may be raised about the second, and then about the third, and so on to infinity. So no general criterion of truth could be guaranteed by anything other than itself.

The first comment these contentions should provoke is that they rest upon an arbitrary and peculiar conception of what a 'criterion of truth' should mean, which it is not necessary to accept, and which *in fact* they refute. They presuppose (1) that a 'criterion' should discriminate, absolutely and finally, between truth and falsity at its first application; (2) that it should do so irrespective of, and prior to, experience; (3) that the truth it guarantees should be absolute. Thus a thoroughly uncritical and old-fashioned notion of truth is presupposed, and a thoroughly *a priori* notion of a 'criterion.'

It should be noted also that this notion of a 'criterion' rules out, without examination, the possibilities—(a) that the 'criterion' should be a continuous process gradually sifting the true from the false, (b) that this process should operate in the course of experience, (c) that the 'truth' it attained should be merely better than, or superior to, the error it eliminated, without claiming to be absolute, though it might, of course, be conceived as indefinitely increasing in value and so approaching absoluteness 'asymptotically.' It is clear, further, that this notion betrays its rationalistic bias in refusing to envisage any possibility that experience could have any bearing on the problem of truth. It conceives its 'criterion' as deciding between truth and falsity entirely *a priori*, with no recourse to experiment or experience. And this assumption must be set down as a prejudice which is not warranted by the etymology of criterion. A 'criterion' should mean merely 'a means of discriminating,' and should beg no questions as to how the discrimination is to be effected. By indulging in this prejudice, moreover, the whole argument against a criterion finally gets into a pretty conflict with itself and with the philosophy that generates it. The deepest craving of all *a priori* philosophy, and of the Kantian in particular, is to emancipate itself from experience, to get itself into a position whence it can predict the future *without* having to wait and see what happens, to allege principles which will legislate for all experience and which we may be *assured* no course of events will disobey. It should, therefore, *desire* to find a 'criterion of truth,' in order to be able to discriminate between truth and falsity in a similarly high-handed manner. When, therefore, it incongruously denies that such a criterion is attainable, it does indeed (indirectly) acknowledge that truth is too empirical to be fabricated wholesale by any *a priori* machinery invented by philosophy; but it casts a fatal slur on its whole enterprise of *a priori* prediction of the course of events. If no test of truth can be trusted in advance of the facts, why should we be asked to put our faith in any 'category'? It is fair to conclude, therefore, that the *a priori* objection to the idea of a criterion of truth has *failed*.

But we should not be discouraged. With a more modest con-

8

ception of a 'criterion,' and a less impracticable conception of 'truth,' our search may yet succeed. Let us, therefore, cease to assume that a 'criterion' must be absolute and admit as a 'criterion' any test that will in any way, or to any extent, help us to sift the true from the false. We need, then, no longer demand of it that it should be inherently infallible, or should instantly yield truth absolute: it may now reckon with probabilities and progressively verify the truth-values which it apprehends. Thus if we can find a test which will eliminate *half* the sources of error every time it is applied, and which may be applied as often as we choose, it is evident that it will steadily increase the value of our beliefs, doubling with every application the value of our 'truths' and halving the possibilities of error, so that even though we started with a belief which seemed as likely as not to be false, after, say, a dozen applications of our criterion we should get from it 'truth' that was at least $\frac{4095}{4096}$ 'pure.'

Now it is 'truth' of this sort, never 'absolute' but always progressive and indefinitely verifiable, that the investigations of the sciences yield. The chemist can never get any substance absolutely pure; but he can reduce impurities to less than an assigned amount, so that it may be taken as practically pure for many purposes. The physicist cannot obtain an absolute vacuum by pumping air out of a vessel, nor can he reach the absolute zero of temperature; but he can get very near them, and can hope to get still nearer by further improvement of his apparatus. Why, then, should not logic learn this lesson from the sciences, and be content to accept 'criteria' which operate in this way? It should not disdain to study the ways in which, in fact, truth is made, because they do not conform to abstract definitions of 'criterion' and 'truth' which were laid down without reference to the facts of knowing. Both in the sciences and in ordinary life we need criteria of truth; but we need only ways of testing truth-claims which will sift the valuable from the worthless, and will progressively augment the value of the former. Thus the infinite *regress* is a bogey which may be eliminated from the quest of knowledge; what to apriorist prejudice appeared as a vain search for an absolute criterion that would enable us to *start* from absolute truth is converted into the infinite *progress* which is exemplified in the sciences. 'Absolute' truth will then appear, not as a presupposition which has to be granted before we can begin to know, but as the aim and ideal towards which our knowledge moves.

The contention that every criterion needs a further criterion to guarantee its authenticity is vitiated by a similar prejudice. It is not necessary that every criterion must be tested by another, any more than it is necessary that a truthful witness must call up further witnesses to attest his veracity: what is necessary is that his testimony should function as true, and should stand all the tests to which it is subjected. The right demand, therefore, to be made upon a criterion, the true test to which it should be subjected, is that it should be self-applicable and should stand *its own* test. If, therefore, our criterion be 'self-evidence,' then that the self-evident is true must itself be 'self-evident' (which it is not!). If it be 'working,' then the test of working must itself 'work' (which it does!). There is an illegitimate circle only if we assume that every principle must be known to be (absolutely) true *before* it is used. For then its successful use can have no logical value; it can add nothing to its certainty, and proves nothing that we did not know already. It cannot, therefore, assuage any doubts that may have survived the principle's self-assertion. But if it is possible to assume a principle hypothetically and experimentally, and to watch it growing certain by use, our method is sound enough; it is just experimental and begs no questions.

We may conclude, therefore, that there is nothing absurd in looking for a general criterion of truth, provided that we are willing to conceive our criterion in a reasonable way, and to put up with such truth as the sciences provide and as suffice for the purposes of ordinary life. And this carries also with it the conclusion that an adequate theory of truth is an indispensable desideratum of any logic worthy of the name. We shall have, therefore, to examine, in our next chapter, the *dicta* which pass muster as theories of truth.

CHAPTER VII

THE THEORIES OF TRUTH

1. The seven theories of truth ; 2. (I) Truth as a property of judgments and propositions ; 3. (II) Truth as apprehension of reality ; 4. (III) Truth as necessity of thought : (*a*) Its genesis ; 5. (*b*) Its difficulties ; 6. (*c*) Its explanation ; 7. (IV) Truth as intuition , 8. (V) Truth as correspondence with reality ; 9. The ambiguity of 'reality'; 10. (VI) Truth as 'independent' of us ; 11. The meaning of 'independent'; 12. (VII) The Coherence theory of truth; 13 Coherence a formal criterion ; 14. Coherence a psychological criterion ; 15. Coherence an imperfect test ; 16. Coherence scientifically obstructive ; 17. The self-contradiction of coherence ; 18. Coherence ends in scepticism.

§ 1. The Seven Theories of Truth.

In examining the theories of Truth we must bear in mind two vital points. No theory can claim to be adequate unless it is (1) more than formal, and unless (2) it is applicable.

By a *merely formal* theory we shall mean one which holds, merely in virtue of their form, of all judgments and propositions, whether they are in fact true or false. By taking 'truth' with such formality any such theory is taking it as truth-claim, and reducing it to mere verbality. To this procedure it is a fatal objection that it *fails to discriminate* the true from the false, and so cannot aid us in our endeavours to do so. An *inapplicable* theory, on the other hand, is one which refuses to adapt itself to the conditions of human knowing; it will have to be pronounced simply meaningless. It will be found that the current theories of Truth without exception succumb to one or other of these objections, or even to both.

We shall have to examine in all seven theories of Truth, to wit that (I) truth is a property of judgments or propositions; (II) truth is apprehension of reality; (III) truth is necessity of thought; (IV) it is an intuition; (V) it is correspondence with reality; (VI) it is independent of man; (VII) it is coherence of thought. Of these the fifth and the last will demand the fullest treatment.

§ 2. (I) Truth a Property of Judgments and Propositions.

This criterion of Truth may claim at any rate to be strictly logical and to involve no metaphysics. But it is also wholly formal: it is as true of false judgments and propositions as of true that truth or falsity is predicable of them, as it is not of questions, wishes, and commands. So the fact (if fact it be) that only a judgment (or a proposition) can be true-or-false does not help us to distinguish a true judgment from a false.

It may further be remarked that though (or, perhaps, because) the theory is of venerable antiquity—it traces its pedigree back to Aristotle—it is as a logical doctrine a trifle crude. It at once gets into difficulties when the question is raised whether truth and falsity are not predicable also of *perceptions*, and when it is asked to decide whether it regards perception as judgment, or not. The proper answer to this question, that *for certain purposes* perception is judgment, for others not (Chap. XI, § 10), no Formal theory can venture to adopt.

Moreover, it is far from evident that truth and falsity have nothing to do with anything but judgments or propositions. The importance of *postulates*, which are a sort of imperatives, in laying the foundations of scientific systems can hardly, nowadays, be overlooked. The impetus given to inquiry by desires and wishes can hardly be pronounced entirely irrelevant to a logic that concerns itself with actual knowing. And only the narrowest Formalism can sever judgments wholly from the trains of thought in which they occur and the questions which they are meant to answer, and treat them in abstraction as self-dependent entities. It is true that we do not often call questions true and false; but we do discuss whether the *right* questions have been put and whether *false* issues and problems have not been raised.

Looking at the matter broadly we find that truth and falsity are incidents in cognitive inquiry; and this is far too much of a whole to make it desirable, or even possible, to restrict the predicates 'true' and 'false' to a single portion of it. A logic that observes the facts of actual knowing may fairly be required to envisage cognitive process as a whole, and to consider 'truth' as its *success* and 'falsity' as its *failure*.

Finally, we should question whether this theory is entitled to lump together judgments and propositions, and to assume that truth and falsity are predicable equally and in the same sense

of both. To this facile assumption, which is typical of the underlying verbalism of all Formal Logic, it may be objected that it
fails to distinguish the *real* meaning and truth of judgments
from the *potential* meaning and truth of propositions. Yet the
two are quite different, and it is most improper to confuse them.
For example, the meaning, and with it the truth, of propositions
like *it is hot* and *it is two o'clock* flagrantly varies with their use;
they both depend on *where* on the surface of the earth the time
or the temperature has become a subject of inquiry. So *both* can
be true and false simultaneously, though in different places
(Chap. VIII, § 4) ; but *per se* and in abstraction from its use
neither proposition can be said to be either true or false. To call
it either is to misapprehend the relation of propositions to truth,
and to judgment. A proposition is never more than *potentially*
true; it becomes (actually) true if it is used in a suitable context,
but then it turns into a judgment. Moreover, it is always possible
to use it unsuitably, and to misapply it; if so, it will become a
false judgment. Propositions, therefore, should not be called
universally true or false; their truth-or-falsity is entirely contingent on their use.[1] If, therefore, we apply the predicates
true and false to judgments, we should carefully refrain from
applying them to propositions, or, as Mr Bertrand Russell calls
them, 'propositional functions'![2] It is clear, then, that in many
important respects this theory of Truth is woefully inadequate.

§ 3. (II) Truth as Apprehension of Reality.

Another Formal theory of Truth, which has, however, a metaphysical or ontological rather than a logical aspect, is provided

---

[1] Cp. further for this—*The Two Logics* in *Mind*, No. 141.

[2] I am aware that Mr Russell himself distinguishes 'propositions'
and 'propositional functions.' But I do not find that he ever distinguishes 'judgments,' 'propositions,' and 'propositional functions'
simultaneously. Moreover, all his 'propositions' are, in fact, 'propositional functions'; they all contain variable terms whose meaning
and truth depend on the use made of them when they are judged.
There is no real difference between the 'propositional function' ' X is
a man ' and the 'proposition' ' Socrates is a man '; the latter also
becomes false if the ' Socrates ' in question happens to be an ape or
an ass.

by the doctrine that truth is essentially of reality. True judgments, that is, refer to objects and apprehend them; they are cognitive of reality or fact. This formula seems at any rate to have the merit of abstaining from the popular confusion of reality and truth, though upon investigation it appears to convey but little information. For its distinction between truth and reality seems to be only nominal. It conceives each of them in terms of the other, and so tells us the nature of neither. 'Reality' is the object truth aims at; but 'truth' is *any* aiming at an object, *including* that ordinarily condemned as false. For, unfortunately, a false judgment also has an 'object' which it apprehends, though it is not the *right* object—not the object its maker wanted and aimed at—and so defeats his purpose. But for the purpose of this theory anything before the mind when it thinks must count as an 'object.' So it is quite formal and undiscriminating. *All* judgments, true or false, are believed, when made, to aim at and apprehend some sort of object and to refer to some reality.[1] But this is a purely verbal fact which in real knowing may well be taken for granted. The question which really perplexes the knower is as to the status of the 'object' he judges 'about.' Is it real or illusory? Is it the object he aims at or another? In a 'false' judgment it is clearly illusory and defeats his purpose; yet he could not know it was 'false' by looking at its form. It claimed to be true and to apprehend reality, like the best of 'true' judgments. This claim was false, its knowing apparent, and its reality illusion; but it was not to be distinguished from a truth by the formal assurance that 'judgment is about reality.'

The underlying difficulty, then, of this theory is that *all* objects judged about, however unreal, fictitious, and illusory, must be accorded *some* status as 'reality.' They are all good enough to be judged 'about.' And they may all be judged about truly or falsely. It is quite possible to judge falsely about a fictitious object. We may assert, for instance, that Rebecca in *Ivanhoe* married the Templar. But we may also judge truly; as e.g.

[1] Strictly this holds only of judgments made in good faith. For the analysis of the lie, see Chap. VIII, § 19.

that Centaurs were anthropocephalic equines, and the Minotaur was a bull-headed anthropoid. In short, the ontological unreality of an object does not render it logically unreal. For logic the utterly unreal cannot be judged, and whatever is judged about has some sort of reality. But for this very reason the formal, logical, reality-claim has no logical interest; our concern is always with the question *to which* of the many orders of 'reality' our judgments may rightly be referred.

§ 4. (III) Truth as Necessity of Thought: (*a*) Its Genesis.

This theory also has an ancient pedigree and a long history, in the course of which it has so infected the roots and coiled itself around the core of Formal Logic that they seem inseparable. It originated at a time when 'schools' were a luxury of 'leisurely' slave-holders, who could afford to scorn servile 'work' and to imbibe the 'liberal' education that stamped them as free men. Accordingly the schools of Greece, and especially of Athens, devoted themselves zealously, for lack of chess and bridge, to the game of 'dialectics.' It was great fun, and an excellent trial of wits; but at first it suffered from the drawback that *there were no rules*. Of course every one wanted to win, and to know that he had won, and to *compel* his opponent to own himself beaten. But how was he to know he had got the better of the argument? So a demand arose for 'valid' reasoning, *strong* enough to extort a confession of defeat from the vanquished in debate, and its discovery became the great *desideratum* of Greek logic.

This desire for compulsion was a main source of the belief in 'necessary truth.' It could not be satisfied by the Socratic game of 'question and answer,' nor by the Platonic 'division.' But after a generation or two Greek ingenuity proved equal to the demand, and Aristotle supplied the syllogism as a form that would satisfy all requirements. After that Necessity could claim to be enshrined in the very centre of the temple of Truth. For the syllogism was a form of reasoning in which there was no drawing back once its premisses had been admitted: its conclusion followed of necessity, and no one could deny it. So once you had entangled your opponent in a syllogism you could force him to surrender at discretion. Moreover, this 'necessity' was also 'truth,' *if* you had taken the precaution to equip yourself with true premisses. And in 'scientific,' though not in 'dialectical,' reasoning one always started with true premisses. So one's conclusions always arrived at 'necessary truth.' In this way necessary truth became the ideal and aim of Logic, which for over 2000 years was fascinated and dominated by the syllogism.

No wonder, then, that logicians came to regard necessity as the hall-mark of truth, and felt themselves entitled, nay, necessitated, to define truth as 'that which we are necessitated to believe.' Necessity became the favourite noun of Logic and 'must' its favourite verb; 'contingent' truths and probabilities were looked down on with contempt. Because such truth was not 'necessary' it was deemed worthless.

§ 5. (*b*) Its Difficulties.

Nevertheless it may be doubted whether, but for the accident of its history, this theory would have commended itself as an attractive and plausible account of truth. It would rather have occurred to us to pry into its implications, and then instead of welcoming it we might have rejected it with scorn and indignation. For after all it prompts to some awkward questions. Thus : (1) Is it really a good reason for calling anything true that we cannot help thinking it? (2) Does it represent truth in an attractive light to make it compulsory, and does it reflect credit on the lovers of truth to represent them as *forced* to embrace it? A little reflection on these questions may greatly abate enthusiasm for this theory of Truth.

(1) That we cannot help thinking a thing is not surely a proof of its truth : primarily it is only a psychic fact about the mind that feels necessitated or compelled. As such it is of interest to psychology; but its logical bearing remains obscure. The logician should inquire what is the value of the guidance it affords, if it is adopted as a criterion of truth. When we think as we think we must, do we think rightly and successfully? So soon

as we inquire thus, we encounter cases where psychical necessitation seems anything but conducive to truth. We find
asylums full of lunatics full of delusions, who cannot help
thinking what the outsiders (who are deemed sane) think false.
No doubt the lunatics are (as yet) in a minority and under
restraint; but is that cogent proof that their convictions are
false? Is truth to be equated with the most bigoted beliefs of
the largest number? And even if the necessitation became universal and *all* were necessitated to hold a belief, would that
make it true? Might not the psychic mechanism of all afflict us
all with systematic delusions? Conceivably we might all be
necessitated to think what the course of events was continually
refuting, say, that perfect happiness was attainable on earth.
Should we not then resemble the lunatic who was obsessed with
the idea that he was made of glass, and would break if he sat
down, and whom no amount of contrary experience could
disabuse of his delusion? Why should not our 'necessities of
thought' conflict in similar ways with the course of events?
If they did, would they remain 'truths'? Clearly they would
afford no guidance except by contraries. We should have to
set aside their claim to apprehend reality, and to ignore them in
practice, and to act *as if* they were *not* true.[1]

Now, of course, it may be admitted that, in a world shaped by
natural selection, no strong and general impulse of our nature
is likely to be entirely misleading; because in that case it could
hardly have been developed. The very fact, therefore, that we
have developed thought goes a long way to show that thought
has proved itself a good and serviceable instrument of vital

[1] Here again we come upon the problem of Cassandra, and of how
she could neutralise the delusion inflicted on her by Apollo. She would
act rightly if she did the contrary of what she was doomed to believe,
and so acted *as if she thought* her prophecies were coming *true*. So, in
the problem of the crocodile who had embezzled a baby but promised
to return it if its mother would tell him truly whether he intended to
do so or not, we should advise the mother to assert, as her only chance
of recovering it, that he *did* so intend. If the crocodile denied it, the
mother should deny that he spoke the truth; the crocodile might then
keep the baby, but could not contend that he had established a logical
right to do so.

adjustment in the past, and may be trusted to lead us fairly right in the future. Still we trust it to yield us truth, not because it says so, and says it cannot help itself, but because we have tried it and it has helped us and we have found it trustworthy. In other words, we believe our truth not because it claims to be 'necessary,' but because we find it works.

(2) Our second question makes the suggestion that it might be better tactics to represent truth as attractive rather than as compulsory. Is it not, after all, a hideous caricature of truth and a cynical libel on man's attitude towards it, to represent truth as something to which we have to be compelled? Is argument merely the logical form of bullying? Is our 'truth-seeking' wholly hypocrisy; is truth repulsive to the natural man, and something he would never aim at could he but help himself? This sordid theory seems, no doubt, to have the syllogism's support; but it may prove to be a false analysis even of that. At any rate it seems most unwise to represent truth as something hateful and unattractive and us as reluctant to welcome it. And it is surely in flagrant conflict with the facts: for in general truth is good and desirable, and men in general desire it.

§ 6. (c) Its Explanation.

The notion that not love but force is the source of truth would seem to spring from (1) exaggerated emphasis on exceptional cases, and (2) from misinterpretation of the ambiguous term 'necessity,' which should mean '*need*' rather than '*compulsion*.' [1] It is observed that there are *unpleasant* truths which extort recognition from us, and it is inferred that *all* truth must be of this nature. But this overlooks the *normal* genesis of truth. A 'truth' is normally the end-term of an inquiry—that is, of an effort of truth-*seeking*—which has investigated some subject of interest to the inquirer and has ended successfully. Being the happy ending, therefore, of such an inquiry a truth is as such satisfactory, good, and desirable. How, then, do 'unpleasant' truths arise? They are 'unpleasant,' not *qua* satisfaction of our truth-seeking desire, but

[1] Cp. *Personal Idealism*, p. 70, *n.*

because in some circumstances they may thwart our other desires. Our cognitive interest is not the sole constituent of our complex nature, and what satisfies it may be anything but pleasing to our other impulses. And these may retaliate by calling it an *unpleasant* truth. Even so it may be, and often is, *relatively* pleasant, pleasanter and better than ignorance or error on the same subject.

One sweeping illustration may suffice to vindicate this analysis of 'unpleasant' truth. Suppose that all science and philosophy conspired to point to the conclusion that pessimism was the true view of life. That would be a supremely unpleasant truth to issue from our cognitive endeavours. But would it be accepted as truth? Hardly. Not only would every step on the way to this conclusion be bitterly contested, but, when it had been irrefragably established by reasoning, there would ensue an irresistible revolt of feeling. Nearly all would insist that science *must* be somehow wrong and that there must be *some* way out of pessimism. They would vote such philosophy 'false,' and would take refuge in a *religion* which transcended and transmuted its pessimism. Such a religion could always be got, because our knowledge can never be conceived to become so complete as not to admit of being rounded off with imaginative and hypothetical additions that would transform its character. These completions would be *postulates* (of 'rationality'), but they would receive much confirmation. For our supposed religion would have far more vital value than the pessimistic truth: its believers, therefore, would survive in virtue of their belief. When they alone survived, or had converted all the rest, what would have become of the 'truth' of pessimism? Can truth be claimed in any sense for that which cannot be made to work and *nobody* believes? Our illustration is by no means fanciful; it describes pretty accurately what in essence men have always done, and the vital function of religion in sustaining the human struggle with the ills of life. True, rationalism may object that this refutation of pessimism is not *rational*; but does it make the world *more* rational by contending that what men have always done has been *always wrong*?

We may conclude, then, that the erroneous belief in the unpleasantness of truth can be completely accounted for.

The belief that truth is pervaded by an inherent necessity is more difficult to dispose of, and demands subtler considerations. For at first sight the existence of logical necessity and its culmination in syllogistic reasoning seem beyond dispute. Yet it may be argued that the facts will support a better interpretation.

(1) It should be noted that by 'necessary truths' we need not mean 'truths which are forced upon us'; we can mean, and should mean, '*truths which we need.*'

(2) It is remarkable that in a normal train of thought which arrives at its destination without hindrance there develops no feeling of necessitation. It has not got to go where it arrives, but goes where it *wanted* to go, and attains the 'object' it *desired*. A feeling of 'must' arises in it only when it encounters an obstacle, and then the feeling is rather that it 'must' remove it or get round it than that it 'must' go on and cannot help itself.

(3) On the other hand an appeal to 'necessity' is commonly introduced when we wish to communicate to others the course of a train of thought. Our motive then is that we want the others to follow us, and think that they will do so more readily if they are told that there is no choice and that they *must* go that way than if we merely recommended it to them as a pleasant excursion conducting to a destination worth reaching. Intrinsically, however, there is no 'necessity' about, i.e. no need for, this way of putting the case, and if the others were more amenable the prospect of attaining a *desirable* conclusion might prove a stronger and more attractive motive than the plea of compulsion.

(4) Especially as logical necessitation is not nearly so potent as it is thought to be. Even the syllogism is not the formidable instrument of coercion it was so long believed to be. Its 'necessity' is not absolute but conditional. Its conclusion is 'necessarily true' *only if* its premisses are true, and these can only transmit the truth they have. But are we *ever* in a position to start our argument from premisses that are absolutely true?

If this may be disputed and denied, we can be under no necessitation or obligation to accept *any* syllogistic conclusion as true. As a matter of fact, whoever does not want to accept a syllogistically proved conclusion has merely to question the truth of its premisses and to demand proof thereof; when he is offered it he asks for further proof of the premisses that proved those of the syllogism to whose conclusion he objected. As this procedure may be carried to infinity, it is clear that the syllogistic form is not really cogent and able to compel assent: an unwilling disputant cannot be brought to his knees by it. Of course, if we *choose* to accept the premisses, the conclusion follows; but not because it had to, but because we wanted it.[1]

(5) Thus the belief in 'necessary truth' results from a 'telescoping' of two standpoints. To the truth-seeker it means the truth he needs, and when he finds it he is not constrained but glad. To the propagandist it serves as a convenient cover to his plans to win assent, because its impersonality is less likely to arouse his hearer's *amour propre*. He says 'we *must* think' when he really means '*I* want to think, and want *you* to agree with me.' Thus the 'necessity' is essentially *for export*.

§ 7. (IV) Truth as Intuition.

Intuitionism is a theory of Truth which was forced upon Logic by the defect in the Syllogism mentioned in § 6 (4). Aristotle saw that proof of syllogistic premisses must not be allowed to develop into an infinite regress, and hit upon the expedient of stopping it by alleging that sooner or later ultimate truths must be reached which would need no proof, because they were self-evident. The perception of these he ascribed to the highest of human faculties, intuitive reason (νοῦς). Since then Logical Intuitionism, not content with the odd, though apparently obvious, fact that some truths are self-evident, has tried to argue that all are. Of course this is not an easy thesis to

---

[1] We need not here raise the question whether the syllogism is in fact so 'valid' a form that no truth can be lost in it; ' Sidgwick's Ambiguity ' seems to confute this claim. Cp. Chap. XIV, § 4; XV, § 4.

establish, even if it can be made out that all inferred truths must be *intuitively apprehended*, and that 'truths' which cannot be are not really true at all. But we need not follow the theory into these contentions, if we can show that its principle is thoroughly deceptive and its explanations are *nowhere* sound.

Let us take it, then, at its strongest, and start with the self-evident intuitions of mathematics. Is '2+2=4' an intuitive truth? Assuredly. It is immediately apprehended. Its truth is admitted by all. It is certain. It is self-evident. It depends on nothing else. It is an unquestionable truth in its own right.

May we infer, then, that immediate apprehension is an adequate logical criterion? Does it never play us false? Does it never *mis*apprehend? Are *all* intuitions true?

If *not*, the first thing logical Intuitionism is bound to provide is some means of *distinguishing* true from false intuitions. If it finds such a thing, *that* will be its true and ultimate criterion of truth, and it may scrap 'intuition' or reduce it to a probable indication of the true test. If it *fails* to find it, it must uphold the truth of all the intuitions anyone has.

But is this possible? Can we not confront all the intuitions which are true with others which are equally self-evident, but false? Is 2+2=4 any more self-evident than 'two bodies cannot occupy the same space'? Yet the latter is merely an apparent fact, resting on crude observation and confuted by experiment, e.g. when hot platinum absorbs (occludes) several hundred times its own volume of hydrogen gas. And besides, is even 2+2=4 true *because* self-evident? It seems so, because we are all familiar enough with arithmetic to do easy sums without reflection. But is not this self-evidence psychological? Is not 2+2=4 logically deducible from the system of common arithmetic with its postulates and definitions and rules of addition?

And would it remain true if some one invented, or found a use for, another arithmetic, resting upon other assumptions? The thing can be done; it has been done in geometry. That the angles of a 'triangle' are equal to two right angles is now true only in Euclidean geometry, and has become false in non-Euclidean.

If Intuitionism cannot furnish a criterion of true intuition, can it not at least *publish a list* of true and genuine intuitions? It has never done so, either in logic or in ethics. Or rather, its attempts to do so have revealed nothing but the hopeless dissentions among intuitionists. We are told that the list cannot be published, because we (often) penetrate to the truly self-evident principles only at the end of a science, and the principles *we* start with are not necessarily *its* final principles. But is not this to make intuitive truth essentially relative to the state of a science and to subject intuitionism to empiricism with a vengeance? We then may ask: But can we in this way ever conceivably reach *final* truths that can *never* be improved on?

Moreover, does any science ever come to an end? If not, how can *we* use the test of self-evidence? It is now purely *ex post facto*, and assumes the *completion* of knowledge. But this renders it inapplicable to *our* knowledge. It thus defies both the conditions laid down in § 1: the 'self-evident' is both true and false and therefore formal, and it cannot be used as a test, because it has to be tested itself. Indeed, once it is admitted that *claims to self-evidence* need testing, like any other, the real test of Truth becomes whatever tests seeming self-evidence.

The truth, of course, which the logician (as usual) has been trying to evade, is that 'intuition' (like 'necessity') is primarily a psychic fact to be considered psychologically before logic should attempt to exploit it. And, psychologically, intuitions are a very mixed lot. Some of those prone to them, mostly women, find they can trust their intuitions (or think so); in others, mostly lunatics, they are so dangerous that their owners have to be put under restraint. We are often regaled in dreams with intuitive certainties that far transcend anything we get in waking life; but alas! when we awake, such 'truths' are apt to grow absurd.[1] In short, psychology furnishes singularly little warrant for the attempts to assign logical value to intuitions.

Lastly, it should be pointed out that the appeal to self-evidence is profoundly demoralising. It tempts us to dispense

[1] Cp. *Formal Logic*, chap. xviii, § 3.

with critical examination and to allege intuitions for whatever we may wish to believe. Thus it fosters dogmatism and narrow-mindedness, which are so bad for science.

§ 8. (V) Truth as Correspondence with Reality.

This would seem to be the commonest of all the theories of Truth, and embodies itself in a variety of formulas. It declares truth a 'correspondence' or 'agreement' or conformity of thought with 'reality,' an *adæquatio mentis et rei*, and leaves it open whether thought is to 'copy' or 'represent' 'reality' or 'reality' thought. It also leaves indeterminate the meaning of 'correspondence,' etc., and of 'reality' (like the second theory, § 3), and its real meaning and value will largely depend on the interpretation put upon them. But its commonness attests its plausibility and its persistence its survival value.

In considering it we must distinguish sharply between two cases: (1) the 'correspondence,' etc., which constitutes truth may be alleged to hold between contents of the field of knowledge, between the perceptions of various senses, between sense-perceptions and memories or thoughts, between various departments of thought, between the thoughts and perceptions of one man and those of another, between 'theory' and 'practice,' etc.; or (2) a 'correspondence' may be alleged between any or all of the contents of our knowledge and a transcendent reality to which it is supposed to refer.

(1) Now in the former sense correspondence is a test of truth in constant use, and no exception need be taken to it. We habitually test truth-claims by what we *call* 'correspondences,' 'agreements,' 'representations,' 'copyings.' Thus my 'idea' of a house is true if it corresponds with the 'real' (perceptual) house. If I remember it with six windows when it only has five, my idea of the sixth window is false. It does not 'correspond' with the 'reality.' A map is true (or 'correct') if its symbols 'correspond with' the features of the country mapped, and enable us to find our way about it. That *sugar is sweet* is true, if all *agree* about its taste. If I infer that I have ten shillings in my pocket because I remember I had twelve yesterday and

spent two, and then count them, if I judge that two florins are equal and then superpose them, the test of truth I use is a 'correspondence.' So a prediction *was* true, if it comes true afterwards; a collation of a manuscript is a 'true' (though not a photographic) copy if it reproduces all the letters of its original, though not necessarily their shapes. The vital point about all such testing and such 'truth' is that both remain wholly *immanent* in human knowledge. The thoughts and perceptions which correspond are mine or those of others. The 'real house' which corrects my memories is a house I can go and look at, the others to whom I can appeal are persons in our common world, the truths I assert are asserted about my experience and my life in the world I inhabit. Nowhere do I refer to anything really 'transcendent'; and this is why my account 'works.'

(2) But so soon as transcendent terms are introduced its meaning seems to break down. If the house is taken, as in Locke's 'representative realism,' metaphysically, as an ultimate reality or thing in itself which would exist just as well out of relation to my knowledge, the 'correspondence' becomes unmeaning. For I then at once get three terms to correlate: first, the house as it really is in itself; second, my 'idea' of it, i.e. my perceptual house; third, my ideas of this 'idea,' i.e. the house as I conceive or remember it. Truth, moreover, will now depend on the relation of the second and the third to the first, the 'real' house. But, from the nature of the case, I have access only to the second and the third, and their relation to the first is only an act of faith (or a superstition). The latter may agree as before, and be true in practice; but they will no longer satisfy the demand for theoretic truth. For *ex hypothesi* their claims to truth can never be tested. I cannot compare a thing within my ken with another which transcends it, to observe whether they 'correspond,' or whether the former is a good copy of the latter. I can never know the house as it is, since I know it only as it appears to me, i.e. to my senses. Thus the 'idea' of the house becomes an impenetrable screen between my thought and the real. I can no longer say, I can

no longer test, whether my idea 'corresponds with reality.' Truth has, in fact, been rendered impossible and unknowable by definition.

Why are we so prone to fall into this absurdity, why are we tempted to take the 'correspondence' thus? Because there *is* a certain transcendence involved in knowing, which we mis-interpret. When I perceive an object and take it as real, I take it as transcending my momentary act of perception, and as revealing a more or less permanent existence. It is, therefore, 'independent' of my *perceiving*, and perhaps of me, if it is *really* 'real,' and not illusory. But it remains an 'object of perception,' and an illusory object also has this same 'inde-pendence' of the perceiving, and 'transcends' it. Moreover, *this sort* of 'transcendence' and 'independence' does not expel any object from my experience or preclude its immanence in the world I know. It does not raise it to the *otium cum dignitate* of the thing-in-itself. The object is 'transcendent' and inde-pendent, epistemologically, not ontologically, and we must not pass fallaciously from the epistemological to the metaphysical sense of 'transcendence.' It is by doing this that realist meta-physics stultify the conception of truth as correspondence. So long as 'correspondences,' 'agreements,' and 'copyings' are taken *pragmatically* as relations which *work within* human ex-perience they will describe one side of truth.[1]

---

[1] It is sometimes argued that in spite of these difficulties a real transcendence and correspondence is involved in some of our beliefs. E.g. (1) When we 'remember' the past, the thought or image is of a past which no longer exists and cannot be 'recalled.' The present thought or image merely claims to be representative of the past, but its credentials cannot be examined, nor can the 'correspondence' of the representative with its original be tested; so truth about the past remains really 'transcendent.' (2) To each self the existence of other conscious beings must similarly remain really transcendent.

To (1) it may be answered that, paradoxical as it sounds at first, all truth-claims about the past, when disputed, can be tested only in the future. Consequently when the correctness of my present memory of the past is questioned, it will always be verified or refuted by sub-sequent action on the hypothesis that it is true. If this action prospers the truth-claim of our memory is vindicated (Chap. XIX, § 7).

As for (2) it may be best to admit frankly that we have no absolute

Whether they describe this aspect in the most appropriate terms is another question. For, taken in this way, 'correspondence' and 'agreement' seem to shade off into the intellectualist notion of 'system,' i.e. into the Coherence theory on the one side, and into the humanist conceptions of harmony and verification on the other, and the stress seems to fall, not on the relation of copying or representing, but on the *congruity* between the factors in knowing, whether that be conceived as complete or as merely intellectual.

§ 9. The Ambiguity of 'Reality.'

The failure of the correspondence view of Truth, then, would appear to be essentially due to the ambiguity and trickiness of the terms 'transcendent' and 'independent.' But it contains other pitfalls also. We noted at the outset that its formula was indeterminate on the subject of 'reality.' Does it take 'reality' *formally* and mean to include anything that *claims* reality? If so, it will have to include dreams, illusions, and hallucinations; but how will it help us to distinguish them from perceptions of true reality? If it tries to restrict itself to the latter it encounters the same difficulty. It simply must provide a criterion to distinguish between apparent and real 'reality' before it becomes applicable at all. But if it could do that the whole problem, not only of Logic but of metaphysic, would be solved; the trouble, however, is that the deceptiveness of the

proof of the existence of other minds. But neither have we any absolute proof that constituents of nature, down to the atom and the electron, have not *all* minds (of sorts) inhering in them. Both these possibilities retain a certain ' theoretic ' interest, because they serve to remind us on the one hand that the suggestion that our entire life is a dream cannot be disproved, and on the other that the line we draw between the animate and the inanimate is based on practical considerations only. Practically these doubts do not, at present, matter, because our ordinary beliefs are in both cases sufficiently supported. We have a strong craving to believe in other minds, and, having adopted the belief we find that it gets all the pragmatic confirmation possible. Whoever is not satisfied with this undertakes the burden of devising a more convincing proof, which, again, is not practically needed, because the evidence we have is found sufficient by all, even by himself in his more normal moods.

apparently 'real' infects all the criteria that are suggested.[1] The truth is that in one, the lowest, sense of 'reality' all 'unrealities' possess reality (Chap. XI, § 13). *As experiences*, dreams, illusions, and hallucinations are real enough; they are also real as factors in the course of reality. And so far as we recognise them as such and do not attribute to them any higher degree of reality they are known *truly*. What we need is not a general assurance that the true stands in a relation of 'correspondence' with the real, but specific apparatus for sifting reality-claims and determining the sort of reality that is indicated in each case.

Lastly, it should be observed that the essential *crux* of the Correspondence theory, the reference to what transcends human knowledge, does not exist merely for metaphysical realisms. It is found also in idealisms which allege the truth of *our* thought to depend on its relation to an Absolute Thought. The conception of the latter does nothing to render our thinking true, unless our thought can show how it grasps the Absolute Thought and perceives the 'correspondence' between the two.[2]

§ 10. (VI) Truth as 'Independent' of Us.

The difficulty of a transcendent correspondence between human thought and that which is supposed to validate it and render it 'true' recurs in an aggravated form in the 'Independence' view of Truth. This is current in two forms, according as truth is regarded as depending on the conformity of our thought with independent Ideas or with independent reality or 'fact.'

To the former variety of the view beautiful and permanently fascinating expression has been given in the philosophy of Plato. According to Plato true reality is to be found, not in the world

---

[1] E.g. the whole argument of F. H. Bradley's *Appearance and Reality* collapses in view of the simple consideration that the absence of contradiction cannot be used to distinguish 'reality' from 'appearances,' because it cannot be assumed that the 'contradictions' which are taken as proof of unreality and error are themselves 'real' contradictions. In Bradley's own book they are mostly 'dialectical.'

[2] Cp. *Studies in Humanism*, p. 122.

of sensible appearance but only in the supra-sensible order of
Ideas, which stand in eternal and immutable relations to each
other, whether they are apprehended by man or not. Thus
truth and reality are altogether independent of us, though at
times, by a divine and ineffable grace, one of these eternal reals
may be revealed to a mortal and fill his soul with truth, so that
he is enabled reverently to 'partake' of it. The situation lends
itself to brilliant and poetic description in Plato's hands; but he
struggled in vain to connect the sensible world he so resolutely
condemned with the Ideal world he had postulated. Once he
had separated them he deprived himself of the means of rendering intelligible their correlation: for it is clear that all his
terms—'participation' ($\mu\epsilon\theta\epsilon\xi\iota\varsigma$), 'imitation' ($\mu\iota\mu\eta\sigma\iota\varsigma$), 'presence'
($\pi\alpha\rho\sigma\upsilon\sigma\iota\alpha$), 'exemplar' ($\pi\alpha\rho\alpha\delta\epsilon\iota\gamma\mu\alpha$)—are but metaphors to bridge
the gulf he had created; and his bridges never span it.

Apart from this special *crux*, which Plato perceived more
clearly, and struggled with more gallantly, than any of his
followers, his theory has to be taken as essentially a form of the
correspondence theory. For though Plato does not explicitly
discuss how the ideas in the soul are related to the Ideas in the
'supercelestial place,' it is clear that *our* ideas must derive their
truth from their correspondence with *the* Ideas. For, if truths
exist independently of us, our judgments can be true only if
and when the relations we predicate copy those which eternally
subsist among the Ideas. Each man's ideas, therefore, have to
be reproductions of the eternal Idea. A correspondence with
the independent and absolute Truth is thus demanded in place
of a correspondence with absolute Reality or Fact.

This alternative form of the Independence theory does not
improve the situation. Absolute fact is just as hard to come by
as absolute truth. It is, no doubt, a general belief that when
we discover a 'truth' we apprehend a 'fact,' and that the existence of a fact is quite independent of its apprehension; but this
belief will not stand much reflection on the actual procedure of
our knowing.

In the first place (1) we can never take for granted that we
are in possession of absolute fact. The 'facts' we start from are

only apparent 'facts,' and retain their inverted commas however much they are criticised and purged, even though we feel confident that the 'facts' we end with are 'the real facts' at last.

Secondly (2) it seems plainly false to call either our *terminal* or our *initial* 'facts' independent of us and our manipulations. The former depend on the judgment and skill with which we conducted our inquiry, on the *data* we selected, on the observations and experiments we made, on the confirmations we exacted. They are thus essentially dependent on and relative to the process by which they were ascertained. They involved valuations by human investigators at every step; they were preferred to rival allegations, and sustained by our belief that they would *make good* as the *best* account of the problem they referred to. They are, therefore, the outcome of the state of knowledge which they consolidate, and remain relative to that. But much the same things must be said about our *initial* 'facts.' They were not *given* us as absolute facts to start with but *chosen* by us as likely to prove relevant to the aims of our inquiry—not *data* so much as *sumpta*. And they had previously been established as 'facts' by processes similar to those which we continue to use. Finally, we have no assurance that they are destined to remain 'facts' in future. Whenever the knowledge which acknowledges them becomes progressive we may advance beyond them or develop and transform them in the strangest ways. So our 'facts' may cease to be facts, as has constantly happened to the 'facts' of our predecessors.

Thirdly (3) we can say, of course, that the 'facts' we now take to be real represent and approximate to the *real* facts, which are truly independent of us and to which the Independence theory really refers. But is not this a mere act of faith? Moreover, it clearly involves the 'correspondence' view of truth. How can we ever ascertain whether our 'facts' are truly representative of 'the real facts'?

§ 11. The Meaning of 'Independent.'

The attempt, therefore, to vindicate 'independence' for truth seems to break down. Any truth which is *relevant* to us must be *relative* to us, and is so far humanised. But, as 'independent' is a highly ambiguous word, it may be possible to distinguish its chief meanings and to show that the Independence theory of truth arises out of confusing them, and so to account for its vogue. At any rate *three* senses of 'independent' should be distinguished.

(1) Taken strictly, it should mean '*wholly unaffected by.*' This is the sense in which it is used in metaphysical refutations of 'pluralism.' Now, in this sense, it is perfectly clear that Truth cannot be 'independent.' For everything is affected in some way or other by other things, and two independent things could not co-exist in the same universe.

(2) Neither can Truth be 'independent' in the sense of '*unrelated.*' A double relation seems to be essential to truth. (*a*) There must be a person *for whom* it is true, and (*b*) an object *about which* it is true. Truth is about 'reality' or 'fact' (§ 3); but it has also to be *judged* so, and *we* have to take the responsibility of deciding whether seeming fact is real (§ 10). 'Fact,' therefore, must be relative to our knowledge and 'truth' must be knowable by us. Both these relations must be frankly avowed.

(3) When truths are *called* 'independent,' what is really meant appears to be merely that they do not remain *tied* to the acts of apprehension or judgments of value which generated them. Once acknowledged, they do not pass away with our judgments and acts of apprehension, but persist and take their place in a more or less stable order of experience or realm of knowledge which we labour to extract from the flux of appearances. Of this order real things and truths form part. Once they are established in it our action can henceforth take them for granted. Thus the truths of arithmetic remain true and do not vary with every blunder in addition, even though arithmetic is a human invention in the last resort. This is what the Independence view should mean if it is to mean anything.

But in this *tenable* sense the 'independence' (as before the 'correspondence') still falls *within* experience and is *not* 'transcendent.' *We* attribute it to some of our judgments because of their superior value and staying power. '$2+2=4$' is independent of my present feelings in a way 'I am hot' is not; but the difference between them depends on empirical differences in the behaviour of the things they refer to; for if beings that can count and have temperature sensations were to disappear both judgments would lose their meaning and become impossible.

Now the error of the Independence theory lies in construing this third sense of independence as if it covered the first two, and reduces it to their absurdity. It does this because it has left out of account the *history* of the 'independence' assigned to some truths. It is really a selective valuation. It means that it has been promoted to the rank of 'independent truth,' because it has worked so well and become so important. But we no more *started* with a knowledge of what truths were 'independent' than we knew what truth-claims were true and what appearances indicated real objects.

§ 12. (VII) The Coherence Theory of Truth.

The Coherence theory of Truth often tries to elude pursuit by flights of metaphysics, but its claim to acceptance really rests on the authority of the sciences. It is plausibly asserted that the sciences all form coherent systems, and inferred that if these could all be made to cohere together the resulting science of metaphysics would embrace all knowledge and achieve absolute truth. This argument, moreover, is taken as so nearly self-evident that little or no inquiry is bestowed upon its details. Nevertheless it is thoroughly questionable at every step, and indeed dissolves into a tissue of logical incoherencies held together by psychological prejudice. Its case may be met by showing that, as a test of truth, Coherence is (1) formal, (2) psychological, (3) imperfect, (4) scientifically obstructive and misleading, (5) logically self-contradictory, and (6) conducive, not to absolute truth but to scepticism.

§ 13. Coherence a Formal Criterion.

(1) That Coherence as a criterion of truth is Formal, i.e. stops short at truth-claims and ignores the distinction between real truth and error, is easily shown. Even if it is admitted that

truths cohere, it is no less plain that errors do so likewise. Nor is it hard to see the reason why. *All* psychic processes, true or false, tend to cohere, because the human mind has achieved a considerable degree of unity, and so incoherence, when it is noticed, jars upon it and feels unpleasant. We try, therefore, to avoid it, and to that extent can all claim to be 'logical.' By trying to make our beliefs 'coherent' we mean 'harmonious.' Beliefs tend in consequence to conglomerate, and to form systems which have considerable power to assimilate what fits in with them and to extrude what does not. But all this is quite irrespective of the truth or falsity of our beliefs. It does not serve to discriminate coherent truth from coherent error. Hence the coherence test fails in the primary function of a test of truth.

§ 14. Coherence a Psychological Criterion.

(2) That Coherence is a thoroughly psychological criterion is already plain. Since all psychic processes cohere, coherence alone will not distinguish any special 'logical' coherence which is taken to be a mark of truth from the merely psychological coherence which supports error as readily as truth, and varies with the history and habits of each individual mind. No wonder such attempts as Formal Logic makes to establish this vital distinction are pitiable failures.

It attempts to account for the course of thought by logical necessitation, but we have already seen (in § 5) the weakness of the theory which attributes the course of thought to necessity and compulsion. We have also seen (§ 6) that even in a formally complete syllogism the logical necessitation is by no means absolute. And before we have committed ourselves to that 'form of reasoning' there is always ample scope for human choices and logical alternatives. The premisses of every syllogism have to be *selected* and put together, and will lead to different conclusions according as they are correlated with one set of questions, postulates, and aims, or another. Even formally there is no logical necessity to use a proposition, say *All S is P*, as a premiss rather than as a convertend in an 'immediate inference.'

And lastly, what prospect is there of coercing into the fold of logical necessitation the vast herds of reasonings which eschew 'necessity,' whose professed aim is merely *probability*, and which are often accompanied by the clearest consciousness that the probabilities preferred are only slightly greater or more attractive than those which are not adopted ?

The same objection holds against the logical coherence which is supposed to operate within a scientific system. Even if we take the most coherent of such systems, arithmetic, and consider the pure notion, say, of '12,' we do not find ourselves necessitated to select any *one* of the infinity of its arithmetical relations. No amount of contemplation of its properties in the abstract will determine what use will be made of it in an actual inquiry. It may figure as 2×6, or as 3×4, or as $11 + 1$, or as $13 - 1$, or as $\sqrt{144}$, etc.; and what it will actually mean will depend on what it is *wanted for*, i.e. on the purpose of the inquiry into which '12' enters as a relevant factor.

The truth is, of course, that the real coherence of thoughts, and the only coherence that should be called 'logical' (because it is the only sort which has logical value in actual thinking), is the coherence created by their relevance to the interests and purposes of some thinker: but this is *not* the sort of coherence Formal Logic recognises, nor is it a sort of coherence which can be determined in advance without examination of a thinker's mind. Nor does this sort of coherence, which is logical because it is *also* psychological, exonerate the coherence-test from the charge of Formalism. For as logical value may be negative as well as positive, the coherence in question may be that of coherent error as well as that of coherent truth: our only gain is that instead of having to do with a purely formal truth-claim, as likely as not to be false, we have now a truth-claim which its author at least believes to be true. But alike whether coherence be regarded as a psychological characteristic of the workings of minds or as a formal characteristic of truth-claims in the abstract, it cannot be used as a criterion and fails to distinguish the true from the false.

§ 15. Coherence an Imperfect Test.

(3) The admission made in § 13 that truths cohere must now be questioned. It will have to be considerably modified. For not only does it fail to provide a place for isolated facts, like a sudden pang of pain, the reality of which may nevertheless be borne in upon us by experience with irresistible force, or for a truth of perception, such as that a tennis champion has served a fault, but it involves altogether too *static* a view of scientific 'systems' to fit the actual facts. It might perhaps conceivably hold of a *perfect* system (if we can give a meaning to that notion), but it is simply not true of our actual sciences. Our actual sciences are not 'perfect'; they are not complete and closed structures into which nothing new can force its way, but are elastic and growing organisms with insatiable appetites for further truth. Being thus continuously and indefinitely *progressive*, there *must* arise in them questions as to the relations of the old and the new. These relations ought, in a true theory of science, to be friendly enough; for every science ought to be receptive of, and hospitable to, new truth; but it is not hard to see why in fact it often is not. For the new truths are often aggressive; they attack and overthrow old-established errors which have long grown familiar and been so harmonised with the old truths that they seem one system, even when they do not entirely cohere, and the adherents of the old system are loath to part with them.

Moreover, even though every science is in theory elastic, the extending, stretching, and straining of the old system which is needed to fit the new truths into it is often felt to be a repulsive business. Especially by the 'great authorities' in the science, who are naturally well stricken in years and have usually lost in the course of nature the elasticity of mind which would render them hospitable to new ideas. So the inherent possibilities of conflicts between the new and the old are usually realised. There is usually a severe struggle between the conservatives and the innovators which in former days normally ended in the suppression of the latter, but during the last few hundred years has *in science* issued in their victory, and so accounts for the progress of the sciences. But the features of this struggle are always the same. The champions of the new truths demand for them scientific recognition even though they seem isolated and anomalous; the adherents of the old system denounce them as discrepant and incredible and incapable of being accommodated in the system of the old truths. Their assertions are often quite false, because they are themselves psychological conservatives who mistake the rigidity of their own minds for that of the system to which they are attached; but it is evident that this struggle makes highly improbable any premature recognition of new truth.

§ 16. Coherence Scientifically Obstructive.

(4) It is also evident that upon the issue of this struggle the Coherence theory of Truth, if it is accepted, must exercise a pernicious influence; for it *must* be biased against the new truths that seek to intrude into the old system. These of course cannot appear to it systematic enough to be true; they are often unexpected and turn up singly or are discovered bitwise. Nevertheless history shows that they may be none the less true; it has happened over and over again in the history of science that the Goliath of an inflated 'system' has been punctured by a little pellet of new fact. Thus Galileo's first glimpses of Jupiter's moons gyrating in the first telescope were sufficient to upset the vast system of Ptolemaic astronomy, once the protests of pious Aristotelians against the use of this diabolical contrivance had been overruled. Similarly the spirit-possession theory of disease, coherent as it was and congenial with the prepossessions of mankind, has gradually yielded to scientific medicine which, in the beginning at least, could manifest itself only in isolated cures. A more equal and protracted battle was waged between the system of Biblical chronology and the repeated finds of fossils, till by dint of numbers they shattered the category of 'antediluvian,' in which it was sought to confine them.

To sum up, then, the Coherence theory is scientifically inadequate for several reasons. (1) It does not provide for the reception of *isolated* truths at all. (2) It resists the recognition of *new* truths. (3) When, nevertheless, new and isolated truths crop up, it must condemn them as less coherent than the old errors which they are destined to supersede. (4) When it is confronted with *equally coherent* systems which provide alternative interpretations of the admitted facts, it is helpless to decide between them. Now such cases are by no means rare in the sciences. For example, the various metageometries are just as coherent as the geometry of Euclid: they proceed from different assumptions, but deduce their conclusions with equal rigour. From the standpoint of the coherence theory, therefore, they should be equally 'true,' whereas in fact an overwhelming preference is accorded to the Euclidean system by reason of its greater simplicity and convenience. The former of these reasons cannot be advanced in order to decide between ordinary physics and Einstein's explanation of 'forces.' The former assumes a plurality of various forces operating in a uniform space conceived on Euclidean lines; the latter dispenses with the 'forces,' and attributes all that happens to the intrinsic complexity of physical space. Thus each is simpler from one point of view, and more complicated from another, and human 'convenience' alone remains available in such cases as the decisive criterion of 'truth.'

§ 17. The Self-contradiction of Coherence.

Perhaps the quaintest development of the Coherence Theory is, however, that arising from the attempt to take it metaphysically. This lands in flat self-contradiction, as follows. The sciences, as we have seen, being growing structures which are constantly expanding, are never entirely 'coherent.' They are always engaged in assimilating new truth which is not yet completely fitted into the old system. Neither do the various sciences cohere perfectly with each other; this is no wonder, because they have as a rule developed independently and pursued their own interests in a single-hearted manner. So the actual facts of science give the lie to the Coherence Theory. But, undismayed, its advocates take refuge in an 'ideal' system which has all the perfections the actual systems lack. In it all discrepancies and incongruities have been smoothed over and have disappeared; all truth has been moulded into a concordant and coherent whole. Having framed this ideal of a single total truth, they feel entitled to look down on the actual truths of the sciences as partial and imperfect, and declare them infected with incoherence and error.

But they have overlooked that the imperfectly coherent truths of the sciences, which they despise, are among the logical presuppositions of their own theory. Without them their own case breaks down. In order to arrive at the conception of truth as 'coherence,' they *had* to recognise partial truths, and to find that they cohered. They had to recognise, say, $2+2=4$ as a truth of arithmetic to get the idea that arithmetic is wholly composed of such coherent truths. The existence of *truths* (in the plural) thereby becomes a necessary presupposition of their theory, and a premiss in its argument. Yet in the sequel this premiss is disavowed and contradicted. Their conclusion is that no such truths can exist, because no partial truths can be more than partially true, and $2+2=4$ also is no truth in its own right intuitively apprehended, but true only as a deduction from the system of arithmetic. Indeed, nothing less than the totality of truth can ever be absolutely coherent and true. So their 'system' suffers from the logical flaw that if their premiss is true it does not warrant their conclusion, while if their conclusion is true it destroys its own premiss. If the truths of the sciences are really true, we have no right to imagine any other and higher truth; if total truth alone is truly true, then the truths of the sciences were not true, and their coherence is no longer a reason for conceiving truth as coherence and a basis for erecting the 'ideal' of a total truth. Indeed, if the sciences are true in their own right, they cannot submit to dictation from the metaphysical phantom of a total truth. There is, in fact, a logically insuperable chasm between the actual and the ideal, between the systems of the sciences and the all-embracing system, which we encounter frequently (Chap. I, § 15 ; Chap. XV, § 15) and which we have no business to ignore.

§ 18. 'Coherence' ends in Scepticism.

The incoherence of the Coherence theory on this vital point may be ascribed to the psychological glamour cast by the word 'ideal'; but its final fall into scepticism is due to the lure of metaphysics. It is inevitable, if we cling to the idea that only the total truth can be wholly true. For if all partial truth is only partially true, truth must be possessed entire or not at all. No partial 'truths' can be trusted, for their partial falsity may always vitiate their verdict on the very point we are inquiring into. Thus we can know nothing until we know everything. The theory involves a covert postulate of omniscience. Until, moreover, we have made sure of omniscience we cannot safely take a single step to acquire knowledge. But it is equally clear that if we had attained omniscience, there would be nothing further for us to learn. Also that omniscience is humanly impossible. Our whole manner of life and the methods of all our sciences would have to be radically changed if we had to reckon with omniscience as a possibility. This deduction from the Coherence theory, therefore, puts truth completely out of relation to man and renders it unattainable by us.

Whether Total Truth remains a possible conception, and can with meaning and propriety be ascribed to the Absolute remains as a metaphysical inquiry which is at bottom idle. For if we assented to it the absolute truth possessed by the hypothetical Absolute would serve only to cast a slur upon all human truth —including the argument by which it was reached. It would merely reduce us to total scepticism. But the whole procedure seems completely wanton. It is utterly irrelevant to our logical inquiry into what, in point of fact, we men mean when we use the epithets 'true' and 'false.' We plainly mean something, and something important, and our theory of truth should discover what we mean. Any tenable theory of truth, therefore, must be humanist *at least*.

CHAPTER VIII

THE HUMANIST THEORY OF TRUTH

1. Requirements of an adequate theory of truth ; 2. ' True ' and ' false ' antithetical but correlative ; 3. ' True ' and ' false ' as valuations ; 4. Valuation a continuous process ; 5. The relativity of truths ; 6. Discovery presupposes interest ; 7. Humanist definitions of truth : (1) As logical value ; 8. (2) Truth as satisfaction of a purpose or need ; 9. (3) Truth as ' working ' ; 10. 'Use' and 'working' as corollaries; 11. The meaning of 'useful'; 12. ' Truths ' one sort of truth-claim ; 13. The realm of truth-claim : (1) Postulates ; 14. (2) ' Axioms ' ; 15. (3) Methodological assumptions ; 16. (4) Methodological fictions ; 17. (5) Fiction ; 18. (6) Jokes ; 19. (7) Lies ; 20. (8) ' Truths ' and their verification ; 21. The ' working ' of truths ; 22. Truth as dependent on consequences ; 23. The cognitive function of doubt.

§ 1. Requirements of an Adequate Theory of Truth.

Reflection on the traditional theories of Truth should have generated in us an adamantine conviction that any adequate account of truth must exhibit a number of features which are lacking to the theories we have criticised.

(1) It must not be merely formal, i.e. it must distinguish between the true and the false and suggest an applicable way of *testing* claims to truth.

(2) It must concern itself with human truth and its attainment by us, and must not put us off with 'criteria' that are inapplicable and 'ideals' that are unrealisable.

(3) It must not, therefore, take too strictly and too seriously terms like 'independent,' 'transcendent,' and 'absolute,' which are better avoided in accounts of Truth. When, however, they are used, they should not be understood in any sense that would rule out the essential relation to man that renders truth valuable and worth winning. However anxious we may be to affirm the objectivity of truth, our craving must not lead us to leave out the human side of knowledge. To do so simply stultifies a theory of knowledge and renders it irrelevant.

(4) We must take nothing for granted in our inquiry into truth, but must be willing to investigate even the most familiar of the conceptions and distinctions which are commonly assumed. This means that all the traditional rubrics by which

we set our experiences in order are to be conceived as *arrived at*, as crystallising out of our cognitive processes, and as gradually establishing their claims to truth and value. Thus the distinctions between 'subject' and 'object,' 'subjective' and 'objective,' 'real,' 'apparent,' and 'unreal,' 'fact' and 'fiction,' in short, all claims to truth and reality, of whatever sort and to whatever degree, are to be taken as *in principle*, subject to inquiry, criticism, and revision.

(5) We must scrupulously keep in touch with actual human thinking, and must not repudiate or disavow it for the greater glory of some factitious logical or metaphysical 'ideal.' This means that we must be *psychological*, consistently and from the outset, and not merely as an afterthought when our 'logic' breaks down. In particular, we must *not* abstract from the *personal* side of knowing, as Formal Logic tried to do, nor ignore the purposive nature of its processes.

§ 2. 'True' and 'False' Antithetical but Correlative.

Bearing these requirements in mind, let us next study our ordinary practice in awarding the epithets 'true' and 'false.' We shall find that they are both antithetical and correlative, implacably opposed and yet inseparably associated. The raw material of every inquiry contains true *and* false, and our business is to extract the true and to purify it until it is 'true enough' for our purposes, while discarding the false. Thus the process of extracting truth is like the refining of a metal extracted from its ores: there is nothing about it that justifies, or even suggests, the demand for any 'absolute' truth. Indeed, since the purity of any 'truth' and the degree of its immunity from 'error' is always relative to the tests to which it has been subjected, it would seem, even at this stage, that there was really no *meaning* to be given to this demand.

Thus in human thinking every inquiry is inspired by the desire for 'truth' and the dislike of ignorance. But because we know that the true and the false are commingled in our data, our whole search of truth is dominated by the need of escaping from 'error.' And by error we mean whatever frustrates our search. 'Falsity' is failure, 'truth' the success of our enterprise, not vaguely in the abstract, but in the sense of solving the particular problem before us.

'True' and 'false,' then, are definable in terms of the purpose of the inquiry. Whatever is found to thwart or defeat this purpose is called 'false,' whatever is taken to forward it and to lead it to a satisfactory and successful conclusion is voted 'true.' This is the primary use of the antithetical terms 'true' and 'false,' and it is evident that at various stages of the inquiry the same factors of the situation may be valued variously. What we began by judging 'true' may come to seem more and more infected with falsity; what seemed obviously 'false' may be shown to have been a hiding-place for important 'truths'; and when we look back upon a completed inquiry, we may see that we could never have succeeded in it, if we had not been willing to subject our material to continuous and gradual purification and been pertinacious in questioning both self-assertive 'truth' and blushing unobtrusive 'error.'

§ 3. 'True' and 'False' as Valuations.

In the above sketch 'true' and 'false' have clearly been described as *valuations*, as expressions of the approval or disapproval bestowed upon some cognitive operation. They are, indeed, the characteristic valuations, positive and negative, which arise in, and are appropriate to, cognitive process or inquiry as such. If we are willing to take them thus simply to begin with, we shall readily understand not only the apparently paradoxical relations in which they stand to each other, but also the complications which arise from their further use. The nature of 'true' and 'false' as valuations sufficiently explains their correlation. Values always hunt in couples, and imply a tacit reference to their opposites. And they always involve a relation to a valuer: for they are constituted by *his* judgments of approbation or disapprobation. In these respects the true-and-false is perfectly analogous to the pleasant-and-unpleasant, the right-and-wrong, the good-and-evil, the beautiful-and-ugly, and, perhaps we may add, the real-and-unreal. They are all forms or kinds of the good-and-bad which designates relation to a purpose, 'end,' or 'good.' Regarded thus, 'truth' is simply the good or end aimed at in knowing; 'error' its 'bad,' defeat, or failure. The doctrine is as old as Aristotle,[1] the most commentated of philosophers; that it has never been understood simply shows that the understanding of a great philosopher demands something more than the intelligence of a commentator.

We should realise, then, that knowing is always accompanied by valuing. Or, rather, that it *is* valuing. For values are the end of knowing and the desire for them is the beginning, while valuing is an integral part, of every cognitive act. At every step in our knowing we are weighing the alternatives presented to us, and judging them good or bad as means to our end: the question we should ever bear in mind is, *Is S P or P'? Is it better taken as P or as P'?* In short, knowing is essentially a purposive process directed towards an end which the knower conceives as desirable, and desires. He judges the various stages of his progress, as it proceeds, as good or bad, true or false, according as they seem to him to be approaching his end or carrying him away from it. It is not necessary, of course, that his judgments should all be infallible and irrevocable, nor that the complications introduced into the proceedings by conflicts of ends in his soul or by divergences between his valuations and those of others should be considered at this stage. These complications must have been overcome and a working compromise between conflicting claims must have been reached, before we can get at fully recognised 'objective' truth; but for the present it will be more instructive to follow the course of individual knowing.

§ 4. Valuation a Continuous Process.

Valuation is a life-long process. It goes on continuously. Every moment of life is felt to have its value, of one sort or another, positive or negative, and its valuation is an unceasing occupation of every mind. This is true also of the cognitive valuation in terms of 'true' and 'false.' It may start any-

---

[1] E.g. *Eth. Nic.*, vi, 2, 2.

where, and about any object at any time, and need never stop till the desire to know is exhausted. And that need never be.

We should expect, however, any particular valuation to undergo the giddiest variations and vicissitudes in the course of its career. What is called true to-day may be falsified to-morrow; what was 'true' yesterday may be 'false' to-day. So the *date* of a 'truth' is by no means always irrelevant, and the only truths that can plausibly claim to be 'eternal' are those which have been put out of relation to time, by abstraction, to begin with, like the truths of mathematics, nor will even this ensure their acceptance through all time. Similarly, the use of timeless formulas, like 'laws' or 'universals' for guiding anticipation, is legitimate only while we bear in mind that in their application the blank spaces in our formulas must always be filled in by specifying the conditions and values of the particular case: it becomes a sinister superstition when we take it as revealing a changeless constitution of the real.

Abstraction from the *place* of a truth can no more be taken for granted than abstraction from its *time*: indeed, *what* is true will often be found to depend on *where* it is required to be true. What is true in one place may be false in another. And that not merely in matters of manners and customs. So simple a question as, *What is the time?* cannot be answered without regard to the place where it is asked. If it is true that *it is two o'clock* in Oxford, it will certainly be false in New York. And one of the most valuable lessons of Relativity is to have impressed on us that *all* the 'times' are true together in different places, because time is *essentially local*, and we ought to think in terms of *space-time*, which is really one and is divided only by abstraction.

This principle is itself only a case, which happens to interest physics, of a wider philosophic principle, which we may now go on to state. *Every truth is essentially relative to the conditions out of which it sprang and to which it was meant to refer.* So when these conditions change, we must always be willing to revise it and to adapt it to the changed conditions, and when we apply it to *other* conditions we are *making an experiment and taking a risk*, and should not assume *a priori* that it continues to hold.

It serves to guide expectation, but its 'coming true' is a real 'verification' which adds to its usefulness and value.

§ 5. The Relativity of Truths.

Again, therefore, it would seem that the notion of an 'absolute' truth is meaningless. Truths are relative to the state of knowledge which they formulate, and to take them otherwise is to delude oneself. Exemplifications of this may be drawn from every department of knowledge. A few will probably suffice to illustrate this point.

As a boy I learnt that Mt. St Elias, in Alaska, was 19,500 feet high. Years afterwards a new observation knocked it down to 14,500 feet. Then some one went up it 14,000 feet, and said he was nowhere near the top. Of late it has kept pretty steady at 18,500 feet in the geography books. Similarly, the Matterhorn appeared to have grown 21 metres—from 4484 to 4505 metres between my second and my third visit to Zermatt—though I could not discover whether natural expansion or the influence of the hotel-keepers had raised it above the 4500-metre line. But these, it will be said, are all variations in our knowledge. The real height of the mountain itself, which it is the aim of our truth to express, has been the same all along, and has not changed.

Such ways of speaking are of course convenient, and seem sound enough until we ask what 'the real height' means and how it is ascertained. We then discover that it cannot be taken as unchanging, and that the-real-height-*for-us* must vary with our means of determining it. The actual top of a snow mountain varies from day to day; there is now more snow on the top, now less, rocks tumble down, the earth is unstable and the range of which it forms part may be rising or sinking. What, then, is meant by its 'real height'? No wonder one may read in Whymper [1] that "the summit of the Dent Blanche is a ridge, perhaps 100 yards in length. The highest point is *usually* at its north-east end."

'The real height' gets into further difficulties when we consider how the height-for-us is determined. It is obtained by

---

[1] *Scrambles among the Alps*, p. 279. Italics mine.

taking observations with instruments. But no human instrument will measure with absolute accuracy, nor is any human observer capable of it. If, therefore, a trustworthy value for the height is desired, the thing to do is to take a long series of observations (probably all different) and then to take their average, throwing out first any observation which for any reason is considered bad. The assumption is, of course, that over-estimates and under-estimates will occur about equally often and will cancel out. But can an average possibly be 'the real height' which varies not? The very next observation may upset it. In scientific measurement it is further customary to estimate the 'probable error' of the value adopted, and then 'the real height' will appear as something like '18,500±25 feet,' which looks still less like a fact in nature than an average.

Finally, the accuracy of a measurement is not only relative to that of the observer and of his instruments but also to his purpose. No one wants to know the height of a mountain to a millimetre, nor would even the most accurate historian think it possible to discover the exact minute in 1066 when William the Conqueror first set foot in England.

It is enough, then, for Science to get approximate values which can be improved on, if needed and desired, to any requisite extent. 'Absolute' truth means nothing to it; or rather, if it is taken etymologically and literally, it means a patent absurdity, a negation which claims to be 'freed from' all relations, and especially from the vital relation to scientific purposes which creates the value of a truth. A scientific 'truth,' therefore, is always a value, and is always capable of being superseded by a better value. Moreover, even a slight improvement may supersede an old value and render it false. Thus, if 'the' distance of the earth from the sun has been taken as 92,000,000 miles, and if what the astronomers consider a better observation reduces it to 91,430,000 miles, the new value is substituted in the textbooks; yet, for many purposes, 92 (or even 90) million miles may continue to be quite 'true enough.'

Hence it follows that the more progressive a science is the oftener it changes its 'truths,' and the shorter is the life of any one 'truth.' Immutability and immemorial antiquity are only found in the 'truths' of pseudo-sciences, or of sciences like arithmetic and theology, which adopt the policy of avoiding the verbal confession of the changes in the meaning of their terms which their progress entails.

§ 6. Discovery presupposes Interest.

Being purposive and relative to purpose the search for truth presupposes interest. Truth is not forced upon us; it has to be looked for, and often long and strenuously. Psychologically almost any interest may start an inquiry and lead to a discovery of truth. Hence discoveries are never the chance affairs they sometimes seem to be, even if a streak of luck attends their birth. Röntgen was clumsy and lucky enough to put his fingers over part of the vacuum tube he was photographing, but he had the sense to recognise his fingers in the resulting marks on the plate, and to understand that they must be transparent to the rays with which he was experimenting. An Oxford physicist, Jervis-Smith, who actually made the same experiment before Röntgen, did not discover the Röntgen rays because he was less clumsy, and so did not understand the much smaller finger-print left on *his* plate. That was Röntgen's luck; but he made the discovery, not because he was lucky but because he was a good physicist, interested in vacuum tubes and able to handle them intelligently.

We may say, then, that it is always from psychological interest and in the pursuit of some purpose that truths are born. They satisfy an interest and fulfil a purpose. But interests vary and purposes change; so our truths do not always satisfy the purpose we started with in the way we wanted. There is an element of unexpectedness, as well as of luck, about many discoveries. Saul went forth to find his father's asses and founded a kingdom. But only because he changed his mind, and desisted from the pursuit of the asses. Columbus started for India, and got to America. But when he got there he felt he had not sailed in vain, and accepted the Western hemisphere instead of the Orient he had sought.

§ 7. Humanist Definitions of Truth: (I) as Logical Value.

All the characteristics of truth we have been considering in §§ 3–6—its dependence on valuation, its progressiveness, its relativity to the occasion of its use, to the state of knowledge, to the purpose and interest of the knower—are completely ignored by the intellectualist descriptions of knowing which are in vogue. Yet they are far more vital than the definitions we considered in Chapter VII.

It must not, however, be supposed that the Humanist account of Truth is incapable of producing definitions. In point of fact it can provide no less than four definitions or quasi-definitions from different points of view. We can define truth—(1) formally as *logical value* ; (2) psychologically, as *satisfaction of a cognitive purpose* ; (3) materially, as *a truth-claim that works* and is useful ; (4) empirically, as *dependent on the consequences* of taking it as true. As all of these phrases, however, have often been misunderstood or misconstrued they will all need elucidation.

(1) The first of these, indeed, should not need much further discussion after what was said about the relation of logical to the other values in Chapter III and Chapter VIII, § 3. We need only note here the formal character of this definition and the advantages of classifying truth with the other values. To conceive truth as logical value is *formal*, because it does not exclude the possibility that the 'truth' claimed may be false and its value *negative*; so that, strictly speaking, truth-and-falsity is the sort of value which concerns logic. We can also say that logic considers its values as primarily *value-claims*, and proceeds to evaluate them, and so to discriminate the 'really true' from the false pretenders. Secondly, the advantages of classifying truth with the other values in the same genus with the ethical, æsthetical, and pleasure-pain values are manifold. It explains (*a*) the curious vicariousness of the terms of valuation in language. A (logical) proof is not only called 'true,' but 'good,' 'elegant,' and even 'beautiful.' Every schoolboy knows that he may get a sum 'right' or 'wrong.' Conversely, logical terms are transferred to ethical and æsthetical contexts. A statue, to be

'beautiful,' must have the 'true' proportions. A 'false' friend is one who does not wish your 'good,' etc. (*b*) By conceiving truth as a value we implicitly raise the question 'positive or negative?', and indicate the need for distinguishing the 'really true' from what only claims and seems to be true. We can then effect the discrimination by the test of superior value for our purposes. The *truer* is the *better*, and, when the worse alternatives have been discarded, may be called 'true.' (*c*) We can correlate the several sciences of value, and bridge the gap between them and the sciences of fact. For if the recognition of 'fact' proceeds from an evaluation, as was shown in Chapter III, § 3, a fact is a hidden value. The 'real fact' is extracted from a mass of apparent facts. How? By displaying superior value. The 'real fact' is *better value*. (*d*) When truth is recognised as a value we grow readier to observe the frequent contamination of logical with ethical and æsthetical values, and to allow that there is no inherent impropriety in a process which naturally results from the unity of the valuing personality. Thus there opens out to logic a new and fascinating study of the interplay of the various values in what are predominantly 'cognitive' operations, and logic need no longer hesitate to admit that their course is often directed by feeling to a happy ending.[1] (*e*) Lastly, the sway of value can be extended over our whole experience. If 'true' is, like 'good,' 'beautiful' and 'pleasant,' a value, and if all the values are relative to one supreme purpose, 'The Good,' we have, in theory at least, taken an important step towards the realisation of the Platonic ideal of a Reality that subordinates itself to the Good.

In principle, then, truth can no longer be unrelated to good. It is a peculiar and specific form of good. But this is no objection, as F. H. Bradley mistakenly supposes.[2] We may make it as specific as we please, so long as we do not overlook the connexion, hitherto ignored, between the True and the Good. However much it may annoy the intellectualist to find that in point of fact moral and logical values are interchangeable and

---

[1] Cp. *Problems of Belief*, p. 171 f.
[2] *Essays on Truth and Reality*, p. 220.

that the various values work together, these processes must be studied; indeed, protests against their undue contamination are most likely to obtain a hearing if they start from an admission that the true and the good are at any rate commensurable as values.

In conclusion we may sum up this value aspect of Truth by saying that *the true is always good to believe*, and that at any given time it is what it is *best* to believe.

§ 8. (II) Truth as Satisfaction of a Purpose or Need.

By defining it thus we at once connect 'truth' vitally with 'life.' So long as we cling to this definition truth cannot be dehumanised, and the paradise of science cannot be desiccated and devastated by the demons of pedantry. If only our schools would teach the truths that truth is desirable and satisfies, and that knowledge is power, they might kindle much intellectual ardour they at present chill by the intellectualist untruth that the more useless a 'truth' grows the 'higher' it is.

The dependence of every inquiry, of every form of cognitive enterprise, on purpose and on the satisfactions which accrue from the attainment of truth, is too obvious to be directly denied once they are pointed out. But the intellectualist tries to minimise their effect. (*a*) He insists on the "peculiarity" of cognitive purposes; (*b*) he denies that truth, though it depends on purpose for its genesis, remains so dependent "in its essence."

To (*a*) the reply is that cognitive purposes remain human, and cannot be dissevered from the rest of our activities. Nor can our life and nature be divided into a 'theoretic' and a 'practical' half. Processes which are not usually *called* cognitive precede, pervade, and clinch every cognitive activity. Thus every inquiry starts with a question; every judgment is the answer to a question. This is the great discovery (or rediscovery) which modern logic owes to John Dewey and Alfred Sidgwick, though it may lurk also in the *dictum* of Protagoras that about every matter there were two arguments (λόγοι).

Even, therefore, if in theory a rigid line could be drawn between the theoretic and the practical, we should in practice find that 'practical' considerations conditioned our theories of the 'theoretical' throughout. When it is studied without prejudice the human intellect is found to point to practice as the magnet points to the pole: when it *fails* to do so, we may be sure that it has become deranged. Moreover, the intellectualist's descriptions of a 'purely theoretic' intellect unconsciously attest this. It has to be represented as 'divine,' because it plainly cannot be human. For example, Plato's Ideas cannot know the individual,[1] and cannot live with the sensible: he has, therefore, to sky them 'somewhere out of space.' Similarly, Aristotle's 'God' is too perfect to contemplate an imperfect world: but is not this an indirect way of admitting that an intellect able to deal with the infinitely various individualities of our 'contingent' world must be built on other lines?[2]

(*b*) It is subtler to argue that Truth may be intrinsically independent of man, 'in its essence,' though for us it must depend on an interest to attain it. But this contention will hardly bear examination. (1) It uses the vague word 'essence,' which has long ago departed from its original antithesis to 'accidents,' and come to mean merely 'the important part.' And what part of truth is *not* important? Surely, for us at least, its relation to man is the most important part. Moreover, if any part of the concrete cognitive process could be independent of the whole of which it is part, how could it be a part at all? An 'independent' part of a whole seems a covert contradiction. (2) It involves a queer use of 'independent,' which we have found to be a tricky word, in Chap. VII, § 11. Here it is used to dissever a product from the process which alone produces it; but can the terminal point of a line be called independent of the line on which it lies? It is true that sometimes when we have arrived at a conclusion we can see that it might have been reached by other, and possibly better, ways; but in the case of truth this suggestion is meaningless. For there is no other way

---

[1] Cp. *Theætetus*, 209.

[2] Similarly, the ' universal ' minds of the absolutist philosophies and the ' divine ' minds of the various theologies are all vitiated by so radical a difference from the motivation and procedure of human minds that the latter can never reach them by any practicable route.

to attain it but by human effort. (3) The whole policy of treating the 'essence' of Truth as 'independent' of its origin is surely discredited by two dozen centuries of failure. (4) The doctrine in question would seem to lead to some curious consequences. If there can be truth independent of us, there can be unknowable truth. For our inability to grasp it will not detract from its truth. Mr Bertrand Russell has seen this, and boldly gives an example: "All the multiplication sums that never have been, nor ever will be *thought of* by any one, deal with numbers above 1000."[1] His illustration fails by reason of the ambiguity in "thought of." In one sense every arithmetical result has been thought of, in laying down the law or rule for its production. It has not been *worked out*, but it can be whenever an occasion arises. Moreover, if *some* truth can properly be called unknowable, why not *all*? In its anxiety to avoid humanism intellectualism plunges into scepticism.[2]

§ 9. (III) Truth as 'Working.'

It must be admitted, nay, emphasised, that to say that *all truth must work* and *be useful* is not, strictly, to define it at all. It is to insist on a very important and vital requirement which has been unfortunately overlooked; but it has not the *form* of a definition. It does *not* make 'truth' *convertible with* 'what works,' nor *identify* it with 'usefulness,' though from the earliest days this false conversion has been falsely foisted upon Pragmatism. The blunder in formal logic which it involves must be debited to its critics, who have never been able to quote from a representative pragmatist any passage which committed it, though it is common in popular and hostile expositions.[3]

[1] Italics mine

[2] This is notorious as regards the *logic* of F. H. Bradley and H. H. Joachim, and their metaphysic does nothing to redeem the logical situation. For even if we are willing to take it *on faith* that the Absolute possesses absolute truth, this is so far from vindicating human truth that it casts an additional slur upon it. Similarly, the intellectualisms, whose ultimate appeal is to brute fact or 'animal faith,' are logically scepticisms.

[3] This false conversion of *all truth is useful* was, I believe, first alleged by Prof. G. E. Moore in an early review, and first repudiated

It is improbable, moreover, that the charge of 'converting simply' *all truth is useful* into 'anything useful is true' would ever have been brought, if the early critics of Pragmatism had had the vaguest notion of its meaning. For they would then have understood how very complicated were the relations of truth to 'use' and 'working,' and how many interesting and important questions and disputes would arise so soon as an attempt was made to determine what sort of 'use' and of 'working' was to be deemed relevant to the 'truth' of a doctrine. The pragmatists, though it can hardly be maintained that they fully realised all the complications and developments from the outset, suspected many of them, and from the first adopted a classification of truth-claims which excluded the identity of 'truth' and 'working.' So they carefully refrained from defining 'the true' as 'the useful.'

§ 10. 'Use' and 'Working' as Corollaries.

In point of fact the usefulness and efficacy of Truth are merely corollaries from the recognition of personal meaning. For once we admit that every truth must arise from a search for truth, in a context of personal endeavour, it must be related to the purposes of the truth-seeker and seem valuable and useful to him. So soon as we drop the abstraction from the personal context of the actual judgment which Formal Logic makes, we make it clear that meaning depends on application; and application is simply *logical use*. All truth, therefore, must have a use, because it must have a meaning.

Moreover, it is plain that all truth-seeking tries to verify a truth-claim, to answer a question of interest, to satisfy a purpose, to attain an end desired. So whatever is accepted or propounded as true must *have been* useful. I.e. it must have seemed relevant to an interest and valuable as an answer to a question or as an instrument or means to an end. It must have fulfilled

by me in *Humanism*, p. 38 (1903). The controversy in *Mind*, Nos. 83, 84, 86, 88, 89 (1912), between Miss L. S. Stebbing and myself turned on this point. The lady was unable to quote for this false conversion; but she had probably read it in the *index* to James's *Pragmatism*. It does *not*, however, occur in the text.

its immediate purpose. Else it would not have been what was wanted, and would not have been called 'true,' because it would not have worked for the purpose in hand.

Thus use is, quite literally, the *ratio essendi* of truth. No truth can come into being, no truth can be asserted, unless it has been judged useful for some purpose. This use *precedes* its publication, and is unaffected by whatever may befall it later. It may be received with universal applause—a fate which befalls a new-born truth only by a miracle—or it may fail to find acceptance and its maker may, upon reflection, himself withdraw it; all this is irrelevant to its genesis, and belongs to the chapter of the revision and revaluation of truths in being.

It should be noted, lastly, that, with this explanation, the usefulness of all truth becomes a sort of truism. It gets its meaning and importance only from its denial of the Formal view of truth and the fact that so many logicians have not yet discovered its emptiness.

§ 11. The Meaning of 'Useful.'

But when it is urged that the salutary doctrine of the usefulness of truth is really indisputable, care should be taken to interpret 'useful' rightly. It should be taken in its fullest and widest sense. 'Useful' means a means to an end. Psychologically, *any end will do*: it need not be a material good or a pleasure or a matter of dollars and cents, although these ends have often entered into the pursuit of truth, for good as well as for evil. In this strict sense of 'useful,' Plato's *Republic* was the most 'utilitarian' scheme of life ever propounded. For in it every act of every citizen was to be a means to the supreme end, 'the Good.'

Secondly, the relation which makes a thing 'useful' should be taken as strictly a relation to its own, the relevant, end. We should not, therefore, call a book good because it was a good narcotic; for that is not the purpose with which books are written.

Lastly, we should not fail to notice that what is useful for one purpose need not remain so when we go on to the next. And as purposes continually change and develop, the usefulness of truth supplies a further impetus for the progressive changes in our truth-valuations. Similarly, the falling out of use of truths no longer actually required sufficiently accounts for most of the belief in 'useless' truths, which it is the aim of the dictum, *all truth is useful*, to dispel.

§ 12. 'Truths' one Sort of Truth-Claim.

It was stated in § 9 that Humanism was never tempted to convert *'the true is useful'* into the *'the useful is the true,'* because it was always keenly aware that truth-claims are not necessarily true. It therefore recognised the need for discriminating the different sorts of truth-claim, and determining their relations to the sort which is generally called 'truths' (or verified truth-claims). In particular it was admitted, and even emphasised, that all sorts of truth-claim were capable of affecting cognitive operations, and of playing an important part in knowing, without on that account ranking as 'truths.' Thus it was shown, in *Axioms as Postulates*, that the so-called *a priori* 'axioms' were really 'postulates,' and so far from being absolutely proved, or 'necessarily true,' were not true at all until they had received an adequate amount of verification.

Now this means, of course, that 'true' and 'useful' are *not* convertible terms. The truth-claims which are not truths may be 'useful' but they are not 'true.' They are, however, relevant, and even essential, to the establishment of truth. Indeed, they are so important that the nature of truth can be properly understood only by mapping out the whole region of truth-claim, and so placing truth in its proper setting. This is accordingly our next task.

§ 13. The Realm of Truth-Claim: (1) Postulates.

A classification of truth-claims should distinguish, *at least*, between truths, errors, fictions, lies, methodological assumptions, methodological fictions, postulates, axioms, and jokes. It should trace their genesis, and their relations to one another. It should note first of all that all these structures are rooted in the 'subjective' side of the cognitive process. The realm of Truth-claim is a realm of *claims* and implies *claimants*. Moreover, all its structures are *purposive* and involve a truth-claim of sorts, and disastrous consequences may ensue if the particular truth-claim is misconstrued. For example, if a 'joke' is not recognised as such and is taken seriously.

(1) Psychologically speaking, the *postulate* may be regarded as the most primordial form of truth-claim. For in it the truth-seeking impulse finds its clearest expression. To postulate means to be willing (or anxious) to believe something 'desirable if true,' and to try to establish its truth. Postulation differs from mere credulity or 'animal faith' in its willingness *to learn from experience*. For postulates are truth-claims which may be defeated, withdrawn, and modified, as well as verified. What decides on the value of a postulate, and in the long run on its fate, is the manner and extent of its *working*. Thus the notion of 'working' embodies the '*objective*' factor in the process—the reply of nature to our demands.

§ 14. (2) 'Axioms.'

As our questions are often inept, our presumptions presumptuous, and our postulates foolish, the way from the 'postulate' to the '*axiom*' is commonly long and arduous, and many drop out by the roadside. But in idea at least the distinction between the two is not difficult. An 'axiom' should be conceived as a fully verified postulate which serves as a principle for a fully established science. When a postulate reaches this stage its logical character has really been transformed. It is no longer a merely human demand upon nature. It no longer depends on our desire to uphold it, but rests securely on the solid mass of scientific fact it has been instrumental in eliciting. So it can defy its critics by blandly requesting them to provide a substitute that will account for the facts in other and better ways.

But, of course, in actual fact such assured and acknowledged axioms are rare. They are much rarer than they were supposed to be, and are getting rarer the more inquiry is made into the first principles of the sciences and the more attention is paid to alternative ways of comprehending the facts. There is in consequence a tendency to take hypothetically and provisionally even such 'axioms' as are retained; and, as this change of attitude towards them does not involve a change in their verbal formulation, it relaxes the meaning of 'axiom' in the older theory of knowledge as well as in the stricter definition given above. This laxity is both unfortunate and unnecessary, because the drift of the modern tendency can be more clearly and better expressed by using the terms 'methodological assumption' and 'methodological fiction.'

§ 15. (3) Methodological Assumptions.

Methodological assumptions are really forced upon the would-be knower by the feeling of his helplessness when he first encounters the vast flux of happenings. He does not know what to attend to, what to disregard, what to select as significant, how to break up ('analyse') the overwhelming torrent. He simply *must* somehow find some clue to guide him through the labyrinth.

Consequently he is willing to adopt any principle, hypothesis, or suggestion that promises to serve as a guide, and to be of use in analysing the flux. A 'methodological assumption' is such a principle. It is a judgment which is useful, or even needful (*faute de mieux*), but which nevertheless is not trusted beyond the tested sphere of its application. It is not necessary that in using it we should be convinced of its ultimate truth. It is not necessary that it should turn out to be ultimately true. It is enough that we should be able to work with it, that it should serve our immediate purpose, that it should guide observations and suggest experiments. If it can do this, we shall hardly be distressed even to discover that in the end it must be false.

As a matter of fact the fundamental principles of all the sciences are, under modern scrutiny, more and more turning out to be not 'axioms' but methodological assumptions. That is, they are essentially methods of working in the subjects to which they refer. The same fate is overtaking many of the traditional principles of philosophy. For example, the real function of the principle of Causation is plainly methodological. It is simply a general instruction to an inquirer who has picked out of the flow of events some interesting bit or aspect of the 'phenomenon' he wishes to investigate, to look for some anterior bit or aspect, so related to it as to be called its 'cause,' i.e. such that he can predict and control his chosen 'effect' by manipulating it. He thereupon declares the second selection from the flux the 'cause' of the first, and flatters himself that he has extracted a guarantee from the course of events, because 'the effect must follow its cause' and 'the cause must produce its effect.'

§ 16. (4) Methodological Fictions.

But as this case (with many others) shows, the methodological assumption is very often a *methodological fiction*. We may be well aware when we make our assumptions that they are not true, and indeed cannot be completely true, because they have been reached by artificial simplifications which facilitate calculation but leave out certain factors in the actual situation. What explains and justifies this procedure will then be that the falsity of our working assumption may be irrelevant for our purpose, and need not vitiate our result, which may be true or good *enough*. Also a methodological principle may work well and be useful up to a point, and then break down: in this case we are apt to consider it a 'useful fiction,' and to go on using it up to that point. The difference, then, between a methodological fiction and a methodological assumption will be that the former is known to have limits to its working, its usefulness, and its truth: in the case of the latter such limits either do not exist or are not known. The methodological assumption thus represents that stage in the establishment of a principle in which its usefulness is manifest, but it is either not yet certain, or not relevant, whether it is ultimately true or false, and whether it will develop into an 'axiom' or turn out to have been a 'fiction.'

In any case methodological fictions are exceedingly common

in the sciences, as Prof. Vaihinger has shown in his monumental *Philosophy of the As If*. Thus the whole of *applied* mathematics depends on our feigning the objects and processes dealt with to be identifiable with the ideal objects and processes of *pure* mathematics. They never are so quite, and our assumption is known to be false. But if an appropriate selection has been made from pure mathematics our fiction comes near enough to the actual course of events to be extremely useful, and, indeed, indispensable. Thus, when a surveyor maps a country he has to treat his base line as an Euclidean straight line, although he knows it is a segment of the circumference of an earth which is (roughly) spherical. In consequence of this necessary falsification his results *cannot* be right, and in the end he has always to 'fake' them more or less to make his map, which is a fiction also, because on no system of projection can the actual relations of the earth's surface be represented accurately on a plane surface.

So the scientific importance of fictions is indisputable, even if we do not go on to contend that the 'ideal' conceptions of pure mathematics, and indeed all 'ideals,' are fictions, and that all identification involves fiction, because it feigns the non-existence of the differences which always exist between two cases of 'the same.'

§ 17. (5) Fiction.

But, after all, methodological fictions are only a special case of the use of *fiction* generally, and the creation of fiction is a logical topic inferior in importance only to the making of truth. It rests, in ultimate analysis, on our power of *feigning* that to be which we know *not* to be truly real, on our *pretending* and acting *as if* it were. This power is displayed not only in self-deception and make-believe, but in every game and every form of play, and in all the works of the 'imagination.'

Now it is fairly evident that fiction always involves a sort of truth-claim. Not only are the terms true and false freely applied to 'works of the imagination' and of art and to 'works of fiction,' but judgments about them may be as literally true and

false as judgments in any other 'universe of diction.' Whoever
judged that Helen eloped with Hector, or that the Centaurs
were hippocephalic anthropoids, or that Romulus and Remus
were suckled by a goat (like Zeus), would be judging *falsely*.
Moreover, misconceptions about the fictional character of an
object of thought may be very serious affairs: they may mean
failure to distinguish between jest and earnest and fatal confusion about the sort of reality claimed by the various subjects
of discourse.

§ 18. (6) Jokes.

Still more troublesome than the fiction to a serious-minded
logician (who frequently apprehends it as a 'lie') is the *joke*.
For he here encounters an irreducible incongruity between the
verbal truth-claim and the real meaning. The joke does *not*
'mean what it *says*' (Chap. I, § 10; Chap. IV, § 12), and may
mean the very opposite. If it is taken to mean what it says, it is
sure to be misunderstood and to lead to further misunderstandings; if it is to be understood, the first thing to do is to discount
its formal truth-claim. After that its real meaning may be
gathered from a great variety of sources, varying with the particular joke. The context, the situation, the character of the
parties concerned, the sounds of the words used and their
similarities to others, lurking allusions to anything in heaven
and earth, in literature or in common knowledge, etc., all may
have to be considered. But as on principle and by training the
Formal logician is wont to abstract from such things and to
concentrate upon the formal truth-claim, it hardly seems possible
that a Formal logician should as such understand a joke and
the truth-claim it makes, which is itself often the best part of
the joke! His only consolations are that jokes do not often occur
in the logic books and that few would have the face to try a
joke upon a Formal logician.

§ 19. (7) Lies.

On the other hand no such difficulty besets the analysis of
the truth-claim of the *Lie*, and the failure of Formal Logic to

consider it is very remarkable. It must be ascribed to other reasons. It is most probably due to intellectualist dislike of what is *not* a purely intellectual entity, not a creation of 'pure thought,' and plainly involves a reference to 'will.' For the difference between the lie and the error lies in the *intention* of the liar. Lying is voluntary, erring involuntary. The liar *knows* that the truth-claim he makes is false; he means to propound an *un*-truth, an *intentional* falsehood. He is not deceived, like the man who is in error, but is himself trying to deceive. He is not in error himself, but, if he is believed, he is producing error in others. In short, for theory and for practice alike, the lie and the error appear to be very different.

But it would be upsetting to intellectualism to have to recognise *intentions*. So it tries to reduce the lie to the error and to ignore the distinction between intentional and unintentional falsity. This tendency comes out well in the vocabulary of a naturally intellectualist people like the Greeks. The same word 'pseudos' has to do duty for both: it embraces *anything false*, without regard to the circumstances under which the false statement was made or to the state of mind of the man who made it. Most other civilised languages have found it expedient to distinguish the lie from the error, and the *lacuna* in Greek can hardly be ascribed to the fact that the Greeks were unacquainted with lying; for it was an art which they admired and in which they excelled. It is to be connected rather with the general defectiveness of their vocabulary in words for willing and all that is connected with it, which has done much more than is usually suspected to produce the intellectualist bias of the philosophies descended from the Greek.

It must not, however, be supposed that there is *no* likeness between the lie and the error. They both advance *false* truth-claims, and they are both *failures*. In this they resemble the joke. The truth-claim of a joke, if understood literally, may often seem false, and the question, 'Are you lying or joking?' may often be the real issue. But whereas a joke is a failure if its truth-claim is taken seriously, a lie fails if it is *not* so taken.

What distinguishes the lie from the error is that some one, to wit the liar, already knows that its truth-claim is false. In the case of the error this need not be so. For though strictly a false truth-claim can only be called an 'error' *after* it has been detected, there may be a time when it deceives every one, and is accepted by all as a 'truth,' whereas a lie does not ordinarily deceive its maker.

In analysing both the lie and the error, however, it is vital to distinguish the persons concerned, and simply impossible to abstract from personality as Formal Logic tried to do. For the truth-claim of the lie looks very different to its maker and its victim. The victim accepts it as true, until he finds it out. The liar knows that its 'truth' will last no longer; he never took it as true and knew all along what was the true nature of its claim. Consequently he could not use it to claim truth withal *for himself*, however well it served his other purposes. He alone, from the first, knew what it is, viz. the purest example of a man-made 'truth' (claim), and 'all his own invention.' But knowing also that, if detected, it ceases to work, he cannot but regard it with a certain apprehension. It may at any time be found out, and will then probably defeat his purpose, although of course it is also possible that by then it will (like war-propaganda) have served its purpose and done its work. In general, however, the truth-claim of a *detected* lie disappears, and the making of it recoils upon the liar.

On the other hand, an undetected lie is completely successful and continues to pass for true. As no one has detected it, no one is entitled to call it a lie. Suppose I circulate a tale which no one can confute, say that Humanism was revealed to me in a dream by Protagoras himself, and then die without confessing. If it is important enough my 'lie' goes down as truth to history, and is taught as such to all the little boys and girls in the whole civilised world. We may suspect that history is full of such lies passing as truths: but *ex hypothesi* we cannot say which they are. Still in idea the line between a truth and a lie is clear, however hard it may be to draw in practice. Nor does the lie contravene the principle that the formal claim to truth which every judgment makes is accepted while it works.

§ 20. (8) 'Truths' and their Verification.

The subject of *Error* is important and intricate enough to be reserved for a later chapter (IX), but about the genesis of *truths* in the proper sense, i.e. of *verified truth-claims*, something further may fitly be said. It is first to be noted that the process of verification [1] is identical with that of logical 'working,' in the sense of our definition (§ 9), and that it is a process to which no final term need be set. The verifying of a claim to truth by its working may go on for ever, and usually does. Inasmuch as a truth-claim may be false, every 'truth' that is enunciated has to be tested. It has, indeed, been tested already more or less, in its maker's mind, before it was published, as we saw in Chap. VI, § 9. But this does not exempt it from further testing. For it has to maintain its claim to be the most valuable, best, and therefore truest, judgment possible under the circumstances of its birth, not only in the eyes of its maker, but also in the opinion of every one else who is, or thinks he is, a judge of its truth-claim. Moreover, it has to uphold its claim and to preserve its 'identity' in the face of possible improvements. When these amount to what is judged to be practically 'another' judgment, it will suffer rejection, and will be revalued as 'false'; and in a progressive science this fate is sure, sooner or later, to overtake it.

Thus, suppose the question concerns what is called 'the' distance of the earth from the sun, and that on the strength of observations of the kind described in § 5, 'the' distance (a manifest 'fiction') is taken at 95,000,000 miles. As the result of subsequent observations, however, better values become available. 'The' distance of the earth from the sun may successively become 92,000,000 miles and 91,430,000 miles, and each earlier value may become 'false,' merely because a truer value can be stated, even though the improvement may be quite slight and even imperceptible by the methods used at first. In

---

[1] Or 'validation.' But the word 'valid' had better be left to Formal Logic. For 'validity' is its *substitute* for 'truth,' and it will turn out that the 'true' cannot be 'valid' nor the 'valid' 'true' (Cp. Chap. III, § 12 ; Chap. VI, § 3 ; Chap. XIII, § 6).

such cases the old 'false' value may continue to be used in rough calculations as being 'true enough.'

It is plain, however, that this continual shedding of superseded truths is no ground for scepticism; it is merely an incident in the unending growth of knowledge. Every truth has its day, like every dog; but sufficient for the day is the truth thereof.

Thus these cases of truth-claims that are not truths but lies, fictions, methodological assumptions, postulates, etc., entirely preclude the simple conversion of *all truths are useful*. Nor, of course, can truth be defined as 'what works,' seeing that all these other truth-claims 'work' in various ways; we may, however, say it is 'what (at any time) works *best*.' This has the advantage of introducing a reference to values, choices, and the progress of knowledge.

§ 21. The 'Working' of Truths.

One final obscurity, however, remains in the relation between truth and 'working.' What precisely is meant by this vague term? Does *any* sort of working, however alien to the ordinary type of cognitive operation, suffice to constitute a 'truth'? If a powerful State or Church sets itself to persecute an opinion, say about evolution, and succeeds in suppressing it by force, does it render it 'false' by killing all who believe it? Does humanism cease to be true because a powerful ring of philosophy professors have found it unanswerable and agreed to ignore it?

It is regrettable that no sharp-cut answer can be given to such questions. It cannot be denied that persecution has often been successful, and that the cause of truth has had many martyrs. Also the question of the relations of truth to survival-value is perhaps the most difficult of all the questions which can be raised about truth. On the one hand, it is clear that opinions which are directly lethal in their effects on those who hold them cannot be held 'true.' If they do not perish altogether with those who hold them, they can survive only as 'false.' It is also clear that opinions which have a high survival-value will be extensively believed to be 'true,' and that therefore their survival-value must form an important factor in our current 'truths.' But it will not be possible to explain *all* 'truth' as reflecting merely the survival-value of beliefs, unless we suppose also that the cosmic order is definitely such as to *force* a particular set of beliefs upon the mind, and to leave it no choice. And this does not appear to be the case.[1] Our choices and preferences appear to be themselves factors in the survival of many beliefs, and nature appears to admit of a variety of interpretations.

It is better, therefore, to conceive 'working' as a wide genus with a number of species, some of which have not yet been fully determined and are still in dispute. For such disputes there may be good grounds. For the working of truths is really specific in each science, and relative to its peculiar problems and subject-matter. For example, the working and the tests of truth in mathematics are not the same as in biology or psychology. So we should not be surprised to find that there are still greater differences between science and religion. In the one case the relevant working appeals to the senses, in the other to a perception of spiritual value, and, perhaps, to certain incommunicable and apparently self-validating experiences called 'mystical.'

But both are of great vital importance, and their difference does not prevent both 'workings' from being species of the same genus. There may long continue to be disputes about *what* workings are relevant to what truth-claims, but the general logical requirements will remain the same in all cases. In all, claims will require verification, and verification of a definite and appropriate kind, and a dispute as to whether a particular verification is adequate has simply to be fought out by the parties concerned. For example, most people would agree that the belief in the existence of other minds has worked so well that it may be considered to have been abundantly verified; but a few paradoxers may continue to argue for a 'theoretic' solipsism, on the plea that another mind must 'transcend' one's personal experience and so is incapable of being directly verified.

[1] Cp. p. 104 and see *Problems of Belief*, chap. xii, especially p. 182 f.

It may, then, have to be pointed out to them that this belief of theirs does not appear to be genuine; for they do not *act* on their professed belief, and it does not meet the severest of all the tests of belief, that of action.

In any case we may reject as utterly false the calumny that Humanism dispenses with objective tests of truth, accepts everything as 'working,' and allows us to hold true whatever we please. As a matter of fact this perilous privilege is enjoyed only by the apriorist, because he does not distinguish truths from truth-claims and dispenses with verification.

§ 22. (IV) Truth as Dependent on Consequences.

This formula may be dealt with more briefly. Its chief value lies not in what it affirms but in what it denies. By insisting on the empirical testing of truth-claims by the consequences to which they lead, it denies all *a priori* theories of truth. By refusing to let a truth-claim validate itself by its own assurance, it effectively rules out all the intuitionist theories which regard truth as 'self-evident,' and all *a priori* theories which regard 'necessary' truths as imposing themselves upon us by main force.

But like the 'working' formula it is not explicit on the question of what consequences are to count as relevant to a truth-claim. It is obvious, of course, that the *value* of the consequences will make a difference. Consequences judged 'good' will support a truth-claim, while those judged 'bad' will conduce to its abandonment. But it is not necessary to *state* that the consequences must be good; since 'good' simply means 'value,' and we have also seen that 'truth' means 'logical value.' Nor need we say that the consequences must be 'practical'; for *all* consequences, even the most 'theoretic,' become practical in the end, and affect action.

More difficult questions arise when it is asked how the relevance of consequences to a truth-claim is determined and how the connexion of a claim and *its* consequences is ascertained. Here again, as in the case of 'working,' and for very similar reasons, we must be prepared for disputes and for a penumbra of 'debatable truths' which are not recognised by all and are still affairs of party and of opinion. But, on the principle of *sordet cognita veritas*, these are often the very truths to which we are most attached.[1]

§ 23. The Cognitive Function of Doubt.

The prevalence of doubts and disputes does not, however, cast a slur upon truth, and we should not allow ourselves to be frightened out of a cherished belief on this account alone. For doubts and disputes are normal accompaniments of truth-seeking, and in no wise detrimental. There is no stronger stimulus to inquiry than doubt, and, as the Greeks were well aware, nothing is more likely to raise the vital issues to be inquired into than a well-conducted dispute. Doubtless Socrates and Plato exaggerated when they declared that the ultimate truths of metaphysics would reveal themselves to those who practised the art of conversation with attractive young men, but 'dialectic' becomes deadening only when it becomes dogmatic (as with Hegel), and the progress of knowledge has always depended essentially on the doubt which discovers, and the ingenuity which solves, good problems. If therefore we are considering the interests merely of knowing there is little to be said against the habit of doubting.

But, of course, this is not the whole story. Knowing is only *one* of the activities of living, and inextricably entangled in the others. Also, it is far from easy to determine where knowing begins, or ends, and so what operations may or may not have a bearing on it. Our first impressions may be quite misleading, and it would certainly be rash to leave the drawing of the frontier lines round knowing to the prejudices of the academic man. The issue is too important to be prejudged: it can be decided only in the light of much experience.

Nevertheless, if we are willing to make reservations for the doubtful cases, and hold ourselves ready to reconsider all, we are free to admit that doubt may become an incubus when we pass from knowing to acting. It is this that has given a bad

[1] Cp. *Problems of Belief*, p. 42.

name to doubt. For there is then a real danger that under the distraction of our doubts we may act in a hesitating and half-hearted manner. And this may be fatal. When, therefore, it comes to action, we must often act as if we had *no* doubts. We must 'make up our mind' to act resolutely on what we judge to be the *best* belief. And to do this we may have to drop our doubts, or at least to deny them all influence on our acts, and to 'act as if' we did not feel them. Now, this combination of intellectual doubt with confident action is not easy; perhaps only superior minds are psychologically capable of it: so the ordinary man has judged it safer and simpler to condemn doubt altogether. But this is to condemn intellectual activity, and to condemn his mind to atrophy.

The prejudice against doubt, which (to the great detriment of their intellectual development) all the religions have sanctioned, is thus practical in origin and expressive of man's unconscious pragmatism. The theoretic fertility of doubt is plain and undeniable; but it goes for nothing, because men are bent on action.

Nor should this be a matter for unalloyed regret: for it reveals how much more than 'theory' goes to the making of beliefs; how much more exacting a test, even of knowledge, is action than cognition; and how subtle are the interactions of knowing and doing.

For it should not be assumed that when a belief is acted on it is left unchanged. The action will inevitably react upon the belief. It will fortify or weaken it, confirm its 'truth' or convict it of 'error.' It has its reaction on every sort of truth-claim, not merely on the lie, but on the fiction, on the hypothesis, the methodological assumption and the postulate, and can transform their logical status—often insensibly and without our feeling it. This power of action has not passed wholly unobserved, though its universality has not been realised: it has been particularly noticed, and resented, in the case of the suppression of doubts and the practical assumption of beliefs which are not theoretically certain; but logicians would have done better to *understand* the operation of the 'will to believe,' instead of merely denouncing it. In extreme cases, where there is *no* connexion between the belief to be verified and the verifying 'consequence,' it is clear, of course, that exception may be taken to this method of proof. If, e.g., a prophet tried to verify a doctrine that the value of π was $3\frac{1}{2}$ by performing a miracle, it is to be hoped that some would have the strength of mind to urge a *non sequitur*; but the cases actively disputed are not of this kind. They concern rather such questions as whether, and how far, the good consequences and working of a religion can authenticate its Creeds, and they are really disputable because the parties naturally see and emphasise respectively the good and the evil in the system to be tested by its 'consequences.' One may admit in general that the goodness of the consequences of a truth-claim will lead men to overlook the flaws in its logical structure. Perhaps, however, they err, not so much in over-rating the closeness of the logical relation between 'truths' and their 'consequences' and in yielding to persuasion by the latter, as in neglecting to consider whether the consequences which impress them are in fact the *best* that can be observed, and whether they would not follow equally well from some alternative theory.

On the whole, then, we must be content to leave unsolved the general question of how, in the abstract, the relevance of the consequences to the truth-claim they are said to verify is to be determined. In principle, questions of relevance are always disputable, and an argument which takes a sequence as a consequence may always be charged with being a *post hoc ergo propter hoc* fallacy. There is no answer to this charge, save by going into the merits of each case. But the Humanist theory of Truth stands out among its rivals by its willingness to recognise the actual procedures of human knowing and to make the best of them.

CHAPTER IX

ERROR

1. How distinguish error from truth ? ; 2. Formal Logic's failure to discriminate between error and truth ; 3. Formal theories of error ; 4. Plato's struggles with error ; 5. Metaphysical theories of error : (1) Idealistic ; 6. (2) Realistic ; 7. Error relative to a particular inquiry ; 8. The genesis of error ; 9. Error implies relations and a fight ; 10. Minimising the difference between truth and error ; 11. Error as negative value in cognition ; 12. All psychic process liable to error ; 13. Error not purely intellectual ; 14. Error the failure of a thought-experiment ; 15. Errors in propositions and in judgments ; 16. Conclusion.

§ 1. How distinguish Error from Truth ?

The vital problem about error is how to distinguish it from truth, and it is a difficult problem. For error is the twin of truth, and fond of masquerading in its garb; nor can we flatter ourselves that either is truly known until we know them apart. A tenable theory of truth, therefore, must lead to an adequate theory of error; but the maxim *veritas norma sui et falsi* is vain unless our theory of truth *does* effectively distinguish true from false. Hence a logical analysis of the general nature of error becomes an undertaking of the first importance. It is important practically because all desire to attain truth and to avoid error, and it is important theoretically because the theory of error becomes the touchstone of all theories of truth: it is essential to the identification of truth, to its discrimination from error, to the correction of error, and to our salvation from its ravages.

But at first sight such discrimination seems a desperate undertaking, for error seems to cling to truth as does a shadow to the body which casts it. It seems inevitable for a body of truth to be accompanied by error, and it is as natural in a theory of knowledge to treat error along with truth as it is in optics to treat shadows along with the bodies to which they belong. This comparison, moreover, indicates what is, in both cases, a *specific* relation. Error and truth *belong together*, and certain 'errors' belong to every 'truth,' as being relative to one and the same problem.

Actually, however, the connexion between truth and error is much closer than that between a body and its shadow; for once the body has been perceived it is hardly possible to mistake it for its own shadow ; whereas, in the other case, we can never get any absolute assurance that what now seems indisputable truth will not hereafter be found to be infected with error, and what is truth and what error may even, in certain cases, depend on the purpose with which we consider it. Thus, whether A is 'in love' may have to be answered affirmatively or negatively according as his relation to B or to C is in question, and whether he is 'large' or 'small,' will depend on whether he is compared with a pygmy or a whale.

We have, therefore, to bear continually in mind that 'truths' are inherently relational. They cannot be cut adrift from the purpose which their allegation serves, from the situation in which they function as 'truths,' from their reference to the errors which they deny and correct. Nor, again, should it ever be forgotten that any 'truth' alleged should be treated as a truth-claim which needs to be tested and may prove false, and that, even after it has been 'verified,' its truth remains relative to the tests to which it has been subjected, and is liable to break down under new and unexplored conditions. It is, therefore, a signal revelation of the ingrained frivolity of Formal Logic that it should pass over the problem of error so lightly.

§ 2. Formal Logic's Failure to Discriminate between Truth and Error.

Even while we censure the failure of Formal Logic to discriminate between truth and error we should, however, recognise that this failure is consequential. It is a consequence of taking 'truth' merely in the sense of 'truth-claim' and of refusing to go into the evaluation of actual truth-claims. For, from the chosen standpoint of Formal Logic error is invisible. Truth-claims are always formally 'true,' whatever they may be in actual fact. If they happen to be false, they do not betray themselves by any overt sign: if they happen to be true, their formal 'truth' conveys no real assurance of the fact. Formally, then, all 'truths' are equally true or false; formal 'truth' is *not* exclusive of error, and is no guarantee against it.

The reason is simple enough. Formalism has abstracted from the relation by which the value, i.e. the truth-or-falsity of assertions, is determined. It abstracts from their relation to purpose and use. It tries to take them *per se*, and apart from their use and their function in an argument, without observing that it thereby renders their meaning indeterminate and their truth-or-falsity indeterminable. An assertion *per se* cannot be known as 'error.' Neither can it be known as 'truth.' Its *meaning* cannot be determined until it is given a context: but if a meaning could be assigned to it, it would be found to be now 'true,' now 'false,' according to the circumstances. Hence, no amount of 'contemplation' of its 'form' will reveal what it will mean in a context, whether its use will be a success or a failure, whether it will deserve to be called 'true' or 'false.' In actual use not even a 'contradiction in terms' need be always false. It may often be unmeaning, but sometimes true. Thus, even 'this is a round square' cannot be pronounced false *per se*. It is false in a geometrical context, no doubt; but it may be true in London. 'The angles of a triangle are equal to two right angles' is true in the geometry of Euclid, but false in that of Riemann or of Lobachevsky. We have seen (Chap. VIII, § 4) that the truth-or-falsity of 'it is two o'clock' depends on the place where it is asserted.

In short, no one can foresee whether the most palpably 'false' propositions will not some day figure as 'truths' in contexts or for purposes which as yet no one anticipates. And let it not be said that, though this may be true of *propositions*, it does not hold of *judgments*. The 'judgments' of Formal Logic *are* only 'propositions': they do not remain judgments when the person who generates and judges them in the course of a purposive train of thought has been ignored and eliminated. It is clear, then, that Formalism has incapacitated itself by its fundamental abstraction from personal meaning from producing a theory either of error or of truth.

§ 3. Formal Theories of Error.

This, however, does not prevent it from *pretending* to do so. As in the case of truth, it does not admit its failure, but propounds pseudo-theories to save its face, or to throw dust into the eyes of its critics. As the habitual solemnity of philosophic phrasing hinders one in calling them absurd, they have to be treated as seriously as possible.

(1) It is vain to try to cope with error by presupposing the notion of truth. For this will not enable us to *differentiate* between truth and error, or to detect the errors in the current 'truths.' To say, therefore, that Error is avoided or corrected by possessing or discovering Truth is like saying that poverty is cured by acquiring wealth and disease by acquiring health.

(2) To say that a judgment which errs is not a real Judgment nor a 'true judgment,' or that 'opinion' can err, but not 'knowledge,' is likewise verbal, *ex post facto*, and futile. The logicians who, like J. C. Wilson,[1] put forward this Platonic platitude as the last word of wisdom, make no attempt to show that we ever 'judge' in this final and infallible way, or have any means of recognising a bit of 'knowledge,' and discriminating it from the 'opinion' which counterfeits it.

It is, therefore, a further objection to this theory that, even when it is accepted, it proves to be inapplicable. It indicates no way of dealing with the claims of assertions to be 'judgments' and with the beliefs of those who take their 'opinions' to be 'knowledge.' All will naturally begin by claiming that their assertions are true, and that they are not mistaken in their conviction that they really 'know.' Consequently, the doctrine does nothing to abate the chaos and conflict of opinions. Yet, in view of the admitted prevalence of error, all would agree that most of these beliefs are wrong, and indeed are nothing but opinions. They would not agree, no doubt, about *which* were the wrong opinions; for the general admission that it is human to err is in practice tempered by a strong conviction that there is *one* exception to this rule and a widespread tendency to think

---

[1] In *Statement and Inference*.

one knows who the one is. Still, if one looks at the matter impartially, it will be an obvious precaution to take *all* assertions as 'opinions' until they can be shown to be something more. But how will this help us either to segregate those which are truly 'knowledge,' or to evaluate opinions and to distinguish the true from the false?

Lastly, the theory appears to exemplify the fallacy or impropriety of 'arguing in a circle.' Its advocates seem to have overlooked that their belief can hardly be accepted on its own assurance. It, too, must be treated as a mere matter of opinion until it has authenticated the claim it puts forward. So their proof of the existence of infallible Judgment requires us to admit their own infallibility in asserting it. The sharp distinction in kind alleged between judgments and Judgment, between opinion and knowledge, is itself an 'opinion,' and one, moreover, for which no reasons are apparent and which seems to fly in the face of all the facts. For, actually, opinions seem to exhibit every gradation of value from the lowest to the highest, and to be continually passing from one to another and changing their cognitive status. The cause of knowledge, therefore, would be better served by making suggestions for the evaluation of opinions than by making futile and inapplicable distinctions: and the whole doctrine is about as valuable as to say that because the notion of 'diamond' implies preciousness, no 'diamond' can be paste.

§ 4. Plato's Struggles with Error.

Of all the Formal discussions of error Plato's is still the best, the most candid, the most penetrating, the most instructive, and the most exhaustive. In the *Theætetus* (187 C–200 D) he examines every theory which it has ever been found possible to entertain on the lines of the traditional logic. He tries to conceive error successively as lying in the object or in its apprehension, as confusion ('allodoxy,' the taking of one thing instead of another by the mind), as potential knowledge, as an incidental flaw in sensation, as a failure of memory. But he finds that every theory that he discusses lands him in a contradiction, and, moreover, in the same contradiction. *We must simultaneously both know and not know the object about which there is error.*

But this fatal contradiction which wrecks his enterprise may be dissipated very simply. It is nothing at bottom but a simple 'fallacy of division,' which arises from disregarding the *persons* concerned and the parties to the commission and the correction of the 'error.' Taken *collectively*, and without regard to their several points of view, they both know and do not know, as Plato says: but *individually*, *some* know, while *others* do not. The 'error,' thereupon, is seen to exist *by* the former *in* the latter. There is no 'error,' therefore, until *some one* judges 'this is false,' or when *no one* continues to judge 'this is true.' But no one ever judges the same thing to be true and false *at the same time*. While he is in error he does not see the error. It is invisible from his (false) standpoint, and seems to him a 'truth.' When he detects his error and sees the truth, on the other hand, he ceases to affirm his error. He has corrected it, and *now* calls an 'error' what *was* a false truth-claim, but is asserted no longer. When, as is usually the case, there are several parties to the 'error,' its complete analysis requires us to recognise that the one party sees as 'truth' what the other sees as 'error.' But to describe this situation as error is to imply that one party is wrong. It is a partisan description, and it is more accurate to call it simply a 'dispute.' An impartial description should not speak of 'error' until *both* parties admit it. This will only happen when the party who *was* in error sees it. Thus, the correction of an 'error' is strictly always self-correction; and in a sense the 'error,' like the lie, comes into being (as such) only when it is found out.

Plato, however, has frustrated himself by ignoring these personal relations which inhere in the notion of error. He has committed the typical fault of Formal Logic by abstracting from the personal aspect of the judgment and the time-sequence of events in the actual train of thought. By treating it as irrelevant that the person who affirms and the person who simultaneously denounces the 'error' cannot possibly be the same, he has *fabricated* his 'contradiction.'

It was natural enough for him to make this mistake; for the philosophic importance of personality had not dawned upon the ancient world. Moreover, he had already made the same mistake in his treatment of the sensible. This he was led to represent as inherently self-contradictory, because he had *refused it the right to change*, to differ in different places and at different times, and to be used for various purposes in different predications. If the sensible is thus deprived of its reference to time, place, and personality, and if its particularity is thus abstracted from, it becomes a mass of the most various and incompatible qualities; but the facts are mutilated, or, rather, an outrageous fiction is put into their place. It is true that traditional logic has committed itself to both these abstractions—from the occasion, as well as from the person, concerned with a 'truth'; but, so far from supporting each other, each by its failure gives away the other as well. We must conclude, therefore, that here, as so often, the Platonic solution is a splendid failure: one of those failures which, if candidly admitted and taken to heart, is a milestone on the road to success.

§ 5. Metaphysical Theories of Error: (1) Idealistic.

The metaphysical logicians, both 'idealists' and 'realists,' have, of course, theories of error consonant with their prejudices. Fortunately, however, we need not linger over them; for they have very little relevance to our human problem of how errors may be detected and corrected in human knowledge.

For this problem the 'idealists' substitute another, viz. what is the 'ideal' of knowledge, and what is the place of Error in the Absolute, and how may the Absolute be conceived to transcend it? The merely human (or 'practical') problem of how we correct our own, or each other's, errors is relegated to a petulant footnote, as in F. H. Bradley,[1] or given up altogether, as by Prof. H. H. Joachim,[2] who, nevertheless, continues to claim spiritual value for his scepticism.

Now, it would not be fair to deny all value to this idealist

---

[1] *Appearance and Reality*, p. 543.
[2] *The Nature of Truth*, chap. iv.

formulation of the problem of error. The question about the place of error in the Absolute has much the same value as the question as to the place of humour in the Absolute, or the problem of evil in orthodox theology. It is important because it is insoluble, and because it brings out the awkward fact that as the problem to be solved ought not, on the theory, to exist at all, the theory must be wrong.

For, if metaphysical idealism is taken seriously, there cannot, strictly, be any problem of error. It has adopted once and for all the 'ideal' of a single all-embracing Truth which is perfectly coherent and systematic. This alone is strictly true, with a truth which is absolute, infallible, and immutable. But it is also ambiguous and self-contradictory, and, in whatever way it is taken, it does not lead to any way of distinguishing human truth from human error.

If (*a*) the *perfection* of the total truth is stressed, it can plainly yield no theory of error. It will plainly be incapable of error and incapable also of understanding its existence. But if this truth is to be perfect it must fail to be all-embracing; so far from including human truth, it must *exclude* it. For human truth plainly lacks the perfections which distinguish its absolute counterpart. So it follows from the ideal of Perfect Truth that all other truth *must* be infected with error. It cannot be truth at all, as idealist theory understands truth, and the extent of its erroneousness can have no further interest. It is enough that our fallible human truth should be refused recognition and declared unintelligible on account of its fallibility.

(*b*) If the Total Truth is to be really all-embracing, and worthy of its name, it must somehow *include* human truth: but then its perfection goes by the board. For, as human truth is fallible, to include it means to include also human error. The total truth must become infinitely elastic, and must harbour all the judgments that ever claim truth. But this indiscriminate hospitality utterly destroys the distinction between truth and error, and reduces 'truth' to formal truth-claim. Every 'truth' will be true for it, and no 'error' will be in view. Moreover, this all-inclusive 'truth' must appear as a chaos of contradictions; because being one, immutable and timeless, all the truths which are relative to an occasion and are held true under the circumstances of any time or place, will be predicable of it simultaneously and eternally. Thus total truth will have to sacrifice the coherence and systematic order of which it was so proud, and yet will fail to justify the human distinction between truth and error.

§ 6. (2) Realistic.

Realist metaphysicians are not so prone to think that a wild-goose chase of the Absolute is the highest of human activities, but they are apt to get nervous when any human activity is cast for a decisive part in the solution of any problem. Now, in this case of truth and error, it seems at first the path of least resistance to credit the object with the success, and to blame the mind for the failure, of any cognitive process; truth can then be said to be the apprehension of the real as it is and error its contamination by 'subjectivity.' This makes man's essential contribution to knowledge the power of making mistakes. But upon reflection this simple distribution of functions grows less attractive to the realist. After all it leaves the mind with too much power. Even though its activity is merely evil it can still intervene in every operation, if only to frustrate it. The aim of realism, therefore, is to define truth and error in terms of a relation of mind as such to the object *per se*, and to conceive this relation as determined wholly by the object. So the object is defined as what thought grasps. It follows that any relation that exists between them must be truth, if it exists at all, and that error is unthinkable. For a thought that fails to grasp its object is not in error, but in blank ignorance. The source of error, therefore, cannot lie in the object of knowledge or be an anomaly in its constitution. There cannot be objects the apprehension of which creates error, as Plato desperately suggested.[1] For if they are apprehended as they *are*, they are apprehended *truly*. Nor is 'allodoxy,' the apprehending of one thing *instead of* another, truly intelligible. It means nothing apart from the

[1] *Theætetus*, 199 E.

purpose of the knower. If he apprehends an ink-bottle as a whisky-bottle, he is truly apprehending an object, though it may not be the object he *wants*. His 'error' is relative only to the purpose of drinking, if he wants to drink whisky. 'Allodoxy,' therefore, gets its meaning from its relation to a human purpose: the 'other' thing which is *erroneously* apprehended must be the *wrong* thing for a purpose.

It is vain, therefore, to try to eliminate the relation to human purpose from the conception of error. Every 'truth' must serve a purpose, every 'error' thwart it; nor is either understood until the purpose to which it is related is known. A man who is content with everything he gets cannot be disappointed. A man who accepts whatever appears at face-value cannot be deceived. A man who does not want to get anywhere cannot lose his way. A man who does not want to do anything can contemplate all things with equal enjoyment. And a man for whom all truth-claims are of equal value cannot find himself 'in error.' It is because men are *not* thus indifferent to values that they distinguish 'truths' from 'errors.'

§ 7. 'Error' Relative to a particular Inquiry.

Alike, therefore, whether the metaphysician abstracts from purposiveness altogether or merely from the purpose which inspires a particular inquiry, he fails to account for error. For the only sort of error which occurs in actual thinking, and can be recognised and corrected, is that which is relative to the purpose of a particular inquiry and means failure to attain it. As contributing to logical theory, therefore, metaphysics add nothing to the Platonic account examined in § 4. They all make the same abstraction from the knower's personality, and involve themselves in the same incapacity to understand such truth and such error as occur in human thinking.

The only way out of this *impasse* lies in going back on the assumptions common to all these unsuccessful theories. Let us abjure the idea that truth and error exist out of relation to man and his desire to know. They are not irrelevant and indifferent to his purposes. Let us no longer assume that his personality does not affect his purposes, but study rather how the admitted 'truths' and 'errors' emerge from the interaction of different personalities and interests. Let us no longer take knowledge as an 'eternal,' timeless, and unchanging system, but realise that it is the outcome of a living process, of a human activity which is intelligible only in relation to the process which generates it. This whole process is in time, and takes time, and the truth and error predicated in the course of it occur at different stages of this process.

§ 8. The Genesis of Error.

We begin always with a *problem* which we desire to solve. This arouses our interest and defines our purpose, and so provides the motive force for our truth-seeking. To this interest a number of possible assertions seem relevant. We realise that they cannot all be true together, and that many of them must be, while all may be, false; but we need them as a preliminary survey of the subject and to indicate the points to be inquired into. We consider, therefore, all that occur to us, and make a selection. We choose what seems to us the best among them to be affirmed as 'true,' and publish it. Any 'truth,' therefore, always makes its appearance in the world of thought as a *partly verified truth-claim*, buoyed up by the hope that publication may win for it further support.

It may thereupon be accepted forthwith as truth with practical unanimity. But few truths are so fortunate. It is commoner to greet them with rage or derision and to reject them as false or erroneous. This means that their truth-claim is disputed and has to be tested further. They become, at best, *debatable truths*, and the dispute about them continues until the parties to it come to an agreement. They are experimented with, probably in the end by acting on them, and their fate depends on the outcome of such experiments, i.e. on the *value* of the 'consequences' of the truth-claim. If the consequences are favourable they may lead to a complete vindication of the original truth-claim and its acceptance as true. But they are more likely to lead to its progressive modification, to amendments and restatements. For it is not likely that a truth is stated fully and in its best form at the first attempt. And often enough they lead to its condemnation as downright 'error.'

But to call it an error is a one-sided and partisan way of describing a disputed truth-claim. It is a 'truth' for those who believe it, and so long as they believe it. It becomes an 'error' only when it is found out and abandoned. Instead of being valued positively as a 'truth,' it is then revalued as an 'error.' Hence when ordinary speech describes as 'error' a judgment which its maker still upholds, it is 'telescoping' two standpoints. For the maker it is still a 'truth' (-claim); for his critic alone it is 'error.' And the situation is not yet a detection of error but still a conflict of opinion. A values as 'false' what B values as 'true,' and until one converts the other no 'common' or 'objective' truth exists in the matter. When they come to agree a revaluation ensues, and the 'error' is recognised in retrospect, while the new 'truth' is antedated and said to have been true all along.

§ 9. Error implies Relations and a Fight.

Thus an 'error' is always a nest of relations. It involves reference to a problem and a purpose, to a value and to a preferable 'truth,' which is judged true about the same object about which the 'error' is 'false.' It also implies a duality, and usually a debate or dispute. For an 'error' to exist as such there must be at least *two* judgments—one to commit, a second to correct it, and a decision of the question about their comparative value. There need not, however, always be two parties, since it is theoretically possible to discover and correct one's own mistakes. In any case error implies a struggle between rival truth-claims, and the (at least provisional) defeat of all but the 'best.' The victor is accounted 'truth,' the vanquished 'error.'

But this victory need not be either decisive or permanent. Quite a slight superiority may win the title of truth, and quite a slight advance in knowledge may speedily lead to its loss. For truths hold their title only while they hold the field: they hold by the same tenure as the priest of Diana Nemorensis, until a stronger and better challenges and overcomes them. In a progressive science, therefore, truths are short-lived, though the plasticity of language, enabling us to put new meanings into the old terms, leads us to overlook their ephemeral character.

§ 10. Minimising the Difference between Truth and Error.

It is clear, then, that the difference in value between a 'truth' and an 'error' need not be very great or very important. More often than not the 'error' is merely a first approximation to a truth, or an antiquated truth through which the path of discovery has led. Indeed, in retrospect, all the steps that were taken to reach a truth must be described as errors: they may even have been 'necessary' errors, if no alternative route was apparent. It is our duty to condemn them and to abandon them so soon as a *better* truth comes within our ken; but this should not lead us to regard 'errors' as irretrievable disasters. It need not prevent us from recognising that normally the path to truth is beset by errors and leads through errors, and that far worse things may befall a cognitive undertaking than a lapse into error. We may select a bad problem, which proves trivial or intractable and sidetracks the course of inquiry. We may be led astray by the pursuit of irrelevant truth. Infirmity of purpose and vagueness of thought may lead to failure. A lack of courage in pressing our conclusions to their logical consequences may prove an insuperable obstacle to success. A desire to eat one's cake and have it too, a vacillation between incompatible beliefs, may arrest progress and stifle thought. All these things are far commoner and more fatal to success in knowing than straightforward errors which are honestly tested and triumphantly corrected.

Errors, then, are not very tragical affairs provided they can be corrected and 'made good.' And it is far more important to develop a *technique* for detecting and correcting errors than a paralysing anxiety to avoid them, or than to deceive oneself with delusive promises of infallibility. Now this is what modern science has done; it is essentially a method of inquiry rather than a heap, or even a system, of dogmas. It yields not 'absolute' truth, 'inerrant' and 'valid,' unattainable and inapplicable, but valuable truth, applicable and adequate to its problems and in- definitely perfectible. And in the development of such truth the commission and correction of errors are normal incidents. But the 'errors' are no more absolute than the 'truths.'

§ 11. Error as Negative Value in Cognition.

It is clear, then, that error should be conceived, like truth, as a cognitive value. Only it is *negative* value. 'Error' results from a failure to sustain the truth-value that was claimed. It was at first thought true, but afterwards found to thwart or defeat a cognitive purpose, or to be superseded by a better way of satisfying it. So it is discarded, judged to be logically 'wrong,' 'bad,' or 'false.'

Thus an 'error' is a failure of our knowledge to attain its '*object*,' in the sense of its *aim*. It differs from the failure called (felt) ignorance in that it involves, not a feeling of failure or mere vacuity, but the rejection of a positive claim. It differs from the failure called self-contradiction in that it does not dissolve into the unmeaning when detected: an error retains its meaning, but its meaning is seen not to be the right meaning because it is not to the purpose. On the other hand, self-contra- dictions resemble errors in existing as such only when detected by their asserters. 'Lies' differ in that they must be detected by others; but *undetected* errors, lies, and self-contradictions all alike pass for true.

§ 12. All Psychic Process liable to Error.

The account given above of the nature of error is very general: it had to be so in order to be applicable to all cases. But in the concrete errors are as multiform as truths. We can have errors of sensation, as when we dream or are hallucinated. We can have errors of perception, as when we judge a distant mountain to be much nearer than it proves when we toil up it; or judge two lines to be unequal, because they have other lines radiating from them in different ways. We can have errors of memory, as when we 'remember' youthful exploits we have heard about, or others to which we aspired but did not attain. We can have errors of judgment, as when we miss our mark through not allowing enough for disturbing factors, or choose a profession or a wife we come to detest. Errors are common enough even in pure arithmetic, as when we add $7 + 5$ as 10, and so cheapen our bill. In this case we may say, to be sure, we thought we were adding $7 + 3$, and plead 'allodoxy'; but, even so, there enters into our error a real element of failure. For in ordinary counting we presuppose a general purpose to count according to the system of common arithmetic, of which we have frequently tested the value; and *this* purpose is defeated by a false addition, whatever other purpose may be attained.

§ 13. Error not purely Intellectual.

Error, then, is never mere confusion. A mind may be quite clear and quite wrong; or, again, quite confused and yet right. A savage may have a perfectly clear theory of the magical powers of his idol, while a Christian may be hopelessly hazy about his theology without thereby frustrating the spiritual function of his religion.

Now, this seems a paradox only while we cherish the illusion that error must be represented as an affair of pure intellect and as capable of being analysed without reference to the problems, aims, and purposes of the knower who falls into error. If we insist on making this intellectualist assumption, we shall always find error becoming inexplicable, and this is the ultimate reason why no intellectualist theories of knowledge are ever able to give an intelligible account of error, though it hardly excuses the weird concoctions of metaphysical 'eyewash' by which they seek to blind their readers to their failure.

The truth, however, is that the fundamental assumption of all the intellectualist theories is completely false. Error is not an affair of 'pure' intellect at all. In this conclusion, at least, we may agree with the intellectualist. He proves it by showing that, if 'pure reason' is assumed, error is inconceivable. We may prove it by showing how, in the *human* intellect, errors can arise, be tested, and be corrected, just because no intellect is 'pure,' and because our actual human intelligence is entirely *teleological* in its functioning.

§ 14. Error the Failure of a Thought-Experiment.

If philosophers could only be got to examine the hoary pre-judices they have inherited from Greek intellectualism and never tested, they could hardly fail to see that so soon as thinking is conceived as a purposive process, arising in a vital predicament and having a teleological function, the analysis of error becomes clear and easy. An error is simply the failure of a thought-experiment. And as every thought is an experiment suggested by a definite situation out of which it is meant to extricate its maker in the best way he can think of, it is clear that every actual thought (as opposed to a form of words or 'proposition,' which can easily be made 'safe' and indisputable by making it inapplicable and meaningless) runs a risk of failure. If it did not, it would be incapable of expressing any truth worth having, and could not prove a success. If it is a success, it is hailed as a 'truth,' as the 'right' answer to the problem it dealt with, as worthy of belief and applause.

Its success, moreover, has a propitious influence on the fortunes of the 'proposition' in which it was expressed. It, too, is called a truth, and even an 'eternal' truth. The next time a similar situation arises, to which it may prove relevant and with which it may be 'identified,' it is sure to be called upon to help. It may then again function as a truth and be verified once more. Of course, however, we can never be sure of this in advance. For, as both purposes and conditions change, cases of 'the same' are always more or less different, and it is always a question whether the difference between the new case and the old will not prove sufficient to vitiate the inference we seek to draw: we can never, therefore, be assured in advance that the old 'truth' will prove adequate to cope with the new situation. Very often it will have to be modified or developed, and sooner or later it is pretty sure to be misapplied to a case in which it will break down.

In this case it will be convicted of 'error,' and this result may be deplorable or otherwise. It will be deplorable only if it means stark failure—just misapplication which affords no clue to more successful use, and fails to indicate the direction in which the 'ideas' (concepts or beliefs) experimented with require to be modified. But, more often, an open-minded and intelligent inquirer will find his 'errors' prolific of future 'truths,' and there is no reason why a logic willing to observe the procedure of actual knowing should shrink from admitting this. Our 'truths' and our 'errors' are both incidental to our knowing, and are generated in the same endeavour—to wit, in an attempt to know and to solve a problem; both therefore are, and remain, relative to the purposes and stages of our inquiry. Hence, in real knowing, the 'truths' are never pure nor the 'errors' wanton; and this for the same reason, viz. that both must be relevant to the inquiry which engenders them.

§ 15. Errors in 'Propositions' and in Judgments.

Regarded, then, as *propositions*, both our truths and our errors are incidents in our knowing which undergo various vicissitudes. In a rapidly progressive subject or science the errors we encounter are speedily corrected and cast aside and forgotten, unless they have proved stepping-stones to truths. But the truths also are almost as ephemeral: they are continually developing into *better* truths, which take their place and degrade their forerunners into 'errors.' To this development of truths the growth of knowledge sets no end: hence no 'truths' are ever 'absolute.' They are never more than the best solutions known up to date to the problems they concern.

Regarded, on the other hand, as *actual judgments* and as the *acts* of a knower, 'truths' and 'errors' both have the finality they lack as 'propositions.' A 'truth' is (i.e. is believed to be at the time) the best solution of the problem that prompted to its assertion: 'errors' are solutions of inferior value, even though this value may not be wholly negative. In the one case, therefore, a hit is scored, in the other a miss; but in either case the question is settled for the time by the judgment, true or false.

But this finality does not mean that the question may not be re-opened. It only means that when it *is* reopened it may prove to be a different question and may need to be answered differently under the new conditions, and that logic should be aware of this and be chary of calling an 'eternal' truth a proposition which has once worked as true. It should also show itself aware of the long jump it takes in passing from the truth of a judgment in a particular context to the truth of the proposition in which it was conveyed on subsequent occasions for its use, of the dangerous ambiguity of 'truth' when used thus indiscriminately of propositions and of judgments, and of the contentious status of both 'truths' and 'errors' in actual thinking. To say that an assertion actually made is an 'error' is to say that a better judgment might have been made, and implies readiness to make it: to uphold it as a 'truth' is to rebut this suggestion, and to challenge all comers to defeat it. If the judgment made was *not* the best solution, as it was held to be, this challenge will be taken up and the former 'truth' will be overthrown and turned into 'error.'

§ 16. Conclusion.

Thus, then, are truths and errors alike born in, and for, the service of man. There is nothing mysterious or illegitimate about the birth, function, or career of either, nothing that is not easily grasped, provided only that we are willing to look at the course of actual thinking, to recognise its experimental nature, to admit that personal meaning is prior to verbal, to eschew the substitution of 'propositions' for judgments and the muddle this produces, and to discriminate between the senses in which 'truth' is ascribed to propositions and to judgments. The whole difficulty of the theory of error is a gratuitous creation of a perverse 'logic' which begins by abstracting from the most important and valuable features of real thinking, and ends by obliterating the difference between truth and falsity.

CHAPTER X

THE BIOLOGIC OF JUDGMENT

1. The central position of judgment ; 2. The forerunners of judgment ; 3. The genesis of thinking ; 4. Thinking and brain development ; 5. Why and when thinking pays ; 6. On stopping to think ; 7. The new and the old in the thought-situation ; 8. 'Analysing' the situation ; 9. Judgment essentially experimental ; 10. Non-intellectual influences in judgment ; 11. Judgment the end of deliberation ; 12. Judgment a personal act ; 13. The effects of judgment : (1) improve the action ; 14. Judgment transforms also : (2) its maker, (3) his situation, and (4) his terms ; 15. The bearing on logic of this account of judgment.

§ 1. The Central Position of Judgment.

Judgment may justly be regarded as the central theme of logic. For, until we come to it, there is nothing which can claim truth or be convicted of error.[1] And after we leave it we get nothing but concatenations of judgments in inference and proof. Thus Judgment is the central focus to which all the paths of logical inquiry converge, the decisive point where the conflicting logics meet to fight out their differences, and the turning-point whence they diverge into fertility or futility. Naturally, therefore, it has many aspects, and opens many vistas : it can be approached by many inquiries, viewed on many sides, discussed in many contexts.

For a logic, however, which sets itself to study the course of actual thinking, the natural starting-point for its account of Judgment will be a description of the circumstances under which, in real life, Judgment actually arises—the vital situation in which we find ourselves impelled to judge. Having grasped the realities which underlie logical debates, it may proceed to discuss the other aspects of Judgment and the many questions which have been raised about them.

§ 2. The Forerunners of Judgment.

Our account of the function of Judgment in our mental life will, however, have to start a long way back. For there is much

[1] Except Perception, for the relations of which to Judgment, see Chap. XI, § 10.

thinking before there is any judging, and much living before there is any thinking. Even in highly developed minds judging is a relatively rare incident in thinking, and thinking in living, an exception rather than the rule, and a relatively recent acquisition.

For the most part the living organism adapts itself to its conditions of life by earlier, easier, and quicker expedients. Its actions or reactions are mostly 'reflex actions' determined by inherited habits which largely function automatically and are inaccessible to direct conscious control. Moreover, the organism is very far from resembling the fabulous *tabula rasa*—from being an impartial and indifferent recipient of external stimuli. It is intensely *selective*, and responds to some while ignoring others; it is full of 'prejudices,' which prescribe the forms a stimulation must take to be noticed; it is imperious in the *demands* it makes upon its experience.[1] So it finds itself equipped, quite lavishly, with impulses to act and to take stimulations in certain ways, and with urges that are called 'instincts,' without having more than the dimmest consciousness of the reason for them or realising their function and rationality. Nevertheless, these reflexes, instincts, and impulses are biologically valuable, and indeed indispensable; they have been shaped by the organism's mode of life, and generally suffice, under ordinary circumstances, to preserve its life and to perpetuate its kind. They are, therefore, generally speaking, salutary; though it is worth noticing that habits, instincts, and impulses are adaptations to the past rather than to the present conditions of life; consequently they get out of gear whenever the mode of life changes rapidly. The organism is equipped further with a variety of sense-organs, which also have been evolved in, and remain relative to, its past life. Their apparent function is to put it into relation with what is practically taken to be an external world with which it has to come to terms. These sense-organs are not infallible, being liable to various illusions and hallucinations under abnormal conditions; but as a rule we can trust our senses not to deceive us more safely than we can trust our logical faculties.

[1] The eulogistic name for these two is '*a priori* truths.'

The deliverances of our senses, moreover, are not only relative to our past life but also affected by it; they naturally perceive the present in the light of the past. This has the great advantage of incorporating past experience in present perception, but also renders it liable to perpetuate past errors. Theoretically it degrades 'pure sensation' into a fiction of *ex post facto* analysis which could not conceivably occur more than once, and does not actually occur at all.

It follows from this elaborate and admirable organisation of adaptive responses to stimulation that organic life might proceed without thinking altogether. It might present the appearance of a smoothly flowing sequence of perceptions, reflexes, instinctive and impulsive acts, in which there was no need for anything like thought or reason at all. This is, in fact, the way in which most living beings carry on their life, and the plane on which man also lives most of the time.

§ 3. The Genesis of Thinking.

Thought, therefore, is an abnormality which springs from a disturbance. Its genesis is connected with a peculiar deficiency in the life of habit. The latter is admirably adjusted to *stable* conditions, to which it can respond with regular and stereotyped reactions. But what if the conditions should grow variable? The organism must then vary its responses and live by reactions which are modifiable and plastic. It can no longer prosper with machinery which works in a uniform mechanical manner and is insensitive to minor differences. The fish that is organised to snap at every worm and every fly will presently find that it has swallowed one that had a hook inside it. Thus an organisation which achieves adaptation only to the broad general outlines of a situation and fails to distinguish its individual peculiarities no longer suffices.

Whenever, therefore, it becomes biologically important to notice differences in roughly similar situations, and to adjust action more closely to the peculiarities of a particular case, the guidance of life by habit, instinct, and impulse breaks down. A new expedient has somehow to be devised for effecting such

exact and delicate adjustments. This is the *raison d'être* of
what is variously denominated 'thought,' 'reason,' 'reflection,'
'reasoning,' and 'judgment,' and it is the real clue to the
biological value of logic.

§ 4. Thinking and Brain Development.

Thought is the characteristically (though not exclusively)
human expedient, by cultivating which man has established
his dominion over the earth. It arises quite late in the evolution
of life and has rapidly succeeded. Its outward and visible sign
is brain-development; for a life of mechanical reflexes and auto-
matisms needed very little brain, merely enough to innervate
and co-ordinate the motions of the limbs. The great bulk of
the modern brain is needed to obtain the variable and plastic
responses which adapt action to particular situations and display
intelligence. Accordingly, ever since mesozoic times there has
been a development of brain throughout the animal kingdom.
The monster reptiles required very little brain, because they led
an almost completely automatic life and could afford to be very
stupid; so creatures with 100 feet of extension like *Diplodocus
carnegii* could do with a brain no larger than a lead pencil in
their heads, though they needed a larger ganglion behind to
wag their tails. Similarly, the *Titanotheres*, the early ancestors
of the rhinoceros, had only about one-eighth of the brain their
descendant has, although nowadays the latter is reputed to be
one of the stupidest of modern mammals, and it would hardly
be an intellectual treat to meet one.

Brain development, then, has paid all along the line, especially
in the human ancestry. It is, however, a little puzzling to find
that the relatively vast human brain was reached quite early in
palæolithic times;[1] the most probable explanation of this fact
is that now the natural selection of the fitter individuals is so
seriously hindered by the conditions of civilised life that brain
development has ceased, or even become retrograde. It must
also be admitted that the correlation of intelligence with brain
encounters difficulties in detail: Leibniz, Gambetta, and Anatole

[1] Cp. *Tantalus*, p. 20 f.

France had very small brains, and though Bismarck (a big man) had a big brain the size record is held by a hydrocephalous idiot!

§ 5. Why and When Thinking Pays.[1]

Still, on the whole, we can make out why thinking pays. The thoughtful, intelligent action understands and handles the particular situation better and more discriminatingly than the mechanical response of habits and reflexes and can be adjusted better to its particular features. It thus renders possible a response which is more adequate and salutary, biologically. And this has happened so often that the tribe of (potential) thinkers has multiplied and the habit of thinking (on occasion) has established itself.

Thinking, however, is not so much a substitute for the earlier processes as a subsidiary addition to them. It only pays in certain cases, and intelligence may be shown also by discerning what they are and when it is wiser to act without thinking. For thinking always consumes time, and in emergencies we may not be able to afford that, while prompt action of almost any sort may mean salvation. It is quite possible, therefore, to overdo thinking, and natural selection will then repress excessive thinkers. Thus the cave man who deliberated whether he should run away from a cave bear or the modern philosopher who carried his imitation of Socrates to the pitch of meditating on one leg in crossing a crowded street would both be abusing their powers of thought in a way conducive to speedy elimination.

The ordinary man, however, is not so foolish. He only thinks when he has to, and neither often nor long enough, which is why he incurs philosophic rebukes for the rarity of his 'rational' actions. Philosophers, however, have very mistaken ideas about rational action. They tend to think that men ought to think all the time, and about all things. But if they did this they would get nothing done, and shorten their lives without enhancing their merriment. Also they utterly misconceive the nature of rational action. They represent it as consisting in the perpetual use of

[1] Cp. Chap. IV, § 3.

universal rules, whereas it consists rather in perceiving when a general rule must be set aside in order that conduct may be adapted to a particular case. However, whether occasions for thinking are frequent or relatively rare, they are at any rate common and vital enough to make thinking a very important accomplishment; it is well worth while, therefore, to investigate its nature.

§ 6. On Stopping to Think.

(1) The first and most difficult step in thinking is *stopping to think*, i.e. the inhibition or arrest of the natural impulse to react at once. This is difficult because we are constructed for prompt action: the whole lower and more primitive part of our equipment drives us into action, and it is clear that for very many of the ordinary occasions of life the guidance of impulse suffices. Indeed, if we had to choose, we could more easily dispense with our thinking than with our impulses, habits, and reflexes. The power to abstain from instant action, in order first to look, watch, and deliberate, was probably acquired by man when he first took to stalking game; but reflective action still goes sorely against the grain of the ordinary man.

§ 7. The New and the Old in the Thought-situation.

(2) If we have succeeded in controlling our impulse we get a breathing space in which to consider the actual situation. Now if this is really a situation which demands thought, and *ex hyp.* it was able to arrest action, it will always appear as a mixture of new and of familiar features. For, if it had seemed *wholly* new and unprecedented, it would be merely paralysing to both thought and action; if it had seemed wholly familiar it would not have arrested action, but have been dealt with in the habitual way. A situation, therefore, which evokes thought will always seem to be *partly* new and different from anything ever experienced before; and yet not so hopelessly so as to baffle thought.

It will be a *problematic* situation, that raises questions, arouses doubts, induces hesitations, and suggests alternatives; yet it will also suggest analogies, hypotheses, and interpretations to cope with it. The first problem that presents itself will be, What is it really and truly and *essentially*? I.e. what is its *most important part* for us, viewing it as we are, with the purposes we have? Are its likenesses with the past more 'essential' than its differences? And in either case to what likenesses and differences shall we attach importance? And how shall we extract from the past guidance for the future? It would seem that we always have a choice between emphasising its novelty and its familiarity. We can view it either as an old situation in a new development or as a new situation in a familiar light; we can think it as a new case of an old truth or as a novelty to be tamed and reduced to established precedents. Actually the situation will usually be complex enough to warrant either interpretation and to render choice far from easy: in practice, however, it is usually more urgent, and also more interesting, to classify the new than to modify the old. Whichever alternative we prefer, we are essentially concerned with viewing the present situation in the light of past experience.

§ 8. 'Analysing' the Situation.

(3) So we set ourselves to 'analyse' it. This means inquiring what it is, in the sense of how it is to be *named*, or with what words chosen out of the extant resources of language is it to be described *for our purpose*? The latent implication of this procedure is that, once our problem has been duly labelled, the conventional meanings of the words we have used will be a guarantee that its future behaviour will conform to our expectations and enable us to make predictions.

This, however, is sometimes an illusion. For the very case we are considering may force upon us a modification of the terms with which we label it. It is no use arguing that this *ornithorhynchus paradoxus* cannot lay eggs because no marsupials do, or that radio-activity cannot be due to the break-up of atoms because matter is indestructible, or that an origin of species is impossible because it contradicts the very notion of 'species': the history of science has so often and so flagrantly shown the insecurity of arguments resting merely on the analysis of verbal meaning that philosophers should be growing afraid and ashamed of *a priori* metaphysics which are nothing but disquisitions on the assumed meanings of words.

§ 9. Judgment essentially Experimental.

The truth that is overlooked is that in actual thinking all the terms we apply are used *experimentally*. The 'subjects' of the various judgments we tentatively formulate are all extracts from the total situation which strike us as significant: the 'predicates' all indicate experiments with these subjects which seem to us worth trying.

Thus every predication should be conceived as an experiment, which tests at one and the same time an interpretation of the situation inquired into, and the 'validity' (i.e. value) of the terms by which it is analysed. The judgment which affirms it puts an end to a more or less prolonged period of doubt and hesitation, and implies that it is preferable to more or less numerous alternatives; but it is only a provisional solution of the problem, and whether its consequences will come up to expectation and the terms of its 'analysis' stand firm remains to be seen.

§ 10. Non-intellectual Influences in Judgment.

It is a mistake also to represent any inquiry which terminates in a judgment as a cold, calm, dispassionate verdict of pure intellect. So long as we pander to this traditional fiction we shall never understand either men's devotion to truth-seeking or the fatal facility of their lapses into error, or the pertinacity with which they cling to errors when once they have committed themselves. Moreover, it stands to reason that any inquiry must be *interested*, and that a lack of interest is anything but a sure guarantee of truth. Finally, it follows from our account of the genesis of thinking that something 'striking' and emotional must have happened to interrupt the smooth flow of experience and to shock us into thinking. No situation would be inquired into, i.e. questioned, if it did not seem questionable.

Consequently no question, scientific or other, could conceivably arise unless it could somehow make a personal appeal to a mind that raises it. The theory of 'disinterested' knowing fails to explain how any knowledge is possible.

Furthermore, the inquiring mind is filled not only with questions but with other contents it has been considered improper to notice. It is filled also with hopes, fears, wishes, and commands, and all of these play important parts. Hopes and fears steer the course of exploration; wishes adumbrate its end. *Postulates* serve as the great guiding 'principles of rationality,' which are necessities of method and verifiable only after they have been assumed. In addition, every mind inevitably *makes demands* upon the situation which interests it and stirs it up to think; it insists that it *shall* 'mean' one thing rather than another, and shall develop in one way rather than another.

It is not indifferent, therefore, to the alternative judgments it tries to formulate and to compare. They are not all of equal value in its eyes, but some are vastly preferable to others. Hence the mind is not unbiased or unprejudiced, and its thought-experiments are tried in a definite order, an order of attractiveness, while the more repellent or improbable ones are postponed *sine die*.

§ 11. Judgment the End of Deliberation.

Sooner or later, however, the time comes in every situation when thinking has to stop, and action, modified, enriched, and improved by thought, has to follow. How soon will depend on the time there is for deliberation, on the complexity of the influences affecting the mind, and in a general way on the urgency of action; but in the end we must 'make up our mind' and pass a 'judgment' on the situation.

This judgment is a *decision* which leads to action mediated and modified by the thought which has preceded. Of course, if the thinking should *not* modify the action to which the impulses prompted, it is merely a waste of time and worse than worthless. Usually, however, thinking does make a difference, and normally a difference for the better.

The judgment which terminates the period of questioning, doubt, and deliberation, moreover, always selects what seems to be the *best* among the alternatives that have presented themselves to the mind. This claim to value is always implied in a real judgment; for if the judgment adopted had not been thought to be the best some other judgment would have been preferred. In making what he thought was the best judgment under the circumstances its maker may, however, have been aware that it was not completely good and perfectly satisfactory; but this would not have deterred him; it would only make him readier to supplement, revise, and improve his first judgment. Indeed, he may make his judgment largely in the hope of advancing thereby to a better one; he need no more have been under the delusion that his judgment was final because he recognised the value of a provisional decision, than he need have imagined that he had arrived at certainty by making a judgment that by an official fiction puts an end to doubt. In all such cases the verbal form need be no indication of the psychological facts. A judgment formally terminates doubt; but its maker may yet continue to feel it, and may only be acting *as if* he were certain, and in order to *test* his doubts and in the hope of resolving them by action. A judgment claims to be the best *possible*; but it may be only the best *available*, and its maker may know this and be anxious to improve it. A judgment claims truth, but it may easily turn out to be false. Thus the appearance of decisiveness which the passing of a judgment implies is in a way deceptive; it tends to disguise the radically experimental function of real thinking. It should not, therefore, be so interpreted as to prevent the re-opening of any question which the progress of science may demand.

§ 12. Judgment a Personal Act.

On the other hand, there is no deception about the air of personal decision which envelops Judgment. Every judgment is a personal *act*, by which its maker commits himself and assumes a responsibility he cannot disavow. Just because no judgment issues from pure reason as a product of non-human thought, just because every judgment arises as a human response to a particular situation in which some one feels himself personally involved, just because it is stained through and through with the personality of its maker, we have a right to hold him responsible for his judgment. As he is so he judges, and as he judges so he is judged. The judgment is his act, which he chose in preference to alternatives (he was at the very least able to abstain and to 'suspend judgment'), and he must take the consequences of his act, just as the judgment must take the consequences of its truth-claim.

We must disallow, therefore, both the pretences with which intellectualist logic has so long hoodwinked us. It is not true (1) that when we have failed to make the judgment which the situation demanded we can relieve ourselves of the blame for our inadequacy or fatuity by fathering our judgment upon any impersonal, self-developing truth, and pleading that *per se* it was not false. If it was a false move and led astray a train of thought, it was a bad judgment. Nor, on the other hand, is it true (2) that knowledge grows in a wholly impersonal manner, and that the one contribution man can make to the process is the mistakes he makes out of his native stupidity. If, as can hardly be disputed openly, truth-seeking is the purely human undertaking he sees it to be, its conduct rests with him, and both its successes and its failures must be credited to man.

Being thus a responsible act, judgment is inevitably *risky*. All living and all doing involve risks, and in judging, also, we must acknowledge them and boldly take our risks. These begin the moment we stop to think. For after all it may be that we misjudged the situation, and should have done better to act promptly. After that we may make a variety of mistakes by selecting the wrong point as the 'essence' of the situation, and by thinking about it in the wrong terms, by including the irrelevant and by omitting the relevant in our calculations. We may next deliberate too long or judge too harshly. And, lastly, we may choose wrongly and adopt a judgment which turns out to be 'false.' But we have the consolation that if we had refused to run the risk of error we should have missed the chance of attaining truth, and that an intelligent man's intelligent error may in the end be very helpful. On the whole, therefore, the doctrine of our responsibility for the judgments we make should be at one and the same time a stimulus, a warning, and an encouragement.

§ 13. The Effects of Judgment: (1) Improve the Action.

When at last a judgment has been launched upon the world, what of its effects? In the first place it must, of course, be *acted on.* For it has been shown that all thinking arises out of living and for the sake of action, and it follows that it must justify itself in action. If the relation of reflection to action is ignored, the former becomes unintelligible and frequently pernicious. So if the judgment which concludes deliberation were not acted on, the whole thinking process would be reduced to futility and it would become doubtful whether its maker had made it in good faith and really believed it. If it were acted on and did *not* improve the situation, it would be condemned as a mistake and would vanish. A successful judgment, therefore, that *can* maintain its truth-claim, must *improve* the situation from which it springs, and initiate *salutary* changes.

A simple illustration should elucidate the benefit of thoughtful action and the improvement effected by its control of impulse. Suppose a man walking through a dry country on a hot day. When he comes to some water he naturally feels impelled to drink, and if he were an unthinking creature he undoubtedly would drink. But if he is 'capable of reflection' he stops to think about his (particular) situation before he quenches his thirst. It may then occur to him that the water looks rather foul, and that there is a good spring a mile farther on. So he controls himself and 'acts reasonably' by refraining from drinking. If, however, he knew that there was no further water for the next ten miles it might be more reasonable to run the risks of drinking the dubious water rather than die of thirst. Both these cases would exemplify the biological value of thinking and the improved adaptation it enables us to make: the reflective act is clearly more closely adjusted to the actual circumstances of the particular situation (cp. § 5) than the prompting of organic impulse, which merely establishes a general connexion between water and drinking without regard to the special circumstances of the case. The fact that they enable us to consider these is the real justification of 'reason,' 'thinking,' and 'judgment.'

§ 14. Judgment Transforms also (2) its Maker, (3) his Situation, and (4) his Terms.

The salutary changes which a *successful* judgment mediates extend, however, far beyond its maker's impulsive action at the time. A successful judgment will affect also its maker, the situation, and the terms by which it is apprehended. It will always effect more or less of a transformation in the mind that has succeeded in making a valuable judgment, in the reality that confronts the mind, and in the terms the mind has employed.

(1) The maker of the judgment not only *benefits* by his modified reaction to the situation he has thought about successfully, but also *learns* from it, and increases his stock of knowledge and his faith in the value of thinking.

(2) This new knowledge transforms the world in which he lives—i.e. as it appears to him—in a way which he could express by saying, 'So, then, reality was not as I imagined, but as I have just discovered.'

(3) The new knowledge is incorporated into the meaning of the terms in which it was expressed, and so transforms their meaning that they can henceforth convey the new discovery. For in a really new bit of knowledge (alike whether it is new to science or only to its maker) the terms *ex hypothesi* had never before been put together. Symbolically, the judgment *S is P* had not been made. Consequently it was not known that *this particular* S could have *this particular* P predicated of it. But now that the predication has proved a success, the newly established relation between S and P becomes part of the meaning of both terms. S becomes an S-of-which-P-can-be-predicated, while P becomes a P-predicable-of-S. Thus a really significant judgment always changes the meaning of the terms it uses.[1]

[1] Cp. *Problems of Belief*, p. 106.

Under ordinary circumstances, of course, these changes are neither very great nor very noticeable, and this may explain, if not excuse, the fact that logicians have not only failed to notice them, but have actually accepted as the logical ideal rigid terms with fixed meanings incapable of expansion.[1] But a simple illustration will easily convince the reader that our abstract analysis is fully confirmed by familiar experiences. Strolling by the seashore in the company of a zoologist I espy a 'worm' wriggling in the sand and inquire what it is. "It is an Amphioxus." "What is that?" "The first vertebrate." Thus the former 'worm' is at once transformed into a biological celebrity, and henceforth regarded with interest, respect, and possibly affection! And simultaneously the meaning of 'vertebrate' is significantly enlarged and the formerly blank 'Amphioxus' is filled with meaning. If instead of acquiring all this new knowledge from a friend I had found it out myself, the process would, of course, have been more gradual and less dramatic, but its essential character would have remained the same.

§ 15. The Bearing on Logic of this Account of Judgment.

We see, then, that though in origin Judgment is only the final step in securing a better response to a vital predicament in which an intelligent and (potentially) reasoning creature finds itself involved, its logical significance far transcends the immediate need from which it springs. It becomes a vehicle for the growth of knowledge and the evolution of reality—that is, of the real we apprehend; and these logical functions tend to dwarf its primary use, at all events in the eyes of logicians.

In the first instance the immediate value of a judgment is easily determined. It is relative to its effect on the situation which engendered it, and bound up with its success in effecting a salutary change and a transformation desired. If it leads to the right response to the situation which evoked it, it is a *good* judgment, as good as a judgment need be, good for the purpose of its maker, and also 'true'—true because it works a salutary change.

[1] The whole of symbolic logic rests on this false assumption.

But it has also a wider significance for logic. It humanises logic by puncturing the traditional pretence that it is an affair of pure reason apprehending impersonal truth with indisputable cogency. It reveals instead the experimental character of thought, the progressiveness of knowledge, and the plasticity and malleability of the real-as-known. It is, moreover, of the utmost importance that the student of logic should have these features impressed on him thus early. It will help him to grasp the natural continuity of Judgment and Inference, the gradual consolidation of proofs, the accumulation of probabilities, the growth of truths, the purposive manipulation of experience, and the futility of imagining that thought can avoid risks, achieve finality, and come to rest in absolute security. And, above all, it will serve as a steady source of light and enlightenment when we proceed with our archæological explorations into the labyrinthine ruins of the Formal theories of Judgment.

CHAPTER XI

THE FORMAL THEORIES OF JUDGMENT

1. The Formal abstraction from context and its consequences ; 2. The degradation of judgments into propositions ; 3. The meaning of propositions potential only and essentially ambiguous ; 4. Illustrations ; 5. The right use of language ; 6. Classification of Formal theories ; 7. Judgment as a relating of ideas ; 8. The psychological meaning of subject and predicate ; 9. Judgment as primary ; 10. Perception and judgment ; 11. Judgment as identity in difference ; 12. Judgment as true by definition ; 13. Judgment as reference to reality ; 14. Bosanquet's form of the reference to reality theory ; 15. Bradley's form of the reference to reality theory ; 16. The source of Bradley's errors.

§ 1. The Formal Abstraction from Context and its Consequences.

We are entitled to describe as Formal any theory of Judgment which fails to notice the circumstances under which Judgment arises and so is forced to ignore its whole vital and psychical setting, which was studied in the last chapter. This neglect leads Formalism to ignore the influence of context upon meaning, compels it to reduce its 'judgments' to propositions, and finally destroys the distinction between true and false judgments. Indeed its rake's progress ends in a verbally complete self-contradiction, from which there is no escape. Formalism begins by defining Judgment as that-which-can-be-true-or-false, but in the end has to admit that *formally* judgment is always '*true*.' For as it insists on abstracting from the circumstances of actual use, it has no means of testing the formal truth-claim of any judgment, and has to identify 'truth' in its logic with *truth-claim*: yet it is unable to scrap its original definition of judgment as 'true-or-false,' for this is needed in order to distinguish a judgment from a question, a wish, a postulate, and other forms of the imperative and interrogative.

It is equally incapable of stopping short anywhere on the way, once it has taken the fatal step of abandoning the real judgment in its actual setting and full concreteness. It is, of course, tempting to do so, for it seems intolerably pedantic to refrain from talking logic till one has secured an actual meaning, and intolerably laborious to pry into the circumstances of every case; but once abstraction is made from the actual case, logic parts company with meaning. What follows no longer deals with fact, but is mere speculation about potential meanings without any assurance that it is relevant to any actual problem.

§ 2. The Degradation of Judgments into Propositions.

The degradation of Judgments into propositions, therefore, is the first and most fatal error of all Formal theories. It is a very easy error to slip into, and indeed is inevitable, if we ever allow ourselves to waver in the conviction that a judgment is not properly a judgment unless it is being judged, that its meaning is a matter of fact which it is necessary to observe while it exists, and that it evaporates when it ceases to be judged.

This doctrine, however, does not mean, as is sometimes foolishly or disingenuously supposed, that a judgment has only a momentary existence and perishes beyond recall the moment the judging is over. This suggestion does much less than justice to the complexity of the situation and the naturalness of the process which degrades the judgment into a proposition. For in passing out of use and becoming 'defunct' a judgment always leaves behind two relics which continue its existence and may lead to its resurrection. The first is its *memory*, the actual and potential recollection (or record) of the fact that it *was* judged. This will influence all who are called upon to judge in (relevantly) similar situations and remember the former judgment. The second is its *vehicle*, to wit, the form of words by which it was conveyed, or otherwise the 'proposition' which in perishing it generates. This is a permanent memorial of the judgment and a permanent addition to the store of knowledge and the stock of truths, whence it can be taken out at pleasure and mobilised for active service.

There exist, therefore, possibilities of reaffirming the original judgment as often and as continuously as is required. True, such reaffirmations will always be accompanied by psychological differences, such as a growing familiarity and confidence

in its truth, or exasperation with the stupid people who do not
see it, but these differences will not preclude its meaning functionally the same as before. For in actual thinking the assertion
of 'identity' always rests on an exclusion of irrelevant differences. If, therefore, we judge the differences between the
original assertion and its reassertions to be irrelevant for our
purpose, we may continue to call it 'the same' judgment; it
preserves its identity so long as it performs the same function in
its successive embodiments. Thus the identity of its *use* creates
its identity; but only while it 'remains in use.' This phrase,
moreover, acquires the same ambiguity as the 'judgment': a
judgment may be said to 'remain in use,' even when not actually
used, if it is frequently reasserted. The functional identity of the
judgment in its various repetitions has also the logical advantage
that it gives scope for its reconsideration and improvement.
Thus its logical value (truth) may be enhanced, and its verbal
form be put more clearly and forcibly.

It is convenient, therefore, *not* to limit the life of the judgment
to the occasion of its first appearance, even though by so doing
we run the risk of accepting in its stead the form of words in
which it was made, *alias* the proposition. This latter, however,
remains the form in which a historic judgment *was* made, and
also a *form-for-judging* and a *potential* judgment for the future :
the one thing it is not, when it is not in use, is a judgment
proper.

§ 3. The Meaning of Propositions Potential only and Essentially Ambiguous.

This confusion of the judgment with the proposition has very
important logical consequences. For with the lapse in the
status of the judgment goes a change in its meaning. It ceases
to mean what it did; 'its' meaning lapses into potentiality.
Strictly, it no longer means *anything*, because *no one* is meaning
anything with it. It passes from an active and efficacious
existence in the world of action into the shadow-land of dic-
tionary-meaning, which is haunted by the departed and defunct
—the ghosts of living personal meaning. But there it is no longer

unique. It finds abundant company. There flock round it hordes of other verbal meanings, the ghosts of all the meanings which its words have ever conveyed (so far as anyone has recorded or remembered them), and the forebodings of the future meanings which they may develop. Consequently, no one can possibly tell, from a mere consideration of the form of words, which of these meanings will become actual when next the words are used.

Thus the potential meaning of the verbal forms has become *essentially ambiguous*, and a matter of speculation, not of fact. Formal Logic has, very unwisely, yielded to the temptation of trying to capture in advance these elusive ambiguities and of pinning down these vagrant ghosts to a fixed habitation. The task is hopeless, because the ambiguities are infinite and unpredictable. If logic will not stick to the solid ground of actual, personal meaning, it dooms itself to be mocked by phantoms and led astray by will-o-the-wisps. It is utterly futile, then, to discuss the value (truth or falsity) of a judgment apart from the circumstances of its origin and the consequences to which it has actually led, or, in one phrase, apart from its *use* in a context. Without this its meaning cannot be determined, and we do not know what we are talking about.

§ 4. Illustrations.

This very important point will justify, if not require, copious illustration. Take, for example, the proposition 'I believe in the thirty-nine articles.' Who can say what this means *per se*? Without the context, we do not even know whether the thirty-nine articles are in a shop or in a creed. The phrase may be used as an exclamation, a quotation, a sarcasm, a lie, or a jest: the least change of reference, emphasis, or expression may alter 'its' meaning so that no Archbishop of Canterbury would recognise it. What it does actually mean depends on who says it, to whom, when, where, why, in what state of mind. Its so-called plain meaning as a 'categorical affirmative' is at best the *commonest* of its uses; but only a plain man of more than average stupidity (or a logician!) will accept it instead of the actual meanings it bears in its various contexts. And if it is only a rough guide to the latter, what right has logic to treat it as trustworthy? Or, alternatively, to treat a judgment as ambiguous because the corresponding proposition has a plurality of senses, and to exhaust itself in trying, vainly, to exhaust the latter? The proposition is obliging enough to convey an infinite variety of meanings, although the judgment, in actual use, may leave no one in doubt as to its actual meaning: is it not wiser, therefore, to ascertain the latter than the former?

The great range of meanings which the same proposition may convey has not passed entirely unobserved by logicians. Thus Prof. Stout once commented on the vast difference it makes to the remark 'I am going home,' whether it is said by a man in the street or on his death-bed.[1] Prof. Cook Wilson used to point out in his lectures how the meaning of 'Smith is a fast bowler' varied according as it answered the question 'Who is a fast bowler?' or 'What sort of a bowler is Smith?' or 'What is Smith?' or 'Is Smith a fast bowler?'[2] When I first read in James's *Pragmatism* (p. 285) that "optimism is the doctrine that thinks the world's salvation necessary," I thought it should read 'unnecessary,' until I saw that 'necessary' and 'unnecessary' would convey the same meaning *in this particular context*. The same lesson is taught by Midshipman Easy's famous apology to the purser whom he had called 'not fit to carry guts to a bear': to say, "I beg your pardon, sir, you *are* fit to carry guts to a bear," is, in fact, to repeat the insult. More prosaically, the identity of affirmation and denial in a suitable context may be illustrated by taking as our question, *Was A elected or B?*; then *A was* and *B was*, while answering the question, each serves to *deny* the other.

Nor does actual meaning even respect the form of judgment: it is notorious that a common meaning (in England) of *It is a fine day* is simply *Let us talk!* Thus so radical a distinction as that between a judgment and a command is mocked; and we should similarly be prepared to find that judgments may be

---

[1] I cannot remember where. Neither can he.
[2] Cp. *Statement and Inference*, §§ 56–9.

expressed in the form of questions, and questions may be raised in the form of judgments, and that a great variety of meanings other than the ostensible meaning of the propositions used may be intended and successfully conveyed.

It is by no means impossible that the same judgment should mean one thing to one man and another to another. Indeed, it normally is ambiguous in just this way, though not always sufficiently to hurt, for the reason that when minds with a different training and history apprehend the 'same' judgment, its terms inevitably have different associations, and so are understood differently. When such judgments are *intended* to be taken thus differently by various parties, they should be called 'equivocations.'

§ 5. The Right Use of Language.

It is thus clear that what is called 'logical analysis of judgment' is nothing but futile speculation about the possible meanings and uses of a verbal form. It begins only after the actual meaning has been killed. It is only a *post-mortem* dissection, which may reveal the cause of death, but never the secret of life. Hence the 'judgments' which figure as examples in the textbooks are quite irrelevant: they *never* illustrate the process of living thought. They are essentially *dead* things, which no invocation of logical axioms or metaphysical principles can revive. Into their dead husks a multitude of meanings can of course be pumped, to convey which they *might have* served. But these are conjectural and potential; and to discover what the judgment meant we must use it again, and use it in a way sufficiently like its original use to recover its meaning.

It is, moreover, a deplorable mistake to throw the blame for the impotence of Formal Logic on the trickiness of language. Logicians denounce the 'equivocations' of words because these obstinately set at naught their 'ideal' of an absolute rigidity of terms, together with a 'one-to-one correspondence' of a word with 'its' meaning. But it is their 'ideal' which is at fault. It demands impossibilities which are also absurdities. Its implication is that every word, just because it fits the case of its use so perfectly, can only be used *once*, and never again, because the next case, being different, will require another word to express it. Now, this dooms every word to be a ἅπαξ λεγόμενον or nonce-word, and reduces its 'sense' to nonsense. It forms a fiction which defies the facts of language, and is a *foolish* fiction, because it stands in no relation to the nature and the needs of thought.

If these latter are allowed a hearing, a very different valuation of language is reached. It will be seen to follow from the facts that a limited number of words exists and an unlimited number of situations in which these words may be used and may convey meaning, that every word *must* be capable of conveying *many* meanings in different contexts; i.e. it must have an (indefinite) *plurality of senses*. This, however, does *not* mean that it must be ambiguous in actual use: its meaning may then be perfectly clear and fully understood. So the indefiniteness of verbal meaning is not a drawback, but rather an advantage; and it is both base ingratitude and complete misapprehension of the function of language for logicians to denounce words which are obliging enough to lend themselves to many uses. It is just because they are thus plastic that they can be adequate to many occasions; and the masters of language who understand its nature will always find it submissive and sufficient for their needs, and capable of being moulded by use to any required extent.

The way, therefore, to deal with verbal 'ambiguity' is not to make a vain attempt to taboo it in the name of logic, but understand it and to make the best of it. We should recognise that any word which can be used more than once is *potentially* ambiguous; but there is nothing in this fact that need prevent us from expressing our meaning adequately by choosing our words (and our audience) intelligently. The choice and the responsibility are both ours; and if we fail we should blame ourselves and not our tool, language. This is the right inference from the fact that every judgment has a personal origin and is an act for which its maker can be held responsible.

§ 6. Classification of Formal Theories.

With this amount of protest and explanation we may adopt the convention of calling a 'judgment' what is only a proposition, for the purpose of inquiring further into the Formal Theories of Judgment.

These fall into two natural groups according as they conceive Judgment as compound and derivative from earlier, simpler, and more primitive phases of thinking, or as in some sense primary and irreducible. The former theories, when they endeavour to account for Judgment as a combination of 'ideas,' 'concepts,' 'representations,' or 'universals,' clearly betray their linguistic origin; for words are, of course, the models which suggest that judgments are made up of discrete terms. They find it difficult, however, to show that their 'ideas,' etc., are more than verbal. In their second form, which attempts to represent judgment as derivative from sense-perception and as a natural outgrowth of the life of sense, Judgment is reduced to an *event*; this procedure cannot be declared impossible, though its fertility may be questioned. At any rate, it has the merit of raising the question of the relations of Judgment to Perception.

The Formal theories of the second group recognise at least the distinctive nature of Judgment and its cardinal place in logical theory: they may also be looked upon as more nearly approaching the theory of Judgment as an act which was developed in the last chapter. Unfortunately, they fail to recognise how essential in determining its logical character are its appeal to personality and its biological function.

§ 7. Judgment as a Relating of Ideas.

The definitions of Judgment as the result of uniting its terms, and its 'logical analysis' into a union of 'subject' and 'predicate' by means of a 'copula,' are, of course, very old. They go back to the founder of our logical tradition, and to Aristotle's definition of Judgment as a σύνθεσις νοημάτων ὥσπερ ἓν ὄντων. This formula is, however, open to criticism on several grounds.

(1) It is clearly much too vague, both about the unity and about the synthesis of the νοήματα. We need far more information

both about the putting together of concepts and about the sort of unity which is thereby achieved.

(2) There is, moreover, a prior question, a very hornet's nest of philosophic wrangles, about the proper nature of the νοήματα themselves, upon which many generations of philosophers have spent their leisure and their powers, without ever arriving at any clear, intelligible, and accepted conclusion. What are these logical entities which have such abundant *aliases*? Are they thoughts? If so, how do they differ from judgments? Are they *only* thoughts, i.e. 'concepts'? If so, whence do they obtain their power of dictating to the real? Are they themselves reals, i.e. 'universals'? If so, how can they be amphibious, and how are the universals in the mind related to those in the real, either in true judgment or in false? How, again, are the universals in the real related to their exemplifications in particular cases? Or lastly, shall we let at least the cat's head out of the bag by asking whether universals are not merely *words*?

All these questions were unanswerable, and therefore the disputes about them were interminable. The questions had been formulated in a way which precluded the simple answer to which a study of actual thinking leads, viz. that the 'ideas,' etc., are just meanings, the meanings of the words we use to convey our own.[1] These meanings embody past experience, and have been licked into shape thereby; which accounts for their application to reality (or 'real validity'): they are also instruments of fresh thinking; which is why they remain plastic, and why past meanings only yield a *probable* guide to the future. Moreover, as these meanings are only potential, words do not actually mean till they are used. They then *become* 'concepts' in their context, and remain so while they are being judged: this, however, shows that 'concepts' are *not* prior to judgment and that judgments are not formed by uniting concepts. It is one and the same personal act which both forms the judgment and gives the required meaning to its 'terms,' the words it uses.

(3) That the Aristotelian definition is silent about the purpose or aim of Judgment is a grave omission. It leaves the habit of

---

[1] Cp. *Formal Logic*, chap. vii, especially § 9.

judging motiveless and unaccountable. We must endorse, there-fore, the protest of the logicians who want judgments to be some-thing more than a juggling with 'ideas.' As J. S. Mill insisted, we want them to affirm about matters of fact, and not merely to be 'necessary' (but impotent) concatenations of ideas. Judg-ment, therefore, means to apprehend the real, and not merely to refer to it. It means to operate upon the real and to alter it, at least for thought. It is a thought-experiment, and an instru-ment for coping with reality. The purpose, then, of 'ideas,' the sole reason for harbouring them in the mind, is that they are used in judgments which deal with reality. If by our general connecting of 'ideas,' or by our particular connecting of them in a case, we succeed in coping with fact, our ideas are vindi-cated; they prove themselves good and 'true.' But that the judgment's formal truth-claim is thus borne out is something we learn only from experience. It is not inherent in the *form* of Judgment.

Hence (4) this definition of Judgment tells us nothing about the *value* either of judging in general or of any judgment in particular. It is purely formal, and applies equally to true judgments and to false, and suggests no way of testing them.

§ 8. The Psychological Meaning of Subject and Predicate.

Nevertheless, the subject-predicate articulation of Judgment is not wholly worthless: it does refer to a psychological distinc-tion which is made in the thought-experiment called Judgment. Inasmuch as thinking is throughout selective, like our other vital processes, our attention naturally lights upon some striking or attractive feature in the total situation. This favoured feature is thereby singled out to become the 'object' thought about and the subject of inquiry. It naturally yields the 'subject' of the tentative judgments which are considered in deliberation. Similarly, our experiments with this 'subject,' the tentative classifications or operations we perform upon it, find expression in the 'predicates' we seek to attach to it. But when we 'make up our mind' to judge *S is P*, we have ceased to try alternative predicates and launch our experiment upon the world.

The completed judgment, however, is a whole, and has been preferred *as a whole* to alternatives like S^1 *is* P^1 or S^2 *is* P^2. Our deliberation is about the *words* in which to clothe our judgment, but our choice is between alternative *judgments*, and not between *subjects* and *predicates*. The subjects and predicates do not exist in their own right or by their own might; they are only distinctions within the judgment which alone is the primary act of thought.

§ 9. Judgment as Primary.

Theories of judgment as a synthesis, then, are clearly wrong in denying that Judgment is a primary equipment of the human mind; but it may be well to explain further what is meant by calling it primary.

Now Judgment is clearly *not* primary in the sense of *coming first* in the thinking process; it does not come before the meaning and questioning attitudes with which it is bound up in actual thinking. Its proper place is at the end of the tentative exploration and experimentation which precede it: it terminates the inquiry and decides the question. Nor again is Judgment primary in the sense of 'simple' and devoid of a plurality of 'parts' and relations. For even though we despair of compounding it, like the proposition, out of subject, copula, and predicate, or of 'analysing' it into a concatenation of fixed concepts, we must admit that it is always a judgment upon a complex situation to which it refers (Chap. X, § 7). Similarly, it cannot disavow intimate relations with meaning, questioning, perception, experience, and action, which are 'essential' to an understanding of its function.

Judgment is to be accounted primary as a characteristic human attitude which cannot be resolved into any other, and for which no substitute can be found: it is irreducible and indispensable. As such a primary act it is as distinctive as putting a question, formulating a wish, or issuing an order, all of which also find expression in distinctive forms of speech, though few languages distinguish them completely. Moreover, it is as such a primary act that it is the proper vehicle for the cognitive values 'true' and 'false,' though it should be observed that, strictly speaking, it is a vehicle only of *truth-claim*. For although every judgment claims truth in virtue of its form, it is not true in virtue of its form. Actually it may be false, and so its truth-claim may always be challenged. Further inquiry may always be needed to establish its truth or to convict it of error.

§ 10. Perception and Judgment.

Perception also has good claims to be considered a primary process. Indeed, it may be regarded as prior even to Judgment, to which it forms the natural stimulus, while, conversely, it seems no less possible to regard Judgment as prior and as transmuting sensation into perception.

The truth is that the relations of Perception to Judgment seem a little puzzling. A good case can be made out for exalting either above the other, according as we choose one point of view or another, and either for assimilating or for distinguishing them.

Thus we may argue that Judgment is superior to Perception because it is the more intellectual process, and that good perceptions are simply the reward of past success in judging. On the other hand we may retort that Perception is the more valuable because the more expeditious in yielding knowledge, and quote Aristotle for the insight that there are many things we should not think about if we could perceive them.[1] And so the passage of what were at first objects of thought into the sphere of direct perception as they become more familiar may be regarded as promotion to a higher status.

If we wish to assimilate Perception and Judgment we may appeal to the same facts, and point out that Perception, like Judgment, claims to apprehend reality, and is distinguished as 'true' and 'false.' It is indeed nearly as hard to distinguish true perception from false as it is to distinguish true judgment from false, and the fact that a false perception receives a different name, 'illusion' or 'hallucination,' should not blind us to a

[1] *Anal. Post.*, i. 31.

psychological identity which would warrant our calling perception 'true' hallucination, i.e. hallucination which is valuable
and works.

Perception is, moreover, permeated by Judgment and inconceivable without it. For it must be defined as sensation
infected and transformed by thought (judgment). It can then
easily be shown that no sense-perception is ever 'pure,' and
that, even theoretically, pure sensation could not occur more
than once. For the second time a sensation was experienced it
would be tainted by memories of its first occurrence; we should
know what to expect from it and should experience it differently.
Even if no conscious memory were retained of the first experience, there would be organic memory, and the new excita-
tion would travel differently to and through organs which had
been altered by the old.

Indeed, this organic memory casts a doubt even on the
possibility of pure sensation as a first experience: for is not the
functioning of an organ determined from the first by its
structure? And is not this an acquisition made in the course of
racial history? So the organs of sense, and indeed all the organs
of the body, may profitably be regarded as products of past
vital activity, and as embodying the mode of life which seemed
good and worth living to the creatures which grew them. Thus
the eyes of an eagle are evidently adapted and relative to the
ways of an eagle, as those of an owl to those of an owl: the sense-
organs of a man are poorly adapted to his mode of life, only
because he has changed it so radically and rapidly in becoming
'civilised.' 'Pure sensation,' then, may be regarded as a
fiction of *ex post facto* 'analysis' reflecting on the meaning of
the actual process of perception.

It is easy, then, to assimilate Judgment and Perception, but
the question remains open whether Judgment should absorb
Perception or Perception Judgment. We may admit that they
interpenetrate and yet differ about the significance of this fact.
Intellectualist philosophers have mostly assumed that Perception is an imperfect or 'implicit' phase of Judgment, and that
if it could be completely 'analysed' it would resolve itself

wholly into Judgment. But this is not the only nor the most natural and instructive interpretation of the facts. It does not follow that because our present perception *has been* mediated by judgments it now *is* thought. For it now involves no thinking or judging, and its immediate apprehension of the real may be a *higher* state. Judgment may have merely served as the *instrument* by which Perception has developed into its present perfection. And the contrast between the immediate apprehension of the master and the laborious judging of the learner (in all subjects, especially in æsthetics) seems to indicate that the cognitive ideal is more akin to Perception than to Judgment. It is a beatific vision rather than an endless argument.

We have touched on the one outstanding difference between Perception and Judgment, from which important consequences flow. Perception is immediate, Judgment mediate. Now this does not merely mean that Perception is quicker, but also that it is *easier* and *more valuable*. It is free from strain and labour, whereas deliberate Judgment is reached only with an effort and a sense of risk; and, psychologically at least, this is a vast difference. It may claim logical importance also if we recall the original function of judging. We saw in the last chapter that it was a *pis aller* for a smoothly flowing course of experience, forced upon us by the exigencies of life when prompt (perceptual) reaction to stimuli ceased to be salutary and had to be checked, and that when immediate perception ceased to be an adequate guide to action, thinking had to be undertaken and action to be mediated by Judgment. But Perception remains the counsel of perfection, and comes to its own again later. It is, therefore, quite in accordance with this that mediate knowledge should continually tend back into the immediate form of Perception and enrich its contents. The more we judge the more we enrich our perceptions, the more adequately we perceive the more perfect grows our life. We may safely conclude that Perception is not *strictly* Judgment, but that, properly, Judgment is subsidiary to Perception. We need Judgment to extricate ourselves from temporary difficulties, but when we can use it, and in the long run, Perception is the easier, prompter, and biologically more satisfactory process.

§ 11. Judgment as Identity in Difference.[1]

This theory has become the pet formula of Hegelising logicians, and lends itself excellently to their mystifications. By juggling with it and perpetually rehearsing the formula that Judgment asserts an identity in difference, or a difference in an identity, they can easily produce the stupor which is supposed to be the final form of philosophic wonder and the true end of philosophy. The aforesaid stupor usually prevents their audience from inquiring how it may be ascertained *which* of these alternatives is the meaning, either of Judgment in general or of any judgment in particular, or indeed how any positive and serviceable information may be extracted from the formula.

Its sole meaning, at first sight, would seem to be to *deny* that a judgment is an absolute identity. But this is only to deny a meaningless abstraction, for, though absolute identities are not infrequently alluded to in philosophic debate, no one ever troubles to explain what an absolute identity can be. Yet it is clear that if two cases of 'the same' were ever *absolutely* the same, in the sense that there was *no difference at all* between them, they would coincide, and could not contrive to remain *two*. Hence 'absolute identity' means absolute nonsense.

Yet in its very effort to deny it, the formula (being Hegelian, and so uniting being and not-being) seems implicitly to assert it. For if its own doctrine be accepted, and the meaning it gives to 'identity' be substituted in its statement, the formula 'every identity is an identity in difference' becomes 'every identity in difference is an identity in difference'; which is a tautology and meaningless as such. Hence, to give a meaning to the formula we must interpret 'an *absolute* identity is an identity in-difference,' i.e. it is *not* absolute, and there is *no* absolute 'identity.'

Now this is true, but it only shows that the whole meaning and value of the formula lies in its denial of the belief in ab-

---

[1] Cp. also *Formal Logic*, chap. x, especially § 5 and § 10.

solute identity. It has nothing to teach those who do not believe in absolute identity.

Now we have never shared this belief. It seemed to us an obvious delusion that bare identities (or differences) could be of use in thinking. For if they existed, and were arrived at in judging, they would wholly invalidate the form *S is P*: we could only judge *S is S*, as Antisthenes said long ago. But once 'ideas' are recognised as human meanings and their independent existence is disclaimed, *S is P* must mean that we have singled a subject (S) out of a larger context and claim to have so selected it that a predicate (P) (also selected out of the body of our knowledge) holds of it, and may, for our purpose, advantageously take its place. Similarly, the denial *S is not P* means that our purpose requires a distinction, or rejects an identification which might, of course, be tenable in another context. In neither case, be it observed, does the real judgment affirm about S and P in general or in the abstract, or possess truth in virtue of its form. Its meaning is always specific and its truth-claim *risky*. For both our subjects and our predicates, both our identities and our differences (distinctions), have to be selected and risked: but this is just why they are made and are worth making. To make them means: 'to put S as P is disputable, but *in this case* true.'

Or otherwise, if we regard judgment as a human experiment from the outset, we must insist that the identities we use in logic are always made (i.e. postulated), as the differences are distinguished, *by us*. They do *not* rest on a mythical 'identity of indiscernibles,' but on a conscious *disregard* of differences which we take to be irrelevant. We are aware that the differences exist, and that we run a risk in abstracting from them; but we hold that our *purpose* demands this, and trust that the event will be our vindication.

Moreover, in thinking about a given situation requiring us to judge, we are always *interested* in distinguishing our present case (or 'predicament') from others in the past, or in tracing its resemblance with others; or rather, we *place* it and determine its significance by identifying it with some, and distinguishing it from other, precedents. Hence our judgment, when we come to it, will take the form either of bringing our case as species under a genus or of distinguishing a genus into its species. But the judgment, when made, will definitely intend *one or the other and not both*, and to understand it we must know *which*. It is only the proposition which is indeterminate on this point.

This shows that the Hegelian formula has reference only to propositions; it is purely formal, and throws no light on what is actually meant when a proposition is judged. Thus it cannot tell us whether, e.g., 'humanists are pragmatists' affirms an identity in difference or a difference in an identity; to decide this question it would have to know the context. As a matter of fact, the answer depends on the question which the proposition is intended to answer: if it answers 'Is he a humanist or a pragmatist?' it asserts an identity of doctrine in a difference of nomenclature; if it answers 'What philosophers are pragmatists?' it specifies one sort of the genus 'pragmatist,' and so asserts a difference in an identity.

Thus the judgment's real meaning depends on its context and its maker's intention, and the identity-in-difference theory has no means of apprehending it. It stands to reason, also, that it is far too formal to suggest any means of testing the truth-claim of the judgment.

§ 12. Judgment as True by Definition.

In order to get away from the awkward question of how false judgment is to be detected and true judgment is to be distinguished from it, some Formalists have had a brilliant idea. Resuscitating an old Platonic idea they distinguish absolutely between knowledge and opinion, and declare that opinion may err, but knowledge never. Judgments therefore which are, or may be, false are not true judgments, and are undeserving of the title of Judgment. For true Judgment is infallible, because we judge only when we know. Knowledge, moreover, is defined as being *of what is*.[1]

[1] This definition of Knowledge pursues the same end as that of Judgment—that of ruling out error (and its problems) by decree, and

It may be questioned, however, whether this high-handed method of burking the problem of Error can be carried through successfully. (1) It cannot free itself from ambiguity. For it continues to use the word 'judgment' for what is distinguished as true-or-false as well as for what it defines as infallible, and the device of writing the latter with a capital 'J' will hardly appease the critical. (2) The distinction between 'Judgment' and 'Opinion' is not established but only asserted, and it seems odd that it should not have occurred to its advocates that it is itself only an 'opinion,' and that as such it does not share in the infallibility it ascribes to Judgment, but is itself fallible, and even false. For (3) no attempt is made to show that Judgment in the superior sense alleged is ever attained, or indeed is really conceivable. For how could one ever be sure that a judgment was a Judgment? How are we to know when we 'Know'? To wait and see and to say 'it is an opinion' when it *has* turned out false is wisdom after the event, and is no help towards determining the value of judgments when they are made.

But even if we adopted this doctrine at its own valuation, it would only lead us into further difficulties. In the first place, (4) if infallible Judgment and absolutely final Knowledge were given to man, the whole business of judging, reasoning, etc., would come to an end. For (*a*) such perfect knowledge would transcend judgment; it would form a system so closely knit that no part could be taken out of it to be affirmed apart, and (*b*) no one could want to affirm *part* of what he possessed *whole*. Why, then, should he judge? Plato, indeed, the real author of this attitude, saw this: he used the same word, δόξα, for judgment *and* opinion. He saw that the eternity of his Ideal truth excludes all change, all movement, and its wholeness all selection; if,

---

of subjugating the real by a definition. But it is woefully ambiguous. Is its second '*is*' opposed to *isn't*, to *was*, to *seems*, to *becomes*, or to *exists*? I.e. is its aim to deny that there is Knowledge of not being, or of the past, or of appearance, or of change, or of the perceptual world? All these spheres of judgment have been banished from the realm of Knowledge by various metaphysicians from Plato onwards, but one might have supposed it obvious that Logic has somehow to make provision for them. Cp. Chap. IX, § 3.

therefore, one had not got it all, one had not got it at all. The Ideal world excludes even the movement of thought. It is a rigid block of reality that renders knowing irrelevant. Thus are judgment, and *a fortiori* inference, ejected from 'logic.'

(5) Finally, what, on this theory, is to be done with 'opinions'? To say 'knowledge is not opinion' is not to get rid of opinions. Logic is, no doubt, forbidden to notice them; but will not some *other* science then have to consider them, to sort out those which it finds to be true Judgments and Knowledge and absolutely true, in order that they may be admitted into the sacred sphere of 'Logic'? If so, it may be anticipated that this science which does the actual work of logical evaluation alone will matter, even if it leaves 'Logic' nothing but a void to contemplate.

§ 13. Judgment as Reference to Reality.[1]

Of all the Formal theories of Judgment those which recognise that a reference to reality is involved in judgment have at present the greatest vogue. But so strange are the conceptions of reality to which they appeal that it seems imperative, before embarking on them, to get clear in our minds about the meaning of the 'reality' Judgment is concerned with. There are four points we must never allow ourselves to forget.

(1) We saw in the last chapter that Judgment always starts from a vital problem, and is an operation on a real and urgent situation. We predicate only when involved in a 'predicament.' There is no question, therefore, but that we are confronted with a real, a *real-for-us*. We may not (and usually do not) know what sort of reality may attach to it in the end, and it may change like a very Proteus during our struggles with it; but real to us it indisputably was, and *this* reality it cannot lose even if it dissolves into a dream or a hallucination.

(2) It is quite futile to assure us that Judgment is about reality without *specifying* the kind of reality it is about. For if the reality thought about is left quite formal, a judgment may mean anything or everything, and effectively nothing. In the

---

[1] Cp. also *Formal Logic*, chap. viii, § 5 ; and chap. ix, § 4.

widest formal sense of 'reality' any object of thought about which anyone can judge has *some* sort of reality—enough to be judged about. Absolute not-being, a παντελῶς μὴ ὄν, is, as Plato said, utterly unutterable. But anything short of that, even 'nothing' and 'unreality,' are sorts of the real for the purpose of judging. Or, as Formal Logic technically puts it, the Copula always asserts being and every 'universe of diction' has being of a kind. *False* judgments, moreover, refer to reality as boldly as true; only their references cannot be verified and do not support their claims. It is clear, also, that the 'being' predicated need not be (and very often is not) existence in the physical world.

It follows that to ascertain the meaning of a judgment, and then to judge of its truth or falsity, it is vitally important to understand to what universe of diction it refers. The judgment 'a Centaur is an anthropocephalic equine' refers to, and is true of, the world of Greek mythology. 'Spherical' triangles are false in plane, but existent in spherical geometry: that 'triangles are musical' is false in all geometry, but is true in a band. That Achilles killed Hector is true in the *Iliad*. In Homer it is true, in Stesichorus it is false, that Helen went to Troy. In the Bible it is true that Jonah was swallowed by a whale; that I was, may be true of a dream. To judge that Centaurs were pigheaded, or that Achilles died of grief because he could not catch the Tortoise, would be *false* in the same references. One can hardly, therefore, be too particular about one's universes of diction!

Clearly, then, this *formal* reference to reality asserts no existence in the physical world. Physical reality is only one out of an infinite number of realities we can judge about. If, therefore, '*real reality*' is meant, it is untrue that Judgment is always about reality. An erroneous judgment is not strictly about real reality. The formal object may belong to any universe of diction. And *which* it belongs to is what the judgment in real life is testing. We want to know whether what seems real is real, and judge, because we are in doubt about it. Could this be taken as known, knowing would be charmingly simple. We could say 'Knowledge is of objects, and there's an end of it.' But as we

always want to know *which* sort of reality our object has, formal
reality is *never* the object of inquiry. The formally real is taken
for granted. It is at once divided into the unreal and the real,
and each of these is subdivided, until we have found a division
to accommodate the object of our inquiry. Thus the real
meaning, and with it the truth, of a judgment depend on our
placing it in its proper world; and to misplace it falsifies it. E.g.
I may say 'behold a cat,' but if my hearers refer it to the room
they may wrongly contradict me, because my cat may be real
in my mind's eye. Now it is true that the ordinary man assumes
that his senses are trustworthy, that what they perceive may
safely be judged real, and that experience usually bears him out;
but philosophers should not beg questions in this naïvely pragmatic way. They cannot shirk the duty of providing criteria for
discriminating the different sorts of reality. Hence merely to
assert that Judgment refers to reality in some sense is inadequate. Nor can they really plead that their reference is meant
to be purely 'logical' and formal, and that they need not go
into the question how the various sorts of objects are discriminated in reality. For this would be merely to confess that logic
is unwilling, as well as unable, to distinguish between truth and
falsity.

(3) It is vital to keep the reference to reality immanent in
experience and relative to the cognitive process. The real must
not be alien to, and outside, the judging. Else we shall relapse
into the crux about our thought's 'correspondence' with a
transcendent, unknowable, metaphysical reality (Chap. VII,
§ 5). Our reference is merely logical, and is (usually) tested
by perception. A judgment that a house has three storeys is true
if it agrees with what we see.

(4) We ought to realise that the reality which sets us thinking
and to which our judgment refers is initially a *reality-claim*, even
as the 'truth' of the judgment is a truth-claim. It is taken to
be real provisionally, and is real enough to be experimented
with; but its claim may always need testing and may be developed or amended as the inquiry proceeds. Hence what we
took to be our real, the initial real-for-us, may undergo great

transformations, and always emerges from the cognitive operation more or less modified. It is very fallacious, therefore, to lump together under the same title the real as it seemed before, and as it turns out to be after, judging, and to ignore the process and the change. To do so hides from us the efficacy and value of the judging act, and renders its function unintelligible. We must expect, therefore, to find that any theory of the reference to reality in Judgment which fails to be explicit on these four points becomes so vague as to be worthless.

§ 14. Bosanquet's Form of the Reference-to-Reality Theory.

For example, Bosanquet's formal definition of Judgment makes it "the reference of a significant idea to a subject in reality by means of an identity of content between them." [1]

This is a very masterpiece of vagueness. Who can say whether (1) the reference is to an immanent or to a transcendent real and involves a copy theory of truth or not? (2) Is it about the formal object or a physical reality? (3) Is the idea's ' significance' the meaning actually intended in the judgment or merely a potential abstract meaning of the words?

(4) Upon one point, however, Bosanquet seems to commit himself. He clearly takes the identity of content as an already existing given thing and not as the result of a process or act: that is, he interprets the situation in terms of identities, not of *identifications*. In other words, he has a *statical* conception of judging, and this seems to be unequivocally and gravely wrong. For the 'identities of content' are not *pre-existent* to the act of judging, but are made by the judging, which takes the risk of their failing and tests them by the outcome. For example, if I have occasion to judge 'this beast is a dog,' I can certainly be said to 'identify' *ad hoc* 'this' and (my notion of) 'dog'; but I judge because I (or others) have a doubt about it, and the form of my act is no guarantee that I am right. If the animal behaves like other dogs it verifies my assertion, and I *was* right. But if what I called a 'dog' behaves like a jackal, and (say) howls instead of barking, my 'identification' may be wrong.

[1] *Essentials of Logic*, p. 79.

Yet the propositions 'this is a dog' and 'this is a jackal' have the same form: both refer a significant idea to the same sort of reality by identities of content—of which one is false. A historical example will illustrate this further. When the Marcomanni called the lions, let loose on them by the Romans, 'Roman dogs' and disrespectfully slew them, their identification was zoologically false. But it was good for the Marcomanni, true enough for their military purposes, while bad and false for the Romans!

We see, then, that *in a real judgment* identities are not *given*, but *risked*. As we saw in § 11 two things can never be absolutely identical; but they may be treated as identical in a context, where for a purpose we can substitute one for the other and ignore their differences. *When* that is, no Formal Logic, but only experience, can tell us. When an identification succeeds the differences in what we have taken as cases of 'the same' always persist; but they have become irrelevant.[1] By substituting, therefore, *identities* (of what sort not specified) for *identifications* Bosanquet abstracts from the process of thought, slurs over the vital difference between the reality referred to at the beginning and at the end of the thinking, and turns the growth of knowledge into a mystery.

§ 15. Bradley's Form of the Reference-to-Reality Theory.

Although F. H. Bradley and B. Bosanquet professed the same philosophy [2] and were always willing to give each other handsome testimonials, there always remained considerable differences in their doctrines, or at least in their exposition. Being a much bolder thinker, Bradley was not afraid to commit himself, and his expositions have the advantage of much greater clearness. So even where he was wrong he could be seen to be definitely wrong, and was, therefore, much more instructive. His account of the reference to reality in judgment also is much clearer than Bosanquet's, more misleading and more startling. He defines Judgment as "the act which refers an ideal content

---

[1] Cp. *Formal Logic*, chap. x, § 10 ; *Personal Idealism*, pp. 102–3.
[2] For the history of which see *Studies in Humanism*, chap. xii.

(recognised as such) to a reality beyond the act," [1] and soon makes it plain what he means by 'reality.' Instead of leaving it vague and capable of being anything from the formal object (§ 13) to the ultimate reality, he explicitly identifies it with the ultimate reality as a whole, or the Absolute, thus transforming a dull technicality of logic into a highly romantic revelation of metaphysic. This is, of course, calculated to flatter a private person, who learns that even in his most trivial judgments he is pronouncing upon the whole of ultimate reality; but he rarely suspects the abysmal scepticism into which he is thereby plunged.

(1) It conducts straight to the inference that, if so, any judgment about particular reals *must* be false. True, this corollary is a little mitigated by the addition 'more or less,' since error, like truth (from which it becomes indistinguishable), is said to admit of 'degrees.'

(2) Upon reflection it also follows that the whole truth, as it truly is, no man can conceivably enunciate. For if only the whole truth can be wholly true, no judgment that does not sum up omniscience can conceivably be (absolutely) true. Thus Judgment would seem to be discredited rather than explained.

(3) In this general *débâcle* the distinction between true judgments and false disappears. They are confounded together in a common failure.

(4) Indeed the very attempt to judge truly becomes inherently self-refuting. For if the real subject of judgment is the whole of reality, the whole procedure of judgment is radically wrong. It aims at truth by asserting *partial* predicates—a, b, c, etc.—of reality R, knowing that none of these can ever be the whole R. Thus it seeks truth by mutilating reality. Moreover, even if we could predicate R of R we should only arrive at a tautology; and even this would fall short of truth, because we should still in the form of our judgment be asserting a difference between its subject and its predicate which did not exist in the real. [2]

(5) Now, it ought to be recognised as one of the inalienable

---

[1] *Principles of Logic*, [2] p. 10.

[2] Cp. *Appearance and Reality*, chap. xv; and *Essays on Truth and Reality*, p. 239.

resources of logic that, if we do not like the conclusion of an argument, we are entitled not only to question its premisses and to pick what holes we can therein, but also to confute it by the falsity of the consequences it entails. In Bradley's theory of Judgment both are easy. For it has ignored three of the four cautions for which we stipulated in § 13. The real to which it refers all judgments is neither the real for us who made them, nor is it immanent in our experience, nor does it grow and develop in our thinking. The real referred to is indeed specified explicitly, but at the cost of confusing the logical with the meta-physical sense of 'reality.' Moreover, in so doing it is taken as pre-existing the cognitive process and as unaltered by it. Thus an insoluble problem arises as to the 'correspondence' between the changes and vicissitudes of the real-for-us which is involved in the cognitive process and the ultimate reality which is immutable and indifferent to our efforts. In other words, the theory eviscerates all judgments of their human meaning and renders our knowing futile.

(6) We should mention, though we need not enlarge on it, that Bradley's formula, though it rightly calls Judgment an *act*, remains entangled in the obsolete language which regards 'ideal contents' and 'logical ideas' as *things* rather than as *meanings* (cp. § 7). This is an unfortunate relic of the verbal meaning (for words *are* things of a sort), and is traceable to the ever recurring confusion of the judgment with the proposition (cp. § 2).

(7) If *all* judgments refer to the whole of reality they all ultimately mean *the same*, and this is different from what their makers meant when they judged. I.e. their human meaning has evaporated and a monstrosity takes its place. This paradox ought to suffice to dispose of the theory which involves it.

Moreover (8) it would seem to be quite false in fact that our judgments all mean the same or aim at the whole. It would be truer to say they *never* do.[1] Actual judgments always refer only

[1] For even the Judgments which profess the aim of including the whole of reality are, in fact, highly selective, and proceed by excluding vast masses of *data* recalcitrant to the cosmic order arrived at. Hence the paradoxical result that all-inclusive monisms are the most exclusive of all philosophies. Cp. Chap. XV, § 15.

to a *relevant selection from reality*, in which we are interested.
Now this selection may be treated in various ways. It may be
overlooked, as it was by the earlier logicians. It may be concealed, as it is by Bosanquet. It may be disparaged and de-
nounced as a defect, as it is by Bradley. But it should be avowed
and defended. For it is the critical point upon which attention
should be concentrated. It is here that the risk of error and
failure enters our thought, and to ignore it turns the risk of
error into a certainty. Nor can we escape it by professing to repudiate selection. Not even the absolutist philosophers succeed
in avoiding it. What they call the Whole never *is* the whole
(Chap. I, § 15; Chap. V, § 8; Chap. XV, § 12). It is always the
part which *they select* as significant; it never includes what they
dismiss as a μὴ ὄν or a μεταξύ, or an 'error' of an opponent. If
they really tried to include everything in their 'Absolute' they
would turn it into a mere rag-bag long before they had finished.

It is no defect, therefore, that our judgments never attain the
Whole: they would be mad to try to; and if a logician resents
this, what he should dispute is not the 'truth' of Judgment,
but our right to select the relevant (Chap. V, §§ 3, 8).

That Judgment concerns, not the total reality or truth, but
always some relevant *part*, is so obvious that any illustration
makes its denial seem grotesque. If, e.g., we take the judgment
'the black cat has had four kittens in my hat-box' it is plain
to common sense that it does not mean to 'qualify the Absolute' or to add to its very miscellaneous contents. For such
addition is impossible by definition, and the remark is not
meant to be about the Absolute at all. Nor yet did I mean to
declare all I knew. I selected something of interest. And my
meaning can be understood without discussing the metaphysical
place of kittens in the Absolute. It may be that if there is an
Absolute (which merely means, *if our notion of a whole* can be
successfully used upon our experience), it is distantly related
to the kittens: for it has, by definition, to include them along
with everything else. But why drag in these metaphysical considerations? They are utterly irrelevant. They are not what I
meant to tell my hearers, nor what they understood. Moreover,

if they were the only thing worth affirming and the only thing a judgment is capable of affirming, it would be a purely verbal 'truth'; for if the whole tale were a lie, it would still remain as true as ever that all kittens and all hat-boxes are *in* the 'universe.' But this platitude was not what I meant to assert. The meaning and the truth-or-falsity of my judgment had reference to the selected part of the whole which was in the focus of interest, and asserted *that*. Thus it seems to be a plain matter of fact that reference to reality is always (1) specific and selective, and (2) to the relevant part, and *not* to the whole, even of what is before the mind.

§ 16. The Source of Bradley's Errors.

It is not credible, of course, that a thinker of Bradley's capacity should have adopted so amazing a doctrine out of sheer perversity, and there is reason to believe that he was troubled all his life by its sceptical outcome. But he appears to have been led astray, and forced into it, by two mistakes.

(1) The first was his failure to appreciate the function of selection in thought. He had, indeed, perceived from the first that actual thinking always selects;[1] but, unfortunately, he conceived selection as a vitiating agency that 'mutilated' reality [2] and led to falsity.[3] He cannot, however, make up his mind whether this selectiveness of thought is a forced choice due to the mind's 'impotence,' or an 'arbitrary' interference with reality. So at times he is sufficiently under the influence of sensationalism to conceive the judgment situation as a matter of the recognition of *data* given by 'sensation,' without perceiving that the organism's activity really turns all such '*data*' into *sumpta*, and to declare "Do what we will, we cannot take up every single detail of the sensuous mass. We must neglect something; but the dropping of part is the forced selection of the part which remains. Hence we have used compulsory and unwilling abstraction."[4] At other times he declares, "We sunder and divide what appears to us as a sensible whole. It is never

---

[1] E.g. *Principles of Logic*,[2] pp. 108, 114, 485.
[2] *Loc. cit.*, p. 586.   [3] *Loc. cit.*, p. 94.   [4] *Loc. cit.*, p. 477.

more than an arbitrary selection which goes into the judgment,"[1] and asks indignantly, "on what principle do you claim the right of selecting what you please from the presented whole and treating that fragment as an actual quality?"[2]

In the final edition of his *Logic* he upholds his original doctrine, but with less confidence and with a more candid avowal of its difficulties.[3] "Judgment is on the one side selective, ideal, and abstract, while on the other side it is conditioned by that reality which in a sense it fails to include. Hence all judgment is mediated, essentially, though not explicitly. . . . All judgment is of Reality, and that means it makes its idea the adjective[4] of the real Universe. Now it is possible to take the reality, so referred to, as being Reality merely at large and without distinction. The result which follows is that the whole ideal content affirmed tends to fall outside the Reality, which on its side tends in consequence to fade into an empty abstraction." But "in judgment the Reality to which in fact we refer is always something distinguished. It is Reality, as our whole world, but, at the same time and none the less, it is also *this* reality. It is a limited aspect and portion of the Universe." So "reality as the subject of our judgment is always a selected reality," and "all judgment implies and depends on a selection made in Reality. . . This selection further is assumed and is not justified in our judgment; and it never in any judgment can be fully justified or even recognised completely. . . . On the one side it asserts really of the whole Universe. . . . On the other side a total affirmation of the mere whole would itself be nothing. And so judgment, being forced to distinguish and select, is compelled to leave out that which in reality it must include. . . ." It is "about an object. Now an object is not the whole of Reality as that at some moment is experienced immediately. The object omits and ignores whatever in that total experience falls outside its selection." So "this twofold nature of Reality, by which it slides away from itself into our distinction, so as there to

---

[1] *Loc. cit.*, p. 94.   [2] *Loc. cit.*, p. 97.
[3] *Loc. cit.*, *Terminal Essay*, ii, pp. 628–32.
[4] A term which betrays the *verbal* inspiration of the doctrine !

become a predicate, while all the time it retains in itself, as an ultimate subject, every quality which we loosen and relate to it, is, if you please, inexplicable." But it is "a fundamental fact."

Even the most rationalistic of philosophers is always willing to recognise a final inexplicability when a pet theory has broken down! In these passages Bradley very handsomely admits that he cannot escape from selection; but he still sees in the process nothing but a form of compulsion and a source of inadequacy and failure. It does not occur to him that our selection may be intentional and rational and justified by the need for relevance. So he will not concede that we have a *right* to select, and may select with full consciousness, a good conscience, and complete success.

(2) The grounds for Bradley's second mistake are not so easy to expound in his own words, because he does not seem to have been fully conscious of them himself. He was always troubled by the thought that a Judgment "cannot stand by itself." [1] But instead of inferring that, therefore, any real judgment must be supplied with a *context*, he continues, "Asserting, as it does, of the particular presentation, it must always suppose a further content, which falls outside that fraction it affirms. What it says is true, if true at all, because of something else. The fact it states is really fact only in relation to the rest of the context, and only because of the rest of that context. It is not true except under that condition.[2] So we have a judgment [*sic*] which is really conditioned, and which is false if you take it as categorical. To make it both categorical and true, you must get the condition inside the judgment. You must take up the given as it really appears, without omission, unaltered, and unmutilated.[3] And this is impossible." [4] In his revision he adds,[5] "With every judgment we fail more or less to include its conditions within itself, and, with every judgment in the end, we do not and cannot completely know what the entire conditions are." (Is it not enough to know the *relevant* conditions?) He infers that "the more the conditions of the judgment are, or can

---

[1] *Loc. cit.*, p. 97.
[2] If it is true in *its* context, why should it be more ?
[3] Why ?　　　　　　[4] *Loc. cit.*, p. 98.　　　　　　[5] *Loc. cit.*, p. 639.

be, included in the judgment, the truer and more real, the less
condition*al* and the more condition*ed* does that judgment
become." Such is the dilemma which forces Bradley to vindicate a judgment by inflating it into total reality.

Now the tacit assumption underlying his argument is that
every 'judgment,' to maintain its truth-claim, must be eternal,
i.e. able at all times to uphold its *verbal integrity* against change
in the real or growth in knowledge that threatens to put it out
of date. But is this demand made in the interest of the judgment or of the proposition? 'It is impossible to fly' was not
true, according to Bradley, a hundred years ago, because aero-
planes have been invented since. It follows that nothing can be
absolutely true unless it can get a guarantee from the totality
of reality, and that every truth is liable to be upset until it has
taken refuge in the bosom of the Absolute. The fact that there
individual truths cease to be altogether or are so transmuted
that their authors could not recognise them, Bradley is pleased
to overlook. Nor does it strike him that in his search for a
'judgment' that shall be indisputable and irrefutable, not in
virtue of its context, but in virtue of its *form*, he loses sight of
the real judgment altogether and is trying to vindicate a mere
proposition. For clearly a hundred years ago, when flying was
declared impossible, the judgment stated the truth. *Now* a
judgment made in the same terms has become false, for reasons
which can be stated. But the two *judgments* are different,
though they find verbal expression in the same proposition.

Thus the whole Bradleyan theory of Judgment, with all its
tremendous implications, would seem to spring, in ultimate
analysis, from a confusion of judgment and proposition (cp. § 2).
So far-reaching and fatal are the consequences of this insidious
error.[1] But it would have been easy to avoid it if it had been
recognised that the selectiveness of Judgment is merely a case
of the selectiveness of life in general, and that a logic which
disregards the psychological distinction between judgments and
propositions is sure to fall a prey to grammar.

[1] Cp. also F. C. S. Schiller, " The Origin of Bradley's Scepticism,"
in *Mind*, No. 134 (April 1925).

CHAPTER XII

FROM JUDGMENT TO INFERENCE

1. Why no proposition can be always true ; 2. But judgments may be true enough ; 3. The Myth of self-developing thought ; 4. Trains of Thought ; 5. Inference not as such superior to judgment ; 6. Is judgment potential inference ?

§ 1. Why no Proposition can be always True.

We saw at the end of the last chapter (§ 15) what a metaphysical invasion could be let loose on logic by turning the judgment into a proposition and then inquiring into the conditions under which it could be declared 'absolutely' true, so that it would hold literally and *totidem verbis*, in all contexts, uses, and senses. It was fortunate that Bradley's attempt failed on its own showing, because, so far from validating particular truths, total Reality turned out to be 'supra-relational' and absorbed and annihilated all relational forms.

But even if the Absolute had not turned out to be such a ruthless monster, there would have been good logical reasons for the futility of looking for any form of words (proposition) capable of being 'always true' in all senses, contexts, and circumstances. For all forms of words are meant for use, and get their (actual) meaning and truth from their applications. What can be used, however, can also be *mis*used; and so all propositions, when misapplied and misused, are capable of giving birth to *false* or unmeaning judgments. This holds also of the arithmetical 'truths' to which intellectualists cling as the last refuge for the belief in absolute truth. It is quite easy to apply them to objects which do not behave like the ideal units postulated by arithmetic, and consequently falsify the arithmetical inferences it is sought to draw : hence a man who gets two drops of water added to two others to make four may consider himself very skilful or lucky.

§ 2. But Judgments may be True enough.

Fortunately, however, nothing so fantastic as 'absolute' truth is required of judgments in actual thinking. A judgment is true enough for the purposes of human knowing if it is true in its context, and is an adequate response to the situation out of which it arises and with which it is meant to deal. Its adequacy or inadequacy, its success or failure, is never a matter of form, but always a matter of fact. It depends on its consequences, on its 'working.'

Fully to appreciate a judgment's meaning and value, therefore, we must be aware of its context and must ascertain both its antecedents and its consequences. Its antecedents have been described in general terms as a problematic situation in which action upon impulse has been inhibited and reflection has been summoned up in order to improve the reaction; whereupon, after due analysis, comparison, questioning, deliberation, and partial testing, a judgment has been chosen as the best available, and launched upon the world.

This conclusion may be the end of the immediate problem, and may 'settle the question,' though it should be remembered that the truth-claim of the judgment undergoes further testing so long as it and its objects continue to figure in any actual thinking. But the end of a problem is not, therefore, the end of life: life goes on and may always generate fresh problems and incite to further thinking. The actual judgment also may have an intellectual career: it may become an object of further thought, and be debated, verified, modified, and amended, by new thinkers to whose situations it seems relevant. Thus, though it was for the time being a solution of the original problem, it may generate fresh problems and suggest further solutions: we may be stimulated by it to further thinking and driven on beyond it to further judgments. For this situation the logical name is *Inference*.

§ 3. The Myth of Self-developing Thought.

But this account of the genesis of Inference is much too simple and prosaic for Hegelising logicians. They demand a romance of Pure Thought in the Supra-sensible World. So they first kill the real judgment by taking it out of its human context, and then set themselves to revive it magically by the enchantments

of their 'Dialectic.' There is instilled into the form of the
defunct judgment a sort of impersonal non-natural semblance
of life, in virtue of which the lower 'forms of judgment' are
seen spontaneously to sprout into the higher, and finally to
blossom into inference. There is attributed to Thought (which
must, of course, be dignified with capitals!) an inherent pro-
gression, *nisus*, or movement, which raises it from the humility
of the Impersonal through the Demonstrative (in Bradley,
Analytic of Sense), the Universal, the Hypothetical, to the
eminence of the Disjunctive Judgment. This last is said to
imply a System of related 'judgments,' and trembles on the
verge of Inference. Finally, the apocalyptic vision culmin-
ates when the Absolute Thought reveals itself as the Perfect
Syllogism!

The whole of this Myth, however, is a creature of illusion and
idolatry. The hierarchical procession of empty forms is an
artificial fiction: it is made to seem necessary only because the
natural connexion of events in a cognitive situation, the problem-
judgment-verifying-consequences sequence has been ignored,
and the real forces which animate a train of thought are abstracted from. The forms of judgment do not move *per se* nor
develop from one into another of their own accord. Neither
have they meaning and value in the abstract. To come into
actual being, they must be *used*. They pass into use when some
one is found to adopt them as suitable for his purposes. And
then they live and move and have their being, not in a supercelestial Void, nor even in a terrestrial treatise on Logic, but in
a fully concrete train of thought passing through a particular
human mind endowed with interests, purposes, feelings, prejudices, etc. on some particular occasion. Thus the maker of
thought is always man, who animates the abstract forms with
his personality: he remains the master, engineer, and driver of
his trains of thought, unless he abdicates his proper function
of intelligent direction. The concrete actual thought is thus
always an activity initiated for the sake of ends and controlled
by these: *they* determine the employment of every form of
judgment that is used. Hence any account of thought which

obliterates its teleological and personal character is a sheer
fiction, which substitutes mythology for psychical fact. It is
also a harmful fiction, because it distracts attention from the
real character of a train of thought.

§ 4. Trains of Thought.

A train of thought naturally starts from a situation in which
(1) action is not pressing, and there is abundant time for reflection; (2) we cannot think of any single judgment adequate
enough to 'settle the question.' We then have to content ourselves with a preliminary instalment, with a judgment that will,
we think, take us part of the way and be a step towards our goal,
though it will not bring it within our reach. This judgment
becomes, of course, itself a factor in the next situation which
will issue in a second judgment, and so on, until our goal is
reached or our interest is exhausted.

It is evident from this that trains of thought are very personal
affairs. It depends very much on the idiosyncrasies of the
persons who conduct them how long they go on for, how far
they get, and of how much accepted truth they become the
vehicles. There are those who can never stop thinking, and likewise those whom nothing can induce to think. Speaking collectively, however, the amounts and sorts of thinking that go
on depend ultimately on the organisation and demands of social
life. In primitive societies trains of thought had probably to
be short and rare; but the conditions of civilised life enable
them to be drawn out to great length in certain cases; indeed,
a few specialists whom society for various reasons (good, bad,
and indifferent) sets apart for the cultivation of the 'contemplative' life can afford to think all the time, and sometimes
get to like it.

They should not, however, be allowed to grow conceited on
this account. For, *pace* Aristotle, perpetual thinking is not intrinsically a better pursuit than action, nor is it necessarily a
proof of a superior mind to take ten times longer in thinking
over a problem than another fellow. A life devoted to thought,
therefore, need not *ipso facto* be the best. It need not even be

16

admirable, if the objects thought about were trivial or useless. Thus it would be possible to spend one's whole life in calculating the value of π to n points of decimals, and, if a sufficient endowment were forthcoming to support the professorial dignity, men of the professorial type could doubtless be found to undertake this job. It would, however, be interesting to observe how long the π professor could endure his work without going off his head and having recourse either to murder or to suicide. Very likely he would not last at it so long as the expert in fabricating the hundredth part of a pin, whose labour would be hardly more mechanical.[1]

§ 5. Inference not as such Superior to Judgment.

Thinking, then, is not naturally an end in itself, though, like everything else, it can become one under favourable circumstances. Still less is judging, and least of all a train of judgments. Nor are any of these processes good in themselves. The ideal thing (Beatific Vision) in every inquiry would be, if under all the circumstances of life we could immediately and instantly perceive the entire meaning and significance of every situation, and could safely act upon it and thereby attain our end. But it is but rarely that we find ourselves in a situation so diaphanous that we at once know what to do. We must often fall back upon the next best thing. This is first to think, then to judge, and finally to act. But even so much expedition is often inexpedient, and we must then approach our end by a still longer route. So we pass from judgment to judgment, interpolating middle terms and mediating between our first judgment and our last. This is acknowledged inference; but there is nothing in it but aims at action in the end.

It is clear, then, that the transition to inference is not as such a promotion of judgment to a higher rank. It is to be conceived rather as an increased delay before action. In itself it is better,

---

[1] This example should be understood as a parable, though under the conditions of academic life not a little of the pursuit of 'pure' knowledge and 'learning' approximates in character and value to this imaginary case.

because more expeditious, to solve our problem, to attain our end, by judgment rather than by inference, and by perception rather than by judgment. Neither are the 'higher' forms in the Hegelian hierarchy any better than the 'lower.' Their value in all cases depends upon their usefulness, and there would be nothing wrong or intellectually contemptible in never using any but 'particular' judgments at all. Indeed, it may be argued that this is what, in fact, we do in actual thinking. For, to acquire actual meaning, every 'form of judgment' must be used, and used in a particular context upon an actual case. Hence *in their application* all judgments, of whatever 'form,' would appear to be particular, and the different degrees of 'universality,' of which so much has been made, would merely exist in the *unapplied* form, i.e. be purely *verbal*.

What, then, would be the truth about the hierarchy of forms? Merely that language has been more or less shaped to reflect the commoner uses of words and to recognise situations which have become familiar in more or less stereotyped phrases. Thus we can see that the so-called 'particular judgment' is a form for dealing with the behaviour of 'things,' while the impersonal ('it rains,' etc.) is adapted to situations in which it is not possible or desirable to attach our predicate to any speci-fied portion of the real. The 'universal judgment' is essentially an instrument of prediction, like the postulation of 'laws of nature.' It is, however, unfortunate that it beguiles the un-critical into taking it as an absolute guarantee of the future, and does not emphasise the saving clause, *rebus sic stantibus*, which is always implied, nor draw attention to the inevitable risks of prediction. A really enlightened and candid logic ought to warn us that when we make such declarations as 'all men are mortal,' or 'no men can fly,' we are always speaking in the light of actual knowledge, and are *not* presuming to deny that means may be found some day for arresting the physiological senes-cence of the body and training it to repair itself indefinitely. If such a discovery were made, it would, of course, cease to be true in the old sense (or senses) that all men were 'mortal,' and the *dictum* would either have to be scrapped or to change its meaning, like 'no men can fly.' The 'hypothetical judgment' is of value as bringing out the experimental character of all our knowledge, though it hardly does this with all the clearness desirable. Similarly the 'disjunctive judgment' should call more attention than, it is to be feared, it usually does to the existence of alternatives and to the importance and need of choosing *rightly* between them. Both these forms, moreover, affirming as they do the reality of *ifs* and *either-ors*, should be seen to be radically incompatible with the principle of determinism, and should induce the logician to warn the scientist that he must not regard and use determinism as more than a methodological principle, enabling him to calculate and predict the behaviour of statistical averages and of such things as have established habits. In short, the meaning and value of all the miscalled 'Forms of Judgment' are relative to their use, and their use depends on the exigencies of a problematic situation in real life, and not on any intrinsic relationship between the abstract forms.

§ 6. Is Judgment Potential Inference?

May we, in the light of these facts, continue to say that all judgment is potential inference? It seems a gratuitous perversity in estimating the functions of judgment, a strange distortion of simple facts, and a revealing display of intellectualistic bias to put this valuation on the transition from judgment to inference. If it is desired to call judgment a potential anything, why not call it a potential act? For that would at least remind us of the destination and ultimate aim of judgment and inference alike. But it is still simpler to explain plainly under what conditions, and for what reasons, a judgment may need support, and may obtain the support of other judgments, and so develop into an inference.

It is clear in the first place that a judgment will not need support if it really settles the question which it answers. It will require support only if its truth-claim is not accepted, or is not accepted as final. Hence we are not entitled to say that every judgment *must* become an inference, but only that it *may*; it can be turned into an inference *if necessary* (i.e. needed). A judgment has not to be bolstered up by inference if it is sufficiently decisive, if it suffices to guide an action which may be embarked on there and then: it is, moreover, none the worse if it never grows into an inference. Secondly, if a judgment is questioned and needs support, we may strengthen it in two quite distinct ways. We may either adduce considerations, likely to be accepted, from which it will naturally follow; or we may develop it further, and observe what further 'truths' (truth-claims) seem naturally to follow from it. In the one case it will itself become the conclusion (logically) of a train of thought; in the other, the starting-point of such a train: thought in the one case will be *retrograde*, falling back from a contested truth-claim upon others not in dispute, in the other it will be *progressive*, advancing to consequences which will confirm the original judgment. In logical language it will become either a 'conclusion' drawn from 'premisses' which back it, or a premiss leading to further conclusions which 'verify' it.

But it is no special merit in a judgment that it should start a train of thought. On the contrary it is a clear gain if it does not, if, that is, we can reach the right response to a situation by judgment without inference, just as it is a gain if we can act on perception without judgment. For each substitution of a quicker and less mediate process for a slower and more circuitous is a facilitation of mental life and conduces to greater efficiency.

Moreover, it should not escape notice that in one very important respect the simple categorical judgment is in a stronger position than a syllogistically demonstrated conclusion. It implies more certainty and greater confidence in its truth-claim. It stands on its own feet, unsupported, no doubt; but it *needs* no extraneous support, being unassailed and undoubted. If, therefore, it is doubted it collapses; it loses its self-sufficiency and has at once to appeal to the support of premisses whence it may be deduced. This is the real reason why a judgment is always liable to become an inference.

Thus we see that inference implies loss of self-evidence, incapacity for self-support, corrosion and corruption by doubt, and a transformation of factual into 'necessary' truth. But necessary truth is not a stronger and more assured form of truth: a necessary truth is one that has not been able to maintain itself without help, and so has become *dependent* on the premisses from which it follows. This is why an elaborate argument that a thing *must* be is so often far less forcible than a simple statement that it *is*, which has not been sicklied over with subtleties of thought. It is regrettable that our traditional logic should have been so fascinated by the forms of speech, and should consider thought-processes in such abstraction from their actual context and function, that it should not have noticed what makeshifts thinking and inferring often are, and how gladly we do without them whenever we can attain our ends by immediate perception and direct action.

CHAPTER XIII

INFERENCE IN GENERAL

1. The importance of inference ; 2. The psychological genesis of inference ;
3. The genesis of formal inference ; 4. The fictions of formal inference ; 5.
Logical necessity ; 6. Formal validity ; 7. The formal fictions needless, useless, and harmful ; 8. Are forms of inference worthless ? ; 9. The general
validity of inference ; 10. Inference and judgment.

§ 1. The Importance of Inference.

It is in the treatment of Inference that the technicalities of
Logic culminate and fill the Formal logician with pride in the
achievements of his profession. It is here also that he begins to
reveal the hidden ambitions which inspired his industry, to
advance his claim to control the exercise of thought and to
coerce thinkers by his forms of valid reasoning, and his pretensions to dominion over all the products of thought. Accordingly
he assures us that with Inference we enter into the realm of
incontrovertible Necessity, of which he is himself the sole law-
giver, and declares that "a necessary truth is really an inference,
and an inference is nothing but a necessary truth." [1] After this
he proceeds to revel in 'valid inferences' and 'cogent proofs,'
and to lay down the law to thought.

These pretensions, however, demand the most careful
scrutiny. The conceptions of 'logical necessity' and 'valid
inference' cry out for examination, and Logic must not be
allowed to forget that Psychology also should have something
to say about the ways of inference. Logical inference is, in fact,
always rooted in psychological soil, and derives its impetus from
psychological forces. Properly speaking, therefore, 'logical
inference' should be merely that sort of psychological inference which has the good fortune to meet with the logician's
notice and approbation, though actually it is developed into the
chief instrument of his will to power.

Hence a comprehensive view of Inference must set itself to
show not only how inferences naturally occur in trains of

---

[1] F. H. Bradley, *Logic*, p. 236.

thought, but also how the Formal logician, viewing them with his peculiar preconceptions, fabricates out of them the 'logical' and 'valid' inference he deals in, and is enabled to propound an *alternative* account of the course of thought. The psychological and the 'logical' (i.e. Formal) treatments of Inference must therefore be distinguished sharply.

§ 2. The Psychological Genesis of Inference.

Speaking generally, we may say that in real life when a judgment does not at once lead to action it leads to inference. In other words, it leads us on to the next judgment. Hence *any* passage of thought from one judgment to another is, *psychologically*, inference. The question of logical value, of whether any inference is 'good' or 'bad,' is an ulterior one which need not be entertained until we ask what we infer for and what may be done with our inference; it should not affect our recognition of the inferences that are actually drawn.

In human trains of thought Inference occurs for two good reasons: (1) because a judgment has been a failure, and has proved inadequate to a cognitive situation; (2) because it has been such a success that we desire to go on with it and to 'pursue the subject.' Thus, if it is a failure, it has to be backed, if it is a success, to be extended, by others. With these associates it joins up or tends to 'cohere.' This coherence of judgments is primarily a psychological fact, like any other, though it is exploited by a certain logical theory (cp. Chap. VII, §§ 13, 14). As the result of this psychological coherence trains of thought are started in various minds which are purposive teleological processes, and go on till they attain their end, or are definitely defeated and blocked. Calling them purposive means that it is always the reasoner's purpose which selects the materials for his 'system of thought,' holds it together, frames his inference, and directs it either to further inferences or to its application.

Such trains of thought, moreover, are definitely *personal* in character. Their course is determined by the extant *interests* of the mind which conducts them, by its past history, aims, and abilities. Consequently it is found that the inferences men actually draw from any situation vary with their interests; it is only if and when a situation arouses practically the same interests in a number of men, and they start similar trains of thought in consequence, that their inferences will agree, and only if their interests are *known*, that their inferences can be anticipated.

The *value*, similarly, of an inference is relative to its place in the train of thought which generates it. It is good if it conduces to the purpose aimed at, 'bad' if it fails to do so. But, primarily, all *bona fide* inferences (and judgments) are good. They seem 'good' when made, to their makers; else they would not have been made. Nor are they declared 'bad,' either by others or by their makers, until they have turned out badly.

But this primary 'goodness' also is so far psychological; it is a personal conviction springing from its maker's whole personality, and varies accordingly. Hence some inferences are, in fact, better than others—because they are *better born*. They had better makers and a nobler purpose, and were used to more effect. And it is often hard to decide which of several inferences that are equally thinkable it is better to make in a given situation —just because so much depends on the personal capacity of the parties concerned—on their insight, and on the amplitude, energy, and direction of their trains of thought. So the mountain landscape which moves a poet or a painter to an ecstasy of admiration will excite nothing but disgust and condemnation in a prosaic farmer intent on looking for arable land.

But whatever the motives and idiosyncrasies that have led to the making of an inference, its claim to value has to be confirmed by its working. Whether an inference which claims to be good *really is* good is never apparent: its claim has to be tested and verified like any other truth-claim. Thus its real goodness or badness is not determined by its origin, but by the consequences in which it issues and by the whole train of thought and context in which it occurs: it is not a formal quality anyone may perceive by simple inspection of the words employed. The real goodness or badness of an inference, then, is not a primary but a secondary quality, which is established by the testing of its truth-claim.

Having thus traced both the occurrence and the value of every inference to a personal train of thought and to the re-action of a human mind to a vital situation or 'predicament,' have we not completed the material history of Inference? What need is there to superimpose on it any further account in the name of Logic, to fabricate a fictitious scheme of 'logical relations,' and to concatenate artificially sequences of judgments which already cohere naturally? Has not the whole Formal conception of Inference become unreal and superfluous?

§ 3. The Genesis of Formal Inference.

It is evident that Formal Logic cannot welcome such questions which threaten to put it out of business. Nevertheless, when it catches a glimpse of them, which it by no means always does, it does its best to shirk them ; for it has difficulties in formulating a notion of Inference that will pass muster, even in its own eyes. But it is so instructive to observe how the notion of a 'logical' inference, 'valid' in virtue of its form, is generated and used that no apology is needed for a short study of the process.

Of course, the first thing to do is to substitute the proposition for the judgment and thus to sever 'logic' from psychology. By this trick the actual context of the inference, its meaning and its use are abstracted from, and the result is hailed as an enormous simplification and economy of thought. 'Logic' can henceforth spare itself the laborious empirical inquiry into the real meaning, purpose, use, value, and success of the actual reasoning, and confine itself to a compendious form of words that can be taken as self-existent and self-sufficient.

The next step is to consider, quite abstractly, how this form may be related to other similar propositions, giving a preference to those which can be described as standing in relations of logical necessity to each other: these are termed 'logical' *par excellence*, and such transitions are called 'valid inferences.'

The whole process, however, of determining what are the

relations between two propositions, and whether the inference from one to the other is 'necessary' and 'valid,' is purely verbal. It presupposes no knowledge but that of the verbal conventions known as 'the Laws of Thought,' and assumes merely that the (verbal) meanings of the terms of the proposition are known and fixed and that the 'law of Identity' makes it self-evident that any 'A' is A (cp. § 5). Assuming this interpretation, any inference can be adequately expressed in symbolical terms and a 'valid' reasoning will take the syllogistic form *All M is P, all S is M, therefore all S is P*.

Now the 'validity' of this form evidently rests on the soundness of the assumption that the identity of each term is unaffected by the different relations in which each stands in the two propositions in which it occurs. For if M in-relation-to-P differed relevantly from M in-relation-to-S, the middle term would become 'ambiguous,' and the syllogism would get four terms and would break in two. This liability of the middle term to ambiguity in use is a very real difficulty in actual reasoning, and a fatal objection to the belief in formal validity (cp. § 6); moreover, theoretically, similar ambiguities may vitiate the major and the minor terms as well (cp. § 5).

From the notion of a 'necessary' and 'valid' transition from one judgment (i.e. proposition) to another it is easy to arrive at a system of judgments or logical system which can be conceived as cohering, not like the actual judgments in a purposive train of thought, but *per se*, and in virtue of the 'logical' (i.e. verbal) relations between its parts. Thus the psychological coherence of the actual trains of thought, held together in the reasoner's mind by his purpose and his interests, can be superseded by a 'logical' coherence not dependent on any mind, and self-existent logical systems can come into being and cohere with the other fictions of Formal Logic.

§ 4. The Fictions of Formal Inference.

This whole system of fictions, however, has no real justification, and is open to criticism on many grounds. It may easily be shown to be (1) false, (2) needless, (3) useless, and (4) harmful.

(1) Falsity is not, of course, a charge which need be as such fatal to a fiction. For a fiction is precisely an assumption which is known to be false in some respect, though this does not impair, and may even enhance its usefulness. For example, the whole use of mathematics depends on our applying to physical entities the ideal properties of Euclidean space and the 'laws' of common arithmetic, and making the needful corrections when our fictions break down. But it is often overlooked that false assumptions must be recognised as such, and must prove themselves useful, before they can rank as *scientific* fictions; now it is just in these respects that the assumptions of Formal Logic fail. They are deceptive, because logicians are not usually conscious of their falsity; and harmful, because they hide from us the real nature of inference, and hinder the adoption of truer and more useful accounts of this process. The notions of *logical necessity* and *valid inference*, therefore, are worthy of condemnation, not because they are fictions, but because they are *bad* fictions.

§ 5. Logical Necessity.

Of the two great fictions of Formal Logic, the first, 'necessity,' has already had its pretensions to yield a theory of truth criticised in Chap. VII, §§ 4–6. It was there shown that a train of thought is not a series of forced moves; it is not compacted by force so much as by purposive striving and vital need: it is not driven on by a *vis a tergo* from behind, but drawn on by the lure of some desired end, to which its various stages are conceived as means. Psychologically speaking, therefore, it seems plain that a train of thought is a teleological proceeding, nor is there any visible reason why the actual inferences which occur in, and form part of, a train of thought should not be conceived as actuated in this obvious and purposive manner. If, then, the actual connexion of thoughts is psychological and teleological, what need is there to allege any further influence, under the name of 'logical necessity,' to hold together a train of thought that already coheres naturally, and to direct *ab extra* a course already animated by its inherent purpose?

Moreover, the notion of 'logical necessity' appears to be not only superfluous but also ambiguous, like that of 'necessity' in general. Philosophic language is confused by at least five distinct, and often antagonistic, senses of 'necessity,'[1] of which no less than three can take cover under the phrase 'logical necessity.'

(1) There is, in the first place, the teleological necessity which has already been mentioned. In this sense the logically necessary is what is *needed* to carry an argument successfully to the conclusion it aimed at. This is quite the most sensible of the senses of 'necessity,' but, in 'logic,' the rarest. It is *personal*, and implies alternatives. For the reasoner who pursues an end has to choose his means; this leaves him free to choose any means that seem to him suitable, and imposes on him the duty of discerning the *best*. But he may be said to be *compelled* to choose *suitable* means.

(2) There is a common sense in which inference is said to be necessary when the premisses have been chosen, and, *after the inference is drawn*, there appears to be no alternative to it. Thus in the syllogism, when the premisses, *All M is P*, *All S is M*, have been assembled, the conclusion *All S is P* is 'necessary.' This necessity, since it inheres in the form of the argument without reference to its purpose, is *impersonal*. But it is important to note that this sort of necessity does not (*a*) exist before the inference is drawn nor while it is proceeding, nor (*b*) does it at first exclude alternatives. If we start with the proposition *all M is P*, and judge it, we are not *compelled* to go on *all S is M*, and so we need not finish up with the syllogistic conclusion. We are free to branch off in any direction and to go on with *all P is Q*, or *all P is M*, and even if we choose to restrict ourselves to 'formally valid' inferences we can say *therefore some P is M*, which is reputed 'valid,' as an 'immediate' inference. No 'logical necessity' appears until we have decided to say *all S is M*; so its emergence does not really mean that we had no alternative *before* we so decided. Indeed, there is, theoretically, an infinity of alternatives open to one

[1] Cp. *Personal Idealism*, p. 70, *n*.

who starts from the proposition *all M is P,* and he is not compelled to adopt the one he prefers. Thus he may stop thinking,
and act at once. He may 'suspend judgment' and do nothing.
He may embark upon an infinity of probable and plausible
trains of thought leading him in any direction he pleases. Or,
again, he may start conscientious scruples about the truth of
his starting-point, and pry into its grounds—back to infinity.
And finally, even if he chooses to restrict himself to 'logically
necessary' inferences, he can exercise his choice even among
these. Without his aid none of the logical possibilities can become actual, and the 'must' of this 'logical inference' should
clearly be distinguished from compulsion.

(3) There is, however, supposed to be a 'logical necessity'
which is really coercive, and admits of no alternatives. But the
evidence for its existence is not good. It is usually exemplified
by the necessity of the conclusion of a formally valid syllogism
(and of other valid forms), and by truisms like 'everything is
identical with itself,' 'A cannot be B and not B,' 'it must
have happened or not,' etc., which are supposed to be important contributions to our logical enlightenment.

To the former sorts of illustration it seems fair to retort that
they are wisdom after the event, which was not available while
the inference was actually in progress and the issue was in
doubt. And surely the fact that when we have made our choice
the alternatives disappear is no proof that they did not exist
before. As for the truisms which Formalism has exalted into
'laws' of thought, they are pathetically inapplicable to actual
thinking. The Law of Identity is impotent to tell us how much
a thing may change and yet 'remain the same.' The Law of
Contradiction cannot say how quickly A may transform itself
from B into not-B without insulting its majesty; and the Law
of Excluded Middle, for all its insistence that an event must
have happened in one way or the other, is no help to a historian
struggling with two suspect versions of the same events.

The truth is, that this sense of 'logical necessity' is merely
a confusion. *Ex post facto* necessity is a formal characteristic
of certain types of inference which relates them to their ante-

cedents and distinguishes them from other inferences. But it
has nothing to do with the incentives to an inference and its real
genesis. It follows ('necessarily') from the assumptions of
Formal Logic—that is to say, it unavoidably arises if we choose
to adopt them; but we may venture to suggest that in ultimate
analysis it is *essentially verbal*, and expresses merely a convention about the use of words in propositions which has
commended itself to Formal Logic.

Formal Logic begins, as usual, by substituting the proposition for the judgment. It then analyses out its 'terms' and
fixes them. Thereupon, it accepts the identity of the terms
(i.e. of the *words*) as guaranteeing the real and effective identity
of the situations to which the terms are applied. Thus it rests
on the assumption that in thinking we may safely pass from one
context to another if we can establish a common term between
them; that is, if we can find a *word* to act as a bridge. Words
are taken as 'symbols,' i.e. as possessing the valuable property
of preserving their 'identity,' i.e. the same inherent and unchanging meaning, in their various uses. It is then argued that,
if we have the same words, we manifestly have a guarantee of
an identity of behaviour in the objects demonstrated that will
carry conviction and justify prediction.

This assumption of the *fixity of meanings* is derived, very
simply, from the identity of form in words and symbols; it
is ultimately deducible from the 'Law of Identity,' which is
taken as a self-evident and indisputable law of thought. Its
usual formulation, *A is A*, is meaningless; but its actual use is
to justify the assumption that '*A*' *is A*—an assumption which
is always disputable and frequently false.

It can hardly, therefore, be contended seriously that the
assumptions underlying Formal necessity are actually true;
they can hardly be more than 'fictions.' But as such they are
very convenient for Formal Logic. They enable it to keep
silent about the effects of transporting a term from one context
to another, to shirk the whole problem of the relativity of meaning to context, and to burke the awkward questions whether the
'A' it relies on is *rightly* so termed, and whether the change in

its context has not in this case produced a relevant change in its meaning. If the question were raised, it might even be seen to be impossible that a principle should be indisputable *in its application*; but if we abstain from raising it, it will seem undesirable to assume that wherever the terms used in an argument are correctly named and the change of context does not make any relevant difference, successful predictions can be made in virtue of the logical form alone. The syllogism is the stock example. *If all men are mortal*, and *Socrates is a man*, it necessarily follows that *Socrates is mortal*, and the Formal logician also ranks among the prophets!

Or shall it be suggested that he is a false prophet and his prediction is illusory? He has at any rate relied wholly on verbal identities, and committed a number of subreptions and juggles with ambiguous terms. In his major premiss 'mortal' is indeterminate; it may, nay must, mean 'liable to die,' 'doomed to die,' and 'dead,' and any attempt to give it a single or precise meaning is fatal to the argument's 'validity.' In his minor premiss 'man' plainly includes 'dead man'; for that is what *Socrates* has been for a good 2000 years. Permitting this, the conclusion proves that the dead man, Socrates, is 'mortal,' in the sense of 'dead'; or, more briefly, that a dead 'man' is dead. Could anything be more fatuous than this inexorable 'logical necessity'?

If, on the other hand, a *living* man is chosen to illustrate its cogency, the syllogism passes from indisputable platitude to perilous prediction. It undertakes to prove that, because in the past all men have died (except those still alive), all men in the future will die. Here 'mortal' seems mostly to mean 'doomed to die.' But what if medical science learnt so to arrest the senescence of the body that natural death ceased to be a necessity? Will it be contended that this possibility of scientific progress is disproved *a priori* by the form of the syllogism? Or will the syllogism uphold the truth of its prediction by quibbling about the meaning of 'man' and 'mortal,' contending that one not 'doomed to die' ceased to be a 'man,' or that 'mortal' should be taken in the sense of 'liable to die'? In either case has it not to confess that its 'valid argument' has changed the original meaning of its terms without changing its 'form'?

The moment, therefore, we allow ourselves to contemplate cases in which the meaning of terms is ambiguous or undergoes important changes of meaning in consequence of the growth of knowledge or of reality, we discover how far from water-tight is the certainty grammatically guaranteed by 'logical necessity' of this third kind. It turns out to be entirely hypothetical and conditional upon assumptions, as artificial as the rules of a game, which express merely a verbal convention about the use of terms. The two conditions for which it stipulates are, first, that what is called A is really A, i.e. that the terms of an argument are rightly identified; second, that the course of an argument introduces no developments into their meaning such as to vitiate the conclusion we are seeking to draw. The importance of this second condition was beautifully illustrated in the early days of the Darwinian controversy by the anti-Darwinians (mostly Roman Catholics thoroughly trained in Aristotelian logic), who protested that Darwinism destroyed the notion of 'species.' Now it was true that Darwinism had explained away the existence of 'species' in the old Platonic sense as external and rigid natural kinds more real than the specimens which exemplified them and reduced them to conveniences of human classification; but it explained both how such natural groups of specimens arose, persisted, and changed, and also the actual character and affinities of the existing forms of life. So it was really *developing* the idea of 'species' in a fruitful manner, which could not be confuted by any verbal argument based on the *old* meaning of the term which it was rendering obsolete, and it is a thousand pities that logicians and philosophers generally should have been so slow to appreciate its logical importance.[1]

Now the first of these assumptions, that all the objects of our thought have been correctly labelled, is plainly preposterous. It postulates the non-existence of error, and it would be much truer to contend that we can *never* make quite sure that 'A' is A. For all that is ever proved in the best scientific inquiry is

[1] For which see *Formal Logic*, chap. v, § 8.

that we are justified in calling 'A' A in the actual state of our knowledge. There is obviously no guarantee involved in this that next day it may not become better to call A a, or to discriminate it into A^1 and A^2, which may be very different for many purposes. So the proverbial certainty that 'eggs is eggs' is no obstacle to a further division of eggs into 'new-laid,' 'breakfast,' 'confectioners,' and 'electioneering,' etc., all with different properties and uses between which it is wise to discriminate in practice. Similarly, while an engineer may safely hold that 'lead is lead,' and that its atomic weight is 207, a physicist may find it most important to discriminate between 'uranium-lead' with an atomic weight of 206, and 'thorium-lead' with an atomic weight of 208, and the commercial mixture, which averages 207·2.

The second assumption, that the meaning of terms is fixed, is not true of *any* words. Probably the names of natural objects, like 'the sun' or 'the tiger,' come nearest to stability of meaning. But the meaning of 'the sun' is relative to the discoveries of astrophysics, and 'the tiger' is liable to become 'extinct, like the dodo,' and to become applicable to Clémenceau, Tammany, and Princeton. Hence, fixity of meaning can at best be a polite fiction which holds, approximately, in those subjects of discourse in which no appreciable amounts of new knowledge are being generated. For it implicitly denies the *growth* of meaning and the possibility of *learning*, and this denial is never wholly true. In a significant argument the parties to it always *learn something*, and so the original meaning of the terms they used is always being altered for them by its progress. The sole reason why logicians have not noticed this, and have even erected the rigidity of meaning into a postulate of logic, is that they illustrate logical procedure never by actual judgments, significant arguments, and real problems, but only by paper problems, and discuss only unreal questions which no one asks and to which the answers are known.

Fixity of meanings, then, is never a fact. Even as a fiction it is a mistake, because it goes far beyond what is needed. For what is needed for the purpose of comprehension is merely stability enough of meaning to preserve the continuity of the developing thought and to convey the meaning of one party to the other. In the *Amphioxus* example adduced in Chap. X, § 14, the conditions of instruction were fulfilled so soon as the zoologist found a pupil who knew that 'vertebrate' meant 'having a backbone' and was willing to accept '*Amphioxus*' as the name of his 'worm,' although, of course, 'the *Amphioxus* is a vertebrate' would not mean so much to him as it would after he had dissected one. On the other hand, to one who confused 'amphioxus' with 'amphitheatre' the zoologist's remark would seem unintelligible, because the new meaning he was required to assimilate would not be sufficiently congruous with his anterior beliefs.

No doubt this need of using intelligible language imposes practical limits on the rapid development of meaning: but if our aim be to understand cognitive procedure it seems truer to say that in real inference meaning *grows* than that it remains unchanged. The fixity of meanings is at bottom a convention, like a code of law or the rules of a game, and the impersonal necessities of Formal Logic are essentially akin to those of chess: i.e. they are obligatory for those who have agreed to play the game of Formal Logic, but must be used with reserve by those who value language primarily as a vehicle of progressive thought.

§ 6. Formal Validity.

The notion of a 'formally valid' inference is Formal Logic's substitute for truth. Formal Logic fights shy of 'truth' not merely on account of its constitutional inability to devise a tenable theory of truth (Chap. VIII, § 8, *n.*), but also because the notion is far too empirical and 'material' for its taste. In consequence of this substitution, 'validity' is also used in contexts in which the term 'value' would be far more appropriate, while it hardly needs stating that in its technical use 'validity' has departed widely from its original meaning of 'strength.'

In spite, however, of the favour shown it by Formal Logic, the notion of formal validity broke down almost as soon as it was formulated. Aristotle was quite aware that the syllogistic form of 'proof' was incapable of guaranteeing true conclusions unless it was supplied with true premisses, and that to supply them was not easy. If either premiss was challenged it had to be proved by a prior syllogism : this would, of course, require two more true premisses to prove its conclusion. Thus every step backwards *doubled* the number of true premisses required, and manifestly put a premium on pertinacious doubt.[1] To rehabilitate the syllogism and to cut off the infinite regress thus lurking in its form, Aristotle could think of no more satisfactory expedient than the arbitrary assumption that sooner or later propositions self-evidently true and certain would be reached which would form the ultimate premisses of all scientific argument. Thus valid inference was made to depend on acceptance of the intuitional theory of truth, the inadequacy of which was shown in Chap. VII, § 7.

In default of intuitions, the soundest policy for the defenders of formal validity would seem to be to give up the futile search for indisputably true premisses, and to declare 'formal validity' independent of 'truth.' For it does not, at first sight, affect the inherent coherence and cogency of the valid form that its premisses should be hypothetical, doubtful, or even false. It is as possible to argue from probabilities and hypothetical truths as from 'absolute' truths, and much easier, because the latter are admittedly difficult to procure. The only inconvenience this practice entails is that no absolute, but only hypothetical, truth can be claimed for the conclusion of a 'valid' form. But this merely renders Formal Logic more self-sufficing. It can glory in the emancipation of 'validity' from dependence on 'fact' and in the superiority of formal over 'material' truth. It can conceive itself as a pure Formal science to which all the other sciences must do homage, though it affords them no help, sustenance, or guidance. And it may be accounted a further merit of this policy that it enables the logician to adopt the only interpretation of the Syllogism which makes it a significant

---

[1] Cp. Chap. VII, § 6 (4); Chap. XIV, § 2 ; see further, *Formal Logic*, chap. xviii, § 2.

argument, and does not render it either a tautology or a *petitio principii*.[1]

Reflection upon the implications of this interpretation may, however, considerably abate the complacency with which it is viewed by Formal Logic. For, if it can *never* be assumed that the premisses of a syllogism are more than hypotheses, it is clear that the conclusion deduced from them can never be more than conditionally true: whether it is *actually true* becomes a question of empirical fact. Thus we have to wait and see whether it actually *comes true* before we can deem it really true. But is not this to subvert the very notion of *a priori* proof, and to render the actual proof of every 'valid' syllogism dependent on its verification? Now verification, as Formal logicians themselves insist, can never become a formally valid process. It always involves the formal fallacy of 'affirming the consequent.'[2] Thus the truth-claim of the valid form rests in the end on a *formally invalid* process, and this hardly seems to be saving the notion of 'valid form.'

Further difficulties arise *within* the 'valid' form itself when we raise the question, already alluded to in § 3, whether the liability of the middle term to 'Sidgwick's ambiguity' does not amount to a *formal defect* in the syllogistic form which renders nugatory the whole notion of a valid form.[3]

So radical a renunciation of an inveterate belief will not, of course, be easily accepted; but, meanwhile, logicians may be invited to contemplate two further facts which bear on their valuation of formal validity. The first is that formally valid inferences may be quite worthless, and even noxious, in actual thinking; the second, the still more curious fact that most, if not all, of the progress actually made in knowledge is effected by processes which are *not* formally valid.

In support of the former contention it may be shown that an inference may be as right as right can be in form, and may

---

[1] Cp. Chap. XIV, § 3, and XV, § 5 ; *Formal Logic*, pp. 210, 211, 219, and 234.
[2] Cp. Chap. XIV, § 3 ; and *Formal Logic*, chap. xxii, § 6.
[3] Cp. Chap. XIV, § 3 ; and *Formal Logic*, chap. xvi, §§ 6, 7.

follow from its antecedents or premises with the completest 'necessity,' and yet in no wise guarantee the actual value of its conclusion for the purpose for which it is needed. For it may be quite useless and grossly misleading simply because it is not relevant to the situation and its needs. For example, a statistician glancing at his barometer before going out might infer that it was standing lower than ever before that year, and this might so excite him that he would proceed, then and there, to verify his observation, thereby losing his train and missing an important appointment; whereas the proper inference would have been that he ought to take out his umbrella! In such ways there is a vast amount of mischief done in the world by the reasonings of enthusiasts and pedants, which, though not formally false, are not actually right, but at best irrelevant to the needs of the age and a waste of time. Valid inference, then, does not suffice for the right conduct of life, and it is not always competent to explain our actual reasoning. It is *not* good inference in actual fact, but only according to the artificial rules and conventions of Formal Logic. And, as these will not guarantee *de facto* rightness, it would seem to be consistent and prudent in Formal Logic to rule out 'material truth,' and to refuse to take cognisance of inferences *de facto* 'good.'

When we consider these, i.e. reasonings which are found actually to advance the work of the sciences and to increase knowledge, we find that many formally bad inferences do excellent work and are in constant use. They are good enough to satisfy scientific requirements and to lead us right, even though they do not attain to absolute certainty and cannot be made formally 'cogent.' As cases in point may be enumerated *probabilities*, *hypotheses*, *analogies*, and *rough rules* to which exceptions are known or suspected; there may further be added *inductions*, which are never 'valid,' except in the imaginary case of 'perfect induction. [1] Moreover, it was shown above that the syllogism could escape the charge of *petitio* only by becoming hypothetical, and that hypotheses always demand verifications, which can never be formally valid. Hence it

[1] Cp. *Formal Logic*, chap. xviii, § 4 ; chap. xix, § 2.

appears that *no* valuable reasoning is ever really valid, and this ought to go a long way towards reconciling us to the conclusion already hinted at that formally valid reasoning does not really occur at all.

§ 7. The Formal Fictions Needless, Useless, and Harmful.[1]

Although exception cannot seriously be taken to the use of fictions in the sciences, it has always to be shown that they serve a good purpose. If, therefore, it is found that any particular fiction is not needed, cannot be used, and does harm rather than good, it ought to be dropped. In point of fact all three charges can be substantiated against the fictions of Formal Logic.

There is, in the first place, no logical need for them. The actual procedure of our knowing can perfectly well be described without recourse to them. We can observe and study the actual trains of thought in various minds—their motives, starting-points, progress, and conclusions. Moreover, when we have ascertained the facts of actual thinking we can proceed to draw our own conclusions and to *evaluate* the actual process. There is no need whatsoever to suppress it and to substitute for it a fictitious, wholly artificial structure of 'logical' inference, linked up by 'necessary connexions' and claiming 'formal validity.' Nor is there any need to relegate such observations to 'psychology' and to forbid Logic to take cognisance of them. On the contrary, it ought to be taken as axiomatic that it is only after we have ascertained the facts of actual inference that we can safely undertake to evaluate them and to give real reasons for thinking some inferences 'good' and others 'bad.'

Secondly, the reasons for declaring the Formal fictions useless have already been made plain. They are not merely a pseudo-analysis of thought, but even as fictions do not really apply. For the necessary connexions which are alleged to hold between propositions do not really determine the course of the actual thinking, and the formal validity which is represented as the logical ideal is never really exemplified.

[1] Cp. § 4.

Lastly, it is pretty evident that this fictitious account of thought is a very serious hindrance to the study of the real process of knowing. It completely diverts attention from it and produces a quite unwarranted complacency in logicians, while destroying their interest in the real problems and difficulties of the sciences. So Logic being severed from the sciences becomes useless, a mere intellectual (or rather verbal) game with fictitious counters.

§ 8. Are Forms of Inference Worthless?

What value, then, can still be conceded to the study of inferential forms? It is clear that the claims usually advanced on their behalf have had to be disallowed.

For (a) it can no longer be assumed that, provided we get the forms right, 'material' truth ensues as a matter of course. On the contrary, though its forms are right a conclusion may yet be false, and even though its forms are 'invalid' a conclusion may be true, and the inference the best possible under the conditions.

(b) Correctness of form is no protection even against formal fallacy. Even the most valid syllogism may be infected with Ambiguous Middle, a fatal disease, the moment we try to use it. Even a premiss, true in general, may involve a *petitio* the moment we try to prove our conclusion with it. In neither case does the verbal form afford any presage of the coming disaster.

(c) Can we say that reasoning in a valid form is less likely to go wrong? Not even that. The discovery that a form reasoned in was invalid may lead, of course, to a demand for justification in fact, and so increases the burden of proof on its assertor. But, by exciting attention, this may lead to closer scrutiny, and reveal 'material' merits which more than atone for its formal defects.

(d) Even though formal reasoning cannot infallibly predict it may yet guide expectation. With a valid syllogism starting from premisses reputed true our conclusion should come true, unless our argument has a flaw that could not be foreseen. If, therefore, it does in fact come true our faith in the truth of our premisses is confirmed, and they grow more probable. If our expectation is defeated we infer that there is error somewhere; either the premisses are false or some term has grown ambiguous. And the falsity and ambiguity might never have been detected if we had not put these premisses together and assumed the meanings of the terms as we did. We have, therefore, learnt something.

(e) In general, moreover, it may be conceded that formal analysis derives a certain value from intensifying our awareness of what we are doing in our reasoning—of its defects, incompleteness, and risks. Practically the value of this insight is more negative than positive. It renders us less ready to claim too much for our truth, and readier to note how far it falls short of absoluteness. Thus it undermines the dogmatic temper; and this may help us to reason better, if it is true that open-mindedness is a help.

§ 9. The General Validity of Inference.

Using 'validity' no longer in its illusory Formal sense, but either as a synonym for 'value' or dispensing with it altogether, we may raise the question, Why is Inference in general valid?—i.e. why is it a helpful and valuable exercise of thought? At first, indeed, it may seem odd that logicians should raise this fundamental question of logical theory at the end of treatises in which they have deeply committed themselves to the practice of inference; but the marvel is much attenuated when one observes to what weird 'postulates' their prejudices have committed them.

F. H. Bradley, for example, devotes to this question the last two chapters of his *Principles of Logic*. Manifestly implying the 'correspondence' view of truth, he asks, "if in inference the conclusion is made what it is by an arbitrary act, how can any such process be true of reality?" (p. 547), and doubts "if there is such a thing as a valid inference." He declares that every inference falls into three parts—a *datum*, an operation, and a result which must be 'new.' But it 'follows' because it has been dragged out by us, and a conclusion we have *made* we cannot also have *found*. "We did not draw the consequence from the bowels of the premises but inserted a product prepared by ourselves" (p. 553). In short, we have interfered, and that is fatal: "the process is invalid and vicious." For Logic cannot transcend its 'postulates,' and "all logic assumes that a mere attention, a simple retaining and holding together before the mind's eye, is not an alteration" (p. 555), even though it is also "true that all inference is a process of correction. It is true that it cannot ever leave its starting-point quite unmodified" (p. 556). It is a postulate also that "some operations do but change our power of perceiving the subject, and leave the subject itself unaltered. And this holds even where our wilful and arbitrary choice selects the process and procures the result" (pp. 570–1).

The reason for these postulates (or rather for this postulate —for they are really one —p. 575) of Logic is not expressly stated; but we can hardly go far wrong in finding it in the dogma (p. 574) that "every inference is the necessary self-development of a real subject." This "idea of self-development" is said to be "necessary for Logic," though Bradley admits it to be doubtful whether it is "when you insist on a final answer, a consistent idea" (p. 573). At any rate it is quite a neat way of abstracting from the personal side of logic, which Bradley is bent on ruling out.

For he sees that there is a sense in which 'valid' means 'good practically' and 'practical' means 'for working purposes in reasoning,' and this sense competes with 'formally valid' and 'corresponding with reality' (p. 573). By recognising it, therefore, it would be possible to vindicate inference as a successful instrument of thought; but he struggles desperately against it. Even though he admits (p. 583) that, when "both process and result diverge from given reality, they no doubt may be valid in the sense of serving," and "may go near enough to convey the meaning" (*personal* meaning, clearly), he insists that (pp. 588–9) "you cannot plead that, because logic works, logic cannot be wrong. . . . It is practically right beyond all suspicion, but for all that it may rest on theoretical error."

What distinguishes Bradley from other intellectualists is that his intellectualism is not blind and unconscious, but wilful and arbitrary.

It may seem sheer prejudice to insist that its working shall *not* validate a truth, that logic shall postulate, against the plainest facts, that thought shall not alter its *data*, that human activity shall only be regarded as *vitiating* any result it enters into; but Bradley sees that any lack of resolution at this point would mean irretrievable surrender to the logic of voluntarism. So he prefers a (disingenuous) appeal to metaphysics, and, ultimately, scepticism.

But this position is really quite weak, and the voluntarist would do well to challenge it. Let him, therefore, point out simply that the whole notion of a self-development of impersonal thought is a fiction, and a foolish one at that. For every cognitive process springs from human endeavour, and the reality of human intervention in it is plain, obvious, and all-pervasive. To our intervention every step in every actual act of thought, every judgment, and every inference, owes its being. To get a judgment at all, some one had to select it from untold possibilities that might have been asserted instead, and to prefer it as the best. Having chosen it, he had to decide how to use it, whether for an 'advance' or for a 'recoil.' In the one case he had to equip it with two premisses, in the other with a helpmate to generate a new conclusion that served his purpose. Of course, in a sense, each step is 'arbitrary'—in the sense in which its synonyms are 'purposive' and 'rational.' Without *such* 'arbitrariness' no one can reason. But the intellectualist is 'arbitrary' in a worse sense; he willfully shuts his eyes to the human activity which engenders and pervades all thinking, to the human action which perceives, picks out, and rearranges all the '*data*' (which are always '*sumpta*,' taken out of a larger context) that form the starting-point of every train of thought. Of course, the process of thought alters its original *data*, but there is no need to apologise for this. It is *meant* to, and, if it did not, thought would not have progressed, and nothing would have been *learnt* from it. Thus its 'practical' working is not a slur upon the truth and 'validity' of inference, but its only safeguard and proper test.

We may surely conclude, then, that Inference is 'valid' because, in a general way, it works, because it is a practice which extricates us from many predicaments, adjusts us to many situations in which direct action fails, and conduces to a more prosperous handling of many problems of life.

§ 10. Inference and Judgment.

It follows from this conclusion that in aim and value Inference and Judgment do not differ utterly. Their procedure and functions are broadly the same. Both have their origin in vital situations, and are meant to relate, directly or indirectly, to problems of life. Both, moreover, are essentially experimental and purposive, and aim ultimately at the control of experience. Only, Inference is more circuitous. It prolongs the experiment. It delays action. It tests a truth-claim, not directly by acting on it, but by the aid or mediation of other judgments first. Thus the pragmatic 'consequences' relevant to a truth-claim in an inference are primarily *other* judgments: though ultimately the value of the whole thought-process is decided, as before, by its application or working.

CHAPTER XIV

SYLLOGISTIC REASONING

1. What is claimed for syllogistic reasoning ; 2 The demand for cogency; 3. The claim to formal validity ; 4. Sidgwick's ambiguity of the middle ; 5. The syllogism as a hypothesis not ' valid ' ; 6. More false claims for the syllogism ; 7. The claim to novelty ; 8. The real function and value of syllogistic reasoning.

§ 1. What is Claimed for Syllogistic Reasoning.

This chapter will have to be largely recapitulation. For when alternative logics clash at any point their differences elsewhere are always involved, and we should never have got so far had we not been willing to anticipate, when necessary, exposure of the verbal juggling which is the stock in trade of syllogistic reasoning *as practised by Formal Logic*. But it will be all the easier and better now to pause and to take stock, in order to realise the full contrast between the claims of Formalism and the actual facts of the situation.

Formal Logic has long been in the habit of making very big claims for syllogistic reasoning. It has been represented as 'cogent,' 'formally valid,' absolutely certain, supremely valuable, capable of attaining truth and *new* truth, incapable of losing or wasting any truth it had started with. A further claim to represent the procedure of actual thinking is less confident or more equivocal. All these claims are unfounded, and we have already had occasion to impugn most of them. But they can be abandoned only by abandoning Formal Logic and replacing it by something better.

§ 2. The Demand for Cogency.

The demand for 'cogency' in reasoning dates back to the very beginning of Logic.[1] It was an urgent social need to formulate rules for the popular Greek game of 'dialectics,' which proved to be (under Providence) the parent of legal procedure and scientific method. The 'dialectician' started by conversing (with young men), and found it such fun that he persuaded

---

[1] Cp. Chap. VII, § 4, and *Formal Logic*, chap. xvi, § 2.

himself that he had found a method of discovering truth: actually he was merely analysing (and incidentally developing!) the current meanings of words. At first, however, the game suffered from a lack of rules and the drawback that it was hard to extort a confession of defeat from a beaten foe who had been driven to contradict himself (i.e. had violated the sacrosanctity of established verbal usage). Accordingly there was a great demand for some *technique* of coercion that would *compel* him to own himself beaten.

Aristotle's invention of the Syllogism appeared to meet this demand; so it was hailed with delight and rapidly adopted by debaters of all schools. Moreover, it was applied also to scientific research, and made the basis for the dogma that true 'science' consisted of demonstrative proof. This dogma arrested the growth of scientific knowledge for over 2000 years, and has not yet been wholly discarded by logicians. It would, however, have been far better in the interest of science if *other* analogies latent in dialectics had been detected and exploited instead of this unhappy attempt to represent scientific progress as compulsory. Thus from the need of a subject for debate might have been deduced the scientific need for a *problem*, and this might have led further to inquiries into the choice of a *good* problem. The perception that there are two sides to every question, which had actually been achieved by Protagoras, might have led to a recognition that every scientific interpretation involves a choice between alternatives. The presence of *parties* in scientific research might have been noticed and their effects traced. And a glimpse might have been caught of the deep-seated and far-reaching analogies between a case of a 'law' and a case in the law-courts.

But all these omissions have done less harm than the adoption of coercion as the ideal to be aimed at in knowledge. After laying so much stress on the coerciveness of the syllogism it was vain for Aristotle to protest that all men naturally *desire* knowledge. He had taken the most effective step for frustrating that desire, and untold generations of schoolboys have had cause to rue the day when compulsion was proclaimed the fundamental basis of learning. The ideal of compulsion has wrought havoc with the theory of truth (Chap. VII, §§ 4–6), and has perverted the notion of logical necessity (Chap. XIII, § 5); it makes nonsense of the formal analysis of the syllogism itself.

And, after all, these efforts were pathetically vain. The course of thinking cannot really be represented as utterly necessitated: no reasoning is sheer coercion, nor is any conclusion absolutely cogent. It is true that we naturally think only when we have got involved in a situation in which action is arrested and thought promises to extricate us (Chap. X), or when we have acquired the habit of thinking, and got to like it; but still natural thinking is more conscious of purposiveness than of coercion. The allegation of the latter appears to be merely a polite device for winning the assent of others to what we desire to believe and them to agree to (Chap. VII, § 6); and the only sorts of 'necessity' which are really inherent in the course of natural thinking are the teleological necessity of means to ends and the 'logical' necessity of inference (Chap. XIII, § 5). But the latter is really quite hypothetical and optional: it follows only if and when we have adopted the premisses, and because we are willing to accept the verbal integrity of terms as sufficient proof of identity of meaning.

Against a disputant unwilling to make these concessions the syllogistic form is ludicrously impotent. He cannot be coerced, because (1) he can refuse to admit the truth of its premisses, and can demand a proof of them. It then appears that the syllogism is totally incapable of making good its threats of coercion, and that the unfathomable abysm of an infinite regress gapes within its form. Thus, if the truth of a premiss is disputed, it has to be proved; but proved it can be only by a further syllogism, which will need two true premisses to assure truth to its conclusion. Hence the method of the syllogism is to support the truth of a proposition by conceiving it as a conclusion, and deriving it from two true premisses, and, when these in their turn are doubted, to summon four more propositions to attest them. Thus the demand for true premisses is *doubled* at every step *backwards* the inquiry takes. Forwards it cannot

move at all, because it can never get back to indisputable premisses. So the more we try to prove the more we have to prove,
and the further proof recedes. The more assistance we get the
more we require; the more doubts are relieved the more are
generated. Such is the nature of syllogistic proof! It becomes
futile so soon as it tries to coerce.

No way out of this absurdity, on the traditional lines, has
ever been discovered. Aristotle, who perceived the difficulty,
thought that the infinite regress could be stopped by intuitions, self-evident propositions, which no gentlemanly logician
(πεπαιδευμένος) would question. He derived his belief in
self-proving truth from the 'Idea of Good,' which Plato had
postulated as the sole and supreme principle from which the
whole rational order of 'Forms,' the only true existences, was
to be deduced *a priori*. Aristotle saw, indeed, that deductive
proof demands more than one premiss; but he never saw his
way to publish a list of the self-evident principles on which the
demonstrative sciences could rest. When it is added, further,
that logical cannot be distinguished from psychological intuition, that many false intuitions are alleged, that intuitions are
very variable, and that assent to them is optional, it is clear that
intuitionism is no way of cutting short the infinite regress which
lurks within the syllogism.

The empiricists, very unwisely, adopted the ideal of formal
validity, with an alternative way of securing the truth of premisses. They thought that by resting argument on *facts* a conclusion could be proved, and a universal formula might be
generated by a sufficiency of particulars. But Hume pointed
out to them that even though their formula might hold of all
known cases up to date, this would guarantee nothing for the
future, whereas prediction of the future was precisely the purpose for which such formulas were needed. Past experience
could no doubt engender expectation, but how could it render
expectation *valid*? Besides, it was not observed that the 'facts'
on which demonstration was to rest were at best facts in the
light of existing knowledge, and that only a credulous and uncritical will to believe could take them as absolute.

(2) But even if we waived this difficulty about the truth of its premisses, the syllogism's claim to coerciveness could hardly survive the subtler attack upon its essentially verbal constitution which questions the identity of its terms. Regarded from this angle, its essential procedure seems to be to argue that the *verbal* identity of a term that occurs in two relations necessarily overrides any difference which may be entailed by the two relations, and guarantees the *real* identity of the object it denotes. Only so can it be contended that the difference between 'M-in-relation-to-P' and 'M-in-relation-to-S' is negligible, because 'M is M' for all that. But the evidence that the terms do not undergo any relevant change of meaning in their transfer from one context to another is wholly verbal. What is postulated is that whatever is called 'M' *is* M. So with what is called 'S' and 'P.' So soon as this assumption is questioned, every syllogism lies open to the charge that it is really trying to argue with four or more terms, and its power to coerce permanently disappears. To the suspicion under which it labours there is only one reply, viz. that *in this case* the difference in the two contexts may *in fact* be neglected for the *purpose* of the argument; or, otherwise, that no *relevant* difference of meaning has been developed by the two relations of the term under suspicion. This is to admit debate about the actual value of any 'valid' reasoning, and plainly does *not* vindicate the form: it only saves the argument in a particular case. Moreover, it involves an appeal to the notions of purpose and relevance which are taboo to Formal Logic. It is clear, then, how a disputant may escape coercion by the syllogistic form: he may admit the premisses separately and in the abstract, and yet refuse to admit the conclusion on the ground that the middle term has developed ambiguity and does not mean the same in its two contexts.

(3) It was shown, also in Chap. XIII, § 5, how easy it is to escape from coercion by the pretence of valid syllogisms to predict the future. So soon as the meaning of the terms employed was inquired into, it appeared that the syllogism's claim to predict could not be sustained, and in order to make a show of

prediction it had to use its terms in several senses. For if the real (in the illustration 'man' and 'mortal') developed new qualities, the continued truth of the conclusion could no longer be reckoned on, and the meanings of the terms would certainly be modified.

§ 3. The Claim to Formal Validity.

After Chap. XIII, § 6, the syllogism's claim to formal validity will not need lengthy argument. There are four interpretations of the syllogism: three of these make it a *petitio principii*, and so a formal fallacy; while the fourth makes it depend on empirical verification, and so incapable of formal validity, though capable enough of an indefinitely growing probability.

Of the three former interpretations two are admitted to be fallacious by the Formal logicians themselves; the third is supposed to vindicate the syllogism, though it makes precisely the same assumption as the other two. They can, therefore, all be discussed together. They take the major premiss respectively in extension, as a definition, and in intension. In the first case *all men are mortal* makes an assertion about all individual men; in the second it attaches mortality to 'man' by definition; in the third it states a universal law of nature and affirms a connexion of attributes.

But in all three cases the question ostensibly 'proved' in the conclusion is manifestly begged in one or other of the premisses. Thus (1) if we are entitled to assert of every man that *he* is mortal, we must either already know this of 'Socrates' (or 'Smith'), and so learn nothing, or else we beg the question: in either case the 'proof' of mortality is a farce. (2) If mortality (in whatever sense) is taken as part of the 'essence' of man, and so the major premiss is intended as a definition, the question is begged in the minor, in which Socrates (or Smith) is pronounced to be a 'man.' Or else 'man' is used in two senses. (3) If it is true that every case of a general principle (genuine or alleged) must of necessity exhibit always and for all purposes all the characteristics which are in general found in cases of that kind ('class,' or 'universal'), it will doubtless follow from the universal connexion of mortality with humanity that any man is mortal. But if we are supposed to know this in advance, what do we learn from the conclusion? Where is the inference? If, on the other hand, we do not know this, we once more beg the question.

And in itself this assumption is false, nay preposterous. For it demands a total blindness (which Formal Logic continues carefully to cultivate) to the possibilities of Sidgwick's Ambiguity of the Middle, which forms an insuperable obstacle to the belief in formal validity, and has already been referred to frequently.[1] It is now time to bring out its full import.

§ 4. Sidgwick's Ambiguity of the Middle.

The syllogistic assumption that a general principle (or 'law' or 'universal') must necessarily hold in any case to which it is (rightly or wrongly) applied, without regard to the question whether the special circumstances of the case (including the special purpose for which it is considered) do not render the principle inapplicable, is plainly false. But there is a good psychological reason for this fiction. When we set ourselves to formulate a general principle or 'universal truth,' we do not, and indeed cannot, think of all its possibilities of application; nor do we foresee all the ways of misapplying it. Our formula is always suggested to us by certain cases which we have examined, and it is no wonder, therefore, that it remains relative to these. Nor is it surprising that when it is transferred to special cases, or to a different type of case, it should break down. For what is in general a case of a universal principle need not be so for the special purpose in hand. Thus '*men are rational*' and '*X is a man*' are (and remain) both true in general; but if X goes mad the major premiss can no longer safely be applied to him and the conclusion is falsified. Again, take '*dogs are quadrupeds—this is a dog, ∴ it is a quadruped*': yet, in fact, he may only have three feet, having lost one in a motor accident. Here the 'dog' both is, and is not, a 'quadruped' according to our purpose. If we want to classify him zoologically he

---

[1] Cp. Chap. XIII, § 3 sf., § 6, § 8 ; *Formal Logic*, chap. xvi, § 6 ; and a paper on ' Aristotle's Refutation of Aristotelian Logic ' in *Mind*, No. 89 (1913).

remains a quadruped despite his accidental defect. If we want to take him out for a walk, or to enter him for a greyhound race, he may not retain enough quadrupedality. Of course, we may encounter the retort: "Any fool or logician can see the catch in this sort of thing: had they foreseen these accidents, they could easily have guarded against them, and have refrained from asserting either that *all* men were rational or that X was a man in the sense of a rational being. Even in formal logic some common sense may be taken for granted!"

But can it? Common sense is all very well in real life, and has always known well enough that circumstances alter cases and that what one calls a thing depends on what one wants to do with it, and that a holy day, like Sunday or Good Friday, may be turned into a holiday, if one pleases, and if society permits. But Formal Logic has hitherto frowned upon such matters of common knowledge. Moreover, this defence of the syllogism introduces into logic a new and revolutionary principle and hardly realises the seriousness of the difficulty. Detection of the ambiguous middle may often need material knowledge which is not in the reasoner's possession: the flaw may be revealed only by the going wrong, in fact, of what seemed to be valid inferences. For example, we may argue that *all salt is soluble in water. Cerebos is salt, ∴ Cerebos is soluble in water*, whereas, in fact, it is not. Cerebos is 'salt' for culinary, but not for chemical purposes. Again, it is true that *no mice eat bumble bees. Shrews are mice, ∴ no shrews eat bumble bees*, whereas, in fact, they largely live on them! A good many people could not detect this fallacy, because they do not know that shrews are only popularly 'mice' and really 'insectivores.' Yet, if at a picnic a lady had been frightened by a shrew, and a professor tried to reassure her by telling her a 'shrew' was *not* a 'mouse,' what would she reply to the fatuous pedant? What would most people make of this?—*Treason is a capital offence. To libel the King is treason, ∴ to libel the King is a capital offence*.[1] Here a knowledge of the law is needed to detect the

[1] Cp.   " Treason never prospers : what's the reason ?
            When it prospers, 'tis no longer treason."

ambiguity of treason. Lastly, until a few years ago the most competent chemical experimentation would invariably have shown that the atomic weight of 'Lead' was 207·2, and have justified the belief that all lead had this weight: it needed quite a new type of experiment (physical) to discover 'isotopes' and the difference between 'thorium-lead' and 'uranium-lead,' and even now this difference has no importance commercially.

Furthermore, this fatal formal flaw in the syllogism defies formal classification. It may be treated as a formal fallacy of ambiguous middle. But it may even more suggestively be conceived as a fallacy of 'Accident,' i.e. as a misapplication of a rule to a case where, owing to special circumstances or reasons, it does not hold. Now this is not strictly a 'fallacy,' i.e. a formal error in reasoning, at all, though it is (illogically) classified by Formal Logic as a 'material' fallacy. In actual fact there is no formal difference between a 'fallacy of accident' and a 'valid syllogism' which is a sound and legitimate protest against misapplying a rule. Only the conclusion does not happen to come true: when this *has* happened we can go back upon our premiss and declare our rule has been misapplied. But we could not have known this in advance. For every new case of a rule differs somewhat from the old ones, and, *qua* different, may elude, defeat, or correct it. All inference takes these risks, and logic should endeavour not to conceal *them* but to warn *us*.

Whatever, then, it is called, the difficulty remains that in *all* reasoning we are liable to fall into what is either a 'fallacy of accident' or an 'ambiguous middle.' In face of which does not the postulate of the identity of the middle term, the confidence that anything called 'M' *is* M, seem uncritical and silly? The right moral for logicians is that we should always consider the actual case in the concrete and the personal meaning in its context, instead of confining our attention to the verbal meaning of abstract formulas. When we consent to do this, it ceases to be either a 'fallacy' or even a paradox that a principle which holds in general should fail in a special application.

Now, curiously enough, the precariousness of general rules in their application to cases was fully recognised by the founder of logic, when he was not writing logic. Although he had laid it down in the *Prior Analytics* that contradictory propositions (A and O, E and I) cannot be true together, Aristotle, when he was writing ethics, quite saw that a general principle does not guarantee all its applications, and that the general truth of a principle is not demolished by its failure to hold in a special case. He gave, indeed, a wrong explanation of it, attributing it to the inferiority of the 'contingent matter' of practical life which baffled the 'form' prescribed for it by the rule; but he recognised the fact very handsomely. Hence his doctrine that what is true—or good or beautiful—in general (ἁπλῶς, which should not be mistranslated 'absolutely') need not be so in a case (τινί or κατὰ συμβεβηκός).[1] Generality is predicated of a rule without regard to its application; it holds of its unapplied condition, without contemplating particular cases at all. Hence Aristotle can even say [2] that external goods are in general (ἁπλῶς) *always good* (ἀεὶ ἀγαθά), but not always good for a particular person (τινὶ δ' οὐκ ἀεί). This would be nonsense if ἀεί meant 'in all cases.' But it means 'universally,' and calls attention to the fact that our 'universal laws,' moral and scientific alike, may fail to fit the peculiarities of special cases. In ethics this generates the great problem of casuistry, and leads Aristotle to deny that ethical rules have 'exactness' and to demand a μολίβδινος κανών,[3] i.e. a flexible standard which is adjustable to the particular case. Aristotle was, however, wrong in thinking that this problem is confined to ethics; it occurs no less in logic. Here, too, rules have to be devised and applied and cases to be decided; and we often learn that we mistook them only from the disappointment of our expectations and the empirical disproof of our conclusions by the course of events. These exceptional cases both test the rule we have used and warn us not to rely on rules pedantically. And they should affect logical theory profoundly. In the first place they demand a modification

---

[1] His ethics are full of this doctrine. E.g. *Eth. Nic.*, 1151 b. 2, 1152 b. 27, 1129 b. 3. Compare also *Topics*, ii, 11, which deliciously declares that "it is not in general admirable (καλόν) to sacrifice one's father; but it is among the Triballi," where it was a tribal custom.

[2] *Eth. Nic.*, v, 1, § 9.　　　　　　　　[3] *Eth. Nic.*, v, 11, § 7.

of the traditional doctrine that contradictory propositions are incompatible. For an unapplied universal principle and the special case which limits its application may well be true together—each in its proper sphere. Secondly, if in *any* syllogism the middle term is liable to develop ambiguity in use, and if for proof of this we must await experience, unable to foresee it though able to recognise it after it has occurred, the theory of knowledge is vitally affected. Our predictions can no longer be absolute. Our truths remain improvable and our knowledge dependent on the course of events. Universality is reduced to a claim which remains, at best, hypothetically true—unless and until something happens to defeat it. And, of course, no verification of a hypothesis ever yields an absolute truth.

§ 5. The Syllogism as a Hypothesis not 'Valid.'

May we say, then, that Sidgwick's Ambiguity implicitly but completely discredits the formal validity of the syllogism? The orthodox analysis declares that "if the middle is ambiguous there is no syllogism. But if the middle may always be ambiguous is there ever a syllogism?" [1]

This doubt is only strengthened by the fourth way of analysing the syllogism (§ 3 *init.*), though at first it seems the only way of rehabilitating it. This way starts from two common-sense perceptions which Formal Logic treats as taboo. It realises, in the first place, that the human mind can reason hypothetically and may draw its hypotheses from almost anywhere, and secondly, that it may adopt absurd hypotheses just for the fun of playing with them.

It is, therefore, open to Formal Logic to adopt its absurd hypothesis about the syllogism, together with its other fictions and conventions, such as verbal meaning, true premisses, the 'truth' of 'propositions,' etc. But it cannot make them work. Nor can it extricate itself from the charge that its 'valid' reasoning invariably begs the question.

In real life, however, none of the difficulties incidental to the Formal analysis can possibly arise. No one is going to try to

[1] *Formal Logic*, p. 199.

prove the mortality of 'Socrates' (in any sense of 'mortal') unless there is a *doubt* about it. It is only when such a doubt has arisen that the syllogism about Socrates's mortality becomes psychologically possible and logically valuable. For the major premiss then ceases to be an assured truth to be assumed without question, and becomes a hypothesis which it is desired to apply to a doubtful case. The charge of *petitio* falls to the ground. The conclusion cannot be taken as an already known truth. It will be true only *if* its premisses are true. We have to wait till it *comes true*. The syllogistic deduction will guide our expectation and enable us to predict, conditionally; but it will always need confirmation in fact. It is only, therefore, when we ignore personal meaning and are content to juggle with paper 'propositions' that syllogistic 'proof' is, *a priori*, complete and assured; in real reasoning the doubt and the empirical confirmation are essential both to its existence and to its value.

But, of course, they are fatal to its claim to formal validity. The verification of a hypothesis always involves a formal 'fallacy.' It 'affirms the consequent.' It argues that because the observed consequences are compatible with the truth of the hypothesis the hypothesis is true, without showing (what is, indeed, impossible) that there may not be other and better hypotheses with which they are also compatible. So proof by verification is always incomplete; the verification of a hypothesis goes on for ever. At no point can we stop it on the plea that we have had enough and are fully convinced of its truth. That would be merely psychological, and logically the confirmations of a true hypothesis continue to accumulate. Verification, in other words, is as long-lived as science. But it is death to 'validity.' The fourth way of interpreting the syllogism, then, does *not* vindicate its formal validity. It only explains its function, use, and value; but all except Formalists will confess that this is much better.

§ 6. More False Claims for the Syllogism.

In § 1 were mentioned further claims injudiciously made for the syllogism as interpreted by Formalism, such as that it yields absolute certainty and new truth, and is incapable of losing truth. All these claims also are untrue, and have really been disposed of in rejecting the claims to cogency and validity.

It is untrue that a syllogistic conclusion is absolutely certain. For its certainty is conditional, and if its premises were not absolutely certain its conclusion is likewise conditional. Moreover, we have seen (§ 2) that no premises can be rendered absolutely certain.

What is more, the demand for certainty involves a false ideal. Its adoption is one of the many harmful confusions of logic with psychology which are generated by the refusal of Formal Logic to face the psychological facts. The search for truth is tiring, and even the most zealous truth-seeker may from time to time crave for a rest. He then longs for a final truth in which he can rest and be thankful. So he is dazzled by the ideal of complete, absolute, and final certainty. But he is then allowing his personal feelings and weaknesses to prevail over the interests of science. Science rises above our human frailties, and does not need to postulate an end to knowing. Though man-made, it does not depend for its continuance on any man. Hence it is right for it to adopt an ideal of unending progress, and, if this can be had at the cost of abandoning the wild-goose chase of final truth, it will not hesitate in its choice. Now unending progress is precisely an implication of the voluntarist theory, which interprets the syllogism as the experimental verification of a hypothesis capable of becoming indefinitely more probable, though never absolutely proved. Truth-seeking, therefore, should repudiate the postulate of certainty as the ideal of human indolence and cowardice.

It is untrue, further, that by mere reasoning we can attain real truth. We can at most establish what may be expected if the fiction of the fixity of terms holds in this case. And even this is established only subject to the further condition that no ambiguity has sprung up in the middle term.

For the same reason it is untrue that the syllogism cannot lose a truth it started from. Its premises may both be true separately and in the abstract; yet, when put together, they may yield an ambiguous middle and lead to a false conclusion. So it *can* start with truth and arrive at error by apparently 'valid' reasoning.

It is untrue, further, that, as understood by Formal Logic, syllogistic reasoning has either logical value or psychological capacity to describe actual reasoning. It has nothing whatever to do with actual reasoning, and can make nothing of it, because it has abstracted from all its essential demands. It recognises no personal meaning, no problem, no purpose, no experiment, no consequences, no verification. Its 'analysis' is wholly fictitious and artificial, and its artifices shed no light on any actual procedure. They merely form a word-game.

It is untrue, lastly, that the Formal analysis of the syllogism can account for the generation of *new* truth. Its pretension to do so is old—as old as the syllogism—but it has never been found capable of clear and convincing statement. It deserves, however, a section to itself.

§ 7. The Claim to Novelty.

In words Formal Logic admits the need for novelty. It *talks* about it profusely. It declares that the conclusion of a valid inference must be *new* as well as proved. It requires 'induction' to elicit *new* facts.

But soon it hints that there is a 'paradox of inference' arising from the latent *conflict between the two postulates of novelty and validity.* If a conclusion can be called a valid inference from true premisses it must be contained in the premisses, while, if it can be called new, it must go beyond its premisses. So it is involved in a dilemma. In the one case, how is it new? in the other, how is it valid? What seems at first a plausible compromise, that the novelty is always psychological and does not reside in the logical situation but only in the minds that come to apprehend it, would seem to be ruled out by the attitude of Formal Logic to psychology.

In *Formal Logic*, chap. xiv, § 4,[1] I formulated this antinomy as being that "psychologically there must be novelty," because

[1] Cp. also Chap. XVI, § 8.

no sane mind would reason except in order to obtain or convey information; while "logically there cannot be novelty," because neither in the abstract 'form' nor in the system of 'eternal' truth can the 'conclusion' and the 'premisses' exist apart. And I accused Formal Logic of floundering about between these alternatives "in helpless inconsistency."

This attack appears to have been thought less unanswerable than the rest of *Formal Logic*; for in a review in the *Athenæum* of 24th April 1912 a reply was attempted. The (anonymous) reviewer (an eminent Cambridge logician) told Thackeray's story of the Abbé and the Duke, who was his first penitent and confessed to a murder, and declared the conclusion "startlingly new to all the persons concerned"—"except the *abbé* and the penitent himself." So then it was *not* new to science, not a discovery *in rerum natura*, but a novelty only to some, and not even the most important, of the parties to the argument!

Again, before accepting the syllogistic form as a method of proving new truth, we have to consider whether its conclusion is not only new but also *proved*, not merely verbally or dialectically but *in fact*. The real logical question is whether syllogistic evidence ever *suffices* to prove a fact—in this case the actual identity of the duke and the murderer—not in logic, but in fact. If it does *not*, the traditional belief that a syllogistic conclusion can prove truth of fact must be abandoned.

Now, surely the evidence it proffers is woefully deficient in this respect. The events related might all have occurred, and yet the conclusion drawn by the *abbé's* audience might still be vitiated by a failure to consider a number of alternative hypotheses that might also account for the facts narrated, and so might render their conclusion actually false. Thus (1) the priest may have been mistaken *in good faith* about his first penitent: he thought it was the murderer, whereas it was the duke. Similarly (2), the duke was mistaken: he thought he was the priest's first penitent, whereas it was the murderer. (3) The duke's confession may have been a mistake, because the man left for dead recovered. (4) The duke was suffering from temporary insanity, and confessed falsely; or (5) he lied. Lastly

(6), the *abbé* may have lied, and the duke have supported him in his endeavour to shock the ladies. Clearly, then, the conclusion is anything but cogent and a 'necessary truth'; for all its verbal 'cogency' it is *not* necessarily a truth of fact.

In his preface to Miss Jones's *A New Law of Thought*, p. vii, Prof. G. F. Stout gives a better example of formal novelty. A remarks to B "that woman there is a scarecrow." B replies, "Sir, that woman is my wife." Conclusion: "My (his) wife is a scarecrow!" Here *both* parties learn something new. For even though the husband was probably aware that his wife was no beauty, he did not know that she could excite such interest in a stranger. Yet what is learnt is only new to two human minds, and is relative to their respective ignorance. It leaves the lady's looks objectively unchanged.

At this point, however, the question is likely to be raised whether such psychological novelty is not enough, and is not all that can fairly be demanded of any argument. With this suggestion it might be well to agree, though it is clearly one of those irruptions of common sense that make such havoc of Formal Logic. If logic is concerned with the motives and procedures of human reasoning and knowing, it is unanswerable; if with the self-development of abstract 'forms of thought,' it is intolerable. But we should by now have made up our minds to choose between these two alternative theories of the meaning and value of syllogistic reasoning.

§ 8. The Real Function and Value of Syllogistic Reasoning.

So we observe that the demand for novelty cannot be withdrawn; that for formal validity can be. The hope of attaining new truth, or of imparting welcome information, is the psychological stimulus to all actual inference; but formal validity is the fabulous monstrosity that is found only in the logic books, and does not exist in actual thinking. If it is frankly 'scrapped,' the real function of syllogistic reasoning becomes quite easily intelligible.

It was shown in Chap. X that we judge only when we think we can adapt ourselves better by reflection than by immediate

action, and in Chap. XII, §§ 5, 6, that we have recourse to inference only when we think that simple judgment is not sufficient;
whence it follows that all thinking is at heart a practical experiment which aims at adjusting action better to the realities of
life. Its ultimate test, therefore, is always *empirical*: we have to
learn from experience whether we have judged and reasoned
rightly. We deduce our conclusion, and hope we have anticipated the future; but we have to wait and see whether our prediction will come true. Hence the claim to foresee with complete
a priori certainty is an illusion.

All our reasoning is hypothetical and experimental. We are
not absolutely sure either of the truth of our premisses or even
of the meaning of our terms in the contexts in which we try
to use them. But we are free to try if we are willing to learn.
Hence we may claim the utmost latitude in experimenting with
hypotheses, provided they entail observable consequences which
test them.

We may start with any proposition, and make it either a conclusion or a premiss. To take it as a conclusion means to explore
its connexions with the body of recognised knowledge. We
then look for two other propositions from which it can be deduced and which will support it and vouch for its truth. This
procedure strengthens its logical status, because a disputant
ready to reject an unsupported proposition may hesitate to
treat thus the conclusion of a formally valid syllogism: he would
then have either to find some flaw in the syllogism or to dispute
one at least of its two sponsors. In this way we can, by reasoning,
build up a body of coherent truth-claims which stand and fall
together and will not lightly be rejected. It is true that these
systems will be hypothetical, and that the argument always
ultimately rests on the verbal identity of the terms employed.
This may always be contested, because a difference in context
may always engender a relevant difference in the terms, and so
there is always in fact a risk, though it may be concealed in
words, in arguing from one case to another. But before these
possibilities of error can vitiate an argument they must be shown
to affect the actual case. It is clear, further, that in this pro-

cedure the reasoner's choice of premisses is limited by the existence of established bodies of knowledge, and that the motion of thought is *retrograde*. Such trains of thought may discover new relations, but hardly new facts, and are fitly called *recoils*.

Reasoning, however, can also make *advances*. If we do not tie our hands by accepting the impossible condition that premisses are not to be used until they have been proved absolutely true, it is easy enough to argue *forwards*. We shall, then, take our first proposition as a premiss, and try to associate it with another from which conjoined together some interesting conclusion may be deduced. The process need not be 'valid,' and the conclusion may be 'only probable' (as when it has involved an undistributed middle); but it is essential to observe whether it occurs in actual fact. Moreover, it is evident that we have an enormous freedom of choice in experimenting with premisses; for they may be derived from any quarter, and antecedently quite improbable conjunctions may prove fruitful. Our initial choices in any inquiry will be largely determined by our interests and preferences, though in the long run they will be objectively controlled by the nature of the subjects of inquiry and the success or failure of our experiments. It is clear that such 'advances' are not made by any formal process or impersonal necessity, but rather by guess-work, luck, and the inquirer's genius.

CHAPTER XV

THE THEORY OF PROOF

1. The ideal of proof ; 2. Syllogism as proof ; 3. The syllogism's failures :
(1) begging the question ; 4. (2) The liability to ambiguous middle ; 5. (3)
The infinite regress in proof ; 6. Can intuition save the syllogism ? ; 7. The
inductive proof of premises ; 8. The cure by systematic coherence ; 9. The
illusions of systematic coherence ; 10. (1) Why circular reasoning is fallacious ; 11. (2) Enlarging the circle futile ; 12. (3) An all-inclusive system
inconceivable ; 13. (4) Is reality one system ? ; 14. System and proof : (A)
The testimony of science ; 15. (B) The incompatibility of systems and the
system ; 16. The self-contradictions of the system ; 17. The moral.

§ 1. The Ideal of Proof.

Closely connected with the theory of the syllogism is the
theory of proof. It was Aristotle's discovery of the syllogism
that infected logicians with their craving for 'valid' forms of
reasoning, and inspired them with an ideal of proof or demonstration which determined their attitude to all questions of
knowledge. The ideal proof was to be coercive and conclusive,
to render its conclusion necessarily true and unconditionally
and absolutely certain. No intelligence was to withhold its
homage from it, or to question its finality. It was the only
thing in Logic worth having, and no price was too high to pay
for it. Compared with it, all other reasoning was negligible
or despicable. Inductions, probabilities, postulates, hypotheses,
analogies, verifications, were all of no account in the eyes of
pure logic and of the true logician. They all fell short of complete 'validity.' They all lacked 'cogency.' They all took risks.
They could neither compel nor assure the mind that trafficked
with them. Proof—absolute, irrefragable proof—alone was
worthy of logic's ambition; for it alone could form the basis
of science. With it, true science became possible—a science that
proceeded infallibly from assured principles to an absolutely
certain conclusion by an irresistible demonstration. Without it,
the sciences became playgrounds for the vagrant fancies and
varying hypotheses of erring mortals, and refused to reveal any
immutable and eternal truths on which the mind could rest and
a fabric of knowledge could be reared.

§ 2. Syllogism as Proof.

Hence the enormous importance of the syllogism. In it logicians thought that they had got hold of the very form of ideal proof. They believed that the conclusion of a valid syllogism was proved absolutely. No one could reject it, once he had committed himself to its premisses, which were linked to its conclusion by so adamantine a necessity that no thought could break its bonds. It was, therefore, a necessary truth, equipped with absolute cogency. Its truth was undeniable, and could shatter all the assaults of scepticism. It was true, no doubt, that the truth of a syllogistic conclusion was *dependent*, and transmitted to it from its premisses. But this was merely to say that it was inferential, and it did not matter. For no doubt could insinuate itself into the firm texture of the syllogistic fabric. So no truth could be *lost* on the way from the premisses to the conclusion. It was true also, of course, that the formal validity of the reasoning was independent of the actual truth of the premisses. It was, indeed, one of the glories of the syllogism that one could argue just as validly from false premisses as from true, from doubtful premisses as from indubitable. So it was better in one's search for truth to start from absolutely true premisses. But there was no difficulty about that. For there was surely an ample supply of true propositions to serve as premisses. If anyone questioned them, their truth could be proved. For had not the syllogism provided the form of proof? At first, then, it seemed that the ideal had been attained.

§ 3. The Syllogism's Failures: (1) Begging the Question.

And yet reflection, some of it dating back to Aristotle himself, has shown that in a variety of ways the syllogism fails to attain this ideal. It turns out that a valid form *can* lose truth, its supply of true premisses *can* be cut off; nay, the very validity of the syllogistic form *can* be disputed (Chap. XIV, §§ 2, 3, and 6). Thus it fails alike in its form and in its presupposition; and, moreover, its failures are not gratuitous: they are demanded by its use in actual reasoning. Yet what better testimony could there be to the fascination of its form than the fact that, despite its notorious and gross defects, it still retains its place in logical instruction?

(1) The first objection which has forced itself upon the attention of all but the most fanatical admirers of the syllogism assails its claim to be in any way a form of proof. It proves nothing, as we have urged, because it assumes the very point to be proved. Or, in other words, the ideal form of proof commits the formal fallacy of 'begging the question.' More precisely, if it does *not* do this, it proves nothing new, nothing we did not know already, and miserably fails to understand the growth of knowledge. 'Demonstration,' therefore, is either a futility or a fallacy, and any 'valid' syllogism will reveal this. Reverting to the time-honoured argument about the mortality of Socrates (a singularly inept example, because the fact that Socrates has been dead so long renders it hopeless as a vehicle of *new* knowledge), if we *know* that its hero has been defunct for some 2000 years, we learn nothing from it: whereas, if we think that he is still alive, and are trying to prognosticate his future by this form, it is clear that we have no *right* to assert in the major premiss that *all men are mortal*, unless we have already ascertained that *every* man is mortal. Thus the mortality of Socrates, so far from being proved, is itself a presupposition of the truth of its major premiss.

The situation evidently is a piquant one, and has led to endless attempts to justify the syllogism by enabling it to rebut this charge of begging the question. Most of these are so verbal, tortuous, and obscure that they serve rather to discredit logic, and would fail in their object, even if they were sound. The rest, in so far as they are relevant at all, all reduce themselves to the *three* expedients examined in Chap. XIV, § 3. It is clear, in the first place, that the interpretation of *all men are mortal* as an enumeration of particular cases will not do. It is fatal to construe *all men are mortal* in denotation, as a proposition about individuals (Chap. XIII, § 5). It is therefore taken, somewhat awkwardly, as a statement, not about all *men*, but about the essential nature of man. This, however, is ambiguous, and may be taken in two ways.

19

(*a*) If it is taken strictly, as part of a definition of man, it will indeed follow that no being that is not mortal can be called a man, and that *if* Socrates *is* a man he is of necessity mortal. But if so, the argument now begs the question in its minor premiss, when it asserts that *Socrates is a man*, without establishing our right to call him so. For all that the 'form of proof' can tell us to the contrary, therefore, the best reasoning might all consist of laying down arbitrary definitions and then assuming that they must hold when applied to reality, which appears to be the logician's conception of mathematical 'demonstration.'

(*b*) The third way of interpreting *all men are mortal* is to take it as stating a general law of nature under which the case of Socrates is brought, and this then seems to afford to our conclusion the guarantee of an established order of nature. When, however, we raise the question whether the general value or truth of such a rule can be taken to guarantee its application to *every* case, including the cases where the subject of the argument is a case of the rule for *some* purposes though *not* for others, or is mistakenly taken as a case at all, we realise (though most logicians do not!) that the syllogism once more begs the question, in a *third* way. For it now asserts, without proof, that the case under consideration is *not* so exceptional that the general rule fails to apply to it, and implies that we were *right* in taking it as a case of the rule. This may be so in the case of Socrates, as of Tom, Dick, and Harry in the past; but it would clearly have been false of Enoch, Elijah, Tithonus, and the other heroes who escaped death: it might, moreover, become false, of some men or of all, if Mr Bernard Shaw's 'Ancients' were evolved, or if medical science discovered how to arrest the physiological decay of the body. Again the syllogism *fails* as a proof, because it begs the question it claims to prove.

(*c*) There remains, however, the fourth way of saving the syllogism, which was examined in Chap. XIV, § 5. If we take the premisses as the statement of a *hypothesis* and the conclusion as *conditional* on their truth, the whole argument becomes an *experiment* to be verified empirically by the *coming true* of the conclusion. Here there is no begging of the question, because there is no assumption of the truth of the premisses, but a confession of doubt which the conclusion tests. It is only when we do *not* feel certain either that *all men are mortal*, or that *Socrates is a man* in the sense in which 'man' implies mortality (say, because being 'dead,' he has returned as a 'ghost') that a real argument is conceivable, and the syllogism can be *used*.

But this interpretation of the syllogism is an avowal that the conclusion is *not* absolutely proved. It is hypothetical and needs verification. So the formal ideal of proof is abandoned, and the syllogism is thrown over as an example thereof. It becomes merely a form in which a thought-experiment is conducted, and its conclusion serves merely to guide expectation. It predicts what should happen if its premisses *were* true, i.e. *true enough* to lead to the conclusion; but it no longer postulates their absolute truth, and relies for their actual truth on the empirical verification of its prediction. Now verification, as we saw (Chap. XIV, § 5), is always afflicted with a formal flaw; and, if it is the best the syllogism can do, the ideal proof of Formal Logic is *never* realised.

§ 4. (2) The Liability to Ambiguous Middle.

(2) A further formal flaw inherent in the structure of the syllogism is its liability to Sidgwick's ambiguity of the middle term (Chap. XIV, § 4). If in actual use its middle may always become ambiguous, the general truth of a proposition used as a premiss ceases to guarantee the truth of its applications; and if a proposition found true in one relation and context may become false in another, the validity of the syllogistic form becomes questionable. For it always argues from what is true in one relation to what is true in another, and proffers no proof of this assumption beyond the verbal identity of the terms. Yet it is a matter of common notoriety that the meaning of terms is often relative to their context. A man who is 'rich' in Iceland would hardly seem so among the multimillionaires of New York. A man who is 'big' in Lilliput would not be so in Brobdingnag. A man who is 'healthy' at sea-level would not be so 20,000 feet up

Everest. Clearly the *logical use* of any term involves an assumption and a risk—the assumption that it will hold in the context to which it is transferred, and the risk that it will not. Moreover, any use of the syllogistic form implies a claim that two propositions may be picked up anywhere and put together, and will thereupon be found to apply to a new case differing more or less from any hitherto observed. Now, these propositions may be abstractly true, and may still remain true separately: they may be true so far as we know, and may have worked quite well up to date; yet they may yield untrue results in the particular (new) application which we contemplate when we combine them. They may then become quite misleading and effectively false.

Thus, to revert to the example given in Chap. XIV, § 4, though it is in general true that *men are rational*, and even indisputable that *Smith is a man*, the inference that *therefore Smith is rational* may fail because he happens to be a howling lunatic. Thus two 'true' premisses, when combined, lead to a false conclusion. The explanation is, of course, that truth in general is no guarantee of truth in a particular case, and that what is a 'case' of a rule for some purposes is not so for the purpose in hand. Such failures of syllogistic proof can, of course, be explained. We merely say, "Oh, the middle term *was* ambiguous. It ought to have been symbolised not by M and M, but by M and μ. But the mistake was unavoidable, because we could not have known this in advance of our experiment; we could find out only by trying." But this explanation does not dispute that the syllogism as a form of 'proof' has played us false.

So we should proceed cautiously on the assumption of the 'law of identity.' That *M is M* wherever any 'M' occurs rests only on the slender basis of a verbal identity and on our imperative need of something to link S to P. Our assumption is really methodological, and always takes a risk. Unless we take this risk, our past experience cannot be brought to bear on our new case at all. The application of a principle to what we believe, or hope, will prove a new case thereof, always must be

risked. In 99 cases out of 100 our experiment succeeds; in
the hundredth it fails. But it may then teach us more about
the variety of nature and the elasticity of principles than we
could ever have learnt from monotonous success. So our
failures should not seriously distress us : we should resign ourselves to an occurrence we have no means of foreseeing or
averting, but we can fairly require our logic to warn us against
this possibility and not to conceal it.

But to Formalist theory this discovery is a terrible blow. It
implies a fatal flaw in the form of the syllogism. It explodes its
claim to absolute truth. It reveals that, however true and
absolute and undeniable a principle may seem to be in itself,
it cannot transmit these qualities to its applications. It cannot
protect itself against misapplication and confutation by the
course of events. Moreover, it exposes formal principles to a
singular temptation. As this risk is inherent in their *use*, the
only 'truths' that can never be refuted and can retain their
claim to absoluteness will be those which are utterly inapplicable, and can never be used under any conditions. We have a
choice, therefore, between (a nominal) 'infallibility' and use.
The theorist succumbs to this temptation and chooses infallibility. Hence, both logic and ethics teem with principles which
have been rendered impotent and inapplicable, in order that
they might never play us false. Yet their part is none the less
grotesque. For inapplicable principles are in the end unmeaning. And, admirably as they befit a Formal logic which
abstracts from meaning, there is no place for them in a logic
which concerns itself with real knowing.

§ 5. (3) The Infinite Regress in Proof.

It would seem, then, that the internal economy of the syllogistic form rejects the ideal of proof it was chosen to exemplify;
properly understood, it points rather to an experimental use
of the form, and conveys a warning against the risks this entails.
Are its external relations to the truth any more favourable to
the ideal of proof ?

After all, the syllogism never professed to yield unconditional

proof. It guaranteed truth to its conclusion only hypothetically, if its premisses were true; or rather, if we might make
bold to assume their truth. Ordinarily this guarantee is enough,
because the truth of the premisses is taken for granted; but
many things are ordinarily taken for granted which would be
hard to prove. And the logician cannot afford to be so lax. He
should not simply assume that there are plenty of absolute
truths lying about to be argued from, but should inquire into
the truth of this assumption and into the consequences of
challenging the premisses of a syllogism.

He would then find that the syllogism at once develops the
curious disability already discussed in Chaps. XIII, § 6 and XIV,
§ 2. When the truth of a premiss is questioned, it is natural to try
to prove it. But, owing to the form of the syllogism, proof will
require a supply of *two* premisses from which the disputed premiss may be deduced. These also will have to be absolutely true,
if the first premiss is to be so. Moreover, as *both* of the original
premisses may be challenged, we are really called upon to find
four true propositions to guard our original conclusion against
the first onset of doubt. Thus the syllogism stands revealed as
a self-defeating form of reasoning: it 'proves' a disputed proposition by turning it into a conclusion deduced from two
others, and, when these are disputed in their turn, it asks for
four more, and so on; thus its requisitions on absolute truth
are doubled at every step it is driven backwards (Chap. XIV,
§ 2). It is certainly a very odd way of acquiring certainty, and
the objections to its procedure are obvious.

(1) Its method is ruinously expensive, and must speedily
exhaust the largest capital of absolute truth to which any
philosopher would lay claim.

(2) It indefinitely postpones the beginning of knowing, and
renders it conditional upon the completion of an infinite regress.
Its entire motion is plainly *retrograde*. It does not *advance*
towards new truth, but *recoils* further and further the more it is
pressed. It appears, therefore, to be singularly unfit to illustrate,
or to sanction, the progress of knowledge. If we cannot begin
our advance till we have got back to absolutely sure foundations,

and must begin our knowing from absolute truths, we shall never make a start.

(3) In order, therefore, to extract from the syllogism an analysis of the *growing* knowledge embodied in scientific proofs, it must be radically reinterpreted. A way must be found of converting the *infinite regress* of its vain search for unquestionable premises into an *infinite progress*. Fortunately this is easy. We have merely to permit the *hypothetical* use of premises; that is, the very same expedient which rebutted the charge of *petitio* (§ 3). If our premises may state a hypothesis, the question of their initial truth loses all its terrors. For truth becomes not our starting-point, but our aim. Provided that our hypotheses can be used (and if not they are vain), the verifications their truth-claim receives in its use will confirm their claim, and gradually establish it beyond all reasonable doubt. We have merely to allow such verification to *count*, and to abstain from dismissing each piece of evidence as it accrues, on the ground that in itself it is not cogent or conclusive. But this will be the real difficulty with apriorist logicians. This use of hypothetical premises means cancelling the demand for initial certainty and truth. It means *experiment* and the perils of experiment. No wonder this expedient, simple though it is, never entered the mind of a Formal logician as an effective way of rescuing the syllogism from its *reductio ad absurdum*. They tried instead a couple of blind alleys.

§ 6. Can Intuition Save the Syllogism?

Aristotle, after a certain amount of coquetting with the inductive proof, to be considered later (§ 7), determined to cut short the infinite regress of disputable premises by inventing a faculty to do the trick. He predicted that sooner or later inquiry would come upon propositions which were true in their own right, and neither demanded nor permitted further proof or test. They were self-evident, self-testing, and self-proving, and their perception was intuitive. Being immediately apprehended, they were absolutely certain, infallible, and undeniable. Themselves indemonstrable, they provided a secure, immovable, and immutable basis for demonstration, and it was only when a body of knowledge reached them that it became worthy of the name of Science. Sciences, therefore, were coherent structures of demonstrated necessary truths, deduced from such indemonstrable premisses. Whatever could not be so deduced was not science, and every science was in principle finite and capable of completion. For from a finite number of premisses only a finite number of conclusions could be proved.

To apprehend these self-evident principles Aristotle providently provided a special faculty. He called it Νοῦς, which is best translated as 'intuitive reason,' and regarded it as the loftiest part of our mental equipment. It was more certain than the demonstrations resting on the principles it apprehended, supreme and infallible, the ultimate guarantee of truth. Thus did Aristotle think, amid the applause of many generations of logicians, that the syllogism could be rehabilitated and the ideal proof attained.

Yet at best he had only cured one of the syllogism's maladies, the infinite regress inherent in the attempt to start from certainty: he had done nothing to justify it as a vehicle of the infinite progress of scientific knowledge or to make its internal relations 'valid.' Moreover, Aristotle had to pay a heavy price for his rescue of the syllogism.

(a) He had to introduce an incurable dualism into knowledge. The immediate truths of Reason forming the first principles of knowledge differed in kind, in value, and in faculty from those of mediate reasoning deduced from them. This, perhaps, might be regarded as an inconsistency and inelegance rather than as a serious objection.

But (b) it was distinctly serious that the existence and infallibility of intuitive reason were merely postulated and not authenticated, and most serious of all that in its use this fictitious faculty was completely futile. For no means existed of applying it to any question so as to safeguard any disputed truth. In the end its ultimate appeal was from logic to psychology; for the fact that we feel immediately certain of the truth of certain propositions or experiences is primarily a fact of human psychology.

Moreover, this feeling attends a great variety of experiences. All have probably experienced it in connection with the illusions of dream-life, in which intuitive certainty runs riot and imposes on us the most fantastic absurdities. It is a habitual ground of belief with a large number of persons, especially of the feminine sex, who rely on 'intuitions' because they are too lazy to reason.

It is extremely liable to morbid perversion, as in the intuitions of the insane. It frequently proves misleading or false, even in the sane, when they trust it to authenticate the truth of propositions which seem to them self-evident. Thus our belief that two bodies cannot occupy the same space seems obvious and self-evident enough; yet it rests on quite inadequate experience, and may be shaken by quite easy experiments. Our belief that $2 + 2 = 4$ exhibits both self-evidence and the highest degree of certainty; yet its truth really depends on neither of these, but on its deduction from the assumptions on which our number-system is built. It is not too much to say, therefore, that for some 2000 years reliance on self-evidence has deceived philosophers as to the nature of mathematical truth. It cannot, in view of these familiar facts, be maintained that a proposition is true because we 'feel it in our bones,' unless some way can be devised of differentiating logical from psychological, true from false, intuition. Yet believers in intuition make no attempt to provide such a criterion; they do not even publish lists of true intuitions. For all these reasons we may fairly conclude that the appeal to intuitions is uncritical, illusory, and futile.

§ 7. The Inductive Proof of Premisses.

If Intuition is unable to establish the truth of our premisses, can we induce Induction to perform this service? At first sight inductive reasoning seems to be manifestly invalid. It is an attempt to reason from some cases to all, otherwise to a principle that applies to all cases, past, present, and to come. And its procedure is not only invalid, but also fallacious. It warrants arguments like "it is very improbable that the solar system will ever come to grief by a collision with another star, for it has never done so yet "; or, "it is very unlikely that I shall die in my sleep, for I have now gone to bed over 30,000 times in my life, and found that I always woke up alive next morning." There is plainly a logical jump from some cases to all, and all the cases are never known. Nor does Hume's question, "Why should the future resemble the past?" receive an answer. Accordingly, there is a pathetic paradox about the attempts of logicians to extract from induction a foundation for valid inference, and they would long ago have desisted from them had they not been so desperately devoted to their conception of valid inference. At present there is something very near agreement that no 'valid' transition exists from the particular cases which point to a universal principle to the logical proof of that principle, though not all would infer from this that induction was logically worthless.

The reason, moreover, for this agreement is sufficiently plain. If the truth of a universal principle has to obtain always and everywhere, wherever and whenever there exists what may be taken (or mistaken) for a 'case' of that principle, it is perfectly plain that from no amount of inductive observation can we validly infer the principle. For the number of our observed cases can never be more than an infinitesimal fraction of the possible cases; and the belief that our inductive basis is a 'fair sample' of nature as a whole, and can go bail for the rest, merely begs the question. It assumes, first, that nature is such that fair samples of it can be taken—i.e. that it is not liable to irruptions of incalculable novelty—and this assumption can hardly rank higher than a convenient methodological fiction; and, secondly, that in our actual evidence we have been lucky enough to obtain a fair sample. Such assumptions are no doubt convenient, but they can hardly pretend to be valid and irrefragable. Besides, how would they help us, if it chanced that the next case we encountered and endeavoured to investigate by their aid did *not* happen to be a fair sample? We have seen that special cases are by no means uncommon (§ 4), and the fact that they are also *hard* cases only renders it more desirable that our logic should undertake to cope with them.

Whoever is not convinced that there is no valid bridging of the gulf between *some* cases and *all* may further be invited to contemplate a still more radical objection. No argument from 'facts' or 'cases' can conceivably attain to formal validity, simply because 'facts' and 'cases' are not found in nature, but have to be constructed. They are not conceivable without a great deal of intellectual manipulation, which transforms the 'given,' and uses operations entailing at every step a possibility of error. Hence our 'fact' is always more or less 'faked,' our 'case' is always more or less 'prepared,' and, unless they were, we could not argue from them. At the beginning of every inquiry the 'facts' are always allegations, and usually replete with error and misconception; it is only the *success* of the inquiry which sifts the 'real' facts from the facts so called. The admission, therefore, that something seems a fact to some one is far from making it a valid foundation for an argument. The more so that any fact, whether apparent or real, can come into being as such only by a mental operation. It has to be 'recognised'—that is, it has to be *discriminated* from the general flux of happenings in which it comes, and *taken* as a fact. Thus it is always a product of a *selection*. And *selection* is always a *risky* process, which involves alternatives and infinite possibilities of error (Chap. V, § 4). From the same *data* a variety of selections may be made, to be recognised as 'facts'; and assuredly with different interests we shall select differently. Moreover, the selection we make may always be *wrong*. It may leave out, or include, too much. It may omit the vital point, or swamp thought in masses of irrelevance. Even if it only views matters in a false light or puts a wrong emphasis upon them, these defects may suffice to baffle an attempted argument from 'facts.'

Moreover, the unwarranted assumptions lurking in the notion of a 'case' are no less serious. It is sheer assumption that a given situation may be taken as a case of any law at all. Having assumed that there must be law (for the methodological reason that otherwise we could not reason at all), we next encounter the more ticklish question—'what law?'—and have to *choose* our law. Any 'law' we try begins as a hypothesis, which we *select* from a number of alternatives because it finds favour in our eyes and is the *best* we can think of at the time. If it happens to be wrong, our 'case' will prove to be recalcitrant to our 'law,' and we shall make no headway. We must then experiment with another law, and hold ourselves ready to scrap it so soon as it ceases to work or a better swims into our ken. And even when we have got hold of a law that works adequately for the generality of 'cases,' we must keep a look-out for the *exceptional* case which defeats the law, and the *ambiguous* case which may be brought under several laws, and raises a dispute as to which classifies it best. It is clear that all these procedures are fallible, and that none can lay claim to formal validity or absolute proof: when its actual procedure is studied, inductive reasoning does not even pretend to be a 'valid' process.

The attempt, then, to prove universal truths by way of induction fails; at best it can but be pathetic self-deception, at worst it may be direct dishonesty.

§ 8. The Cure by Systematic Coherence.

It is no wonder that from the first attempts should have been made to render inference inexpugnable, without recourse to fictitious faculties and dubious psychological dogmas, by developing the implications of its inherent structure. Syllogistic proof plainly relies in part on the *esprit de corps* which pervades the body of our truths: a challenged truth summons a couple of its kin to bear it out. In other words, proof implies the *coherence* of truths, and the thought easily suggests itself that systematic coherence may be proof enough, and indeed the essence of all proof.

This contention is quite plausible, and must be taken very seriously. It has at present the support of all the most consummate logicians, who, indeed, would hardly allow anyone else to rank as a logician at all. And their idea is of the most venerable antiquity; for Aristotle already had to struggle against those who thought that it was proper to 'argue in a circle,' and to establish the truth of a group of propositions by the mutual support they yielded to each other. Aristotle rejected this view as a 'fallacy,' but he had not encountered its modern refinements; and in any case it is deserving of careful examination.

So let us raise the question *de novo* whether the proposition C may not be proved by deducing it from A and B, and then B by deducing it from A and C, and finally A by deduction from B and C. True, we do not thereby gain a proof of any one of them which is *independent* of the truth of the others; strictly speaking, we only prove that A, B, and C stand and fall together. But do we really need such proof of their independent truth? Is it not enough that they form a system of coherent truths, and is not systematic coherence in the end the essence of real truth? We hesitate to content ourselves with this merely because our systems are too small; they seem liable to foreign invasion and overthrow, because we feel there is so much they do not include which might upset them. But the cure for this weakness is *more* system and *more* coherence: if we could *complete* our system of knowledge and render it *all-embracing* would it not become certain and unassailable? And would not our reasoning then be completely valid? Circular argument, therefore, is fallacious only if the circle is not large enough; make it as large as the universe and it becomes the acme of proof!

So the logician, rising in thought (or imagination) to the possession of such an all-inclusive system, can revel in the consciousness of a perfect order, in which every part is sustained by the support of every other part, and in turn sustains it; in which nothing is amiss and nothing can be altered, because to alter it would derange the whole, and in which every objection can be silenced by the grim alternative 'that or nothing.' In such a system [1] no part can be denied, because to deny it would subvert all knowledge, and no one can get a standpoint outside the system to subvert it. The systematic whole, therefore, is unassailable and indubitable. From this secure and exalted standpoint the logician can look down with pity and contempt on the cognitive operations of inferior mortals. The laborious investigations of the sciences look to him like the wanderings

---

[1] Or should we not rather say—' in *this* system ' ?

of babes lost in a forest of uncomprehended fact. The vain struggles of the syllogism to establish its validity exemplify merely the futility of 'linear inference.' He interprets syllogistic reasoning as groping for the conception of systematic coherence. Its essence is to show how the premisses go bail for the conclusion. C gets A and B to endorse its claim to truth: the importance of this is that, once it is 'proved' syllogistically, C can no longer be rejected save at the cost of rejecting A or B, or both. In other words, it is strengthened by the systematic coherence of all truth, though, he would hasten to add, a syllogism was still very remote from the full-orbed security of his all-accommodating system. It is only when the cost of rejecting anything is the rejection of everything that anything is proved. Thus on the choice between 'this or nothing' rests the validity of proof.

He would then graciously admit, no doubt, that, as a matter of prosaic fact, the perfect security of perfect proof had not yet been achieved, because no system of knowledge (with the possible exception of his own philosophy, if he is a metaphysician!) was as yet all-embracing; but he would live in hopes, and would hold that, as an ideal at least, his conception of proof as systematic coherence was irrefutable.

§ 9. The Illusions of Systematic Coherence.

In spite of this impressive argument, a question may be raised whether this conception of valid proof is itself valid. The father of logic was familiar with essentially the same idea, and rejected it as a 'fallacy,' which has ever since been listed as that of 'arguing in a circle.' It seems incumbent, therefore, on the advocates of proof by systematic coherence either to explode this fallacy or to distinguish their notion of proof from that of circular argument. This ought not to be a difficult achievement for men who can distinguish between a 'good' and a 'bad' infinite; after that, why should it be hard to distinguish between a 'vicious' and a virtuous circle? Still, at first sight, it seems a little odd to turn a fallacy into a valid argument, nay, into the pattern of all proof by mere enlargement of the circle.

To test this matter we shall do well to inquire how, and how far, the conception of an all-embracing system is really thinkable, and, if it is, whether reasoning in such a system would be the ideal proof, necessarily cogent and indisputably valid. For this purpose it will be necessary to examine—(1) why precisely an argument in a circle is regarded as fallacious; (2) whether the objection to it, whether sound or not, can be made to disappear by enlarging the circle; (3) whether a system truly all-inclusive can be conceived, and how; (4) whether the real must be taken as forming such a system; and (5) whether, accordingly, the idea of such a system yields the true theory of proof.

§ 10. (1) Why Circular Reasoning is Fallacious.

It is obvious that if anyone feels doubtful about the truth of a proposition, his doubt can be assuaged by summoning up other propositions which he accepts as true and showing that they support the proposition doubted. For he may then be compelled to drop his doubt under penalty of losing truths he values. But even so he always has a choice; he may either now accept the truth he had doubted before, or he may now reject the truths he had accepted before, because he finds them in such doubtful company. So his doubt *need not* be assuaged by an argument which merely purports to show that the truth of proposition A is bound up with that of B and C. He can simply say: "Well, that is a reason for doubting B and C as well! The mere fact that a number of lying witnesses all tell the same tale is no reason for believing any of them." It is true that if he wishes to retain his belief in B and C he may now *prefer* to accept A; but he is perfectly free to repudiate the whole system. The fact, therefore, that he has this choice confutes the contention that he is coerced by an argument of indisputable validity. Consequently, reasoning in a circle is not *as such* a cogent form of argument, nor is it 'valid' in the sense of coercive. Nor is argument in a system, which does not (so far) differ from it in form. Formally both lack coerciveness, and neither can appeal to Formal Logic, which has no use for any argument, however natural and persuasive, that does not use force, and insists on treating the human reason as Roman Law treated the slave, and on holding its testimony worthless unless it has been extracted under torture.

To meet a charge of circularity or to bolster up a disputed system it is *not* enough to argue within the system: it is necessary to find *outside* support, which will fit into the system and remove objections, and will not be itself disputed. Thus the system defends itself, not passively by its mere coherence, but *actively* by showing capacity for expansion and by assimilating what was *independent* fact or truth, and so satisfying the objector who had refused to accept its own testimony to its truth.

§ 11. (2) Enlarging the Circle Futile.

Our analysis of the objection to circular argument should throw light on the consequences of enlarging the circle. The larger the circle can be made, the larger the mass of truths supporting the disputed proposition and the greater the cost of rejecting it. The doubter naturally, therefore, grows more reluctant to make the sacrifices his doubt entails. But this reluctance is psychological, not logical. Logically he is still able (and entitled) to reject the whole coherent mass, which still floats in the air of hypothesis and is not anchored to the solid ground of fact. A disputable proposition does not become indisputable by taking to itself other propositions which are no less disputable; for the whole system may only be a case of coherent error.

§ 12. (3) An All-inclusive System Inconceivable.

But will this reasoning hold if all conceivable propositions can be summoned to support the challenged truth, and the objector be confronted with a truly all-inclusive system? To answer this question we must begin by inquiring what is *meant* by an all-inclusive system.

(*a*) It obviously cannot mean one that includes the objector, objection and all. For then the doctrine would become a truism; if the objector and his objection have been absorbed into the system the opposition to it will, *ex hyp.*, have vanished.

(*b*) The utmost we can suppose is that the system becomes so inclusive that it leaves the objector no ground outside it to stand upon. This would render his objection *illogical*, though, even then, it may remain psychologically real. This seems, at first, a logical possibility. But is it thinkable that a really stalwart objector can ever be wholly deprived of his *locus standi*?

To deprive him of all standing-ground outside the 'all-inclusive system,' the latter would have to develop two further qualities which are not usually held to be, and are certainly never shown to be, consequential on this notion. (1) It would have to embrace not only all real things but also all imaginable things. And (2) it would have to make good its claim to be the *only* system that could perform these feats.

(1) For, unless it performed the first feat, the objector retains his right to put himself, in thought, outside the system, and to postulate reals that will not fit into the system seeking to coerce him. Even if he could be forbidden to do this, he could not be prevented from passing judgment on the system as a whole. His judgment will be a value-judgment, of course, but so is every other judgment—nay, the belief in the system itself. Moreover, he will always have at least two alternatives. He can approve or disapprove. If he approves, he cancels his objection and comes back into the system, *voluntarily*; but it can hardly be called indisputable merely because no one chooses to dispute it. If he disapproves he can give reasons. He can also state the conditions under which he would accept the system, and imagine additions to it which would transmute it into something acceptable. But by so doing he would be refuting its original claim to all-inclusiveness. If he remains intransigently in revolt he likewise refutes the system's claim. For, to be truly all-inclusive, it has to include in itself the denial of itself. But this renders it self-contradictory, which is precisely what it was assumed not to be.

So there seems to be no escape from the conclusion that two standpoints remain thinkable—that of a submissive part of the system, and that of the recalcitrant rebel. Moreover, their valuations may well be diametrically opposed, so that what is

20

true for the one will be false for the other. Hence, once more, the system will not be able to be all-inclusive. It will not be able to validate the judgments that reject it. But whether it rejects or accepts them, it will, in fact, refute itself.

(2) The above considerations are really enough to dispose of the assumption that there is *only one* genuinely all-inclusive system and that no *alternative* ways of systematising truths are conceivable. The uniqueness of a system is even harder to prove, and even to conceive, than its all-inclusiveness. For alternatives prevail throughout the field of knowledge. No conceivable system is so rigid that it absolutely determines the place of a given fact, and no necessary inference leads from all-inclusiveness to absolute determination. All our experiences and all our 'facts' can be interpreted and correlated in a variety of ways. They may be viewed from different standpoints, by different methods, in different orders, with different purposes; and what one system rejects or abuses another may welcome and exalt. Hence systems which are technically all-inclusive, i.e. which conceive themselves as such, may exist in the plural.

Thus the course of events may be ascribed to causation or to chance. The causal relation may itself be conceived as mechanical or as teleological. The manifestations of intelligence may be set down to consciousness or explained away after the fashion of 'behaviourism.' Any event may be conceived as completely determined or as partly indeterminate, the reign of law as absolute or as modifiable by 'miracle.' Novelties may be recognised or tabooed. Most flagrantly of all, every event, nay every event conceivable, may be valued as good or as evil, and fitted either into an optimistic or into a pessimistic scheme of interpretation.

There are, then, plenty of alternative ways of compiling coherent systems; but there is no proof that only one of these can be all-inclusive. In theory, at least, the notion of an all-inclusive system may have a plurality of exemplifications, and the choice between them remains open. Hence the mere formal notion of 'system' is powerless to settle disputes about a contested truth;

it may cohere with one system and not with another, and both may claim to be all-inclusive. It is only when both parties to the dispute have accepted *the same* system that an appeal to systematic coherence ceases to be a fallacy of arguing in a circle. But even then its proof is not 'cogent' and indisputable.

(c) If all-inclusiveness is to mean that the system is *closed*, and not to be extended by taking in new fact, a doubt arises whether such a system can be valid, or even thinkable. For it would seem of necessity to argue in a circle. No doubt an all-inclusive system *should* be 'closed'; for, if it admitted anything further or new, it would thereby admit that it was not all-inclusive before. But if its all-inclusiveness is taken thus seriously, it cannot come to terms with a critic who condemns appeals to a system he questions or rejects as false, and a deadlock ensues. He demands independent evidence of its truth, and rightly, because he doubts either its all-inclusiveness or its truth, or both: but the system cannot proffer it, because it claims to have already included all truth and to have left none outside. It thus refuses to submit to any independent test or to listen to objections; so the critic, being refused satisfaction, is naturally driven to accuse it of arguing in a vicious circle. He is even entitled to charge it with self-contradiction, because its claim to all-inclusiveness is confuted by his inability to accept it. Logically his very existence ought to be inadmissible, though this is probably not the reason why Formal logicians are so reluctant to reply to criticism and so long-suffering in their lofty silence.

Thus the all-inclusive system seems to be caught in a dilemma. So long as it remains open to argument it cannot form an all-inclusive system: it has to concede the existence of extraneous truth, capable of confirming (or confuting) it: so soon as it claims to be all-inclusive, it closes itself, begs the question of its truth, and raises the question whether the mere existence of criticism is not a confutation of its claim.

This question must be answered in the affirmative. Though humorous, it is a *mauvaise plaisanterie* for a system to claim all-inclusiveness while its claim is actually being contested. While it is not disputed, there is nothing to discuss; but if it *is* contested, this is a proof that it *can* be contested.

Can it even be conceived to become indisputable? Hardly. For even if a system were admitted to include all the facts, it would not follow that all its interpretations and valuations were right. By adopting a different interpretation or valuation an alternative system might always be constructed which would dispute its claim to truth. Hence, however extensive and complete a system was conceived to be, it could never grow to be *unique*, and so could never make out a *cogent* case for itself. There would always be other systems making the same claims, and we should be free to choose between them. An all-inclusive system, therefore, to which no alternative is conceivable, is *not* conceivable.

§ 13. (4) Is Reality one System?

But perhaps it may be argued that, nevertheless, it may be real. May not reality form a system which in point of fact admits only of *one* interpretation? That is what every true metaphysician believes at heart about his own metaphysic; but every metaphysic, in fact, refutes the belief. For, though all metaphysics claim to be coherent, they never are completely; though they all claim to be all-embracing, they never are; and though they all claim to be uniquely true, not more than one of them can possibly be true (on their own assumptions), and it is more than probable that all are false. It seems fantastic, therefore, to identify the ideal of an all-inclusive system uniquely true with any actual system of philosophy.

Furthermore, the assumption that there is a totality of reality, or otherwise that the real indisputably forms an unambiguous whole, is highly questionable. It is a pure assumption of which no proof is ever offered, and it seems to clash with a number of obvious facts. Thus (*a*) many of the constituents of the real appear to have a character which forbids their union into a whole. For example, space, time, and number. All three appear to be infinite, and an infinite whole is self-contradictory nonsense. (*b*) Other reals appear to be highly recalcitrant to fusion

with their kin into a real whole. For example, the complete
fusion of two minds, with all their idiosyncrasies, limitations,
errors, delusions, etc., into one, would seem to be unthinkable,
except under conditions which would amount to annihilation of
the minds said to be united. When the 'spiritual nature of the
Absolute' is scrutinised, it is found to mean nothing but a
common grave for such spirits as we know. (*c*) The Absolute
does not really form a unifying principle which compacts the
real into a 'universe.' It is too indeterminate; we can conceive
a variety of ways of unifying the real (§ 12), to each of which a
different 'Absolute' will correspond. 'The Whole,' therefore,
remains a hypothesis to be verified (or not), and a logical species
to be exemplified in a variety of cases. Hence the mere notion
of a totality of reality has not the strength to bludgeon philosophers into agreement.

§ 14. System and Proof: (A) the Testimony of Science.

The prospect of finding in the idea of system a pattern of
perfect proof has clouded over considerably, but we are still
far from having faced all the logical difficulties it involves.

(A) In the first place, the transition from the actual facts of
systematic coherence to the ideal of an all-inclusive system was
allowed far too easily. It involves a logical jump which is not
only *invalid* but positively *false*. It is, moreover, invalid in
several ways.

(1) There is first the minor point that it is not valid to argue
from the dependence of a conclusion on its premises to a dependence of the premises on the conclusion. For the relation
need not be reciprocal (or 'symmetrical'). Thus the very
notion of systematic coherence is not arrived at validly.

(2) That truth is system is inferred from the systematic
character of the sciences; but the inference is false. For the
sciences never rely for their truth on their systematic character
alone; they always demand, more or less, in one way or another,
application and verification *as well*.

Nor are they ever *perfect* systems; indeed, with their actual
procedure they cannot conceivably become such. They all

accept many *data* on the mere warrant of experience, as sheer facts, without deducing them from their system. Even geometry takes the existence of space as empirically given, and does not attempt to prove that it cannot have more than three dimensions. Also, they admit facts without requiring them to cohere. This is, in fact, the way they *grow*. But if they really relied on the systematic character of truth, they would have to reject all new facts and all new truths, simply because they did not cohere with the old beliefs, but corrected them (Chap. VII, § 17). Actually this is just what the conservative party in every science always tries to do to novelties, often with success; but what it shows is not that the belief in system is the basis of truth, but that it may easily become a source of error.

No *growing* science, therefore, is ever quite coherent: some adjustments in its system are always going on, in order that it may accommodate new truth. And if it be retorted that a *perfect* system would not be forced to such accommodations, it would only be made clear that no perfect system would be capable of growing, nor its devotees of *learning*. It would differ radically from the sciences, which are conspicuously capable of instruction, growth, and progress. So in the end it would remain a fact that scientific truth is an insecure and unstable jumping-off place for the theory that perfect coherence means absolute truth.

(3) Moreover, this invalid jump has a surprising reaction on the sciences. It is something of a boomerang. It arrives at the conclusion that a perfect all-embracing system alone can be strictly true, and that the sciences cannot claim such truth because they are partial and partially coherent. But does not this conclusion *discredit* the premises from which it started, the truths of the sciences? If "only the whole truth can be wholly true," the truths of the sciences are no longer capable of being true.

Yet the ideal of a perfectly coherent system was drawn from the actual systems of the sciences. If these are now invalidated, no true conclusion can be drawn from them. The belief in Coherence, therefore, becomes groundless. Or rather, it becomes a conclusion which confutes its premises, and so destroys itself.

Thus the attempt to establish the coherence ideal both presupposes and *discredits* the truths of the sciences; and must do so. For, unless it presupposes them, it has no starting-point; unless it discredits them, it gains no supremacy. Actually it does not discredit science only because it is so self-contradictory that it discredits itself.

(4) It is an illusion to think that the conception of systematic coherence can be validly used to test imperfect systems. It is often argued that because of two theories one is more coherent or more inclusive it is therefore nearer than its rival to the complete truth, and that the order of coherence in theories is also their order of merit. But this is not a valid inference. We cannot assume that the road to truth runs in a straight line, that we are approaching truth at every step, and that every apparent approach is really on the road to success. The best road may be a winding one, and its curves and spirals may often seem to take us away from our objective, while the short cut which seems to lead directly to it may encounter an insuperable obstacle further on. One might as well assume that the right route up a mountain must always be one that goes straight for the summit, whereas it may only lead to the foot of an unclimbable cliff, and the true *route* may lead a long way round up a lateral *arête*.

This simple consideration, which is never mentioned by those who glibly talk about 'degrees of truth' they have no means or intention of measuring, really disposes of the assumption that we can declare one theory truer than another, in the sense of coming nearer to absolute truth, without having previously reached the latter; and the history of the sciences fully confirms this inference by furnishing many examples of theories which have long seemed all but completely true and have then had to be discarded, while others which looked quite unpromising have in the end proved far more valuable.

Thus the whole early history of physics is one long illustration of the *failure* of the direct approach to physical reality. It was natural for man to suppose that the course of nature, to

be knowable by him, must be closely analogous to human
nature, so that power, volition, striving, and desire could reasonably be attributed to all the 'forces' of nature; that colours,
sounds, smells, and tastes really resided in the bodies which
displayed them; and that his immediate experiences of qualities like hot and cold, dense and rare, hard and soft, were
obvious clues to the behaviour of the real. Yet experience
proved that all these conceptions led nowhere. The science of
physics made no progress till they had been abandoned. The
right way to progress lay through a very inconspicuous side
track which did not tend to harmonise man and nature, but
regarded as real nothing but the mechanical conceptions of
matter and motion and the postulates of their indestructibility
and conservation, to the (apparently absurd) point of leaving
no room in its materialistic scheme for the mind which had
excogitated it. Upon these assumptions the mechanical theory
proceeded, almost to completion. It then led to the discovery
of facts, still more remote from direct experience, which have
scientifically superseded it. We have no organs at all for
directly apprehending 'electricity,' and yet the 'electrical
theory of matter' admittedly explains and transforms the
mechanical theory. It reduces its dogmas to statistical averages
and rough approximations. Neither the indestructibility of
matter, nor the conservation of mass, nor that of energy, is
any longer thought to hold exactly. Indeed the ingenious
theory of Sir J. Jeans supposes that it is the continuous *annihilation* of matter that keeps the sun shining. Not to be outdone,
Prof. Millikan interprets the highly penetrating 'cosmic rays'
he has studied as indicating a *reconstruction* of matter going on
where they originate. Thus physics is in doubt whether to
attribute the empirically given consumption of energy to the
destruction or to the construction of matter; and, for the time
being, is trying to have it *both* ways. The present 'facts' are
amiably ambiguous enough to fit into either 'system.' The
obvious incompleteness of the new theories of physics is, however, a logical merit. They make no illusory claim to finality.
No one professes to know what electricity is in itself. It is

just a key that gives us access to nature's working, and all that the physicist cares about is that it should be a *convenient* key, in terms of which he can manipulate all physical reality.

Even more instructive, perhaps, is the history of the theory of light. It has been a protracted struggle, with many vicissitudes, between two *analogies*, the one ascribing light to an emission of particles, the other to an undulation of an (imaginary) 'luminiferous ether.' This struggle, which dates back to the days of Newton and Huygens, has ended, for the time, in a deadlock. There is a large body of known facts which fit well into the undulatory theory. There is a growing body of known facts which fit only into an emission theory. But the two theories are undeniably incompatible, nor can *either* accommodate *all* the facts. These, however, are far more certain than any theory which 'explains' them. Here, then, we have a signal example of how incoherent and recalcitrant to system truth may be. We shall, of course, continue to hope that some day some genius will devise, or some piece of luck reveal, a theory that will accommodate all the facts and show us how light can (be or) resemble both a projectile and a wave; but, meanwhile, the actual situation vividly attests that mere insistence on the coherence of truth is impotent to get a science out of its difficulties.[1]

§ 15. (B) The Incompatibility of Systems and the System.

(B) The numerous logical flaws we have detected in the attempt to represent an all-inclusive system of coherent truth as the acme of proof all at bottom spring from a single fault of method. They have all assumed that there is a logical connexion, rather than an antithesis, between such a system

---

[1] Philosophy as a whole may be regarded as remaining involved in a very similar condition to the theory of light. From the first the conflicting systems of metaphysics have offered incompatible interpretations of the *data*, to which some have done more justice in some respects, others in others, none in all. A dispassionate survey of the doings of philosophers could not but conclude that though all these systems might contain some truth, and must contain enough truth to satisfy their authors, none could be true absolutely and for all.

and the systems of the sciences. But in fact the structure, method, and logical character of such a system are hopelessly at variance with the actual procedure of our knowing.

All our actual knowing is *purposive*. Scientific systems, therefore, are meant to satisfy various scientific purposes, which determine their character and to which they are relative. The better a system fulfils its purpose the better it is. It should follow that a *perfect* system would be one that satisfied *all* purposes; whereas, in fact, the alleged all-inclusive system satisfies *none*, except the craving for something all-inclusive, and cheats even this.

Again, all our actual knowing is *selective*. It always clears its way to truth through a jungle, by *selecting a part* from a larger whole, cutting out the superfluous, neglecting the rubbish, leaving aside the irrelevant, concentrating upon the 'essential'; throughout it operates upon wholes in a wholly different way from that assumed by the theory of the all-inclusive whole. It distinguishes, moreover, between two wholes which concern it: (1) the whole which is before the thinking mind—the *psychological* whole; and (2) the whole of reality (if reality may be taken to be such as to form a whole)[1]—the *logical* whole.

But neither of these wholes is ever *relevant* to any inquiry, neither is ever the real subject of a judgment. No one ever tries to blurt out all he has in mind: for he is interested only in judging about the part which immediately concerns his purpose. This is true even when he professes to be judging about the whole. For he is then thinking of its wholeness, without reference to all its details, and so omitting much. So no judgment ever truly claims to include the whole, because no judgment ever truly *aims* at including it. Not even the philosophers most addicted to discoursing about 'the Whole' have any real intention of including it. The Whole they talk about is always a very selective affair. It does not include the great masses of reality that conflict with their idea of a beautifully ordered system. It does not include errors, discrepancies, contradic-

[1] For which see § 13.

tions, imaginings, fictions, fancies, delusions, ravings, 'appearances' of any sort. It does not include, in particular, the beliefs of their opponents. It is always reality *optimi juris* they mean; so much so, that in the end it usually seems to include little more than its advocates' personal preferences and convictions.

No charge of falsity, however, can be based on this procedure. Our judgment's refusal to grapple with the totality of reality is no confession of inadequacy, but rather its best proof of intelligence and prudence. It means that we claim to have selected out of the infinity of conceivable judgments the one which is best adapted to our purpose, and have rejected the rest as irrelevant. Our problem in logic, then, is never how to attain the Whole, but always how to select the *relevant part* (Chap. V, § 3). This selection, of course, involves a risk, the risk that what is excluded as irrelevant may turn out not to be so: but this risk must be taken in all effective reasoning. Had we to contemplate the totality of reality in every aspect before hazarding any judgment, our thought would be paralysed, and we should never arrive at a judgment at all. But the failure to achieve this impossibility does not *vitiate* our judgment. It is valuable and 'true' if it does what it was intended to do, and achieves the purpose with which it was formulated.

The sciences, similarly, are all based on selections and assimilate the real selectively. Each begins by selecting some aspect of reality as worthy of study and by abstracting from the rest. Thus geometry selects the spatial aspect, biology the living, physiology the bodily, psychology the mental, and so forth. They form their 'systems' by devising assumptions that enable them to arrange, predict, and control the phenomena that interest them, and give no thought to the question whether the various assumptions they severally make are congruous with each other. For this problem forms philosophy's special job, for which, *en revanche*, the details of the sciences are largely irrelevant.

Thus the selections on which the sciences rest are all *purposive*. They are also *risky*. For there cannot be any *a priori* guarantee that a science will begin by making the right, or the best, selections, by including everything that will further its purpose, and excluding all that will hinder it. In point of fact all sciences go astray in their initial stages, and wander, often for ages, in the wilderness of uncomprehended fact and the deserts of illusion and false analogy. But this too has its compensations. Because a science is partial and does not try to embrace the whole, it can embrace more than it did, and so can expand and progress. And when it is attacked, it can summon assistance from without its borders, and search and hope for reinforcements that will defeat its critics. The same effort will also acquit it of the charge of arguing in a circle. It has preserved the capacity of growing, of learning, of improving.

The ideal all-inclusive system, on the other hand, *cannot be selective*. It cannot be partial, because it must include the whole and can tolerate no selectiveness in the structure of its whole. It must include, *ex officio*, not only all that is, in all its features, but all that is apparent (seeing that appearance also is a sort of reality), all that is conceivable, all that is imaginable, however mistakenly or perversely. It must assimilate without discrimination, not only what is significant and valuable, but also what is meaningless and worthless. All this it must do by the very law of its being, under penalty of failing to be what it essentially claims to be.

Evidently such a 'perfect system' would be a perfect chaos: for what alone distinguishes a system from a chaos is precisely that it selects what it judges to be the relevant parts or aspects from the total material before it, and arranges them in an appropriate order for a purpose. This, accordingly, as we saw, is what the sciences all do. But no all-inclusive system can do it. It has to include everything and can dismiss nothing as irrelevant, least of all the objections of those who question it. So it flatly contradicts the process whereby systems are produced, and becomes a rag-bag Absolute and an absolute rag-bag which can have no meaning for our thought. The rubbish it is bound to include springs up and chokes whatever germs of truth or sense can germinate in such a wilderness. To appeal to a 'system' of *this* sort in order to validate our reasoning is farcical, and would be taken as a sorry jest if the philosophers who do it could be suspected of making a joke.

Thus, in method, structure, and logical character alike the systems of the sciences, and the System of the philosophers are divergent and antithetical. The former are willing to run risks and to take them as tests of their truths: the latter evade all tests, and aim at escaping from all risks into a system which shall provide in advance against all conceivable danger. The structure of the former is teleological, purposive, and significant; that of the latter mechanical, aimless, and meaningless. Logically the former disdain formal validity and confess to taking risks and making experiments, whereas the latter prides itself on its pursuit of its unattainable, illusory, and worthless ideal of formal validity.

§ 16. The Self-contradictions of the System.

What more remains to be said about the all-inclusive system? May it be pointed out that it has been convicted of self-contradiction in *four* distinct ways?

Thus (1) to maintain its claim to validity, to meet the charge of circularity, it must be capable of expansion: yet its official all-inclusiveness forbids it to expand.

An ordinary, that is a scientific, system of belief defends itself when attacked by extending over the ground from which it is assailed: i.e. it *expands* itself, and it can do this precisely because it did *not* include this ground before. This same procedure also shows that it was not really a closed system, but open to objection and to argument and capable of expansion. It was in principle an *open* system. But if it had tried to maintain itself by arguments resting on its own contentions, it would have been arguing in a circle, and would have carried no conviction. Nor can it have been *perfectly* systematic, seeing that it was capable of an improved restatement which included more than it did at first.

In all these respects, however, the all-inclusive system is differently situated. It must be *closed*, because *ex hypothesi* there is nothing outside it over which it can extend. Whatever objections, therefore, it encounters, it must argue within itself, i.e. in a circle. It offers its reasons only to those who have already accepted it, and is powerless to persuade any others. If to escape from this reproach, it opens and expands itself, it at once sacrifices its claim to all-inclusiveness. Thus it never escapes from the fatal contradiction that to avoid circularity it must be capable of expansion; to be all-inclusive it cannot be.

(2) In ultimate analysis the notion of a system is found to presuppose those of selection and relevance; but these implicitly *exclude* all-inclusiveness. Thus an all-inclusive system is really a contradiction in terms: to become a system, it must select; to become all-inclusive, it must not.

(3) It was shown in § 15 that systems are formed to satisfy purposes, and that a *perfect* system should satisfy *all* purposes, whereas the all-inclusive system satisfies *none*. The truth is, that it is rendered so self-sufficing as to become perfectly useless; for all its uses are illusory.

(4) It seems a comical ending to the pretensions of the all-inclusive system that what is alleged to be the final form of coercive proof should turn out to be in form a 'fallacy' and in substance a doctrine incapable of proof and even of statement as a valid reasoning at all.

Now, self-contradiction is not strictly a proof of *falsity*; for it may be merely verbal. But it shows at least that, so far, no *meaning* has been expressed, and renders it incumbent on those who have chosen to express themselves in self-contradictory terms to explain what, if anything, they meant. Until they have done so the coherence theory of proof may fairly be dismissed.

§ 17. The Moral.

What finally is the outcome of this protracted struggle to propound a form of valid proof? Its moral surely is that of which we have already caught a glimpse in Chap. XIII, § 6. It is high time we renounced the ideal of *formal validity*—altogether. The programme Formal Logic set itself has ended in flat failure. It set aside the ways of actual thinking in order to grasp the glittering ideal it had assumed: but its ideal has proved unattainable and self-confuting.

Not, indeed, that it was wholly false. It embodies a modicum of truth: but the truth it embodies not only fails to warrant the doctrine derived from it, but definitely points in a different direction. Thus the syllogistic form becomes invalid only if it is applied to the 'absolute' truths alleged; it is quite well suited to the statement of hypotheses (§ 5). Again, induction from 'facts' which are taken as cases of a general principle is a plausible and effective way of establishing or confirming such a principle: it becomes inadequate only if it is forced to keep up the pretence of being a 'valid' process. Lastly, the doctrine that truths cohere and form systems is true enough, if it is allowed to observe the conditions under which such systems are formed and can grow. It is only when it is puffed up into an all-inclusive system, which cannot be a system but only a chaos, which cannot select or grow or improve, that it becomes grotesquely false.

Moreover, these objections to the notion of formal validity are in no way sceptical. They are all urged in the interests of real knowing. Formal validity is a false ideal, because it shuts out the actual processes whereby our thought-experiments are conducted, and hypotheses are suggested, tested, improved, and verified in the unending progress of knowledge.

And Formal Logic is a false logic, because in its wild-goose chase after formal validity it ignores the actual difficulties, trials, and triumphs of our knowing. Our reasoning need *not* be *valid* to be *valuable*, a good proof need not be coercive to be persuasive and even convincing, and a truth may grow more probable and certain throughout the ages, without ever becoming absolute. On the other hand, our thought must be authorised to run risks, to show enterprise, to aim at ends, and to satisfy demands; it is not the *safest*, but often the *boldest*, thought that is crowned with success. For in the adventures of thought, as of the battlefield, fortune favours the brave.

CHAPTER XVI

VALUABLE REASONING

1. The failure of ' proof ' is the opportunity of ' discovery ' ; 2. Wanted, a logic of discovery ; 3. Novelty in thought ; 4. The conservative bias against novelties is psychological ; 5. The logical case against novelty ; 6. Novelty in reality ; 7. The proving of discoveries ; 8. Probable reasoning not mathematical ; 9. Probability as a practical conception ; 10. Postulation and the ' will to believe ' ; 11. The great postulates ; 12. Hypothesis ; 13. Analogy ; 14. Verification.

§ 1. The Failure of 'Proof' is the Opportunity of 'Discovery.'

Is the failure of the theory of Proof, which was traced in the last chapter, the end of Logic? Does the scrapping of 'validity' entail a total loss of 'value'? By no means: it is the beginning of what best deserves the name of Logic and does it most credit—the study of valuable reasoning and real knowing. So long as Logic was fascinated by the ideal of Formalism and the attainment of valid forms and coercive proof monopolised logical attention, not even the plainest facts about our actual knowing could be noticed, and no attempt could be made to evaluate the really valuable procedures by which truth is augmented and confirmed.

So it passed unnoticed and unmentioned that knowledge is actuated by a *desire* for truth, that it is an *activity* spurred on and guided by *postulates*, that it needs the stimulus of a *problem*, that it demands *novelties* and seeks new truths, that it is throughout an *experimental* and *progressive* process, and that verification has no end. The will to know starts with little, but craves for much; though it is content, if need be, to start from the humblest and insecurest beginnings, it is literally *insatiable*, and is never lulled to sleep even by the highest achievements. So the collapse of 'validity' is really a gain: it clears the way for 'value,' and leaves us free to enter on the path of discovery.

§ 2. Wanted, a Logic of Discovery.

The Formal logician's infatuation with 'proof' had blinded him to the need for discovery and to the absurdity of substituting for the discoverer's actual procedure his own *ex post facto* version, rearranged as a logically cogent 'proof,' from which even the veriest duffer could not withhold his assent. He was always seeking for some formal, mechanical, *a priori* process that should be safe and fool-proof, without reflecting that a fool-proof proof would be a proof for fools, and that an intelligent inquirer is ready to take reasonable risks. Nor was he conscious of any incongruity in illustrating logical method by discussing problems which the sciences had already solved long ago, and in elaborately demonstrating truths which were already perfectly familiar to every one.

What is wanted is something utterly different from such puerilities. We want a logic that will start from our actual procedure in knowing, and will study how we make discoveries and assure *ourselves* (and not an absolute and absolutely idiotic 'mind') of their truth. We need, in other words, a Logic of Discovery, which realises that discovery is the primary and vital aim and need of truth-seeking, while 'proof' is secondary and can wait—even till the day of the last judgment. It is probable, moreover, that careful observation of how discoveries are made will suggest to us sundry ways of *improving* our procedures, and so will attach normative corollaries to our descriptions. For *intelligent* reflection is not idle but practical, and really to understand a procedure we must employ it and see what happens, or, in other words, *experiment* with it.

Such a logic of discovery is not as yet in being. It is too antithetical to that of Formal proof in all important respects to be entertained until the latter has been honestly discarded. It will not be *a priori*, but empirical; that is, it will not attempt to dictate to nature and to predict the future by the mere magic of verbal spells and the coercion of 'correct' definitions, but will ever be willing to learn from experience, and to modify or abandon even its most assured assumptions and beliefs whenever it becomes possible to change them for the better. It will not be coercive, but attractive. It will not aim at indiscriminate total inclusion in a chaotic whole, but at selection of the relevant and valuable. Its reasonings will be not 'safe' and timid, but

21

bold though 'risky'; not 'absolute' and certain, but probable, convincing, and satisfying; not 'infallible' in the abstract and futile in fact, but applicable in fact though questionable in the abstract; not '*valid*,' in short, but *valuable*.

Nor can any reason be given why such a logic should not be recognised. It already exists in fact and is in common use: only when blinkers are worn is it not seen. It is taboo in the text-books of Formal Logic, but its exclusion is sheer prejudice: for its adoption would not only vindicate the logical value of common-sense reasoning and of the procedures of the sciences, but yield a far more rational account of the very forms to which Formal Logic appeals. Thus it relieves the syllogistic form of the charge of *petitio* by taking the premisses as hypotheses to be tested (Chap. XIV, § 5). It transforms the retrogressive search for indisputable premisses into the unending progress of scientific verification (Chap. XIII, § 6). It baffles the assaults of ambiguity by admitting the risk of ambiguity in the abstract but requiring the ambiguity to be shown in each actual case. It puts verbalism in its place, and relieves Logic of a vast mass of pseudo-problems by refusing to accept propositions instead of judgments as authentic examples of thought. And, finally, it brings out forcibly how much more vital to reasoning are novelty and progress than proof and assurance.

§ 3. Novelty in Thought.

For convincing psychological reasons novelty is an indispensable ingredient in actual thought. A rational being only thinks when he is buoyed up by the hope of attaining (or imparting) a new truth which is relevant to the actual situation in which he (or his audience) finds himself involved, and only a lunatic would propound irrelevant truth which had no bearing on these circumstances. This is the reason why we discuss what is doubtful and seek for what is unknown. Moreover, it was seen from the first that the syllogistic form must come to terms with the demand for novelty. The conclusion it reaches must be somehow 'new.' Aristotle was not, however, very exacting in complying with this demand. He declared merely that the conclusion should be 'other' than the premises, and apparently any verbal change would have contented him. He was thus enabled to avoid the prolonged controversies which have troubled later logicians as to how much, and what sort of, novelty was to be required from a syllogism, whether the novelty was to be psychological only (to some or all of the parties concerned), or whether, in addition, there was to be recognised a specifically 'logical' novelty which was new to science, or even *in rerum natura*.

It was shown in Chap XIV, § 7, that the attempts to render the demands of novelty compatible with those of formal 'proof' failed: it must now be recognised that the traditional theory of 'Induction' is no more capable of satisfying them. This theory has pertinaciously attempted to claim formal validity for its procedures, and novelty had to be sacrificed in the attempt. It first tried for a 'perfect' induction, resting on an exhaustive enumeration of all cases. This cannot be denied to be formally valid, but it can be denied to occur in fact; and it is obvious that it teaches us no new truth. If exhaustive enumeration is required to make induction 'safe,' we shall have to wait till man is as extinct as the dodo before it can safely or truly be affirmed that 'all men are mortal' (='dead').

All the other interpretations of 'induction' involve risks, arising from the possibilities that some of the cases relevant to our inquiry have been overlooked, or that the 'law' to cover them has not been rightly formulated. So every attempt to argue inductively from 'new' cases or to new laws has to run the gauntlet of the formidable questions—How do you know that your cases are rightly selected and your laws rightly formulated? Since both 'cases' and 'laws' involve selection and selection always involves a possibility of error, no formal *technique* can ever assure our reasoning's *de facto* rightness. Hence we may always find our old ideas and formulas breaking down, when applied to new cases, under the strain of further use.

When this happens, the whole subject has to be reopened. We have a choice between three alternatives, between which it is often hard to decide. (1) We may scrutinise the 'facts' and

repeat our observations until they can be brought into conformity with the law. We thus prefer the 'law' to the 'facts,'
and modify the latter till they fit it. But (2) it is also possible to
change the law until it fits the cases. And lastly, (3) we may
change our views of *both*, until they are brought together by
mutual concessions.

No one, moreover, can predict which will be the right procedure on any occasion. Methodologically we prefer the least
upsetting alternative. This is usually to suppose mal-observation
of the case. But we may have to change a 'law,' reluctant as
we all are to discard one that has a record of good service. Such
reluctance is, of course, a psychological factor; but psychological
factors play a great part in the making of all truth. Thus we may
as well recognise the fact that in matters also of scientific discovery there is always a conservative as well as a liberal party to
be considered.

§ 4. The Conservative Bias against Novelties is Psychological.

When viewed with a Conservative bias, *growing* knowledge
will naturally seem suspect; for we shall be most impressed with
the *discrepancy* between the new evidence and the old doctrine,
and disposed to declare that the new must be either itself false
or what renders all else false. We shall overrate, therefore, its
logical shortcomings. Yet with a Liberal bias, hospitable to
novelties, the *same* evidence will look very different. It will
seem adequate and the opposition to it merely perverse. The
Liberal will set himself to stress the *continuity* between the new
and the old, and will refuse to take the old system as fixed and
settled and its truth as final and unalterable. He will insist that
it must be *elastic* enough to extend itself, if required, over the
new discoveries, and will deny that they will, in the end, be
found to strain it beyond endurance. He has faith that the new
will always turn out to be, in a manner, old, and will show itself
assimilable: the old system will be able to embrace the new, if
it tries. At worst, inquiry has merely to be continued for the
new facts to grow more certain, coherent, and intelligible, and
to form a new system. Thus the doubts and commotions which

attend discovery should not distress us: they are normal, and
prove nothing against its truth. They merely mean that our
native indolence is shocked by the summons to readjust ingrained beliefs.

As a rule, therefore, the Liberal bias is to be preferred. Undoubtedly the ideal of scientific method is untiring open-
mindedness and willingness to explore all avenues to discovery,
and readiness to adopt whatever interpretation works best; but
actually the great authorities in every subject are usually too old
to take to novelties with a good grace, and hence prolonged and
often repeated struggles are necessary before a new truth is
admitted, whenever it chances to have any emotional interest
or to bear on any disputed point (Chap. VII, § 15).

§ 5. The Logical Case against Novelty.

Conservatism, however, is not merely psychological; a logical
case can always be made out for it. For our whole logical
apparatus seems at first sight to be incapable of dealing with the
new and to be devised to hide its existence from our eyes. Consider, for example, the implications of the assumption that whatever happens must be such as to be a 'case' for a 'law' or
'universal.' Is not this really to assume that the new must be
the old in disguise? And is it not to ignore the new *qua* new?
If so, is it not the *method* of Logic directly to defy the psychological facts of immediate experience? For everything we
experience feels *partly* new, and this part is often disconcertingly
large.

Nevertheless a deeper analysis of thought will show that not
only psychology but logic also may, and even must, recognise
novelty.

(1) The analysis of actual thinking shows that novelty is not
an incident merely of Inference. It appears already in Judgment.
For no judgment is made unless it is thought to convey some
novelty. A sane mind has no other motive to judge. All real
judgments, therefore, as opposed to forms of words, are 'synthetic' in Kant's sense. They were meant to *add* to (some one's)
knowledge.

(2) The subsumption of the new under the old is misinterpreted by Formal Logic. It does not mean what Formal Logic supposes. It does not mean that the new is old *in fact*: it only treats it *as if it were* old, in order to forecast its behaviour on this hypothesis. It is not dogmatic, therefore, but methodological and experimental. We try whether the 'new' case can be brought under the old rule, and thereby test both the rule and the case. Moreover, this implies willingness in us to modify our views of *both*. In the normal growth of knowledge such modification is the outcome; the 'facts' grow more assured and the 'laws' which 'explain' them get a firmer grip.

Thus the real meaning of the logical or thought-experiment is that this willingness to learn exists. But this is not revealed by the verbal form of the assertion. It lies in the asserter's mind, and is an attitude thereof. It is nothing, therefore, a verbalist logic can perceive; psychological insight is needed to detect it. Hence no Formalism can understand how novelty gets either into the syllogism or into the sciences which acquire new knowledge by their dealings with reality.

It is clear, then, that several sorts of novelty are relevant to Logic. There is first the psychological craving for novelty which is an effective stimulus to thought. There is, secondly, the novelty which attends every process, not only of thinking but even of experiencing, the flavour of novelty with which every event enters into personal experience. This also is psychological, but it may be nothing more. For what is new to the individual is not necessarily new to science; he may 'discover' only what is already known. Nor need what is new to science, the 'logical' novelty which is reducible to law by being taken *as if* it were no novelty at all, be a new development of reality; the real may have long exhibited the behaviour which has at last been 'discovered.' We are apt to take as a real change what is a change 'only in our knowledge.' Strictly speaking, however, a *merely* psychological novelty does not exist. For a change in our knowledge is always a change in *us*, and so a change in reality. Thus the question of novelty in thought naturally leads on that of the generation of novelties by changes in reality.

§ 6. Novelty in Reality.

Philosophers have, of course, tried hard to dispute the change in reality and the reality of change. Ever since the Eleatics avowed the motives of the typical metaphysics in their crude *naïveté*, they have argued that novelty could not be truly real. Being was one and the same, now and for evermore, and if facts defied this dogma so much the worse for the facts! To a critical eye, however, this dogma is little more than an assumption. It is the simplest of assumptions, doubtless, and so methodologically the first to be tried; but it is not necessarily the truest. Its claims should not be allowed to stand against positive evidence to the contrary. Its methodological character does indeed entitle us to go on using it, even where the facts are against it; but it will then be used as a *fiction*. And other possibilities are worth exploring.

Now that the idea of a cosmic 'evolution' has, tardily, got into our heads, we find that there is quite a good case for the ultimate reality of novelty. But if novelty is a fact, it is a very important fact. (1) Thus it will enable us to justify our stubborn faith in freedom, the belief that our actions are not all fully determined by antecedent events. The new and the free converge, and, in Bergson's theory of freedom, become indistinguishable. (2) Our eyes open to the fact that human nature really changes. For if we can change our acts, we change our habits, our tastes, and finally our nature. This is just what 'evolution' means; it is what man has done in becoming man, and since—too slowly, no doubt, but surely, continuously, and the more rapidly the more intelligent he grew. (3) The capacity for new adaptations is not confined to man. Animals, too, are clever enough to effect them. Thus the swallow soon discovered what conveniences telegraph wires were to sit on and eaves to build under: the sparrow has become an inveterate townee who never yearns for a week-end in the country. Within the last forty years the seagull has learnt to prefer the filth and plenty of Westminster to the unpolluted solitudes of the unharvested ocean. But the most shocking case, perhaps, is that of the Kea parrot. He had always been a good vegetarian, like the rest of his tribe, until sheep were brought into New Zealand. Then he developed an unnatural taste for mutton kidneys, and used his beak for hacking them out of the living sheep.[1] This rendered him unpopular with farmers, and implacable war was waged upon him. The Kea has now become rare (except in the mountains), and so his change of habit was not such a good adjustment to new circumstances as he may have supposed.

How far down the scale of being does this capacity for creative innovation extend? It is hard to say, because scientific observation of nature is so recent and has been so inadequate. However, it is probable that the various disease-germs have all *adopted* their present nefarious mode of life—some of them, like the tetanus germ, have not yet become wholly parasitic—and it has definitely been recorded that even lowly fungi can be taught to change their habits. Thus we may read in *Nature*, No. 1792, p. 429, that "purely saprophytic fungi can be educated to become parasitic by sowing the spores on a living leaf that has had injected into its tissues a substance positively chemotactic to the germ-tubes of the fungus experimented with. By similar means a parasitic fungus can be led to attack a new host plant. These experiments prove what has hitherto only been assumed, viz. that parasitism on the part of fungi is an acquired habit."

(4) It is not, therefore, by any means a self-evident truth that the habits of the *inanimate*, alias the 'laws of nature,' can undergo no change. Human experience of the ways of nature has been much too brief and much too prejudiced to warrant any such assumption. Indeed a suspicion has in recent times arisen that the laws of nature may not be as immutable as was supposed. Several of our sciences have come upon phenomena which pretty clearly point in this direction. It is no longer biology alone that is impressed by the evidence for 'evolution.' Astrophysics finds itself observing 'stellar evolution.' Chemistry finds that the relations of its 'elements' are highly

---

[1] It has recently been found that the magpies in some of the Western States of America are (in the last ten years) acquiring a very similar habit, and attacking cattle and horses. Cf. *Nature*, No. 3044, p. 336.

suggestive of their evolution. Above all, the discovery of 'radio-active' substances makes cosmic history as essential to the understanding of the present in physics as it is in psychology. Modern science has ceased to stress the 'eternal' order of nature, and views it as a historical process in 'Space-Time.' It is not too much to say that for it every 'atom' is what it is in virtue of what it has been through. An atom of 'lead,' e.g., is the lead it is because it has been generated by the disruption of an atom of uranium, or of thorium, so many æons ago. It had a beginning at a definite date, and it is very likely some day to have an end: to speak, therefore, of its term of 'life' is far more than an analogy. Moreover, it is possible that radio-activity is an *acquired* habit, and likely enough that it is not confined to the substances in which it has been detected: there are other indications, also, that the whole cosmic machinery is running down. Either, therefore, the physical world had a beginning, or the 'laws' that formulate its happenings now have changed. A still bolder line of speculation already looks to the 'annihilation' of matter as the source of the energy which the stars are able to radiate so lavishly and continuously. This argument is open to the objection that there may be an as yet undiscovered compensatory process by which atoms are reconstituted; but the former 'axioms' of the indestructibility of matter and the conservation of energy are more or less openly abandoned.

They should never have been taken as axioms, nor even as facts; for they had never really been proved. All the 'proofs' given of them always presupposed the principles they supported, and so begged the question. They were in truth nothing more than methodological principles, and there is really no reason why the working principles of sciences should ever be taken otherwise. A scientific principle is a much better instrument of exploration when taken methodologically than when taken dogmatically; for it does not then close our eyes to alternative possibilities, and leaves us free to use incompatible principles wherever this is (temporarily) convenient, without allowing progress to be paralysed by 'contradictions.' But so soon as a working principle is valued in itself and irrespective of its services, it swells into an overweening dogma, and becomes a superstition and an obstacle to progress. Nor need we fear that the use of the belief in the invariance of natural law will be endangered if it is taken methodologically. Even if the whole weight of tradition were not behind the belief, it would be secured against frivolous rejection by its superior convenience. No one in his senses is going to change a good working principle unless he sees his way to a definite improvement, simply because of the amount of recalculation the change would involve. Moreover, it is evident that the great bulk of the real does not change appreciably or to an extent that would falsify our predictions over short periods of time, so that it is empirically feasible to take the ' laws of nature ' as invariant.

On the other hand we must be prepared to find, if the evidence is good enough, that physical reality also really changes its modes of behaviour, like psychical reality. It will naturally follow that we must provide ourselves with a logic that is able and willing to take into account this feature of the real in its theory of proof.

§ 7. The Proving of Discoveries.

It is pretty clear that the proving of discoveries and novelties will involve some recasting of the old logic, just because it was so uncannily successful in working its fiction that the new was only the old in disguise. Logic will have to be frankly adapted to the apprehension of the new. But this process should not require any very serious extension of the conclusions already reached. For, as a result of Chap. XV, the notion of 'proof' has already been greatly relaxed, in order to preserve its utility.

Formal proof has proved a chimera altogether. Nothing can be proved absolutely, either by 'induction' or by tracing back its premisses in a vain and endless regress, or by postulating a perfect system, or by just declaring the last premiss we have strength to reach self-evidently certain. Induction is not formal proof, 'system' means rotation in a circle, the search for premisses means retrogression instead of progress, and 'intuition' is unabashed assertion. The right way to make sure of a truth-claim is to move on with it and to verify it progressively. But such verification is not formal proof, and never becomes formally flawless. It is, moreover, far more empirical than any procedure inductive logic ever contemplated: for it admits that experience has a use in confirming (or undoing) even 'syllogistically proved' conclusions.

Consequently the real function of formal proof is hypothetical or dialectical. It is hypothetical, if the premisses are understood to formulate a hypothesis, of which the conclusion anticipates the consequences before they are observed: it is dialectical if it formulates the falling back of a disputed truth-claim upon the support of unchallenged (verbal) truths. Now this occurs much oftener in dialectical discussion than in the exploration of nature, and this is, no doubt, why the Greeks discovered it. The implied purpose is, not to *discover* a novelty but to *assure* it. Our question is not—'have we here a *novel* truth?' but 'have we a novel *truth*?' The inquiry is not into the novelty of the claim but into the truth of the novelty. This 'truth' is 'proved' by exhibiting its connexion with truths already accepted. Clearly it is thus deprived of its independence and absoluteness; but it is also backed by the whole strength of a system with which it stands or falls. We thus fortify the borders of knowledge and defend its outposts, without, however, removing the conditional character of the whole system and its logical dependence on the continued success of its working; so it in no wise amounts to, or tends to, the Formal 'ideal' of absolute unconditional proof.

It is, moreover, easily adjusted to the procedure of scientific discovery. In discovery, our main interest is in the eliciting of novelty, in the extension of the bounds of knowledge. Our attitude is one of inquiry, not of *ex post facto* reflection or criticism. We desire and purpose to discover *new* truth, and all our emphasis and attention fall on the *novelty*.

Hence the problem for our Logic will be—How can it so adjust itself as to regard this aim as attainable? Clearly it must not lay down conditions which would render discovery and novelty impossible. Nor must it ignore the process of change. It must not, therefore, demand initial certitudes: it may well content itself with initial probabilities, being mindful that every inquiry springs from a doubt.

We may very well admit, therefore, that we start from insecure ground, with wild hypotheses, with questionable 'facts' that are at best anticipations of the 'real facts' and may not turn out to be facts at all, with brute facts for which no reason is apparent. But all this does no harm, provided we are led on to something solider. For a starting-point should not be taken as a resting-place but as something to be got away from as speedily as possible. It is only stationary structures that require fixed foundations. But there is nothing stationary about a science. It has no use or need for premises, fixed and unalterable, upon which to 'build.' Even its initial assumptions should be taken as *meant* to be tentative, open to revision and capable of improvement; or alternatively, as fruits of *successful experimentation* with principles that would yield a science. As it develops, its 'facts' and its 'laws' change, multiply, and grow—together. Its coherence is not structural and static, but more like that of a living organism. This explains why it can radically transform every part, without affecting the vitality and value of the whole.

Thus the sciences are comparable, not to stable structures, but rather to streams that carve their own beds, and gather volume and momentum as they go. They are essentially *enterprises*, and, if they are successful, provide us with certainties resulting from the continuous testing of their assumptions ('principles'), *data*, and doctrines by their outcome and working. These scientific certainties are never absolute, but are often sufficient for our needs. And, of course, the hope of further improvements never dies.

§ 8. Probable Reasoning not Mathematical.

The shifting of the focus of logical interest from 'proof' to discovery means, *inter alia*, the substitution of *probable* for 'valid' reasonings. If 'proof' is no longer required to be

absolute and coercive and fool-proof, and derives its value from
being sufficient for a purpose and progressive, probable reasoning need no longer be despised and ignored. Once we sincerely
and completely renounce the false ideal of validity we must face
the fact that, if we reason at all, we must argue from, with, and
about probabilities.

But probability is an obscure, and perhaps an abstruse, conception. Logicians proper have almost entirely ignored it:
psychologists have shown no curiosity about the nature of the
feeling of probability and the conditions under which it arises
in the mind, and, with hardly an exception, the mathematicians
who have dabbled in logic have devoted their attention exclusively to a single and special case of probability. By restricting themselves to judgments of probability about matters
in which the alternatives can be counted and the chances admit
of definite estimation and, therefore, of mathematical treatment,
they have produced an illusion that the subject is essentially a
branch of mathematics. Their special cases, therefore, bulk
largest in the highly technical literature of the subject. But
they are neither the commonest, nor the most important, nor
the most fundamental cases. A few of the mathematical
logicians have perceived this. Mr J. M. Keynes, for example,
in his admirable *Treatise on Probability*, conceives 'probability' as an objective relation between evidence and conclusions derived from it, which is irreducible and should be
taken as one of the indefinables of logic, but notes that "mathematicians have employed the term in a narrower sense; for
they have often confined it to the limited class of instances in
which the relation is adapted to an algebraical treatment." [1]
He takes this as the "most fundamental sense" of Probability
(p. 11), and emphasises that "we cannot analyse the probability-
relation in terms of simpler ideas. As soon as we have passed
from the logic of implication and the categories of truth and

---

[1] *Op. cit.*, pp. 5, 6. Following the Cambridge tradition that logic
deals with propositions, not judgments, he calls both evidence and
conclusions " a set of propositions "; but this terminology may be
ignored without loss.

falsehood to the logic of probability and the categories of
knowledge, ignorance, and rational belief, we are passing to a
new logical relation in which, although it is logical, we were not
previously interested, and which cannot be explained or defined
in terms of our previous notions" (p. 8). It is of this wider
sense that Bishop Butler's declaration holds that "probability is
the guide of life."

Mathematical probability arises out of this more basic sense
by a series of easy reflections. Probabilities are felt to differ in
force, weight, and value, and to admit of more or less. This
suggests quantitative treatment, and it is an easy further step
to seek to evaluate these quantities numerically and to express
the quantitative differences between probabilities in definite
figures. In certain artificial cases this can easily be done. If, for
example, we take a full pack of cards and draw one, we can say
that the probability that it is the king of hearts is $\frac{1}{52}$, that it is
a king is $\frac{1}{13}$, that it is a heart is $\frac{1}{4}$, that it is red is $\frac{1}{2}$; thus the
whole mathematical theory of probability follows.[1] In other
cases no such definite values can be assigned to our probabilities. Thus we may discover a stationary population of
1000, of whom 20 regularly die a year; but we cannot usefully
infer from this that the probability of the decease of a particular
member of this community within a year is therefore $\frac{1}{50}$; for
he may be at death's door already, or may be a youth with good
prospects of becoming a centenarian. The mathematical theory
of Probability, therefore, must be regarded as a special development, determined by the technical interests of mathematicians,
into which we need not, for our purposes, enter. It does
not attempt to answer the wider questions how and where
the notion of Probability originated and found its way into
logic.

[1] But it does *not* follow that the mathematical theory will be really
applicable. So soon as we try to use it, e.g. to determine whether a
series of guessed cards was fortuitous or shows evidence of ' telepathy,' we again encounter ' psychological ' factors, in the shape of
' number habits ' and a preference for guessing aces, which upset our
calculations.

§ 9. Probability as a Practical Conception.

Seeing that mathematics is competent in one sort of Probability alone, and that logic despairs and declares Probability an 'indefinable,' the field seems to be open for constructive suggestions. Accordingly, we may venture to suggest that the notion of Probability was originally a *practical* one, that it is deeply rooted in the exigencies of life, and that its natural affinities are with the taking of chances, the running of risks, and the desire to anticipate and control events.

In support of this suggestion it is significant that the word 'probable' originally means nothing more than 'what can be approved.' Now, what can be approved is clearly relative to the situation in which one finds oneself. But for æons before he ever dreamt of devising mathematics man found himself involved in a great variety of practical situations in which he had to take terrific risks, to take off-chances, to act on vague estimates, guesses, hopes, and desires, to form anticipations and decisions on a basis of ignorance and avowedly defective knowledge. He simply *had* to become expert in estimating probabilities. But where was he to find clues to guide his decisions? At best the (often superficial) regularities of nature were taken as grounds of expectation, and postulates of enduring centres of activities ('things,' 'substances') and unbreakable ('causal') connexions erected thereon. It is clear that whatever confidence in the cosmos man could muster under such conditions must have been based on faith and courage rather than on knowledge and exact calculation, and that any feeling of 'certainty' that grew up in the most sanguine could hardly be more than subjective infatuation.

Under such unpromising conditions, then, did the habit of estimating probabilities and of reasoning about them grow up. Man was forced to cope with probabilities, because there were no certainties to be had. He simply had to develop (good) judgment in taking risks and estimating chances and probabilities in order to survive. The 'practical' certainties of life and the 'theoretical' certainties of the sciences on which we now rely have all been won from the chaos of casual happenings by slow and painful efforts. These efforts have left their imprint all over human mentality, and have stamped themselves on the underlying conceptions of our modern theories. They have moulded, amongst others, our sense of the 'probable,' and we can always fall back on vague forecasts, prompted by unanalysed experience, whenever the conditions do not admit of exact formulation and the hypothetical certainties deducible from the well-tried theories of an established science. We then revert to the primitive condition in which every event seemed random and every act ran incalculable risks, and the consciousness of chance and risk dominated life.[1]

Nowadays, of course, the situation is widely different. The habit of reasoning from and about probabilities, and estimating them numerically, has established itself, and transformed the surface of life. There is hardly anything for which quotations may not be had. Even in the probabilities least susceptible of mathematical accuracy monetary values are current and business can be done. It is not merely that the bookmaker will estimate the chances and quote the odds for and against the success of teams, horses, and dogs, and that insurance companies will insure against all risks, from fire and burglary to twins. Stock exchange quotations claim to appraise from day to day the present value, and forecast and discount the future, of all securities and most businesses. The daily quotations of the market-prices of all commodities lay claim to equate the relation between supply and demand for long periods ahead, and it is to be noted that they are more and more becoming world-prices, and that the difference between buyers' and sellers' prices tends to get narrower as markets grow larger and knowledge of the conditions affecting values grows. In short, all the innumerable and enormously varied transactions of human affairs rest upon and deal with probabilities.

---

[1] The close connexion between these two notions survives in French, which uses *hasard* for *both*. The German '*wahrscheinlich*,' though it does not reveal so much of primitive mentality, yet brings out its latent subjectivity. The 'probable' is what 'seems true,' but maintains itself only in a certain percentage of cases.

Now it is pretty clear that all these things have nothing to do either with mathematics or with certainties. All these probability estimates are neither infallible nor 'formally valid' nor 'cogent' nor mathematically accurate. But they are efficient and valuable and trustworthy and definite enough to support and carry on the very complex order of civilised life. They are the sort of reasonings we actually use in dealing with the problems of our life, and compared with them the alleged cases of exact calculation and necessary truth have a strangely unfamiliar, artificial, and pedantic air. They have to be elaborately fabricated, and no one but a professor would expect to encounter them among the real problems of his actual thinking. And even theoretically their claims are deceptive and misleading. Mathematical exactness remains a postulate and a fiction. It holds of the ideal abstractions of *pure* mathematics, but often enough leaves us in the lurch when we apply it to the reals we try to treat mathematically. Again, 'necessary' truths are all of them *dependent* on the assumptions from which they derive their 'necessity.' It is always conditional and hypothetical and experience always has the last word in the vital question whether our hypotheses and postulates and ideals *apply* to the real. So soon as, therefore, we really try to *use* them scientifically, their 'necessary' truth becomes a precarious experiment and reduces to a probability. The truths of all the sciences are in a like case. If we bear in mind their origin and history, we see that they always remain relative to the evidence which has 'proved' them and raised them to the rank of recognised truths. In each case definite and limited numbers of observations and experiments have to be rejected or invalidated, or certain definite assumptions to be withdrawn, in order to undermine the ground on which they stood and to deprive them of their status. They are true *if* such and such assumptions are made, *if* such and such observations were good, *if* such and such experiments were free from hidden flaws. The moment these things are called in question their 'truth' has to be proved all over again. Even, therefore, when they are not actually questioned, their truth should not be regarded as more than 'probable,' i.e. as what

22

is approved as best worthy of belief in the actual state of the science. *All truths are probable* [1]—in a higher or lower degree, and our measurements of that degree again are only probable. A logic that studies actual reasoning, therefore, will not scorn to deal with probabilities, and that whether their chances are capable of exact mathematical statement or not.

§ 10. Postulation and the 'Will to Believe.'

Once it has emancipated itself from the obsession with 'validity' there is no reason why logic should refuse to recognise the right to postulate. For to postulate is simply to *demand* what one wants, and why should one not ask for what one wants, if one is candid enough to confess it and honest enough to recognise that it does not follow that one gets it because one has asked for it? On the other hand, there is no sense in abstaining from demanding what we want, because our over-scrupulous abstention from trying to get it may be the very thing that prevents us from getting it. So the right to postulate belongs inalienably to the logic of desire and action, and initially there is no need to limit it. We may try all things, holding fast to what is good.

But after a postulate is made, it had better listen to the comment of experience. If our demand is foolish, it will meet with no response, or encounter hostile verdicts. We shall then do well to reconsider it. It does not follow that it should at once be scrapped, for it may be a very valuable postulate which we are rightly loth to renounce; but it may be better to modify it, and it will almost always be well to modify the methods of verification we have tried: by exploring further possibilities, by trying other and subtler methods, we may often succeed in extorting a favourable response. Moreover, we shall generally find that it is fairly easy to obtain for our postulates a certain amount of what may be taken as confirmation from experience.

---

[1] Including this doctrine itself, which does not shrink from submitting to the test it proposes. For if it should become possible to find flaws in this demonstration and expedient to modify or withdraw it, to do so would be quite in accordance with the principle enunciated.

For as our observation is selective, and we can and must exercise the right of rejecting what seems irrelevant, anomalous, and distracting, the evidence that tells against an important postulate often has much less than justice done it. Cases arise also of a clash of postulates.[1] Here we naturally try both to eat our cake and to have it, as we may do by taking methodologically one (or both) of the conflicting postulates. Even where we have to choose, we are apt to retain the postulate that seems to us most congenial.

Thus the process of postulation is very far from being inerrant and formally valid. It is full of risks and possibilities of error. It affords ample scope for the distinction between intelligent and ill-judged postulation. But all this does not entitle Formal logicians to give themselves airs of superior rectitude. They are fully as liable to err in postulating as other folk: perhaps if anything rather more so, if one allows for the effects of self-conceit and of blindness to pitfalls in promoting error. There is in truth *no* mechanical safeguard against error, no fool-proof device that will protect stupidity and guarantee success in knowing. This warning indicates the debit side to the right to postulate and to run any risk that seems worth taking.

The right to postulate, to which voluntarist logic assigns such a cardinal function, made its logical *début* under the title of the 'Will to believe.' But, as its author (William James) was quick to recognise, this name was not a good one. It aroused the hostility of the anti-religious, and, by simplifying overmuch, proved misleading. James's contention was really that there existed a psychological will to believe and also to disbelieve, which was a universal feature of our human endowment, but completely vitiated the customary intellectualist accounts of belief as a purely rational procedure. James went on to show that on this *psychological* basis a *logical right* to believe might be erected if the proper logical precautions were taken. These he proceeded to enumerate, such as that the exercise of our will to believe is adapted to certain occasions alone, that whatever we

---

[1] As between the libertarian postulate of freedom and the determinist postulate of calculability.

believe we believe at our risk, and especially that in the end what controls our acts of belief and determines their viability and value is always experience and the consequences of *acting* on a belief. But because his doctrine outraged the feelings of his intellectualist critics and challenged *their* dearest beliefs, it was misunderstood and misrepresented to an incredible extent. This reception was really an excellent testimonial to the soundness of James's contention, but we may avoid it by substituting the coldly logical and less ambiguous 'right to postulate' for the more inflammatory 'will to believe,' and by explaining that neither phrase commits us to anything but a recognition of the activity and enterprise which underlie and actuate our knowing.

§ 11. The Great Postulates.

Every postulate has, as we have seen, a psychological origin. It comes into being because it has commended itself to its maker's mind, and issues from his total personality. But its genesis is only the beginning of its career. Once propounded, it has to undergo a severe, and theoretically unending, process of natural selection. It is tested by its working, by the consequences of taking it as true. It is to this process that it owes the logical value to which, if successful, it attains. And, of course, of the postulates actually put forward, those that survive this testing by experience are relatively few. Even of these few a good many are not fully verified, for confirmation admits of more and less, and others linger on rather because they have not been scientifically disproved than because they have shown themselves scientifically useful. The (complete) teleological interpretation of nature is a good example; for while it would clearly make the course of events more congenial and more intelligible, our science is not yet able to use it effectively. Others again, like the 'postulate of immortality,' are psychologically so attractive, at all events to many minds, that they can survive a good deal of negative experience.

The postulates in scientific use are, of course, among the few survivors. Though many of them are nothing but hardly disguised conveniences of research, like the assumption of determinism, and most of them admit of alternative forms, they may in general be regarded as the outcome of long experience in the working of a science and as having met with large amounts of confirmation. They have often shown themselves so useful and become so familiar that no one dreams of disputing them. Hence it is easy to deceive oneself about their logical status. They can easily pass for self-evident 'axioms,' and it requires penetrating criticism to bring out their real nature.

In an introductory work like ours we can hardly embark on an exhaustive examination of the 'principles' of all the sciences, in order to show that they are without exception experimental postulates that have been hallowed by success, and that even now their value is largely methodological: we must be satisfied to take as a single example the common-sense view of the world which is presupposed and built upon by all the sciences, even though they are, not infrequently, led to repudiate or to revise their foundations. All our common-sense beliefs about the world are full of lurking postulates, practically service-able, but rough and methodological. 'Things' ('substances'), 'causes,' 'effects,' 'events,' 'laws,' 'space,' and 'time' are all of them, in Bergson's happy phrase, *découpages* hewn out of the immediately given flux of crude experience by postu-lations. They all derive from the fundamental postulates that the world is knowable and that we are entitled to take experience not as a whole but *bitwise*, or that we have a *right to analyse*.

It should at once be observed that this assumption about the way in which our cognitive activity sets itself to fashion an intelligible world out of crude experience is the exact converse of the Kantian method. The latter did not really start with experience as it would actually present itself to a mind beginning to know, with the chaotic confusion of a 'psychological baby,' but took for granted the common-sense *analysis* of experience, which had already turned the original chaos into an interacting world of things and persons extended in space and enduring in time, and sought to rescue it from the criticism of Hume. Hume, similarly, had presupposed the common-sense analysis and sought to carry it to what seemed to him its logical conclusion by resolving also its remaining *continua*, the self, space and time, into atomic 'things,' 'events,' 'impressions,' and 'ideas.' To confute this Humian exaggeration of common-sense analysis Kant had to insist on the need for *connecting* principles to compact together the Humian 'mind-dust'; so his whole *a priori* machinery was composed of '*synthetic*' principles. We need not here consider whether the Kantian machinery can be made to work; it is enough to point out that if our *datum* is *a continuum*, our problem is not how to invent enough synthetic principles but how to justify our actual practice of analysis.

To this question the simple answer is that analysis is forced upon us by our sheer inability to take our experience as a whole and to handle it effectively as such. So we assume that it may be taken in pieces and that whatever stands out and interests or concerns us specially may be singled out. We also assume that this treatment is not resented by cosmic happening as a whole, and that everything but the object (or 'subject') of our inquiry may be neglected for our purpose. Thus a *postulate of irrelevance* supplements the postulate of analysis. Unless we made these assumptions we could not speak of 'things,' 'causes,' and 'effects' at all, nor trace 'causal connexions' between them. We could not even isolate 'events' from the flow of happening.

Yet these assumptions are not only methodological, but largely fictitious, as modern science has come to see. Our 'analyses' never really sever their objects from the flux in which they live, but only lift them up into the focus of attention. What is taken as 'irrelevant' is never more than relatively so, and its irrelevance may disappear so soon as our purpose changes. It is strictly false, moreover, that either things or persons exist in isolation: even for common sense, they exist in the *continua* of space and time and in a social medium. For the purposes of physics, indeed, their isolation has completely broken down; 'atoms,' 'electrons,' and their like are no longer independent 'substances,' and have become *places* in 'fields of force.' The *continua* of space and time have also been traced to postulation. They are derived from the immediately given perception of *motion*, and built up by the assumptions of Euclidean space and Newtonian time into separate principles of cosmic cohesion. But these assumptions are no longer adequate for modern science, which has shown precisely what are the postulates of Euclidean geometry, why it is convenient to ascribe them to physical space, and where they break down. It has also discovered the limits to the conceptual separation of space and time and the physical complexity of the problem of motion. The results have been the reinstatement of 'space-time,' and the revolution in physics known as 'Relativity,' in order to accommodate the empirical facts of motion. But even the physics of Relativity take no account of psychological complications, and fall short of the complete relativity formulated long ago in Protagoras's 'Man is the measure of all things.'

The postulate of *causation* is not really worthy of the masses of philosophic controversy it has generated. The primary problem which it raises is really that of our right to break up the flow of happening into events. It is vital for us to claim this right, because we should be practically paralysed if we could never reason about anything less than the totality of reality. But after we have taken this necessary step, the rest is comparatively easy; we can take our selected 'events' as 'effects,' and allege 'causes' to 'explain' them. In this procedure an 'effect' is any event we wish to regard as 'caused,' while a 'cause' is anything that enables us to treat (for any purpose) events as 'effects.' Thus 'effects' are nothing without 'events' and 'causes' nothing without 'effects,' while causal analysis is nothing but a device to break up the flux. Moreover, as historically 'cause' has stood for any device that would do the trick, and by itself seems to be void of meaning, it does not appear that the causal postulate adds anything much to the general postulate that the world is knowable, which may be said to be implied in every effort to know. Its philosophic reputation is undeserved.[1]

The notion of '*law*,' similarly, is primarily a methodological device, like so much of our scientific apparatus. Having observed the regular occurrence of some (at first, a very few) events, we can erect a postulate that all events shall be regular

[1] See, further, *Formal Logic*, chap. xx, especially §§ 6–8.

and calculable. Our aim is to be able to make predictions, and the 'law' is primarily a formula which makes prediction possible.[1] When it succeeds, we say we have found the law; when it fails, we seek to amend our formula until it fits the facts. But we never sacrifice the demand that all events must be subject to law, because we will not give up the hope of prediction. Nevertheless, we are not wholly unprepared to recognise an element of fiction in our postulate; for if it were pressed to the utmost we see that it would conflict with other postulates which we also value. If every event is taken to be capable of absolute prediction, we must sacrifice the postulate of freedom and the reality of novelty (§§ 3, 4); and this will seem to many too high a price to pay. So we content ourselves with taking it as a methodological assumption which, in certain cases, proves a fiction.

Besides the postulates of common sense there are many others of a general sort, which we tacitly imply in knowing. Thus it is a methodological postulate that the world is knowable. The 'Laws of Thought,' to retain any meaning, must be taken as postulates.[2] All use of conceptions ('universals') implies the postulate that there shall be events a^1 and a^2, so related that they can be treated as 'cases' of the conception A. There are also plenty of unnecessary and mistaken postulates, such as those of Formal Logic and other pseudo-sciences, and there is abundant occasion for the exercise of sagacity and critical judgment in the choice of postulates. Nevertheless, there can be no doubt about the value of postulates in general, nor about the controlling part they play in knowing.

§ 12. Hypothesis.[3]

The mental attitude expressed in the making of hypotheses has plainly no pretensions to validity or cogency. It is rather a

---

[1] The objective counterpart of ' law ' is ' habit.' But this does not give us the same assurance. For, though things have habits, they may *change* them, and so defeat our predictions (Chap. XVIII, § 17).

[2] See *Formal Logic*, chap. x, especially §§ 10-12.

[3] See, further, *Formal Logic*, chap. xxii, § 3; and the article on " Hypothesis " in Singer's *Studies in the History and Methods of Science*, vol. ii.

play with possibilities which the Formal logician must look down upon as mere guessing. Nevertheless, it is lacking neither in logical allies nor in importance for real knowing. Its logical kin are not merely playing, feigning, and guessing, but also doubting, questioning, postulating, and experimenting, and all these are important activities in the eyes of a voluntarist logic. Their value resides in their capacity to *transform the face of the given*, and so to arouse the mind from the inert contemplation of appearances. They all involve mental *activity* instead of dull acquiescence in given conditions. And the mental activity they involve can in every case be made subservient to the ends of knowing.

A hypothesis, as the word implies, is a sup-position, a support laid down for us to step on in the prosecution of an inquiry.[1] Moreover, 'supposing' is also a form of make-believe that occurs in play. We shall not, therefore, go far wrong in sup-posing that hypothesis is a creature of the imagination and intended to help us on our way.

As I have elsewhere said, "the mental attitude which enter-tains hypotheses and can take 'fact' as hypothetical and possibly unreal, means an intellectual revolt against mere givenness. It has become critical of appearances, and has partially freed itself from the oppression of brute fact. It meets reality with an active response, and does not merely submit to whatever comes along. It feels free to anticipate reality by its guesses, to question it, to experiment, to take liberties with the given, to distrust and doubt appearances, to rearrange the world, at least in thought, to play with it, and with itself. For Hypo-thesis is a sort of game with reality, akin to fancy, make-believe, fiction, and poetry. In the hypothetical attitude 'facts' have ceased to be accepted at face value, to be just fact, and become capable of being *symbols*, whose suggestions are more important than their bare existence. Whatever they may be in reality,

[1] This derivation comes out well in the first use of the word in Plato (*Rep.*, vi, 511 B), where "stepping-stones and starting-points" (ὑποθέσεις καὶ ὁρμαί) are to conduct us to the "unhypothetical" first principle which confirms our guesses.

they are no longer *fixed* in the mind, but afloat; not being fixed ideas, they can be moved about and played with. But, like games in general, this play has a serious function. By loosening the connexion between what the real is (or seems) and what we think about it, it enables us to think it other, and *better*, than it is; and so, guided by our hypotheses and 'ideals' (which are postulates), we can set to work to *make* it other, and better, than it was." Thus "it is by this hypothesis-building habit that science touches poetry on the one side and action on the other." [1]

Plainly, then, a hypothesis is a guess, not a matter of knowledge, a child of doubt and hope. It is tried on tentatively, as it were in play. But the purpose of its use is serious enough; it is an experiment with the real that presents itself. Just as every thought is an experiment, so every conception is, *in use*, a hypothesis. We are not *sure* how it will answer, how responsive the real will be to its demand,[2] but we desire and expect the real to bear out our hypotheses; they partake, therefore, of the nature of postulates.

Such being the nature of Hypothesis, there is little reason to try to hedge it in with rules and regulations. We need not restrict the free play of fancy so long as we are willing to give meaning to its products by applying them to reality and honestly consent to *test* their cognitive value. If our hypotheses are applicable and verifiable, experience will pass a sufficient verdict on their value. As W. S. Jevons said,[3] "We must entertain the feeblest analogies and the merest guesses at truth, and yet must hold them worthless till they are verified." Psychologically, therefore, everything is permitted, but experience sternly sifts our fancies and bestows logical value on a few survivors. This stipulation is simple, but comprehensive and sufficient. As Prof. Carveth Read aptly says,[4] "No hypothesis is of any use that does not admit of verification (proof or disproof) by comparing the results deduced from it with facts or laws. If so framed as to elude every attempt to test it by facts, it can never be proved by

[1] Singer's *Studies*, ii, pp. 429–30.
[2] Cp. *loc. cit.*, p. 425.
[3] *Principles of Science*, p. 593.
[4] *Logic*, pp. 269–70.

them, nor add anything to our understanding of them." Hence, "to be verifiable a hypothesis must be definite," but "except this condition of verifiability and definiteness for the sake of verifiability, without which a proposition does not deserve the name of an hypothesis, it seems inadvisable to lay down rules for a 'legitimate' hypothesis." Nevertheless, meaningless hypotheses abound in theology and philosophy, nor are they wholly unknown in science. The 'Lorentz-Fitzgerald contraction' to explain why the motion of bodies in the (imaginary) 'ether' could never be detected, was a good example, until the situation which evoked it was elucidated by another interpretation given by Einstein.

§ 13. Analogy.[1]

The play of fancy is not in fact as free and arbitrary as it seems. It is aroused by the stimulations of the real and subject to the limitations of our experience. We cannot imagine what is utterly unlike anything we have ever experienced. There must be some sort and degree of *likeness* between what we imagine and what we know. When this basis of likeness is granted us we are said to *argue from analogy*.

An analogy is best defined as a likeness we want to argue from, in order that we may assimilate one part of experience to another and pass from the known to the unknown. This is not the strict etymological meaning of the word, which was 'equality of ratios.' But this only occurs in a few artificial cases, while in the wider sense arguments from analogy are common and indeed universal. For 'inductive' and 'deductive' reasoning are both concerned with the relations of 'cases' to rules ('principles,' 'laws,' 'universals,' etc.), and no two cases are more than 'similar'; hence in arguing from one 'case' to another of the same rule we are always relying on the analogy between them. If the argument succeeds, the analogy is pronounced 'good' (or 'true'), if not, 'bad' (or 'false'). The crucial question is always whether the likeness between the two cases is strong enough to support the transition from the one to the other. Now this is

[1] See, further, *Formal Logic*, chap. xxii, § 4.

always an assumption (or 'postulate'), because no two cases of 'the same' are ever *absolutely identical* (if they were, we could no longer regard them as *two!*), and their logical sameness always rests on abstraction from their differences: thus analogical reasoning always runs a risk. It lays no claim to 'formal validity.'

Bearing this in mind, we shall have little difficulty in deciding the dispute between philosophers as to whether similarity should be regarded as an ultimate fact of perception or as analysable into 'partial identity.' It is not easy to say what meaning can be given to the phrase 'partial identity' in this dispute. It seems implicitly to deny the constant association of differences with identities and to imply the existence of absolute identity. If it means that each of two 'similar' objects is composed, in part, of an absolute identity accompanied by equally absolute differences, the doctrine at once suggests inquiries as to how a thing with such a discordant constitution holds together, and as to what assurance we can have that the differences will not outweigh the identity and so frustrate any argument based on the 'partial identities.'

The truth would rather seem to be that we are always aware of the presence both of likenesses and of differences in our objects of thought. 'Identity' is the postulate of the irrelevance of differences.[1] The question that arises, therefore, is never as to the existence of differences, but always as to their *relevance* and *value*. Is more weight to be given to the likeness or to the difference between two cases for the purpose of our argument? May we abstract from the differences between them, and treat them as cases of 'the same'? Abstractly either contention is always tenable; so, prior to experience, this is an *open* question. It is to be decided by experiment.

Similarities and analogies being thus matters of perception and postulation, we may expect to find considerable differences in the capacity of different minds to perceive them and to select those which can forward their purposes in reasoning. Some will dispose of a wider experience and a more creative imagination;

---

[1] Cp. *Formal Logic*, chap. x, § 10.

some will be acuter than others in seeing analogies, and will show greater ingenuity, sagacity, and judgment in choosing such as will be fertile of valuable consequences. But even the richest minds are limited in these respects, and the objective nature of the real also imposes limits on the success and value of our analogical reasoning which are hard to estimate. Often there seems to be an objective discontinuity and lack of similarity between different parts of our experience, *alias* different portions of the real, and our faith that all reality must be pervaded by far-reaching analogies that knit together its various parts and provide high-roads for our inferences will be baffled. Nor can we have any antecedent assurance that even if such analogies exist we shall be able to discover them; for they may be so impenetrably shrouded from us by the limitations of our senses and our minds that they yield us no important or significant clues to the inner nature of the real. Of course, however, we shall, for methodological reasons, make all the assumptions we need. We shall assume that human life and experience may yield analogies that give us glimpses into the inner structure of reality, that the universe is not rent by chasms no analogy can bridge, and that the analogies which we flatter ourselves we have discovered between its parts are real. But these beliefs are all methodological assumptions, and the marvel is that we have made them work to so great an extent. It is only a voluntarist logic which leaves room for faith and hope and does not forbid scientific reasoning to appeal to the charity that can sanction such perilous procedures.

§ 14. Verification.[1]

It is clear that all reasonings require verification. We have seen (Chap. XIV, § 5) that even the most valid 'deductions' require to be verified because it is no use 'proving' that a conclusion *must* be true, if it does not *come true* in fact. Similarly in 'induction' the *selection* alike of the 'cases' and of the 'laws' and their *relevance* to each other require unending verification; and the same is true of postulates, hypotheses, and analogies.

[1] See, further, *Formal Logic*, chap. xxii, § 6.

Verification, therefore, appears to be the universal method of *auditing* the accounts given of the real by our thought.

Unfortunately for Formal Logic, however, Verification refuses to be represented as a formally valid process. Indeed, it is a formal fallacy. In regarding the coming true of an inferred result as a confirmation of its truth-claim it condenses itself into the formula, if *A is true, B follows; but B follows, ergo A is true*; which is flagrantly an 'affirmation of the consequent,' and a notorious fallacy vitiating all the reasoning which appeals to it!

Formal Logic has detected this defect, but hardly its significance. It does not perceive that it is a challenge to its whole conception of logic which places it in an awkward dilemma. Either *all* reasoning is vitiated by its dependence upon verification, and this would mean scepticism; or *sound and valuable reasoning may be formally fallacious*, and this would mean the end of Formal Logic. To us acceptance of the latter alternative is rendered all the easier and more welcome by the fact that Formal Logic will presumably prefer the former; it will only be a further nail in the coffin of Formal Logic that it should be driven to condemn all our reasoning and plunge into scepticism.

Let us accept, then, Verification as a good and useful process and consider its uses. In the first place, it plainly admits of more and less, and therefore of cumulative proof. Indeed, in strict logic, the process will go on for ever. That is to say, *no* amount of verification of a truth-claim will ever convert the indefinitely growing probability which verification yields into *absolute* truth and certitude. But *psychologically* there is no need for this. As their working prospers and confirmation accumulates we soon come to feel that our beliefs are adequately verified and as true as true can be for us; psychological certainty reduces the chance of falsity to zero.

But, secondly, this psychological certainty does not set in at the same point in all minds or at all times. For some are harder to convince than others who are more sanguine, credulous, or scrupulous; some are bolder and take greater risks, others more cautious and more insistent on safety. Hence there is no one definite point at which verification merges into proof for all minds. For this reason there is, and will always remain, room for differences of opinion about what is proved and true, and logic cannot transcend the limits of personality. Radically different temperaments, like the optimist and the pessimist, the intellectualist and the voluntarist, cannot be coerced into agreement in the inferences they draw, even from the same *data*; at most they may recognise each other's bias and their own, and may agree to differ.

We demand, moreover, different degrees of assurance in different subjects. Where, as in pure mathematics, we are dealing with ideal systems of our own creation, we require complete accuracy, and laugh at the classical scholar who had 'not exactly proved' the proposition set him in Euclid, but 'flattered himself that he had rendered it extremely probable'; similarly, we formulate our 'laws of nature' with an exactness we do not expect to find in any of their exemplifications. In ultimate analysis, no doubt, the application of mathematics to life always remains hypothetical, as does that of our 'laws of nature' to the course of events; but we hold that, *if and in so far as* the laws apply, their results should be exact. In our practical dealings with concrete situations, on the other hand, we realise that we are concerned with probabilities and that 'practical certainty' is the most we can attain, and find that we are often compelled to act on slight ones and to accept verifications which we feel to be far from adequate. Verification, therefore, is largely relative to the nature of the subject-matter.

Lastly, Verification is not only quantitative but also *competitive*. In scientific inquiry there are normally *several* hypotheses to be considered, and it will rarely happen that the results observed will verify them equally. Hence we cannot get away from the questions—which is the *best* hypothesis? and which is the *best* verification? Every accepted truth, therefore, has to be regarded as the victor in a strenuous struggle for existence, in which it has risen to its present eminence by overcoming an indefinite number of competitors which have sunk into the more or less forgotten 'errors' of the past. But for this very reason it cannot disavow its history, and holds its place by the same tenure. To survive it must continue to be the best and strongest (most 'valid') explanation of the known facts. It must be ever ready to meet any challenge from new facts and new theories, and cope with them victoriously. Otherwise it is ousted from its dignity and scrapped. Thus its tenure is precisely that of the priest of Diana Nemorensis, "the priest who slew the slayer and shall himself be slain." And the more progressive a science is the more rapidly does this fate befall its reigning 'truths.' But what reason is there to regret the process so long as it means the growth of science and the replacement of less valuable truths by more valuable? *Our* truths, at least, are not 'eternal'; they arise and perish and rejuvenate themselves unendingly in our service, and the more rapidly they do this the better do they serve us. Verification, then, is the name of the indispensable process to which truths owe their value, and without which no truth arises.

CHAPTER XVII

SCIENTIFIC METHOD

1. Is there only one method of knowing ? ; 2. The Platonic theory of mathematics ; 3. The conflict between the Platonic and the empirical explanation ; 4. The empirical explanation of mathematical truth ; 5. The task of the sciences and of philosophy ; 6. The logical value of incipient sciences : (a) principles ; 7. (b) Facts ; 8. The relativity of fact ; 9. (c) The organic apparatus a presupposition of scientific method ; 10. The fallibility of our organs and the use of instruments ; 11. 'Memory' as a presupposition of fact ; 12. The personal equation and the self ; 13. The power of words ; 14. The power of common-sense realism.

§ 1. Is there only One Method of Knowing?

It has been customary to suppose, ever since Plato and Aristotle, that there are (at least) *two* methods of knowing, and that there is an essential difference between the way in which the mind grasps principles and the way in which it applies or uses them. Hence the deep chasm between '*a priori*' and '*a posteriori*' truth, between 'deductive' and 'inductive' reasoning.

But we have seen good reason to question this tradition in both its assumptions. It cannot be maintained either that the two methods are independent of each other or that by itself either of them yields knowledge. Thus the idea of principles absolutely certain *a priori* has proved entirely elusive. Neither as 'intuitions' nor as 'necessities of thought' have principles been able to make good their claims to possess absolute truth and to be sufficient guides to knowledge. The principles accepted as true all have a long history behind them; they were all conceived in doubt and started life as postulates, and are all now the products and survivors of a secular struggle to know. They have acquired their present value and status by the successful working of the sciences which employ them; their verification has made them 'true.' They are *not*, therefore, independent of the process of experience, but are its finest fruits. Moreover, quite apart from the implications of this genesis of principles, it is untrue that formally valid deductive reasoning from principles is *ipso facto* forthwith true (Chap. XV, § 4). Our best 'deductions' have to be verified, and *gain* in logical value by coming true in fact. Till then they rank merely as intelligent anticipations, which guide expectation but do not coerce the future. They, too, therefore, are dependent on experience.

On the other hand, it has appeared that the attempt of 'induction' to reason from sheer fact is sheer illusion (Chap. XV, § 7). *Absolute* fact is as much a fiction as absolute truth. For in our reasoning 'facts' are never *given* but always *taken*, and often *faked*. At best the 'facts' an induction starts from are a skilful selection from a mass of irrelevant material; but often they are ingenious *fictions* ('ideals' and abstractions), taken as working hypotheses, and (perhaps) growing into 'objective' facts by their successful use. At any rate, every *scientific* 'fact' has had a history which has a bearing on its logical value; it, too, must be regarded as the survivor in a struggle for existence.

Accordingly our two methods draw together. They betray their human origin and likeness. Neither will work without the other. They are plainly meant for each other. They interpenetrate and fuse.

It follows that the method of knowing is really *one*. We never rely entirely on the native powers of the mind, on the infallibility of our intuitions—in other words, on our native impudence. Nor do we ever merely abase ourselves before brute facts.

Our procedure is always more intelligent, critical, and self-respecting. We always experiment with selected demands and try them upon selected facts. We are always armed with a hypothesis, and usually have alternatives in mind when we question nature. The point of our question is always aimed at some subject of interest. Knowing is essentially a rational, purposive *activity*, and to leave out the teleological and the activity factor, as intellectualism does, alike in its sensationalist and in its rationalist forms, is a false abstraction and a fatal mistake.

It need not be denied that this procedure is risky. Inquiries inspired by desires may go astray. Our desires may prove too selective, and may blind us to factors in the total situation which should not be overlooked. But exhortations to be 'dispassionate' and 'disinterested,' and solemn warnings of the type "Beware, young man, lest you find what you are looking for," are merely fatuous. For there is no other way of inquiring but that of asking the questions one is interested in getting answered, and there is no way of so emasculating the human intellect that it no longer feels any passion or desire and grows *indifferent* to truth. The attitude described as 'dispassionate' inquiry is really one of high internal tension, and, when we look closely into it, the profession of dispassionate neutrality towards vital problems always turns out to be a cloak for a lurking interest that is ashamed to face the light of day.

The proper way to guard against the dangers of over-eagerness is not to force oneself into the attitude of a weather-cock and to turn in any direction winds of doctrine may chance to blow, but to allow experience of the working of our anticipations and ideas to determine their status. In other words, we should seek to verify our postulates and cultivate open-mindedness. In detail, the expedients by which we extricate ourselves from error and secure ourselves *are* the methods of the sciences.

§ 2. The Platonic Theory of Mathematics.

It would hardly be respectful, however, to adopt this attractive simplification of the problem of knowledge without due consideration of the claims made for an important group of sciences, the mathematical. Ever since the days of Plato, who was followed (with for our present purpose unessential variations) by Aristotle, the case of mathematics has seemed peculiar to philosophers. The mathematical were taken as the typical, nay, strictly as the only, sciences. They were thought to proceed by deduction from absolutely certain, *a priori*, and self-evident principles by cogent demonstrations, and to be wholly composed of necessary truths. Plato, though not Aristotle, further held that ultimately there was *only one* principle from which all scientific principles should be deducible (the Idea of Good) and that its nature was metaphysical. Thus philosophy was represented as the sole source of certainty and the foundation of all the sciences. It is no wonder that so flattering a theory proved popular among philosophers, and, thanks to Euclid, a devout Platonist, this theory of mathematical truth was also accepted by mathematicians for over 2000 years; still it remained a philosophic, and specifically a Platonic, theory. So we may describe as *Platonism* any theory of the sciences which regards them as dependent on principles or resting on 'presuppositions' which are self-evident or *a priori*, and as standing in need of a metaphysical deduction in order to become truly certain. The opposite view, that the sciences are independent sources of knowledge and their principles are successful postulates, while the function of metaphysics is to combine and harmonise their results and not to 'prove' them, may be called *empiricism*. It is suggested primarily by the natural sciences, but it has, of course, to explain the peculiarities of mathematics.

§ 3. The Conflict between the Platonic and the Empirical Explanation.

A clear-cut issue is thus before us. Are there *two* sorts of science—the *a priori* and the empirical—and is there no one scientific method, or is the Platonic theory of mathematics erroneous, and is scientific procedure in mathematics essentially the same as in the empirical sciences?

Inquiring into this dispute we may ask (1) whether Platonism gives an adequate explanation of the facts both theories recognise, (2) whether Platonism can dispose of the case for empiricism, (3) whether the converse is not true.

In answer to the first question we may note that, strictly speaking, the Platonic theory leaves as unexplained miracles both the initial discovery of scientific principles and the progress of the sciences. For if it is true, as Plato declares, that scientific principles are entirely dependent on the one metaphysical principle of the Good, it becomes inexplicable how they can be discovered, even as 'hypotheses,' until the Good (on which they all depend) has been discovered, and how the sciences can progress when the Good has *not* been discovered. The actual progress of the sciences should, therefore, be impossible. Hence the history of science shows that there must have been some way of establishing scientific principles *otherwise* than by deduction from metaphysics, and the thought easily suggests itself that experience of their working is really the agency which confirms hypotheses and turns our guesses into 'principles.'

Thus a complete empirical explanation becomes quite thinkable, whereas a complete Platonism, denying all logical value to experience, remains incredible. Even a moderate Platonism remains a dualism, and is at a loss to explain how experience can co-operate with *a priori* truth in the formation of knowledge.

§ 4. The Empirical Explanation of Mathematical Truth.

On the other hand, empiricism has little difficulty nowadays in supplying a complete alternative to the Platonic theory and explaining how mathematical principles may be suggested, tested, and established, by experience.

(1) It can no longer be conceded that mathematical truth is *sui generis*, purely *a priori*, ultimate and unanalysable. Its necessity is merely that of inference : it flows from the definitions which lay down the rules for the game of mathematics. Euclid's postulate, the famous 'axiom of parallels,' is merely a definition of Euclidean space. If we adopt this definition, that the internal angles of a triangle should equal two right angles is a necessity of precisely the same sort as that a king should be mated if he has no valid move under the rules of chess. The definitions of mathematics look less arbitrary than those of chess, only because they have a more serious purpose; but both alike are suggested by experience.

(2) As the name continues to testify, 'geometry' once meant 'land-surveying,' and had the utilitarian purpose of measuring and comparing areas, while arithmetic was a way of dealing with empirical things which allowed themselves to be treated as units for various purposes. Thus the function of mathematics was to calculate the shapes, sizes, motions, and behaviours of physical things. It greatly simplified their manipulation, although (as Plato perceived) no real ('sensible') thing

is ever reducible to the mathematical thing which takes its place in our calculations.

(3) Mathematicians are now quite clear that mathematical definitions and postulates admit of many alternatives; the choice between them is determined by the purpose to which they are to minister. The assumptions of Euclidean geometry and common arithmetic are the simplest, and for most purposes the most convenient, of these alternatives, because the easiest to apply to the real. But it is meaningless to ask whether they are 'true' in any other sense, nor are they logically obligatory or superior to the other alternatives. They owe their privileged position and their identification with reality to their practical, not to their logical, superiority.

Thus the fundamental principles of mathematics are assimilated to hypotheses which have been verified, and differ from other hypotheses only in their antiquity and in the amount of verification they have received. They resemble hypotheses in six important respects.

(1) Like other hypotheses those of mathematics had not only to suggest themselves to the human mind and to issue from the human imagination, but also (2) to be stimulated by some empirical cue. Actually it was long experience of *things* in the physical world, which spontaneously grouped themselves into classes and were *almost* indifferent to the way they were moved about, which suggested to arithmetic the hypothesis of *units*, *entirely* alike, and utterly unaffected by any manipulations. So arithmetic became the science of what followed from postulating ideal units and counting them. The counting was an ideal process, and the units were idealisations which did not occur in reality; but the manipulations of arithmetic were applicable to the 'things' which had suggested them. Similarly spatiality is a constant attribute of things : they are extended and stable, and can be moved quite easily in physical space (if not too large); this empirical character was warrant enough for geometry to imagine an ideal space in which shape is conserved absolutely and the 'axiom of free mobility' holds without reservation. The axioms and postulates of Euclid, therefore,

are imaginative constructions suggested by experience. They
were originally hypotheses; but they were a great success, and
proved applicable to many aspects of physical reality. Thus
(3) they were relevant to scientific problems and applicable to
the real, which is perhaps the most valuable requirement in a
good hypothesis. Yet (4) they were not, and were not intended
to be, copies or replicas of sensible reality; for to insist on
slavish imitation in a hypothesis is to clip the wings of the
imagination and to rob it of its elevating power. It is enough
that the real should show 'approximations' to the ideal qualities we demand in mathematics : it is idle to expect perfectly
straight lines and plane surfaces to occur in a three-dimensional
real which is the battleground of a variety of 'forces.' But
though the real never attains to the ideal and is never mathematically 'exact,' the latter may enable us to forecast the
behaviour of the former; in which case it is said to be 'verified'
by its usefulness. Thus (5) the principles of mathematics are
verified by their use, like other truth-claims. Not (6), however,
absolutely. They may become indispensable, practically certain,
and psychologically unquestionable; but in theory, at least, it
remains thinkable that better assumptions may be devised or
that characteristics may be discovered in the real which lend
themselves better to interpretation by non-Euclidean mathematics. In Einstein's physics this case may perhaps be said to
have occurred; in any case it is clear that the usefulness of our
mathematical principles was our reason for declaring them
'true.' We must, therefore, contend against Plato that here,
too, the conclusions are more certain than the premises from
which they were deduced, and that it is the scientific success
of the mathematical sciences which authenticates their principles, and not the infallibility of the principles which guarantees
their success.

§ 5. The Task of the Sciences and of Philosophy.

Having thus vindicated the unity of scientific method, we
may proceed to describe it. The sciences all arise out of the
gradual articulation of the gigantic problem which the world

presents to any intelligence that tries to live in it. In the beginning there was just the one problem of life, with philosophy as the attempt to solve it. But out of this situation grew the special sciences, practically independent and each concerned with one aspect of the whole treated in abstraction from the rest and developing its own assumptions, its own methods, and its own inquiries. This is the present situation ; but in the end we may hope that there will be a sufficiency of sciences to suggest to a philosophy which undertakes to interpret and co-ordinate their answers an adequate answer to the total problem.

Thus, in a sense, Plato was right. The sciences did historically arise out of philosophy, if we assign this name to the inquiry into the whole problem of life: but it is *not* true that they remain logically dependent on their genesis. On the contrary, philosophy in the end becomes dependent on the sciences, which, when they have done their work and achieved their several ends, always leave over a further problem—that of the combining together of the deliverances of the special sciences (together with any other relevant evidence from direct experience) into a single consistent and adequate interpretation of life. *This* sort of philosophy is not *pre-scientific*, like the first, but raises an ulterior question which the scientific specialist may ignore, and the scientific worker may do well to forget while at work, because it transcends the scientific standpoint, namely, the question of the vital significance of scientific results.

So scientific method in the strictest sense is limited at both ends. It starts from a pre-scientific situation which gives it its subject matter and initial problems. It ends with a final problem of the correlation, harmonisation, and valuation of scientific knowledge, which can neither be solved without scientific method nor yet by that alone.

Sciences, then, are to be understood as special methods for dealing with special problems, and essentially partial ways of concentrating upon the objects of interest and of inquiry they select from the vast and apparently unlimited *continuum* with which the real confronts us. This selection has at first a great air of randomness, and in its initial stages the growth of a science seems highly contingent. Historically speaking, it would seem, a scientific 'principle' may arise out of anything and come from anywhere. It may be suggested by anything. Sheer guesses, fantastic and false analogies, the intuitions of a poet, the revelations of a prophet, the intimations of a genius or a lunatic, may figure in its pedigree, and start it. Its genesis is a psychological, not a logical, process. It owes its whole logical value to what happens to it *after* it has been suggested. For when suggestions have been harnessed in the service of a science or a problem, they have to *work*, and cultivation tames their wildness. Those which remain incurably wild or idle are finally discarded; those which serve the purpose of the inquiry are trimmed and trained and verified continuously, until the most exacting sceptic can find no word to say against their respectability and 'self-evidence.'

Thus the logical value of scientific truth is a growth and an achievement: it is not the *premisses* of our science which are certain but the *conclusions*.

§ 6. The Logical Value of Incipient Sciences: (*a*) Principles.

Consequently, we can observe marked differences between the principles of an old and of an incipient science. The former (usually) present themselves as a single coherent system, unmoved by any breath of doubt, undistracted by any hint of alternatives. The latter seem a battle-field of rival principles, a confused struggle of parties contending for their favourites, while even the most honest and scientific inquirers are at a loss to select the best among a number of tentative alternatives.

It is, however, clear that it is precisely these disputed principles which show us how a science is made and enlighten us about its logical structure. It has been a great mistake for logicians to take their illustrations of scientific knowing from established sciences. They solemnly inform the scientists that Queen Anne is dead, as it were, and bestow their *ex post facto* blessing on such procedures as have succeeded.

Thus the so-called logic of science has hitherto been written merely about discoveries already made, and *not* about their making, about which it is merely remarked that the process is not logical. As Prof. M. R. Cohen sarcastically says, "The Canons of Induction teach us how to discover the cause of typhoid or some other disease of which the cause is already known; they are silent about the cause of cancer and the methods by which it is to be investigated."[1] But how can the method of scientific inquiry possibly be illustrated by an account which expunges from the record all the risks, perplexities, hesitations, errors, and failures which beset the exploration of an actual problem? Thus is the *experimental* nature of thought hopelessly obscured. Our examples should be chosen from live questions still in dispute, in which the principles to use are still hypotheses, in which the postulates have not yet grown axiomatic, in which the 'facts' are still suspect and largely spurious. Hence there is much more logic to be learnt from psychology than from mechanics; and from psychical research, where all is doubtful, facts, principles, observations, analogies, experiments, and results, where prejudice, fraud, mendacity, self-deception, and hallucination are rampant, where hardly anyone is exempt from some noxious form of bias, than from a subject like mathematics, where emotional interest is at a minimum and everything appears to be settled—everything, at least, that is allowed to be mentioned in a text-book. Psychology and psychical research are logically so instructive, just because in them the battle of the principles has not been decided and questions of method are still being agitated. For it is in regions where we have slowly and painfully to feel our way that we become most acutely conscious of the need for care at every step we take, and are most willing to explore alternatives which may be improvements; where he sees a made road straight before him the logician ceases to be an explorer whose advice and observations may be of value to explorers, and is forced into the superfluous and ridiculous *rôle* of endorsing discoveries others have made and of logically 'demonstrating' what is already scientifically assured.

He also incapacitates himself for understanding the revolutions which sometimes occur even in established sciences when

[1] *Journal of Philosophy*, xv, p. 673.

the adoption of one of the suppressed and forgotten alternatives to the reigning principles suddenly becomes expedient. For he cannot explain how it is that though of the utmost 'theoretic' importance they avail so little to disturb the 'facts' of the science and the confidence with which it is regarded in 'practice.' He thinks that the Copernican revolution should have gone far to discredit astronomy, the Darwinian to discredit biology, the Einsteinian to discredit physics, the revulsion from Euclid to discredit mathematics. Instead of which all these sciences are more flourishing than ever. His whole difficulty arises out of his refusal to admit that principles are really selected for their empirical merits as working hypotheses. So he does not see that quite small improvements in the recognised 'facts' may entail a revolution in their 'explanation' and properly produce a radical transformation of the underlying 'principles.' This may, nevertheless, leave the main body of the science unshaken and intact, because the 'fundamental' principles were never more than convenient assumptions serving to hold together the admitted 'facts.' The real lesson of such occurrences is that experimentation with 'principles' is always in order, even though it is often too arduous to be prosecuted, and that their revision is always thinkable even though there is not often any need to undertake it. The logical outcome clearly is that the truth of scientific principles depends on the use made of them and on the success with which they have worked.

§ 7. (b) Facts.

Reflection on scientific method has been dominated and distorted by two delusions. The first, which has just been examined, is that we can start inquiry with assured principles which are self-evident and need no testing and may be taken for granted. The second, which is its twin, is that we can start from assured and solid 'facts,' which impose themselves on us and speak for themselves. Both these delusions are corrected by the doctrine that initially we *experiment*, more or less wildly, alike with the 'principles' we postulate and with the 'facts' we recognise, that facts and principles are only factors in scientific method, remaining relative to each other and to the state of our knowledge, without ever arriving at real finality so long as knowledge grows. Both are rooted in a pre-scientific situation from which their problems spring, and are in truth to be understood and used as what the jargon of philosophy calls 'categories.' Thus it is out of its psychological urgency that the logical value of our knowledge grows.

In spite of this insight, however, we may readily admit that scientific inquiry often appears to start from 'facts,' or what we are pleased to take as 'facts' for the purpose of the inquiry. Whether this is consciously realised or not, such facts are always problematic, always provisional, and always suffer transformation more or less as our knowledge grows. At the outset this factual subject-matter is plainly pre-scientific and of very inferior logical quality, and quite unfit to prove any principles 'valid,' though it may suggest them to the eye of faith. This alone is enough to defeat the enterprise of inductive logic in extracting valid principles from facts, and justifies the veil of obscurity drawn over the origins of the sciences. It is wisdom and the instinct of self-respect that prompt the sciences to forget them. For only so is it possible to uphold the ideal of fact, stern and unbending, deaf to the allurements of theory, and adamant to the appeals of human emotion.

It is this ideal fact which is referred to when science is said to have unbounded respect for fact, to be devoted to its study, to lead to a loyal recognition of fact as the finest fruit of scientific training. Such fact is to be a pure *datum*, absolutely *given* and in no way *fabricated*. We are to have no say or choice about it, and to have done nothing to make it fact. Nothing *faked* is to count as *fact*.

But how does this ideal itself accord with the actual? The 'facts' the sciences have accepted at various stages of their career have been very different. At best they have been ephemeral, more often they have turned out fancies, fictions, fakes, fallacies, errors, superstitions, delusions—everything, in short, that is abhorrent to the scientific soul. From this condemnation only the reigning facts are exempt, to which we (rightly) pin our faith because they are the best we have; but in the light of their history must we not admit that sooner or later they, too, are fated to be superseded like the rest? And what is to be done about it?

The most obvious thing to do is to hush up the trouble, and to hope that it will not become public. The sciences, like the theologies, are human enough to try to conceal their difficulties from the uninitiated, and by a lavish indulgence in technical nomenclature they often succeed. Another favourite expedient is to institute a Draconic purge of 'facts,' and to endeavour to find a fact which shall be, like Cæsar's wife, above suspicion, so hard and solid that it can be trusted to stay fact, come what may.

So the whole pack of sciences start on the trail of absolute fact. But, alas! their history records no triumphs in this quest. However deeply they dig down they never seem to get to the bottom of any fact and can never produce an absolutely final account of it. Our actual scientific facts are no more above suspicion than was Cæsar's wife: they entertain relations with gross fictions as equivocal as Pompeia's were with Clodius.

§ 8. The Relativity of Fact.

It is high time, therefore, that logicians realised what the sciences are by now accustomed to confess, viz. that the actual scientific 'facts' are never absolute. They are always relative to the state of the science in which they figure, to the organs and methods by which they are discerned, to the conditions under which they are observed, to the instruments by which they are measured, to the theories in terms of which they are described, to the experiments from which they have resulted, to the history, bias, and aims of the science by which they are recognised. Hence if by 'facts' we mean the facts recognised at any time by any science, every science must admit that its 'facts' have undergone progressive transformation, and seem bound to change further as its knowledge grows: nor need it hesitate to admit that the facts as they appeared at the beginning and as they turn out to be at the end of an inquiry may often differ *toto cælo*.

In view of the logician's reluctance to face this relativity of 'fact,' it may be expedient to give some illustrations. When the plain man asks the scientist the plain question, "What is the colour of blood?" he expects the answer "red." Does the scientist give this answer? No, he knows too much. So he answers: "If the blood is that of a mammal and not of a caterpillar, and is seen by an eye with normal colour-vision and in daylight, you may call it red." Again: "Is matter indestructible?"—"It would seem so, under terrestrial conditions, so far as our finest balances can tell us; but now that we can observe much minuter losses, we should add: 'Only if it does not happen to be radio-actively disintegrating.' And it is probable that the stars are radiating away their substance in the form of 'light,' and quite plausible to hold that inside the stars matter is being annihilated all the time." "Is fever the disease I am suffering from?"—"Fever is a symptom of many diseases." "Have I 'typhoid' then, or 'dysentery'?"—"Both are names for the mischief made by half a dozen sorts of microbes." "Is 'witchcraft' a fact?"—"No, you must not call it that: it is no longer orthodox, though until two or three hundred years ago you might have been burnt for not doing so, even in the most civilised countries of Europe. You should now call it 'hysteria' or 'hypnotism,' though in another two or three hundred years these terms are quite likely to sound as vague, absurd, and unscientific as 'witchcraft' now does to our medicine-men." "Does the sun attract all bodies in the solar system?"—"If they are not so small that light-pressure prevails over gravitation." "Do you and I see the same rainbow?"—"That depends on whether we can agree about what we call 'the same.'" "Was Columbus the first European to discover America?"—"Unless you prefer to believe that Eric the Red got there some centuries before." "Who started the War?"—"Be careful to consider what and where you are before you answer, for the accepted truth on this point is regional." "If history is never impartial and everywhere suspect as *une fable convenue*, may we appeal to psychology to yield us absolute facts?"—"Nay, nothing is more likely to disabuse you of the belief in absoluteness." "How so?"—"Why, it frequently fools the axioms of mathematics. If you move a pair of compasses across your skin, you feel it has one point or two according as you move over one part of the body or another. Again, arithmetically $0+0$ always $=0$, but two flies crawling over you unfelt while they are separate become psychologically perceptible when they crawl together. So when Euclid confidently argues that if $A=B$ and $B=C$, A must equal C, psychology triumphantly retorts that in all magnitudes taken as equal by our senses or our instruments there may lurk unperceived differences which become apparent when A is directly compared with C, and hence A may nevertheless be larger than C."

"Lastly, am I in motion or at rest?"—"Wretch, you are plunging into a hornet's nest of problems. Have you never considered that the earth is revolving on its axis and circulating round the sun, which is travelling in space as part of a galactic star-cloud, and moving relatively to an unknown multitude of other systems? No absolute motion has yet been discovered and there are no means of detecting it, if it exists. Will you not, therefore, tell me relatively to what frame of reference you wish to know your motion or your rest? For only so has your question any meaning." "Well, then, can you tell me how many stars one can see simultaneously on a fine night?"—"You may think you see several hundreds at the same time; but you really see them as they *were* when their light started on its journey to your eye. So you see them all at *different* times, the moon as it was $1\frac{1}{2}$ seconds ago, the sun as it was 8 minutes ago, a distant star as it was thousands of years ago. 'Simultaneous' has become an ambiguous word, and time as relative and local as motion. The principle of Relativity is a gallant attempt by physics to explore the far-reaching paradoxes which this fact entails!"

We may safely conclude, therefore, that for scientific method 'facts' are relative to the 'theories' that deal with them, to the laws which explain them, and to the general state of knowledge and of the society which recognises them. It is vain to seek for a 'fact' in which no theory is lurking in order to build

a science on a fixed foundation. But neither is there any
'theory' which is doomed to remain such and may not hope
to rise presently to the rank of 'fact.' All the conceptions used
in scientific method get their value from their use as instruments
of knowing.

§ 9. (c) The Organic Apparatus a Presupposition of Scientific
      Method.

The same function may be claimed also for a number of
other presuppositions of actual knowing which are often overlooked. Thus it is to the organic apparatus of the senses and of
the bodily structures generally that we are indebted for our
primary *data*. It is indispensable and invaluable, because we
could hardly live without trusting it. Yet the sciences speedily
discover that it is by no means perfect and infallible. Our
senses are strictly limited in their range and highly selective,
responding only to a minute fraction of the stimuli they might
notice.

For example, this is how they treat vibrations. They are
noticed as 'noises' if they are very slow, as 'tones' if they
are faster than 32 per second, and as the rate of vibration increases they get higher and shriller up to about 40,000 per
second. After that silence: the ear shuts up shop, and will
hear no more of vibrations. When, however, certain other
processes, now denominated 'ether-waves,' begin to hum at
the rate of about 390,000,000,000,000 per second, the eye wakes
up. It sees 'red.' It goes on seeing all the colours of the
spectrum up to about 770 billions at the violet end. But at
either end of the visible spectrum there are known to be further
vibrations of what is called 'invisible light,' because it is
refracted and reflected and generally behaves like light. It is
light in all respects, save that the eye does not respond to it.
The 'infra-red' rays are, however, perceived by the skin as
'heat,' though it wholly boycotts the blue end of the spectrum
which, therefore, yields 'cold' light without heat, while the
'ultra-violet' produce chemical effects which are salutary or
injurious to the human body ('tan,' vitamin D). Indirectly

we have obtained cognisance of vibrations with frequencies as slow as $12\frac{1}{2}$ billions per second and as fast as 100,000,000 billions ('cosmic rays'), so that, if we take the visible spectrum as an octave, there are 5 octaves below and 18 above the limits of vision. Clearly, then, our organic recognition of vibrations is very discontinuous; we have no organs for the direct perception of most of them. Nor are we sensitive to the ultimate fact of physics, 'electricity,' or the electrification of bodies as such, which is presumably why we were so much slower in utilising this great force in nature than the electric ray and the electric eel.

Now the selectiveness of our organs seems to be merely capricious and accidental, till we reflect that it is biological and adaptive. Our eyes are adjusted to the sort and intensity of light which the sun pours upon the earth, and in general, in so far as our organs are shaped by the life we have led and represent adaptations to modes of life that were chosen—or at any rate preferred to extinction—by our ancestors, it may even be said that their selectiveness is volitional. Man's organs, like those of other living beings, are relative to his mode of life. He has not the eye of the eagle and the keen scent of the sleuth hound or of the blue-bottle fly, because his ancestors never needed to develop eagle eyes and blue-bottle noses. Their habits were arboreal; and so we have prehensile thumbs, and an eye that is a good judge of moderate distances and an aid in hurling missiles.

But man's supreme organ is the brain, the seat and instrument of his intelligence, and the philosophic worship of 'reason' is merely a misconstruction of this vital biological fact. As we saw in Chap. X, §§ 2-4, man is emphatically the animal which lives by his brains, and, though civilised life has fostered many ways of sucking those of others, the ultimate basis of progress is destroyed if brain-development is arrested. It is also obvious that the direct dependence of our factual *data* on our organism and their ulterior dependence on our mode of life form an insuperable bar to the belief that 'pure' theoretic knowledge of total reality is the end for which we are constructed and what our organism is fitted to achieve.

24

§ 10. The Fallibility of our Organs and the Use of Instruments.

Our senses are not only selective, but also fallible. Not only are they easy to deceive—a fact which is the basis of the art of conjuring—but they spontaneously show us a whole host of illusions—straight sticks bent in water, parallel rails converging in the distance, and the like. All, moreover, are subject to hallucination, which is often hard to detect. It is no wonder, therefore, that, from the early days of Plato and Democritus, philosophers, rationalists and empiricists alike have deplored their deceptiveness. Nor did the scientists deny it: only, instead of merely bewailing it, they sought for remedies that might protect us against the cheats of the senses.

For this purpose they invented a great variety of instruments, which enormously extended the range and accuracy of our senses and the exactness of our observations. Metaphorically, as well as literally, we are now armed with spectacles in our contemplation of the real. This use of instruments is the great difference between ancient and modern science.

But instruments do not fundamentally alter the problem of knowledge. They do not absolutely guarantee either exactness or immunity from error. Thus (a) while it is true that the more exact we make our instruments the more minute grow the quantities they enable us to measure, yet the more numerous also grow the sources of error we must guard against, because to a fine measurement errors become relevant which were not appreciable in a rough one. Thus the curvature of the earth's surface does not matter when one is marking out a tennis court; but it becomes relevant when one is measuring the base line for a trigonometrical survey.

(b) Every instrument has limits to its exactness, and these are not merely practical. They may be inherent in the theoretic structure of the instrument. Thus no microscope could conceivably render visible structures no larger than the wave-length of light, nor is it probable that any balance will ever measure the loss radio-active substances undergo by emitting a particles, even though we (by other methods) actually count the number expelled per second, and can thus show how rough and fallacious were the old proofs of the indestructibility of matter.

(c) When we want accurate observation we have soon to recognise that the conditions are so complex and so variable that anything may upset them. The least variation in temperature or atmospheric pressure, for example, produces variations that vitiate an experiment and defeat our expectations of uniformity. Hence we find that no two observations ever agree exactly. If they did we should suspect that they had been 'faked,' like two completely concordant tales by supposedly independent witnesses to a complicated transaction. The vaunted regularity of nature is in a sense always faked. It is a regularity not in the crude facts of observation but in an artificial extract from them, a formula derived by taking the mean of a number of observations, after excluding any which for any reason are considered anomalous and 'bad,' duly *weighting* the remainder, allowing for the probable error both of the observations and of their mean, and finally imposing on them some 'law' to which they can plausibly be held to conform. The actual observations, even so, will probably be compatible with a number of 'laws,' and the one chosen is always preferred for reasons which may be sound but are pretty sure to lie beyond the observed facts.

(d) However fine we make our instruments and however carefully we observe and correct our observations, we come sooner or later to a point at which we rely once more on the observer's senses. For he has to read off the record of his instrument. Now, every observer has his own idiosyncrasies about this, his own rate and mode of recording, and organs with a constitution and sensitiveness peculiar to himself. Any divergence or anomaly in these respects will entail personal errors; or will at least involve a *personal equation* which will enter into all his measurements. It can be ascertained, not indeed absolutely but relatively to the personal equation of another observer; but the *dictum* of Protagoras remains fully true. Not only is man the measure of whatever objects he studies, but in the last resort every man is the measure of what is real for him.

§ 11. 'Memory' as a Presupposition of Fact.

Besides the sense-organs other constituents of our complex nature enter into the 'facts' Scientific Method deals with. Thus *memory* is as indispensable a presupposition of knowledge as sense-perception: without it mind would be narrowed down to the pin-point impression of a moment. We could make no plans and forecast no future, having no record of the past. A certain *retentiveness*, therefore, is a postulate of effective knowing. But so is a certain capacity for *forgetting*. A literally photographic and indelible memory would be an intolerable burden, and by retaining the past too vividly would paralyse action in the present. We, therefore, neither wish nor need to remember everything, and, as Prof. T. H. Pear well says, "a good memory should be serviceably selective . . . and the art of forgetting is but the inner aspect of the art of remembering." [1]

Being thus selective, memory can hardly lay claim to infallibility; but failure to remember all that is relevant to a present situation is far from being the only 'trick' it plays upon us. It is apt to remember what is irrelevant and inopportune: it is often almost as *creative* as imagination, and 'remembers' what never happened at all. And it habitually enters into present perception and plays a great part in shaping it: all we perceive is perceived in the light of a past more or less consciously remembered; which is why no two minds perceive quite alike, and why there is a historical side to every fact recorded in every science, though the natural sciences often find it convenient to forget this (Chap. XVIII, § 10). This influence of the past on the present, to which Mr Russell has given the name of 'mnemic causation,' is usually beneficial, because it enables us to bring old knowledge to bear on a new situation, but there is always a risk that it may take the form of distorting preconceptions.

A further reason why memory cannot unreservedly be trusted is that what goes under the name is very ambiguous and really complex. At least five distinguishable processes or acts are comprised under the name of 'memory.' (1) There is,

[1] *Remembering and Forgetting*, p. 13.

first, the retentiveness, which makes *living* matter able somehow to retain past impressions and so teachable. This is the only sense of 'memory' which lends itself to associationist and materialist interpretation, for it may (at a pinch) be ascribed to a physiological alteration in brain tissue which results from its functioning. (2) There is next the judgment of memory, which arranges the raw material provided by memory in the first sense, and refers the surviving traces of former experiences ('images' and what not) to a personal time-order and objectively *dates* them. (3) There is the more or less obscure, but purposive, process, which accounts for the general relevance to the mind's actual situation of the memories which come up; this process is plainly not random, and without it memory might easily be useless or worse, because *irrelevant* recrudescences of the past might often be fatal to present action. If the process of 'remembering' were really mechanical, we should expect our memories to crop up quite at random without any special reference or relevance to the actual situation; the fact, therefore, that (on the whole) they do not reveals its purposive and teleological nature. (4) This comes out still more strongly in active *recollecting*, which is conscious striving to bring about the relevance of our memories to a present we desire to act on. (5) There is, lastly, the postulate of the trustworthiness of memory. Now this is assuredly a fundamental postulate, for, if we could not trust our memory, knowledge would be restricted to judgments about present experience. Still this postulate is not wholly true; our memory may play us false and its products are not always trustworthy. But being a genuine and indispensable postulate it is not dropped when it is found to be fallible; so long as it is true enough to be useful we try to guard ourselves against its tricks (as in the case of the illusions and hallucinations of the senses) by elaborating substitutes and checks and tests of its veracity.

§ 12. The Personal Equation and the Self.

The fact that for good or ill every mind suffers from 'mnemic causation,' i.e. perceives its present in the light of its past, renders it impossible really to eliminate the personal equation in any knowledge. We may, indeed, pretend we have done so, and flatter ourselves that we have guarded against the worst deceptions of personal abnormality, but do so only by accepting some one else's perceptions (much as a colour-blind person may concede the 'normality' of *superior* powers of colour discrimination), and this only substitutes personal equations which yield *better* standards for worse. It is also true that the sciences often talk as if personal equations could be got rid of altogether, and as if they aimed at purely objective and completely depersonalised knowledge. But this notion is a pure abstraction, and actually a fiction. It does not actually occur, and cannot be made a condition of the possibility of knowledge. In actual practice the sciences do the best they can with the minds they get, and take their standards from those whose workings seem most valuable.

So the *data* of knowledge are never really depersonalised. Nor is complete 'objectivity' reached. Impersonal objectivity remains a *fiction*; the objective world remains relative to a subject in the background, however much he strives to efface himself. There is no thought without a thinker, no observation without an observer, not even a dream without a dreamer, and no object without a subject. To this extent at least philosophy is justified in criticising the fictions of science.

But it cannot be said that philosophy has made a success of explaining this ineradicable relation of subject and object, and of describing the nature of the self or soul in intelligible terms. Western philosophy never even discovered the fundamental problem of the self until Descartes. Even then the self was valued merely as a specific against philosophic doubt, and described metaphysically as 'spiritual substance.'

Now this description has its roots in very primitive thinking. For man at first spontaneously conceived himself on the analogy of the natural things it was so vitally necessary for him to know and control. But in forming the notion of 'thing' he had implicitly projected his own unanalysed self into nature. It was the experience of his self-identity that suggested the existence of 'things' in nature that could change and yet remain 'the same,' and thus led to the recognition of 'substances' underlying the changing 'appearances.' For only his own inner life could yield man a direct model for the notion of persistence through change. 'Soul-substance,' therefore, is the product of a double process of interpretation by analogy; first the attribution of a persisting self-like support to the phenomena of nature, and then the assimilation of the self to the supposed substances underneath the external world, the two together constituting primitive animism. So the self became a 'soul,' easily identifiable with the life and the breath, a thing-like entity among other things, which though normally resident within the body was in principle detachable, and could wander forth in sleep for perilous adventures in all the realms of being. In view, moreover, of the manifold risks of mortal life it seemed prudent to cast about for a securer receptacle than the body for the precious soul, and so the wily medicine-man or magician frequently found it better to keep his soul (in some durable shape) safely locked up in a secret place, and then felt sure that nothing could endanger his life. Of course, if some enemy got hold, say, of the crow that was the sorcerer's soul, and wrung its neck, the sorcerer would incontinently fall down dead. This ancient theory of the soul remains familiar to readers of fairy tales.

It had, however, considerable drawbacks. Quite apart from the confusion of internal and external, of psychical and physical, which it involved, it did not really explain the soul's relations to its conscious states, and what was meant by its 'having' them. By conceiving the soul merely as a *thing*, and therefore an *object*, it disabled it from becoming a *subject*, and so from observing and contemplating itself. Nor could it explain how the soul's changing states were attached to its unchanging substance and could fuse with it into a unitary being. When a change occurred in a soul, did the whole soul change or only part, and, if so, was there no change in the relation between the changing part and the unchanging 'substance'? The problem of unity and plurality in the soul, of the relation of the parts ('faculties,' 'elements,' etc.) of the soul to the central unity was similarly insoluble, and in general the soul-substance theory could neither account for the epistemological relation of subject and object, nor yet justify the common-sense belief in the practical unity of the personality.

It thus challenged the attack of an 'analysis' which triumphantly demanded to be shown an unchanging item in the soul, and, when it could not be produced, proceeded to dissolve the mind into a series of 'impressions,' 'ideas,' or 'events' (Hume, J. S. Mill, Bertrand Russell, etc.). But this analysis also was totally incapable of explaining how this series of events could be compacted together into a mind that is *aware* of its history and serial nature.

The epistemological problem of the self was handed on unsolved to the Critical philosophy of Kant. Kant *more suo* declared its solution to lie in an *a priori* necessity of recognising a synthetic principle, which he called the Transcendental Ego or Synthetic Unity of Apperception. This did not aspire to be a substantial soul, but it was the subject presupposed in the knowing of every object, and nothing knowable could free itself from its grip. This correlation of subject and object is usually taken to solve the epistemological problem of how the mind can know its objects, and also as a proof of idealism.

Yet it was very far from being satisfactory in either respect. Though it got analytic idealism out of the Humian *impasse* and provided his dissected objects with a subject, it failed to establish any real priority of mind. It left the subject as dependent on the object as the latter was on it. Nor did it really provide common sense with its chief *desiderata*, with a self that was a unity of subject and object and that *really belonged* to the individual states of consciousness which it unified. For to exemplify the Transcendental Ego as an epistemological function was *not* to have a self of one's own that could possess and cherish its experiences. There was nothing in Kant's argument to prevent a single Ego from supplying the needs of all the minds in existence, and Fichte could promptly turn the Transcendental into a metaphysical and Absolute Ego, indistinguishable from the *Atman* of Indian philosophy, and this was not in the least what the ordinary man aspired to or supposed himself to be.

William James took a decisive step in advance by emending the psychological description of the self which both Hume and Kant had mistakenly presupposed. He gave up the fiction of the discontinuous states of consciousness and described the mind as a *continuum* or 'stream.' He distinguished also between the self-as-object or the '*Me*' and the self-as-subject or the '*I*,' and included in his psychological description the fact that the whole stream was always *owned* by an *I*. But, presumably, in order to emphasise his correction of the Humian 'series,' he described the *I* as a *succession of I's*, each handing on its possessions to the next, and passing into the *Me* (in retrospect) as it passed away. And he made no attempt explicitly to elucidate the unity of the *I* and the *Me*.

Nevertheless James's psychology implicitly contains the answer to this final puzzle. We have merely to read his account of the self in the light of his distinction between the focus and the fringe of consciousness. The contents in the focus of the mind's attention are always surrounded by a fringe of objects not attended to, which fades gradually into the impenetrable gloom of the background. The objects 'before the mind,' i.e. attended to, are exquisitely unstable and continuously changing; but the background is ever felt to be present, and is never seen to change. *Ex hyp.* it could not be, for if we tried to observe its contents, to see whether they changed, they would at once come out of the background and into the focus. Our inference, however, that the background is always the same, and never changes, may well be an illusion. It takes unobservable change as absence of change, and this we may see to be a mistake, if we consider all that happens in a shifting of attention. Not only do new objects come before the mind, but the old ones disappear. Where do they go? Where can they go but into the background, into the unconscious depths of the soul? But there they are not lost; they lie hid, but may be summoned forth again when needed, and 're-collected.'

It is thus the nature of the mind or soul to exhibit a continual ebb and flow between the contents which are actually before the mind and those which remain potential in its unconscious recesses. They cannot all be actualised together; we cannot express all that we are in the fleeting consciousness of any moment, and we realise ourselves in a *succession* of states. It is this fact which gives rise to the division into the *I* and the *Me*, and produces the illusion of an unchanging *I*, inactively watching and indifferently sustaining all that happens in the soul. But really the *I* and the *Me* are *one* : they are consubstantial and share in the same contents and *together* constitute the soul. Both moreover change, though the changes in the *Me* are observable and those in the *I* are only inferred. Further, each *Me* properly belongs to its *I*, and each *I* is the *I* of a particular *Me*; each soul is completely individual throughout. Thus the *I* is, as Rutgers Marshall declared, simply "the field of inattention." [1] The total self divides into the *I* and the *Me* merely because its life is manifested as a succession in time which is at no moment expressive of *all* its powers. But could it transcend this restriction, the dark inscrutable background which envelops our actual consciousness would evaporate; it would be taken up into the light, and would cease to be a torment. We could then identify ourselves wholly with what we actually were. [2]

Our solution of the problem of the Self clearly has important logical consequences. If the self which is the presupposition of all knowing is an individual self, and not a transcendental function or a metaphysical Absolute, logic should clearly expect psychological differences in the thinking of individual knowers, and should be prepared to consider how they may best be discounted or brought into agreement. It will no longer do to take for granted the facile assumption that all minds think alike and that the introspections of a single philosopher can legislate for all the realms of knowledge. It will be necessary to recognise that all knowers are subject to bias, not only personal but also social and political, and that all these forms of bias must be

---

[1] *Consciousness*, pp. 39, 42, etc.
[2] See, further, *Humanism*, p. 225.

evaluated in each case. For example, the conflict between the conservative and the innovating attitude enters into every problem of scientific inquiry. It is evident, also, that our conclusion will be a valuable and indeed decisive reinforcement of our earlier contentions (Chap. IV) about the personal character of meaning and the purposiveness of all knowing. A voluntarist logic, therefore, will welcome the opportunity of explaining why it is that differences of opinion are so persistent and that truth so extensively and so long remains a partisan affair. This is particularly marked in the beginnings of scientific inquiry, because we begin with little or no experience of the consequences of the sorts of bias and of the various attitudes towards the object of inquiry, and therefore cannot evaluate them. But, as has been remarked, the initial stages of a science are logically the most instructive, because they generate most doubt and create a tension in the mind. When a science has succeeded and attained to undisputed truth it asserts its independence of its makers, and generates illusions about the nature and value of its methods, while the fact that there is no longer any dispute about its results causes our logical vigilance to relax.

§ 13. The Power of Words.

We have by no means exhausted the list of the equipment or luggage which the scientific knower carries with him on all his explorations, whether he knows it or not. His personality represents a highly individual and never completely analysable factor; his language, on the other hand, is his means of communicating with other minds. Properly used, it is a precious assurance of social support; but it is also what drags him down to the common level, and veils his individual vision. It is *was uns alle bändigt das Gemeine*. If he can master it and use it skilfully, he can convey his meanings and communicate his discoveries; if he fails, he is lost and starves in a desert of sterile verbiage. So, sooner or later, he discovers that *les paroles sont faites pour cacher nos pensées*; the great instrument of expression can be made to conceal our thoughts, or, not infrequently, their absence.

It has taken science weary ages to see through the Great

Illusion woven by words and to learn that verbal reasoning is no proof of anything, and even now philosophy hates to admit that it cannot stand against experience. But verbal reasoning can deal only with the meaning of the *words* it uses, and this could embody no knowledge but that which their inventors had: it has no power over the future, and cannot predict it; any new discovery may confute it and force the scientific knower either to scrap his old words or to transform their meaning by using them in new senses. Actually he does *both*, and which of these policies he adopts appears to be very much a matter of chance. But both have drawbacks. If he keeps on coining new words to express his discoveries, he becomes a specialist whom only his equals (if he has any) can understand: if he develops the meanings of old words, he may cause confusion, and will certainly incur the charge of misusing words and destroying established meanings. All verbalists will condemn his thought as self-contradictory and incoherent, and will refuse to listen to novelties that find expression in such improper terms.

From Formal Logic, in particular, he must expect no mercy. For the *fixity* of verbal meaning is one of its fundamental (though unavowed) assumptions. It continues to swear by the 'Law of Identity,' without investigating what it can mean. Actually it relies throughout on the identity of terms which are taken to 'mean the same' in different contexts in order to justify inference from one case to another. If this verbal identity of two cases of what is called 'the same' is not accepted as an unquestionable guarantee of validity, the whole fabric of Formal demonstration crumbles.

But modern science finds it growing harder and harder to believe that reality can be controlled so easily, by just laying down the meanings of words, out of the plenitude of our power over them and the fullness of our ignorance of nature. So to a typical 'ontological' proof (by pure logic) that the world is one because there can only be one 'universe' which (by definition) is the totality of reality, it is tempting to retort, "But how do you know that anything conforms to your definition? I admit that verbally 'universe' implies unity, but how do you know that it *applies* to the real? Or otherwise, that you are *right* in conceiving the real as a world or totality?"

Words, therefore, are not instruments of prediction or control, and the attempt to use them as such is not science but magic. It is the fatal superstition which vitiates all *a priori* reasoning. Scientifically any *application* of the 'law of identity' runs a risk of refutation by experience. The 'law' is not a fact nor a controller of fact; it is a methodological assumption, a fiction, or at best a postulate. Nothing, not even a self, remains absolutely unchanged for two moments together; so the *logical* identity of two 'cases' of A—a^1 and a^2—is always a fiction. It is often a useful fiction, but it can only mean that *for our present purpose* the differences shall be taken as irrelevant. But this postulate may, of course, always be disputed, whenever the 'law' is applied. So the indisputability of *A is A* subsists only so long as no attempt is made to use it.

The Law of Contradiction is afflicted with a similar fatuity. It says 'nothing can both be and not be.' But anything that can change or have a plurality of relations defies it. It can both be and not be with the utmost ease. It is at one time, and not at another. Or in one respect, and not in another. Or in one place, and not in another. Or for one purpose, and not for another. Or in one context, and not in another. If we try to equip our statement of the Law of Contradiction with all the reservations required for its (verbally) valid application, we soon find that there is no end to them, and that we are chopping at a Hydra's heads.

There is, moreover, a fatal objection to deciding scientific questions *a priori* by thus applying 'laws of thought.' In all *growing* knowledge the meanings of the words which serve as its vehicles are developing, and these new developments are sure, sooner or later, to diverge so far from the original meanings that they come into logical conflict with the latter. Whereupon those who cling to the older meanings can cry out upon the 'contradictions' and impossibilities of the subject and take them as proofs of falsity. But they may be only verbal and incidental to the growth of knowledge. The sciences do not shrink from them. They freely recognise 'atoms' that are no longer indivisible, 'species' that are no longer immutable, 'light' that has become invisible: they operate with 'liquid crystals,' 'solid solutions,' and 'unconscious' perceptions and mental processes. All they care about is to get conceptions adequate to the facts, whatever verbal paradoxes they may involve. It is quite legitimate, therefore, to speak of the 'life' of an atom, a mine, or a ship, if the analogies implied therein are found to hold.

Thus the charge of self-contradiction has no terrors for a scientific reasoning that is actively engaged upon facts. It is fatal to dialectical reasoning, because this has accepted the Formal convention of the Fixity of Terms and become essentially *verbal*. It cannot, therefore, defy the verbal conventions expressed in the 'laws of thought.' It has thereby restricted itself to extracting the verbal implications which lurk in the meanings of words, and of course hold only so long as these conventions are accepted. But actually there is always an appeal from the completest verbal contradiction to the facts of the case. So a formal contradiction justifies, not an inference to the falsity of the (apparently) self-contradictory assertion, but merely the question—*What do you mean?* The man who uses contradictory language appears to have broken the conventions for communicating meaning; but as presumably he meant something, he should be given an opportunity of explaining himself. And the question put to him is the sovran specific for clearing up difficulties and misunderstandings, clearing away obscurity and bombast, cutting short dialectics and bringing to light the real issue. It is the chief protection of the critical inquirer against the snares lurking in the verbal apparatus which he cannot but take over and use.[1]

§ 14. The Power of Common-sense Realism.

But this is not all. He not only takes over a language and a formal logic (which is language in disguise), but a whole meta-

[1] For the logical meaning of 'contradiction' see, further, H. V. Knox, *The Will to be Free*, part vi.

physic entrenched in the forms of language. It may be called common-sense realism, and its leading conceptions claim to be, at one and the same time, ultimate realities, logical categories, and grammatical forms. So it believes that the world is composed of a plurality of *things* (substances, substantives) and *persons* (subjects, pronouns), existing in their own right and having *qualities* (adjectives) and *relations* with each other, acting and being acted upon (*verbs*, active, passive, intransitive, etc.) according to causal and teleological laws (which are developed out of our experience of compulsion and willing). As a view of the world this metaphysic has two great advantages.

(1) It is the outcome of man's experience of the world and of his practical dealings with reality. It has, therefore, pragmatic authority, and is not merely an untried theoretical construction. To a large extent it is both a *datum*, from which more refined theories have to start, and which they have to explain, a criterion which can be used to test them, and the destination to which they must return.

(2) It is much more deeply rooted than any competing theory. It is spontaneously accepted and really believed by all, even when they play with other theories; it is, therefore, *acted on*. Consequently it provides the common ground by reference to which all other opinions can be compared. However zealous they may be to transcend it, they will all tend to relapse into common-sense realism at some point, or appeal to it for practical support.

In spite of this dependence on common sense, however, it must be confessed that the sciences modify its beliefs very freely, and often depart from it very widely—quite as far as the wildest metaphysics. The man in the street, for example, would hardly nowadays feel much at home with the ultimate reals and favourite conceptions of modern physics. Needless to say, good scientific reasons are always to be given for such departures from common sense.

Yet in the end the sciences have always to *return to* common sense. They have to vindicate the value of their hypotheses and fictions by their power to transfigure the crude reals of immediate experience, to predict its happenings, and to enable us to control it. For otherwise we get no assurance that the conceptions which our science uses are more than *entia rationis*, calculating counters by which the course of events is predicted, without revealing the inner nature of the real.

Thus the relation of science to common sense involves a two-fold movement: there is first an advance from the common world of common sense to the worlds of the various sciences, which are deemed more real because they are more potent. But, in using the power over appearances which knowledge of scientific reality yields as a test of the truth of our scientific conceptions, we implicitly commit ourselves to the superior reality of the world of common sense, and affirm the supremacy of life over science in the last resort.

Moreover, it would be well never to forget that behind all our cognitive operations lie vast masses of crude experience out of which the world of common sense has itself been extracted as a practically serviceable selection and interpretation. In this murky region, which only the science of psychology ventures to approach, the conventions which underlie the common world of common sense are not yet established; the line has still to be drawn between objective and subjective, real and apparent, perception and hallucination, dream and reality, and the unity of the universe has not yet been adopted as a dogma and enforced by the exclusion of all facts that will not fit into it. Crude experience, therefore, forms a turbulent chaos from which our instinctive love of order shrinks; but a scientific logic should remind us that it also serves as a great reservoir of possibilities to which we may revert when, as sometimes happens, our working hypotheses have broken down and stand in need of a radical reconstruction.

CHAPTER XVIII

SCIENTIFIC METHOD (*continued*)

1. The interplay of 'fact' and 'hypothesis' in scientific method ; 2. Scientific method universally applicable ; 3. Observation and experiment: defined ; 4. The control of emotion ; 5. The need of guiding observation ; 6. The inevitableness of risk ; 7. The limits of observation and experiment ; 8. The operation of hypotheses ; 9. The plurality of hypotheses ; 10. The proving of hypotheses ; 11. The cumulative nature of proof ; 12. Abstraction ; 13. Classification ; 14. Idealisation and fiction ; 15. Laws of nature ; 16. The finding and proving of laws of Nature ; 17. Laws and habits ; 18. How laws apply to cases.

§ 1. The Interplay of 'Fact' and 'Hypothesis' in Scientific Method.

We have seen in the last chapter that scientific procedure is by no means devoid of presuppositions. Scientific method does not start with a clean slate: it inscribes its findings on the much-furrowed wax of a palimpsest. Speaking roughly and in general terms, we may no doubt say that its operations are always reducible to correlations of 'facts' with 'hypotheses'; both terms, however, must be taken very broadly. Under the former we are to understand all apparent facts arrived at in the various and complex ways studied in the last chapter, all *data*, whether given historically or only assumed, all starting-points and stepping-stones that are used to pave the way to discovery. Now it is clear that most of this material has no pretensions to be *final* fact; it is dubious and provisional, and that it is fact at all is plainly a hypothesis. But this does not matter; for what matters is the logical character, not of the initial material, but of the end-product fabricated out of it. The business of Scientific Method with 'facts' is to turn appearances and allegations into the solid structure of a science.

Again, under 'hypothesis' we should embrace interpretations, theories, principles, analogies, postulates, and demands—anything, in short, which can serve to string 'facts' together and to set them in order. Actually these terms differ rather in the directness with which they point to the emotional and volitional factors lurking beneath the surface of the cognitive process than in the cognitive function they are used to describe. In actual use they all serve as *rules of inference*, as *instruments* for working upon the raw material which is 'given,' and as *vehicles* for scientific progress. They are all simply 'transport,' adopted in view of the nature of the country it is desired to explore, in the hope that they will prove suitable. If not, they should be scrapped at once, as also if they can at any stage be improved upon; for they have no inherent logical status, but are just *methods* for use, to be held experimentally.

In their functioning, moreover, they, as also the given they operate on, may undergo any amount and sort of transformation that may seem to be expedient or requisite. Thus 'theories' may turn into 'facts,' and 'facts' be discredited as false analogies and interpretations and the inferences of childish superstition.

§ 2. Scientific Method Universally Applicable.

The application of Scientific Method is universal. Despite the attempts of certain scientists to represent it as something exclusive and mysterious, there is nothing too lowly, repulsive, obscure, contentious, or deceptive to come within its scope. Neither is there anything too 'sacred,' which generally means a fear that the things so denominated cannot bear investigation.[1] Scientific Method is the *only* genuine method of knowing, and will tackle anything knowable. It despises no problem and prejudges no question. It is willing to begin operations on any material it can get, however insecure, dubious, or dull, and to pry into lingering pseudo-sciences like astrology, heraldry, and Formal Logic as zealously as into the most flourishing and progressive sciences. For it has confidence enough in itself to shrink from nothing, and to be capable of *learning* from anything.

Hence the *data* from which Scientific Method starts are neither absolutely 'fact' nor even absolutely 'given.' They are whatever is *taken as fact* for the purpose of the inquiry, and would better be called *sumpta* than *data*. Nor is any inquiry

[1] Cp. *Problems of Belief*, p. 43.

made, in a particular inquiry, as to how they have come to be such *data*. This question does not arise, precisely because they have been accepted, however tentatively, and because any mistakes that have been made in the initial selection of *data* can be put right in the progress of the inquiry. If any doubt arises, it can be inquired into; if any mistake is detected, it can be repudiated or corrected. Science has no superstitious reverence for any one's *data* as such, not even for its own; it feels free to select, reject, and remodel them as suits its purpose and that of the hypotheses and fictions it employs; it retains also the right to go back upon and to revise any conclusion it has reached. For the logical value of its conclusions and of its procedure is in no wise dependent on the *data* it started from: it depends rather on the advance made after *leaving* the starting-point.

All this, however, is not to say that an application of Scientific Method is guaranteed to carry every inquiry to a *successful* issue. Its results may be negative. It may succeed in showing only that the apparently bad material it started with really is bad, and that nothing can be made of it. In many cases this may be a valuable result. In others, in which the alleged facts are very important and interesting, the conclusion drawn may be merely that the method of investigation actually employed should be altered and improved. In neither case, however, is there any ground for intolerance. Those who are not satisfied with any verdict of science, whether positive or negative, should always be left free to work for its revision, if they think it worth their while and they see any prospect of success. For no scientific truth is ever absolute; and proof, verification, and disproof remain intrinsically questions of more or less, and the answers to them appeal variously to different minds. It is far more important not to block any possible avenue to further truth than to obtain a mechanical and official uniformity of beliefs which is not expressive of the psychological facts of human nature.[1]

[1] This remark applies to scientific investigation rather than to moral action. In practical affairs it may sometimes be undesirable to allow full liberty of experimenting to all and sundry on all occasions.

§ 3. Observation and Experiment: Defined.

Observation and Experiment are the traditional terms for describing the scientific treatment of *data*. They denominate vitally important attitudes of mind which dovetail into each other and co-operate closely; but for this very reason it is desirable to distinguish clearly the functions of each.

Regarded psychologically as an attitude of mind, observation is just *watching*, not however with any suggestion of passivity, idleness, or indifference, but an attitude of active *watchfulness*, sustained by a *will to watch* and to delay action. As was suggested in Chap. X, § 6, the capacity for such watching was probably developed in man by his life as a hunter when stalking big game; he then had to learn, as his first lesson in self-control, the need for waiting for his opportunity and inhibiting his impulse to react thoughtlessly to the presence of his prey. It need not be doubted that such self-control was a difficult achievement, and long involved a high degree of internal tension and excitement, essentially akin to that which we may still observe in a pointing dog or a quivering cat about to pounce.[1] Calm and 'disinterested' observation is a 'sublimation' of such activities, and does not annul their primal nature.

Compared with Observation, Experiment is an *intervention*, and expresses a will to interfere with the course of happening. It means an attempt to remould the actual nearer to the heart's desire. But, of course, it does not *exclude* Observation, but rather presupposes it. The outcome also of the experiment must be observed, and any attempt to 'fake' the results of experiment defeats its purpose.

But even here societies tend to overrate the value of uniformity and probably harm themselves more by being intolerant than by being indulgent; for their intolerance is not a fruit of experience but a relic of barbarism and a deduction from a false theory of truth. Those societies which still maintain a censorship of scientific investigation should at least learn to use it not to suppress unorthodoxy (which is generally stimulating), but to curb futility, i.e. the preference for trivial, pedantic, and (relatively) worthless inquiries to which the academic man is naturally prone and on which academic institutions are tempted to set such a high premium.

[1] Cp. H. V. Knox, *The Will to be Free*, p. 216.

Conversely we must recognise an experimental factor in Observation. The concentration of attention in scientific observation is selective, and therefore experimental, and the more intently and selectively we observe the more we depart from the casual and random observation we began with and change the conditions. Moreover, as an inquiry progresses, we learn more and more precisely where to look, we use more and more delicate instruments, and observe more minutely: the eye of the trained observer has much deeper insight. If, then, to alter the given conditions is the essence of Experiment, it is clear that observation grows more and more experimental as a science grows.

The antithesis, therefore, between Observation and Experiment must not be taken as absolute. It is not true that the former is passive, the latter active. Both are active, because in ultimate analysis all life is an activity expressive of an experimental attitude towards the world, and all knowing is a questioning of nature animated by a will to know, which, again, is a manifestation of our will to live.

§ 4. The Control of Emotion.

Just because it is so intimately volitional, the attitude both of the observer and of the experimenter implies a will *not to frustrate itself*. Hence, while the emotions and interests which stimulate to any research are to be cultivated, those which are extraneous and irrelevant have to be repressed, and must not be allowed to incite us to acts not compatible with our purpose. Thus, if we have set ourselves to watch a dog-fight, no sympathy with the under dog must move us to interfere. If a surgeon is operating on a friend, no thought of his pain and danger must be allowed to disturb the cold precision of his movements. Whether we are testing the truth of the hypothesis dearest to our heart, or trying to confute the pernicious errors of our worst adversary, we must emulate the impersonal impartiality of a recording instrument in observing the consequences of our experiments. This is the meaning and reason of the belief in 'scientific impartiality' and 'dispassionate observation.' It demands not only presence of mind, but also a high degree of self-control. But it does *not* mean that the scientific observer must qualify for his task by suppressing his *whole* emotional nature and abjuring all scientific aims and interests. This would be both impossible and undesirable. For his desires may be precisely the motive forces which incite him to research and inspire him with the tenacity to carry it through. They become objectionable only if and when, in the *actual* interrogation of nature, they tend to vitiate the response: they then rank with inattention, carelessness, laziness, indifference, and other sources of error and bad observation.

§ 5. The Need of Guiding Observation.

The fact that a cognitive enterprise may fail from lack of eagerness, as well as from excess, should convince us that observation (and with it experiment) must be *guided* by some clue—of interest, purpose, or previous knowledge. *Random* observation is most likely to be futile and least likely to light upon discoveries. An observer who does not know what to look for will usually fail to see what is going on and will mis-interpret even what little he sees, while his reactions will be unintelligent and determined by his anterior habits. His situa-tion will be typically that of a lay observer of a conjuring trick. He will see miracles and impossibilities happen freely, while what is really done will hit the blind spot in his eyes, and pass unperceived, to an incredible extent. So there will be literally no end to his malobservations and misdescriptions. Now the observer of nature, unlike the spectator of a conjuring trick, does not have to consider an *intentionally* deceptive and dis-tracting procedure; but nature's ways can produce more than the effects of trickiness by their profound alienation from human nature. So, initially at least, the observer does not know where to look and what to attend to; his attention has to be guided to the point which must be discriminated from the irrelevant setting which he can, and should, ignore.

In scientific practice this guidance devolves upon 'theory,' i.e. hypothesis, and the previous knowledge which has suggested

it, thus justifying Aristotle's sagacious paradox that all knowledge arises out of pre-existing knowledge.

But it is clear that this procedure may at times *misguide*, and
cannot claim validity. The 'previous knowledge' on which
we rely to analyse the new problem may be a survival of primitive ignorance, and nothing but a 'superstition'; so it may
mislead us and prevent us from noticing the right clues. Thus
we are plunged into the dilemma that without attention and
the selectiveness which it involves we can make no progress,
but that, with it, we may select wrongly and attend to the wrong
points, and go astray.

Once more, therefore, there is no escaping from risks in
theory. There are, however, in practice, ways of minimising
our danger and increasing the chances of success. As in a
detective novel, the investigator can follow various clues, weigh
alternative interpretations, and entertain several hypotheses
at once, and pit one against the other. This will sharpen his
attention, extend his field of observation, and add to the interest
of inquiry by enlisting party spirit. It will enable him to offer
employment, and perhaps satisfaction, both to the conservative
and to the radical instincts and tendencies. By cultivating a
mind open to competing hypotheses he can obtain, not indeed
a valid guarantee, but an adequate confidence that he is really
observing most of what may be supposed to be relevant at the
actual stage of his inquiry. If it is not, he must go on experimenting and observing till he has gained as much assurance as
he requires.

§ 6. The Inevitableness of Risk.

The truth is, of course, that by no manner of means can we
avoid all risks. Any procedure which rests on attention is
selective, because attention is a volitional attitude which concentrates upon a *portion* of the whole field of observation, and
takes the risk of neglecting the rest. It is, therefore, a sort of
experiment with the relative values of these portions. It backs
itself, as it were, to find the object aimed at in the part attended
to, and to neglect the rest with impunity. It does this because

it knows that our minds cannot cope with the multitudinous claims on our attention otherwise than by selecting, and would be paralysed if they refused to select.

Hence the 'facts' of any scientific inquiry are always a selection, and a very great deal depends on selecting them intelligently. This operation is habitually taken for granted in logical descriptions of scientific procedure. Yet it is often the hardest of all. The logician gaily declares, "Begin, of course, by assembling your facts," and the scientist is lucky if he is not also told that he must assemble them *all* before he is allowed to proceed. Yet this advice is nonsensical, false, and impossible. It is nonsense, because in no inquiry do the facts ever form a sum or whole: those which are valuable have always to be extricated from a morass of others of which the relevance and the authenticity are in doubt. It is impossible, because no scientist can be sure that the facts he has assembled exhaust the subject, and it is false because it misrepresents the logical nature of the procedure used and the facts employed.

In every inquiry the facts actually assembled and argued from are a selection, namely, that part of the visible *data* which is judged *relevant*. Hence the scientist should firmly reply: "But pray, sir, what *are* our facts?" and point out that he only wants facts which are such for the purpose in hand. Also, that every variation in this purpose will entail differences in the facts relevant to it, and a different analysis of the presented mass of *data*.

There is no justification, therefore, for the favourite fancy of inductive logic that facts were to be conceived mechanically and uncritically as a hard, unyielding mass, easy to observe and impossible to mistake. They appear different in the light of different theories, and change their colour and complexion like chameleons. To realise how readily the 'facts' change according to the point of view, we have only to listen to the speeches of contending counsel in a law suit or to the rival accounts of the same events by two party historians or orators; or to read a fine literary study of this situation, such as Browning's *Ring and the Book*. In any genuine inquiry there is always more or less doubt about the 'facts': even in the sciences they often remain in dispute for ages, where conflicting interests are concerned.

§ 7. The Limits of Observation and Experiment.

Our powers of observation are limited by the limits to the sensitiveness of our instruments, and ultimately of our senses; for in the end the latter are needed to read off the records of the former. Our power to experiment is limited by the limits of our control; for it is only where we can control the conditions that we can vary the conditions one at a time and experiment with precision.

But experiment is not always possible: for experimental control is never what we start with, and is often difficult to attain. It belongs to a late stage in the development of a science when we have reason to believe that we have analysed our subject sufficiently to put definite questions to which the results of experiment can return definite answers. It is only at this stage that we can (a) vary the conditions at will, and (b) feel reasonably confident that we are changing only one (relevant) circumstance at a time, which are the two essential requisites of successful experiment. Even so we get no complete guarantee of success. For, even though we have power to experiment, the condition we experiment with may prove unimportant, and, even though it seems single, it may prove to be plural. Like simplicity and complexity, unity and plurality in actual inquiry turn out to be relative to the purpose and the point of view. The typical case in point is the self or soul, which no psychology, from Plato's day to our own, has ever been able to represent either as single and simple or as their opposites *consistently*. Nowadays even advanced sciences like chemistry are forced into similar admissions. Until a few years ago no chemist proposing to experiment with a well-known 'element' like 'lead' would have hesitated to assume that *all 'lead' was lead*, if he had got it chemically pure, which, though laborious, was not impossible. But since the discovery of 'isotopes' he may have to regard every sample of lead as a mixture of 'uranium-lead' and 'thorium-lead,' as probably different in its composition from every other, and so as indefinitely complex. It may still be lead for some purposes, but it is no longer simply lead for others. Its atomic weight, 207·2, becomes a statistical average, while the actual atomic weight of his specimen may be anything between 206 (for pure uranium-lead) to 208 (for pure thorium-lead). Thus 'lead' has become a collective term for an indefinite plurality of sorts of lead, and every sample of it behaves like an individual whose history has to be known to predict his behaviour.

A prudent logician, therefore, will conclude that a thing seems simple only because it has not been inquired into, and single only because no one has been interested to distinguish different cases or aspects of it; further research and more penetrating 'analysis' may be expected everywhere to reveal further differences which may or may not be relevant to a particular inquiry.[1]

So much for Experiment in established sciences where much may be taken as known: in matters where as yet little or nothing is known, we speedily come upon the limits of Experiment. For example, suppose we try to apply Scientific Method to the question of determining whether a certain house is 'haunted,' and what is meant thereby. We start, of course, with the stories that have given the house its bad name; and if we are tactful, pertinacious, and lucky, we may get them at first hand. At this point difficult questions will arise as to the psychology of ghost-seers, and the character, history, and motives of the particular witnesses; but in certain cases the evidence may seem to warrant further investigation. We may even obtain access to the house and be allowed to sit up in it—which is a sort of experiment, but under conditions which are deplorably vague. We do not know what enables people to see ghosts, or enables ghosts to become visible; neither do we know what a 'ghost' is, what his habits are, or with what bait he can be caught. We are experimenting quite at random, and are not likely to succeed. But it is precisely in these initial stages, when a nascent science is trying for experimental control and neither principles nor

---

[1] Hence the 'ideal' of a reciprocating cause which never develops any plurality in its bosom is only a disguise of our old enemy, the final and incorrigible truth. Cp. *Formal Logic*, pp. 305–9.

procedures are as yet established, that research is most keenly conscious of its logical difficulties and that its method comes out most instructively.[1]

§ 8. The Operation of Hypotheses.

We see, then, that scientific inquiry never comes to an end of its dealings with 'fact.' 'What the facts really are' remains a subject of investigation, and undergoes continual transformation as our knowledge grows, i.e. as we become better and better able to predict and control the course of events.

This progressive ascertainment of fact, however, may equally be viewed as a progressive interpretation of *data* by theories which are instrumental in transforming them. These theories also are nothing final or definitive, but hypothetical, experimental, and plastic, and are tested, like the 'facts' they refer to, by the outcome of our operations.

Thus the hypotheses, in the light of which we discern our 'facts,' sharpen our eyes and guide our attention to the vital points to be observed: they select what is taken as fact for the purposes of any inquiry from masses of irrelevant detail. Hence when a knowing process prospers we grow confident that its *data* are real facts, and that its hypotheses are helpful and 'true.' But when the hypotheses tried prove unsuitable, and fail to work and to be verified, it is clear that the use of hypotheses may mislead and wreck the inquiry and blind us to the real facts. Thus our chief instrument of success may also conduct us to disaster. Here, as elsewhere in logic, our tools have sharp edges and must be used intelligently. They become dangerous in some hands, and are in no wise fool-proof and infallible.

§ 9. The Plurality of Hypotheses.

If, however, we are not looking for a mechanical guarantee of validity, we are by no means helpless in this difficulty and can protect ourselves sufficiently. We have simply to accustom ourselves to operate with *more than one* hypothesis. The more

[1] See, further, "Some Logical Aspects of Psychical Research" in *The Case for and against Psychical Belief*, ed. by Carl Murchison (1927).

brilliantly a hypothesis illuminates one portion of the field of inquiry the more deeply it obscures the rest, and hence every hypothesis *blinds* us to those *data*, which it is not interested in and makes nothing of, even while it opens our eyes to those which it selects as important ('essential') and valuable. Admitting this, it follows that the risk of overlooking what may prove to be important may be minimised by entertaining *a sufficient number* of hypotheses, and playing off one against the other.

This suggestion will seem strange only to a mind which has been stiffened and corrupted by an utterly dogmatic education. Anyone who has been trained to observe the actual process of inquiry, will be familiar with the fact that every step in its progress demands a plurality of possibilities and a choice between alternatives. Where there is nothing but a straight course, and no way of departing from it, there is no thought, nor need for thought. But, where a situation has *problematic* features, thought is stimulated and considers what is the *best* view to be taken, until it is decided by a judgment on the whole situation. It is for this reason that every judgment which emerges from such thinking lays claim to the value which is 'truth' (Chap. X).

A certain *technique* in operating with alternative hypotheses arises naturally. In principle every hypothesis that is entertained increases our chances of overlooking nothing important, and improves the prospect of discovery. Nevertheless, the maxim, 'the more the merrier,' does not altogether apply. In practice the psychological limitations of the human mind cut down the number. Usually *two* rival hypotheses, each zealously supported by a party inspired by a natural bias, and offering special advantages in dealing with a burning question, are as much as any science can manage to entertain at a time. But, as each dispute is settled, a further question can be taken up. So the plurality of hypotheses is successive rather than contemporaneous. Nevertheless, a sufficiently capacious mind may do well to remain open to a great range of possibilities, and abundance of hypotheses remains an asset in *theoretic* inquiry.

It may become an impediment when the time for action

comes and theoretic knowledge has to be *applied*. For the consciousness of a number of possibilities may then have a distracting and paralysing effect. Single-hearted resolution in acting upon *one* theory then seems the only pathway of salvation, and this seems incompatible with attempts to do justice to a number of competing probabilities. Psychologically action demands psychological certainty, and so reinforces the tendencies to theoretic dogmatism that its long domination in the history of thought should probably be traced to its supposed practical, rather than to its assumed theoretic, urgency.

Nevertheless, both these assumptions would seem to be equally erroneous. It is unnecessary to base truth upon compulsion, and vain to insist on formally valid theory. Nor is it necessary that the certainty demanded for action should be *theoretic*. There is such a thing as *practical* certainty; it is, in fact, the only certainty we ever feel or can attain. Now, practical certainty can coexist with clear consciousness that the theoretic grounds we propose to act on are only probabilities, and not always even very high probabilities.

Nor, again, is it true that in order to *act* we must feel practically certain. How much certainty we require depends on the circumstances of the case. If it is desperate enough we may have to stake our fortunes on a forlorn hope. Where there is *spes una salutis*, its improbability, and the superior probability of a number of unpleasant possibilities, may keenly impress the mind but need not affect our action. Short of that we often embark on a course of action we know to be risky, *faute de mieux*, or because we like to take chances and enjoy the feel of a daring deed. The popularity of games of chance and of sports with a spice of danger testifies to this trait in human character. It is a psychological blunder, therefore, for the logician to require the scientist to be a coward and to run no risks. He should realise that courage is an *intellectual* virtue as well as a practical, and that the thinker who will not budge till he can start from absolute certainty, and who puts safety first and will run no risks, is very unlikely to make discoveries, or indeed to get anywhere at all.

What, then, is the grain of truth in the doctrine that theoretic uncertainty unnerves practical action? It is surely fatal to those whose will is so weak that they cannot 'make up their mind.' Otherwise there is no psychological difficulty about first considering all the relevant alternatives that occur to the mind, estimating their probabilities, and then deciding on the best course of action and resolutely carrying it out in a single-hearted manner. For that is after all precisely what should happen in all thoughtful action and before every genuine judgment. At its *best* the human intelligence *is* capable of reflecting first and acting afterwards, with a gain in range and without loss in vigour; and, if it finds this difficult, a slur is cast upon the quality of the intelligence. A well-balanced mind strives to combine decision in action with unimpaired receptivity towards the lessons of experience, and is not ashamed to change its course when it finds itself heading for the rocks. It can deliberate fully and then act resolutely, acting boldly but not blindly. The 'purely contemplative' mind, on the other hand, that cannot apply its thoughts to reality is *not* the highest, but forms a specialised and often morbid development that should be controlled both in its own interest and in that of society at large.[1]

§ 10. The Proving of Hypotheses.

It follows, from what has been said about the plurality of possibilities in any inquiry so soon as they are looked for, that the proving of a hypothesis is always a highly *competitive* affair. It is utterly misleading to represent it as a solemn trial and formal testing of a single hypothesis by a jury of rigid and infallible canons of proof, which necessarily ends in its final acceptance or absolute rejection. There are always several hypotheses in the field, and the scientific problem is always *which* of these is to be preferred, on the evidence available. Now the available evidence may vary from day to day; it is also more or less indecisive and ambiguous, in the sense that it will fit into

---

[1] At present the social value of many philosophers, some pedants, and even 'pure' mathematicians, would appear to be definitely negative.

more than one hypothesis with more or less ease. Similarly, our hypotheses are commonly 'ambiguous' likewise in the sense of *indeterminate*,[1] simply because we cannot at the outset formulate them in terms sufficiently prescient of all the developments of the inquiry, and cannot help leaving them vague about what subsequently turn out to be incompatible alternatives. Hence there are often plenty of vicissitudes in the history of a hypothesis.

Nor are we really entitled to assume that either of these 'ambiguities' must be removable within a definite time. The indeterminateness of terms is due to the possibilities of future inquiry, which cannot be set aside by any *fiat* that the terms shall be taken as definite and precise and their possibilities as limited. This is why, in spite of many logicians, 'plurality of causes' can never be ignored.[2] And the elasticity of facts is equally ineradicable. They may continue to submit to several interpretations and to elude crucial experiment. The disputes between optimism and pessimism, determinism and indeterminism, mechanism and teleology, etc., will never be decided by any appeal to the facts. These, moreover, may also continue to be discrepant *inter se*. Some may lend themselves to one, others to another, of two incompatible alternatives. There would seem to be no logical reason why the present conflict between the competing theories of light should not be prolonged indefinitely. For, from our postulate that truth cannot be inconsistent, it only follows that we shall continue to cherish a belief and a hope that ultimately all such conflicting theories may be reconciled or superseded, not that our hopes will actually be fulfilled. Nay, it is not even certain that the real will ultimately allow itself to be grasped by human minds at all. All we can be sure of is that we shall be very obstinate in urging this postulate, even upon recalcitrant facts.

Even in sciences, where truth is not actually in dispute, it remains liable to dispute. For doubts may be raised about the historical evidence on which it rests, and new theories may

[1] For this see *Formal Logic*, chap. ii, § 8.
[2] Cp. *Formal Logic*, p. 306 f.

arise which put a new complexion on the 'facts.' When this happens, we often discover to our surprise how insecure was the ground on which the truth's acceptance rested. Its experimental basis is often very limited, and is always limited in principle by the actual number of the experiments taken as proving it. Established truths, therefore, are always sensitive to any source of doubt or error which may spring up in the evidence on which they rest. For example, the whole doctrine of Relativity rests on the Michelson-Morley experiment and its scanty repetitions: the whole existence of Piltdown man (*Eoanthropus dawsoni*) rests on the correctness of his discoverer's statements about the exact locality in which his fragments were found. There is always, then, a *finite* amount of evidence which has to be impugned or discredited in order to upset a 'truth.'

To upset a truth, however, it may suffice to reinterpret the evidence for it. Let a new theory arise and a new issue be raised, and the old facts will frequently become ambiguous, indeterminate, and insufficient. The old observations and experiments, though adequate enough to decide the points they were devised to meet, will not be relevant to, or decisive of, the new issue. For example, in the long dispute about abiogenesis it has been shown, over and over again, that the positive evidence alleged for it depended on conditions of experiment which were insufficiently stringent to exclude all access of living germs. Nevertheless, its disproof cannot be said to be complete so long as it is possible to invalidate the whole of the negative evidence by the suggestion that the means used to kill all organic germs in the substances experimented with, viz. the prolonged application of heat, would be likely to destroy also the conditions under which the inorganic would become organic. Similarly, in the disputes about fraudulent mediumship, every discovery of a new method of fraudulent manipulation always brings to light a gap in the evidence at this point, and casts a doubt (which may or may not prove well-founded) on all the earlier evidence.

Thus every new theory entails a re-examination and revision of the 'facts,' and, generalising, we may say that no care in observation, no skill in experimentation, can guard scientific evidence against unforeseen objections, new conditions, and unknown possibilities of error. We should accustom ourselves, therefore, to think of all truths as relative to the evidence on which they rest, to the verifications which have confirmed them, and to the alternatives to which they were preferred. By constantly bearing these points in mind we shall get out of the habit of looking for an absolute proof to which scientific methods can attach no meaning.

§ 11. The Cumulative Nature of Proof.

If absolute proof is a chimera, so is a decisive experiment. No single experiment can ever be decisive ('conclusive') however impressive it may seem at the time. For in every science that is not completely explored (and what science nowadays would claim to be that?) there lurk untold possibilities of error: these cannot all be eliminated at the first attempt, and are only realised later. This is the real reason why successful repetition is needed to confirm the results even of the most crucial experiment.

In the ordinary *routine* of the sciences, proof is, accordingly, cumulative. We start in ignorance and perplexity, with doubtful 'facts' and tentative theories, and by working with them gradually transform their logical status. Our evidence grows more solid and trustworthy; of our theories some grow more definite and confident, others fade and waste away. When the balance of probabilities in favour of one view becomes so overwhelming that only the perversest minds can resist its weight, we acclaim an established 'truth.'

It is important to note that in this process we can, and do, utilise evidence which is far from 'cogent,' and may even be very defective. If we are not deceived about its defects, we may find that its various bits do not all have *the same* defects, and that the mass, as a whole, covers the whole ground, meets every objection, and cannot be dismissed. Indeed, in the beginnings of any inquiry, when we are still feeling our way, no other policy holds out any prospect of success. We must use the material we have, and endeavour to improve it; if we rejected

26

it bit by bit, because none of it in all respects attained to our standard (or ideal) of 'conclusive' proof, we should render scientific progress impossible.

For initially our evidence is never perfect : any procedure, therefore, which renders the accumulation of evidence impossible really amounts to a refusal to accept empirical proof. Yet it sounds very specious to declare that bad evidence is utterly unworthy of credence and should be rejected altogether. This contention is sound only if proof must be complete and belief final, and both absolute. But if proof is cumulative and belief a gradual growth, and both admit of infinite degrees, it is invalid and harmful. Actually there are numbers of inquiries in which little or no progress is being made, because the nature of empirical investigation is misconceived in this way, and such clues as exist are not followed up, because the evidence which yields them is not unexceptionable.

Psychical Research is a good example. Here there is probably no single piece of evidence as yet which is individually cogent and which a critical mind ought to find convincing. But, collectively, the evidence is so copious and persists so uniformly through the ages that no candid mind will deny that a case for scientific investigation is made out. Hence Kant's verdict in *Die Träume eines Geistersehers* still stands. "I do not dare," he says, "wholly to deny all truth to the various ghost stories, but with the curious reservation that I doubt each of them singly, but have some belief in them all taken together." [1]

The cumulative nature of proof, of course, explains the paradox, but the whole case is logically instructive. For the mistaken refusal to allow evidence to accumulate can certainly claim the sanction of Formal Logic : so it shows that Formal Logic is not only incapable of assisting research, but capable of actively obstructing it.

§ 12. Abstraction.

We have seen that the main concern of Scientific Method is always with the empirical testing, by the course of events, of

[1] Rosenkranz, *Kant*, vol. vii, p. 77.

a hypothetical interpretation of the selected subject-matter in which a science takes an interest, and, in ultimate analysis, this means what interests those who cultivate the science. The subject-matter, similarly, is whatever a science takes as real or 'fact.' To this primary concern the other processes which are recognised as entering into scientific investigation may be regarded as subsidiary. They do not introduce any radically novel conceptions.

Abstraction, for example, may be conceived as a form of *selection*. In abstracting we select some factor in what has been given in experience, and consider it as if it existed by itself and apart from its setting. Or, we *abstract from* some feature of the given by imagining it absent. The former method selects what is considered relevant, the latter neglects what is considered irrelevant. In both cases, therefore, our procedure depends on the right to assume the existence of relevance and irrelevance. In both cases it means concentration on what is judged relevant.

So understood, the scope of Abstraction is plainly very great. It may be said to occur in all attention, all perception, all predication, all classification. For we never perceive all there is in an object; and if to perceive better we concentrate our attention upon its important aspects, we *ipso facto* divert it from the rest. Consciously or unconsciously, our perception is always selective.

In *predication*, similarly, the situation which yields the *subject* we judge about is always selected from a context from the larger part of which abstraction is made. The *predicate* (experimentally) applied to it is torn from its setting in past cases of successful judging, and transferred to the new situation with which, if the judgment is a success, it coalesces in an enlightening manner (Chap. XI, § 8).

§ 13. Classification.

As for *classification* it plainly rests on enormous amounts of abstraction. In classifying a thing along with others, i.e. including it with others in a class or kind, we always ignore as irrele-

vant—(1) its place, (2) its time, (3) its individuality. Thus we
fabricate 'eternal' and 'universal' kinds, abstract universals,
and substitute them for the concrete individuals we encounter
in the course of events. Whenever we want to handle the real
in bulk, this device is very convenient and successful. But that
for the purpose in hand nothing depends on the object of our
thought being the particular thing it is, at the time it is, and in
the place it is, is of course a hypothesis, or rather a series of
hypotheses. It may sometimes be true, if we happen to have a
purpose for which it is true. Also, if we happen to have made
the right abstractions and selections for our purpose, and if we
are not trying to argue to cases which are too remote in space
or in time.

For scientific purposes classification is often fruitful, because
the purposes are such that abstraction from the object's individuality does not matter. Thus in many sciences, like physics
and chemistry, the 'facts' are really *statistical*: they do not
deal with individuals at all, but with vast aggregates of individuals. If the smallest visible speck of matter is really composed of 20,000 millions of atoms, all our observations clearly
must be true of the *average* behaviour of these, and do not deal
with individual atoms at all. Now, one of the advantages of
averages is that they smooth out individual anomalies, if such
there are. So by experimenting with billions of atoms at a time
the chemist gets an assurance that he can ignore their
individuality.

On the other hand, for other purposes the classificatory
abstraction from individuality will certainly break down. If we
are really interested in an individual we always find that he
departs from the average of his class somewhere. His behaviour
always shows some individual features, and these may be the
very points we are concerned to foresee and control. Similarly,
the abstraction from time and place may break down. Knowledge that a man was a normal baby, and howled in the regula-
tion manner at the age of one, does not justify a confident forecast of what he will do at twenty-one or at forty-one. It may
be true that a mindless thing like fire burns 'here and in Persia,'

but it does not follow that a *man* will behave in the same way in Persia as in Piccadilly.

To meet this difficulty philosophers have made two proposals, neither of which is acceptable to science. (1) They have declared that the individual is as such unknowable, and not a fit subject for science. This conclusion was first reached by Plato (*Theœtetus*, 209 f.) (Chap. IX, § 15), and has often been echoed since. The scientific objection to it is simply that it is untrue. Science does *not* refuse to study the individual case, if it is interesting, as it often is. It could, moreover, do so, even if it were bound always to universalise; for anything it discovered about an individual could easily be universalised, simply *by conceiving it as a case of a kind*: this is easily done, and costs science nothing. The uniquest thing imaginable, a Heidelberg jaw or Trinil skull, can promptly be turned into the 'type specimen' of *Homo Heidelbergensis* or *Pithecanthropus erectus*.

But it need not be. Science can also study the individual for his own sake. Thus the science of psychology *can* set itself to study an individual mind and character, and there are psychologists who do this, often with great ability and success. Only we expect them to entertain us by their writings, and call them *novelists*, and do not make them professors, who are expected to bore us with their instructions.

(2) The second philosophic way of treating individuality is to re-conceive, or rather to re-name, it. It is then called 'the concrete universal,' and is made a text for philosophic sermons. This was Hegel's way, for whom it was an article of metaphysical faith; but scientifically it is useless. It is the mere re-statement of a problem, not a solution. It is a scientific fact that universals are useful for handling individuals, e.g. by classifying them. Our classes, however, are abstract universals, on which the Hegelian heaps scorn because they cannot reproduce the concrete real. He means that no list of qualities, however long, will re-constitute the individual whose qualities are enumerated. To this fact the Hegelian merely adds an assertion that nature *has* performed the miracle we cannot conceive—the individual *is* a concrete universal!

But *we* are as wise as before. We know as little as before *how* the qualities are concretely united. We know as little as before *what* universals are predicable of what individual, and how to avoid the error of classifying by means of *wrong* universals. If we were in doubt before, we are so still. If our problem was to determine whether *Pithecanthropus erectus* was a man or an ape, we are still left to decide it without Hegelian help. For whether he is rightly called a man or wrongly, he is, in either case, a concrete universal, and the scientific question, "A concrete universal *what*? An ape or a man?" does not interest the Hegelian. And the sweeping doubt everywhere nourished by evolutionist discoveries, as to whether individuals are not the only reals *in rerum natura*, and classes only subjective conveniences, survives in full force.

Science, therefore, will do well to reconcile itself to the situation, and to accept any abstraction that will work, without raising metaphysical questions as to what makes them work when they do. It may leave the philosophers to their sterile wrangles about the number, order, and deduction of their 'categories,' which are just classifications too, of doubtful value.

It is scientifically more important to note that every predication is a classification. To predicate *S is P* is to claim that the individual quality of a particular S may properly be expressed by the general term P. When pressed, we have, however, to admit that, strictly, the S is P in its own particular way; it is not P in general, but is the P it is under *these* circumstances. We can only plead that for our purpose this blurring of the actual circumstances does not affect the truth or value of our judgment. In ordinary predication our purposes are far more fugitive and transient than those embodied in the great systems of scientific classification; so it is natural enough that we are conscious of them, while in the latter case we are apt to forget the abstractions we use. It required the Darwinian revolution in biology to disabuse scientists of belief in the eternal validity of their classifications, and to remind them of their practical function.

§ 14. Idealisation and Fiction.

Between Abstraction, Idealisation, and Fiction there are no hard and fast lines to be drawn. By stripping off their actual setting, thought can equally raise qualities to 'ideals,' or reduce them to 'fictions.' The base line of a survey or a tennis-court becomes an ideal line after Euclid's heart by abstracting from its three-dimensionality and crookedness; but it then equally becomes a 'fiction' that can find no home in physical reality. In fact, 'idealisation' and 'fiction' are only opposite ways of *valuing* an abstraction, and the choice between them is often a matter merely of taste.

Consider e.g. an exact measurement, a complete vacuum, a pure mechanism, an elastic body, a frictionless surface, a non-conductor, a perfect gas or fluid, an economic man, free trade, a wise ruler, pure pleasure, perfect health, a disinterested motive: are they to be called abstractions or idealisations? They all occur, and have a valid use, in a respectable science; but they have all to be used with discretion, if they are not to become 'outrageous fictions.' The latter may worm their way even into the haughtiest sciences; even at Cambridge, Mathematical Tripos Papers used to contain questions of the type derided by Sir Oliver Lodge as beginning—'Take a small elephant whose weight may be neglected . . .' One can, of course, construct problems in mechanics in which the weight even of an elephant may be abstracted from, and there is no *formal* difference between a true and a false abstraction and a true and a false ideal, any more than between a true and a false hypothesis or analogy. 'True' and 'false' involve reference to purpose and conduciveness (or otherwise) to that, and the value in each case depends on the use to which the instrument of research is put and on the consequences achieved by its means.

However, even at their best, the sciences remain full of 'fictions' which are very useful and methodologically indispensable. Even our mathematics would be useless and inapplicable, if we did not *feign* that physical objects had the shapes and properties that properly belong to our mathematical ideals alone. The objects of *pure* mathematics are equally abstractions, fictions, and ideals.

§ 15. Laws of Nature.[1]

A law of nature is usually called an observed uniformity, but this is far from being the whole story. Actually any observed law is a form of Hypothesis, or rather the outcome of a series of hypotheses, and it is a pity that inductive logics have generally slurred over what very audacious and complicated assumptions are involved.

We should inquire, in the first place, why it is assumed that there are laws at all. To this question the only answer would appear to be, 'in order that we may be encouraged to search for them.' Now, this assumption is a hypothesis or postulate. It is not a necessity of thought. It is perfectly possible to conceive a world in which nothing happened according to law and every event was an unpredictable miracle. Nor would such a world necessarily be *bad*; it might easily be better than ours. In it we should, however, have to take things as they came; there would be in it neither prescience nor science. If, therefore, we wanted to predict, it would not satisfy us: in other words, 'law' is *a postulate of method*.

Secondly, the general assumption that Nature conforms to law, which is called the Uniformity of Nature, ranks among the principles called *a priori*. It is so called by those who have seen that laws are *not* observed facts but interpretations which have to be read into the facts before the facts will yield them, but have *not* seen that they are read in *experimentally*, and are in no wise certain when first tried, growing certain only gradually by the success of their working.

Moreover, thirdly, this conviction that *there are laws* is no guide whatever to the discovery of the particular laws which we believe to hold in fact, and use to forecast events. Whatever we allege and believe about the former principle, it is admitted that the formulation of particular laws can come only from experience, as a fruit, not of philosophic criticism, but of

[1] See, further, *Formal Logic*, chap. xxi.

scientific research. Even Kant does not deny this, though it did not disturb his philosophic complacency to find that he had assigned 'Law' and 'laws' to quite different sources, crediting the former to an '*a priori*' category of causality, and the latter to 'experience,' and though he has next to nothing to say about the problem of discovering particular laws. Yet this is the essential scientific problem, and, unless the Uniformity of Nature can help us to solve it, it remains sheer eyewash.

Now, actually, belief in the Uniformity of Nature does help to a certain extent. If we had no belief at all in the possibility of such a thing as a 'law,' it would not occur to us to look for a law anywhere. On the other hand, we need not believe in the *universality* of law in order to look for laws in any department of nature in which we happen to interest ourselves. For we wish to be able to control it, and prediction is a condition of control. Moreover, 'law,' as we have just seen, is a postulate of prediction. The assumption of 'laws of nature' is the most successful of the many devices men have tried for calculating what is going to happen. Its aim is to get an instrument for guiding expectation and preparation; we desire prescience to obtain control.

But in the first instance our desire to control and predict may be departmental. We shall then profess indifference to what happens outside our sphere of interest. "Scientifically it makes no difference at all that the investigator of one subject should believe that another (in which he is not interested) is the sport of chance; except in so far as this belief may induce him to confine himself more strictly to his own sphere of the knowable and so promote his efficiency." [1] Belief in universal law, then, only arises with the desire for universal control.

But it is no substitute for detailed search for laws. For "from the notion of Law no laws are deducible." [1] And Scientific Method must, and can, concern itself with the finding and formulating of the particular laws.

[1] *Formal Logic*, p. 311.

§ 16. The Finding and Proving of Laws of Nature.

We have already rejected [1] the notion that laws of nature are just observed uniformities. They can be represented as such only *after* their discovery, when all the bad observations and false clues that attended the inquiry have been eliminated. But what is actually observed is never the law, and is never quite uniform. The crude facts as observed are never exact, and never quite conform to any suggested 'law,' which is an exact formula meant to colligate, *and sift*, them.

Nor is the law finally adopted as the best formula, usually the only one considered. There are mostly several alternatives to choose among, and concordance with the actual observations is not the only canon used. The scientist gives a natural preference to a simpler formula as against a more complicated, not because he imagines nature is bound to follow what seems to him the simpler course, but for the sound methodological reason that it is easier to handle. He knows, also, that observations are not all of equal value; better observers and more favourable conditions make some observations better than others: some, therefore, must be discounted or discarded. As, moreover, no observations can be exact, no two can be expected to yield quite the same values: hence he takes an average, and disregards small discrepancies, until he has reduced his 'facts' into 'good agreement' with his favoured formula.

It should be remembered, also, that his *rôle* was never passive from the first. The 'facts' he started from were the *data* he judged worth arguing *about* and good enough to argue *from*. This initial procedure already involved him in a good deal of *selection*.

Now in a well-established science such selection is pretty safe. We can be pretty certain what *data* are relevant and good. But in the beginnings of any subject of inquiry we encounter masses of non-scientific evidence. This has to be sifted, and, mostly, scrapped. But we must be careful to allow for the fact that, just because there is no good evidence at this stage, the

[1] § 15, *init.*

'real facts,' as they will turn out to be, must be lurking in the *bad* evidence, and have to be extracted out of an ore not rich in precious metal. It is also clear that in contentious matters differences of opinion may begin thus early and involve controversy as to what *data* should be selected. Some inquiries indeed, e.g. in philosophy and theology, never seem to get beyond these initial controversies.

The *data* selected should next be viewed in the light of a comprehensive formula or hypothetical 'law.' The question to be asked—does it fit the facts?—is always a question of more or less. If the values deducible from the tentative law are in good agreement with the observed facts, the law gets scientific status and has to be reckoned with further. On the other hand, the question of its *provenance* is not important. For all that science cares, it may have originated in a dream, like Verner's Law.

For a 'law' may be suggested in very various ways. (*a*) It may be directly and obviously suggested by the *data* (selected as above), and these may suggest no other. But this will be rare.

(*b*) More often the accepted *data* will suggest different laws to different minds, and so start a controversy as to which is the *best* interpretation. Such a controversy may be hard to end, if the parties will not agree about their standard of 'best.' Usually the *simplest* or *most convenient* is preferred. But most convenient *for what and whom?* If the aims and interests of the parties differ, they may differ about the most convenient interpretation. Thus the interpretation of animal behaviour will be very different according as we are or are not willing to admit that it may be 'conscious' and intelligent. 'Simplicity,' similarly, is ambiguous; a theory that is simpler from one point of view may be more complex from another, a case illustrated by Euclid's space and Einstein's.

(*c*) Most commonly, however, the interpretation does not come from the *data* themselves, but from extraneous sources. Of these the most obviously legitimate spring from the general theory of the subject. Thus the extra weight of atmospheric 'nitrogen' was naturally accounted for by the admixture of a heavier gas, and the discrepancy between the calculated and the observed motions of Uranus by the existence of a further planet. But the 'law' may also come from another science, as when Darwin borrowed Malthus's law of population and when biological observations are interpreted by notions drawn from chemistry or physics, and astronomical illusions explained by psychology. And now and again it may be necessary to take up with remote analogies and wild suggestions, and to run counter to well-established principles. The irregularities of Mercury did not prove to be analogous with those of Uranus, but involved the whole of Einstein's theory of Relativity and the end of Euclid's long reign over the space of physics. We should also remind ourselves that in the last decade or two most of the fundamental assumptions of physics, like the law of gravitation, the indestructibility of matter, and the conservation of energy, have been found wanting in accuracy.

The law-making scientist, having got his 'law' to fit his 'facts' without acute discomfort, is tempted to proclaim it as *the* law. But he has also to prove it the *best* law, and to dispose of rival formulas. Or again, *none* of his laws may be a perfect fit. There will then be need for *crucial* experiments and a search for further *data* that will not be so amiably ambiguous as to fall in with alternative laws, but will vote decisively for one.

Now, science hitherto has been singularly fortunate in not encountering many clear cases either of persistent ambiguity in the 'facts' or of failure to find a suitable 'law'; though the present trouble with the two theories of light looks as if it might be fairly persistent. But in philosophy alternative interpretations are normal and practically ineradicable. Definite experiment is almost impossible, the facts are persistently neutral, plastic, and submissive to sweeping interpretations which are hard to prove, because hard to disprove. A philosophic view, when worsted in argument, simply re-states itself in slightly modified language; and if its 'reasons,' as is often the case, are simply *camouflage* for instincts and spiritual cravings, it hardly does even this. For it can always be sure that it will continue to be believed by those to whom it appeals. Hence the great philosophic antitheses, like those between realism and idealism, rationalism and voluntarism, pessimism and optimism, continue their indecisive contests from age to age.

It might be supposed that when a law has been adopted, after the fashion sketched above, it had still to be *verified*. But in reality the whole competition out of which it has emerged *victoriously* is its verification. Of course, if the 'law' is 'true,' it has to continue to maintain itself by its working; for no *final* verification is known to science. If it encounters new 'facts' which challenge it, or new theories which promise more, it may have to fight for its title, and will probably undergo amendment. But if the changes are slight it will continue to be called 'the same' law, and to be verified unendingly.

§ 17. Laws and Habits.

Nevertheless, the use of the term 'law' to denote the device by which our science forecasts the course of events entails serious drawbacks if it is not understood. Thus it tempts us fatally to speak of things '*obeying*' laws, thereby suggesting in nature a respect for the law-giving of human science and in the conforming things a submissiveness to the law which are booby-traps for philosophers and scientists alike. Actually, the law has no police force to execute its behests, and the constitution of nature can hardly be required to recognise our law-giving. *Why, then, do our formulas work?*

The right answer would appear to be, "because things have *habits*." The laws of nature, in so far as they are correctly formulated, are descriptions of the habits of things. Subjectively we *know* them to be convenient formulas which work; objectively we *believe* them to be confirmed habits which seem to be practically fixed.

But we need not ascribe to the things any consciousness of the habits they have. There is nothing shocking in the idea that things may have habits without knowing it. This is only to say they are like us. For we, too, are never conscious of all our habits.

Habit, therefore, implies an analogy with human nature. But we should never shrink from rendering the world more commensurate with our intelligence when we can do so with success. We are familiar with the nature and growth of habit in ourselves. We know how it stiffens and steadies our actions. We have merely to apply this notion to beings much older, stabler, and stupider than ourselves in order to get habits rigid enough to be conceived as 'laws of nature.'

Our procedure may be decried a 'sheer anthropomorphism'; but in ultimate analysis all interpretation is anthropomorphic. It can be nothing else. We can contemplate the world only with the eyes and brains and feelings we have. Human analogies run through all fancy, all fiction, all science, all philosophy; they differ only in their remoteness and flightiness. So science need not be squeamish in ascribing habits to things.

Nor need it take sides in the metaphysical dispute between those who would explain nature in terms of human nature and those who would explain human nature in terms of nature. It is entitled to conceive both 'laws' and habits methodologically, and to use either, as seems convenient. At one time it may reduce all 'laws' to 'habits,' at another all spontaneity to law, without pleading guilty either to anthropomorphism or to materialism. Thus it can legitimately have it *both* ways; for *methods* are public highways, and their use does not imply allegiance to any shibboleth of metaphysics.

§ 18. How Laws apply to Cases.

A second drawback to the use of 'law' in Scientific Method is that already mentioned in § 13. The law seems to be an abstract universal formula, which gets no grip on the particular case. This, however, is sheer misunderstanding. It is an illusion generated by the unwise habit of contemplating the law only in its *unapplied* condition, and *abstracting from its use*. Taken thus it is an empty formula, devoid of any but potential meaning; in fact, in Mr Bertrand Russell's language, a 'propositional function.' But if we want to use it, we fill up the blanks in its formula, assign definite values to its variables, apply it to the case we are concerned with, and observe how it bears out our calculation.

It is quite untrue, therefore, that science is too 'universal' to trouble about the particular case. Properly understood, it is concerned with nothing else. A universal formula that failed to predict particular cases would have to be scrapped. Here too, then, it appears that the *use* of science is an integral constituent of its *meaning*.

CHAPTER XIX

THE CASUISTRY OF KNOWING

1. The value of casuistry ; 2. The revaluation of truths ; 3. The antedating of truth ; 4. Truth and time ; 5. Potential truth ; 6. Action as a test of truth ; 7. Historical truth ; 8. Mathematical reasoning : doubly pragmatic ; 9. Novelty in mathematics ; 10. The importance of system in mathematics ; 11. Mathematical systems man-made games ; 12. The serious application of mathematical games ; 13. The antiquity of mathematics ; 14. The limited application of mathematics ; 15. The alternative systems a recent discovery ; 16. Rationalism's appeal to arithmetic ; 17. Arithmetic and volition ; 18. Arithmetic and experience.

§ 1. The Value of Casuistry.

It is a pity that the study of hard cases, *alias* Casuistry, has fallen into such widespread desuetude. For this much blame attaches to modern moralists. Formerly no moral theory was regarded as complete until it had been applied to life, and had shown its mettle in dealing with hard cases; thus Casuistry provided a real practical test of its truth, and a check on irresponsible theorising. But now moralists fight very shy of mentioning actual cases of conduct at all. For this evasion they give various insufficient reasons; but their real motive may be suspected to be that the prevalent ethics have found the problem of Casuistry to be altogether too much for them. By conceiving the moral act as an application of a moral *code* they had unwarily committed themselves to the formulation of moral *laws* to cover every case in advance of its occurrence; and when this idea was conscientiously worked out, as by the Catholic theologians, the results of Casuistry proved so unsavoury and demoralising that the Protestant moralists shrank from the outcry raised against it. So they confined themselves to talk about 'moral ideals,' without reference to their application, and, to make quite sure that these 'ideals' would remain uncontaminated by the dross of earthly action, they so conceived them as to be *inapplicable* altogether. The typical exemplification of this fatuous policy is the Categorical Imperative of Kant, which is generally commended as the *beau idéal* of a pure morality, instead of being cast aside as totally devoid of meaning.

But the right idea of Casuistry is to be based, not on code law, but on *case law*, since the code arises out of the right decision of the case. In logic, also, it is from the discovery of truths that we learn the nature of Truth. It is, therefore, a perfectly sound idea that theories should be tested by their application to cases, and especially hard cases. It is a test as applicable to logic as to ethics. For in both rules, 'laws' or 'principles' have to be *applied*, and the results of their application determine the meaning and value of the rules.

Hence the result affirmed at the end of the last chapter, that the *use* of a conception is not irrelevant to its *meaning*, but illuminates it, may be generalised: it is entirely proper to test a theory of knowledge by requiring it to deal with hard cases. And in our case of the voluntarist theory of knowledge this procedure is the more appropriate that there have been many attempts to confute pragmatic theories by citing hard cases against them. We shall, therefore, proceed to examine the more notorious instances.

§ 2. The Revaluation of Truths.

The continuous revaluation of truths is an incident in their growth, and when it is remembered that 'truth' is essentially a valuation (Chap. III), the difficulties sometimes found in the process will be seen to disappear. 'The truth' about anything at any time is the *best* opinion, in the actual state of knowledge. But as knowledge grows, this 'best' changes; the old 'best' becomes antiquated, and has to undergo revaluation. The least improvement in the value of our knowledge may entail the scrapping of an old 'truth' and its replacement by a better. But once it has been superseded and its successor has been safely installed in its stead, we can afford to do historic justice, and to admit that what is now 'error' contained much truth, and indeed was a necessary step in the discovery of the new truth.

Valuations, moreover, being relative to purpose, 'truths' change together with the ends to which they are the means.

But they do not change at the same rate everywhere. In ordinary life our ends alternate so rapidly that we cannot but realise the dependence of our means on our ends, and the need for revaluations; indeed, we hardly trouble to call the 'right' judgments which conduct to our ends 'truths' at all. Thus, if one wishes to go from Oxford to London, the 'up' platform is the 'right' one; if to Birmingham, the down; but no *intrinsic* 'rightness' is ascribed to either platform. In the sciences also, which are progressive, changes in value are common and rapid enough to operate as a check on the belief in 'truths' which are independent of the occasions for their use. But in philosophy 'truth' is so stationary, and changes so slowly, that many are beguiled into taking it as absolute. Hence we may say that frequency of revaluation marks the progressiveness of a subject of inquiry.

§ 3. The Antedating of Truth.

This is a consequence of Revaluation. Since the 'truth' is always the best solution of a problem, and is continually being revalued as better solutions become available, it is clear that the best solution would be adopted as true *at any time*, if it is available. If, however, it is not available, it cannot be adopted until it is discovered. When it is discovered and becomes available it is, consequently, *antedated*. That is, we say *it was true* before it was discovered, although we did not know it.

How much a truth can be antedated depends, however, on the circumstances. We cannot say, for example, that Xerxes's 'true' way to force Thermopylæ was to use artillery. Artillery cannot be so antedated as to be a conceivable means to Xerxes's ends. But we can say he *ought* to have used the path over the mountains by means of which the Greeks were finally taken in the rear. For it was available at the time, and only his geographical ignorance of its existence hindered Xerxes from using it. Similarly, truths about objects which we have at various times discovered, like Neptune, the okapi, radium, and so forth, may all be antedated to various dates, because we might have got all the experiences they now yield us long before we did.

In certain cases a truth (usually of the scientific order), once it is discovered, is recognised as so valuable that it would always have been used in the past, and, humanly speaking, will always be used in the future. The truths of arithmetic, for example, can be antedated to any extent, and also extended without limit into the future. They can thus be taken as models of *eternal* truth, be given a superior status, and be promoted out of relation to human affairs altogether. As we shall see (§§ 8–18) this is a mistake, though a natural one.

Sometimes, on the other hand, the antedating of a truth demands nice judgment, and the date is essential to the truth. Thus one watching the courtship of a friend may find it is true that she is engaged to-day; but he should not hastily infer that she had been engaged all along, or even yesterday, for she may only have got engaged to-day. Such cases do not puzzle common sense, but they do perplex logicians who will recognise no mean between an eternal truth and no truth at all. It is no wonder that their logic fails to apply to so temporary an affair as human life!

§ 4. Truth and Time.[1]

Among the abstractions of Formal Logic that from the time context of the actual judgment stands out as an outrageous fiction. For if a truth is to be of *use* at all, it has to be used *at some time*, and it is essential to its truth that it should be used at the *right* time. So the time-relations of our judgments are vital to their truth, and indeed to their meaning. Who can say whether '*it is hot*' is true, or indeed what it means, unless he knows *when* it is said? Only a logic, therefore, which has systematically abstracted from meaning can dare to substitute the monotonous abstraction of a timeless '*is*' for the various tenses of our actual predications. Nor is its abstraction rendered more defensible by the fact that here for once Formal Logic parts company with its twin sister, Grammar.

The situation is greatly aggravated by the further dogma that truth is 'eternal,' and that if anything is 'once true' it is

[1] Cp. *Formal Logic*, chap. xxi, § 7.

'always true.' For the eternity of truth is an unsavoury nest of confusions, from which a brood of paralogisms is hatched. 'Eternal' is a highly ambiguous word, and at least five of its senses contribute to the confusion.

"(1) Eternal is often used as an equivalent of 'everlasting,' i.e. enduring throughout all time. (2) 'Eternal' may mean 'changeless,' or (3) 'timeless,' i.e. that which cannot be an 'event,' or be related to events. . . . But (4) 'eternal' is also used as meaning 'applicable at any time and to any event.' And lastly, (5) 'eternal' may refer to the fixed *dating* of temporal events." [1]

The deep differences which separate these uses may be brought out by illustration. Of the first sense, 'God' and 'heaven,' in their popular conception, may be quoted as examples. Of the second, Aristotle's 'God' and Plato's 'heaven.' Of the third sense, mathematical truth seems to be the best example. For that the angles of a triangle are equal to two right angles cannot be an event: it is part of an ideal system which claims to have abstracted from time-relations once and for all. Of the fourth sense, 'laws of nature' are a good example; for we have seen (Chap. XVIII, § 18) that they are *meant* to apply to events, and do not really abstract from time-relations, except in order to be transferable from one event to another. The fifth is really the most trivial sense of all; it means that if one should happen to sneeze now, it will be a truth to all eternity that one sneezed then!

But this sense, at least, is a clear misnomer. For such truth is *essentially dated*, and its 'eternity' really means its inclusion in a time-order. Truths of this sort, therefore, must be in time, whereas those of the third sort are specially exempted from it. In the first and fourth senses there is an essential reference to time, while the second transcends it. Only the third, therefore, is properly timeless: but it exists only by a *fiat* of ours, and is a voluntary abstraction from time, which, moreover, may also prove to have hidden in it an essential relation to final application (§ 12).

[1] Cp. *Formal Logic*, p. 325.

§ 5. Potential Truth.

We have seen that a tried and tested truth is distinguished from a truth-claim by the fact that it has victoriously emerged from a verification-process which is judged adequate. But need a truth, to remain true, be continually reasserted? No. It has won its title by its services, and retains it also when it is not functioning. It is enough that it should remain *verifiable* and capable of being called out on active service.

Moreover, as William James has pointed out,[1] most of our 'truths' are thus kept in reserve, and only mobilised when wanted. This is why intellectualism fails to see any connexion between truthfulness and usefulness. A truth, while not *in* use does not seem to be *of* use.

But can its use, therefore, be neglected altogether? If it were *never* used, would not its truth soon be disputed or forgotten? If it never *could* be used, would it not become unmeaning? Ultimately, therefore, verifiable presupposes verified truth, and potential knowledge actual, as Aristotle taught us long ago.

Under the requirements of life truths are constantly passing from the actual into the potential state, and back again. Thus, suppose I go for a walk in an unfrequented forest I know well. Absorbed in meditation, I stumble over a stone, and sprain my ankle. At first sight this accident would not be said to have affected my 'knowledge' of the forest. I know its paths, and my way home, as before. But I can no longer *use* my knowledge. I cannot act on it. It has become *potential*. And as I lie groaning on the ground, I realise that it has become irrelevant to my plight. A way out of the wood, which is a 'true' way for one who has the use of his legs is in no real sense a way out for me. I no longer 'know a way to get home.' I have 'lost' the way had. Finally, I give myself up for 'lost.'

Now, suppose a benighted wanderer happens to come along on a horse. He has the knowledge and ability to move, but has 'lost his way.' So his knowing how to move has become as irrelevant to his situation as has my knowledge of the forest's

[1] *Pragmatism*, pp. 214-30.

topography to mine. He, too, 'knows no way out.' But when we meet and join forces, the 'useless' knowledge of both becomes functional again, and we both make our way out. Thus even in potential knowledge it is a latent relation to action which renders it valuable, and ultimately 'true.'

§ 6. Action as a Test of Truth.

The pragmatic theory of truth contends that often directly, and always ultimately, the decisive test of truth is the action which it indicates. As Prof. Loewenberg neatly says, "a truth has not merely to be *asserted*, but also to be *enacted*." [1] What made this theory seem so repugnant to the mass of philosophers was that the learned had long been accustomed to discuss their problems only dialectically—i.e. by words, not deeds—and had got out of the habit of acting on their theories. Thus they had disputed for many centuries about the site of Troy, but it had occurred to no one that the way to settle the question was to go and dig. Then Schliemann came along with a touching but quite 'uncritical' faith in Homer, and dug up Troy at Hissarlik, although expert opinion had decided that it must be at Bunarbashi.

This substitution of action for dialectics is one of the great differences between modern and ancient science. It is very modern, as is shown by the story of Charles II's request to have it explained to him why the addition of a living fish to a bucket of water did not increase the weight of the bucketful. Instead of appeasing the royal curiosity with learned conjectures, the Royal Society performed the experiment and found that the 'fact' was false.

Of simple truth-claims direct action forms an admirable test. But when the claim is more complex we may prefer to argue on general probabilities. Thus if we hear a grossly improbable report, say, that 'there will be a race of motor-perambulators in the Parks on Sunday,' we may infer from our informant's character that the report is false, and refuse to test it by ocular

[1] *The Problem of Truth* (University of California Publications in Philosophy, vol. x, p. 216).

demonstration. Still, this test is less complete, and we take risks. The improbable may happen, and a liar may tell the truth.

A still more complex case is presented by the famous experiment whereby Elijah established Yahveh's superiority over Baal in the eyes of Israel (1 Kings xviii). Even the priests of Baal might have been converted by the fire from heaven if the blood-thirsty prophet had given them a chance. Still, the connexion here between the claim to be tested and the verifying experience was not very direct. An obstinate sceptic might doubt the complete accuracy of the historical record, and explain away the fire from heaven as the first fortunate flash of the thunder-storm subsequently mentioned. Still, scientific experiments, even when crucial, would seem to be essentially tests of the same nature as Elijah's.

Lastly, in extreme cases, we may entirely dispense with direct verification by action, and argue *a priori* altogether. A meaningless miracle, reported by a notorious liar, is disbelieved without further inquiry. Thus if a scout told me: "Have you heard, sir, that the President of St. John's shot an angel in Bagley Wood yesterday?" I should reply, "No, but I do not believe it." I might hold that previous applications of the pragmatic test had made further testing unnecessary. Still, strictly, I should run a risk even here: no merely formal argument about the impossibility of angels or of shooting them would completely confute the story. For if the event *had* occurred it would be *my* notions about miracles and angels that would need revision.

§ 7. Historical Truth.

Historical truth, at first sight, seems a serious crux for the pragmatic analysis of truth. How can truth about the past depend on its consequences? It seems a paradox. For the consequences are in the future, and how can the future alter, or in any way affect, the past? The case is clearly intriguing, and worthy of careful analysis. The objection, moreover, is serious, because there *is* a historic side to any truth ever discovered, and, unless historical truth can be accounted for, the whole pragmatic theory collapses.

(*a*) It will not do to pooh-pooh it by merely remarking, "Oh, history is all 'propaganda' and meant for present or future use!"

(*b*) We should rather note that all beliefs about the past have a *present value* and warrant derived from past *testing*. For every historic truth *has had* consequences which once were future, and *have* tested it; so that by the time it is acknowledged as 'historic truth' it may be said to have undergone pragmatic testing. For example, 'Queen Anne is dead' was news once. It was attested by many who saw what they recognised as her corpse, attended her funeral, and saw George I reign in her stead. Of all these experiences there purport to be contemporary records. Nor has anything occurred since to lead us to doubt the deadness of Queen Anne. Hence this historical truth was verified in the past and continues to be so. It still 'works,' and is supported by our belief in the integrity of history.

Nevertheless, if evidence were got showing that the accepted accounts of Queen Anne's death were untrue, or if a queer old lady turned up and claimed to be Queen Anne, we might have to modify our beliefs even now. The new evidence might turn out to be a fake, and the old lady a lunatic, but their claim, until it was disposed of, would reduce the traditional 'truth' to the position of a contested claim. The truth would be unsettled. We should have to choose between conflicting claims.

Moreover, we cannot shut our eyes to the fact that in many departments of history truths habitually *are* unsettled, and are being altered from day to day. Thus, so far, historical truth is no exception to the type. It is vain to urge that 'the *real* truth could not alter,' so long as we have no means of knowing when we have really and finally reached it. By us at any rate *our* historical truth must be treated as modifiable.

(*c*) This conclusion is a necessary working assumption of the historian, whose occupation would be gone if he could not alter, and improve, the history of the past. He may justify his activities, no doubt, by the plea that he is only striving to get nearer to the real history of events; but for all that the immutable past is an over-belief for him which he does not act on.

The principle he does act on in re-writing history is that all history must be such that the acknowledged present facts can be derived from it. Every historical truth continues to have consequences which may be used to test it, and may lead us to withdraw or modify our acceptance of its claim. A history, therefore, that represented Carthage as defeating and destroying Rome would be false and incredible; it would be refuted by its consequences ; for then half Europe would presumably be speaking a Semitic and not a Latin tongue. Subject, however, to this condition, the historian has a choice between the alternative stories which satisfy it, and can adopt or compile whichever version seems to him best. Thus past events have for the historian a sort of indetermination strangely analogous to that which future events have for the agent, and *for our knowledge* the past is no more rigid than the future.

(*d*) In one important way, indeed, it is clear that the whole past, with all its truths, is altering daily. It is slipping further back into the past, and this entails changes in its character, both psychological and logical. Its memories fade insensibly ; and, after a time, it ceases to be *remembered*, and is only *recorded*. Thus there may still be living a few survivors of the Mutiny who can bear witness to it from personal experience: but when they die its truths will rest on records alone, and will be subject to the tests applicable to these, and not to those for memories. Time, therefore, makes a difference, even to the past.

(*e*) The most instructive way, however, of meeting the contention that future consequences can have no bearing on the past is to examine a concrete case of a historical question or debate. This is the most instructive way, because it requires us to consider an actual case and real problem, instead of a string of paper propositions about history which no one may be interested in enough to believe or dispute. Whenever a real dispute is examined, it will be found that all the verifications actually appealed to are necessarily *subsequent* to the starting of the question; thus, though the truth is *about* the past, its verification, like that of any other truth, is by its *future* consequences.

This fact was once borne in upon the writer by a friend, who asked him whether he had seen a certain eminent philosopher receive an honorary degree. "No," I replied. "You should have." "Why?" "Because he looked like Solomon in all his glory." "Indeed, where did he get the 700 wives from?" "You mean 300?" "No, 700." To decide the historical dispute thus started, I suggested an appeal to some of several Scotsmen present, but to our surprise they all professed ignorance. I then suggested a reference to Scripture, but for a long time we failed to get hold of a Bible. Finally a professor of theology (who also could not decide the question) kindly produced one, and verified *my* contention. Clearly here all the consequences used to test the conflicting truth-claims were future, and (as much as half an hour) subsequent to the beginning of the dispute.

§ 8. Mathematical Reasoning, doubly Pragmatic.

Rationalism still regards mathematics as its citadel, and mathematical truth as the simplest and surest form of truth—absolutely necessary, entirely self-evident, and independent of man and human experience, a model for all other truth to aspire to, nay, as alone strictly knowledge. This valuation of mathematics is very old: it goes back to Plato (if not to Pythagoras), and prevails in Descartes, Hobbes, and Spinoza. It is typically affirmed in Kant's *dictum* that in every science there is just so much strict science as there is mathematics. It leads to a contempt for all truth which falls short of this ideal.

For our pragmatic voluntarism, on the contrary, mathematics is essentially a human device for the control of experience, which exhibits human manipulation in cognitive operation at its *maximum*. For this reason it forms an extreme, rather than a typical, case of knowledge. Indeed, one may say that only complete fiction has more of the human 'making of truth' in its composition than mathematics.

In support of this *dictum* it should be noted in the first place that, so far from dispensing with the pragmatic test in mathematics, we apply it *twice over*. Mathematical truth has a *double* function and value—first in the system of assumptions of which it is part, and then in the purposes of life. A question about the 'truth' of mathematics is, therefore, always ambiguous. It may refer to the vital value of mathematics. If so, we should answer that geometry is 'true' because it is of use in astronomy, in physics, in chemistry, in engineering, and in most of the arts; arithmetic is true because we use statistics, and encounter many things we desire and need to count. This is the answer to shock the Platonist withal.

Usually, however, questions about mathematical truth do not probe so deep. They inquire not into the *further* uses of mathematics, but merely into the nature of mathematical truth *within* mathematics.

We should, then, answer "a mathematical truth-claim is 'true' when it coheres with an established system, or accords with a recognised procedure, which is useful as a whole, in the first sense. If the truth in question supports the system, it is probably true, if it upsets it, false. For the system forms our court of appeal in testing such a truth-claim: we regard it as so valuable that we will not let it be upset."

Usually this guarantee suffices; but it is not absolute. For in mathematics, as elsewhere, truth has to be conceived as progressive. Now, elsewhere, this is easy enough; for we encounter novelties that force us to new cognitive adjustments. But mathematics do not progress thus empirically. Just because they flow from (apparently) arbitrary assumptions of our own making, we will not lightly change them. Any proposed change or modification in mathematical assumptions has to be justified as conducive to the progress of mathematics, before it is adopted.

§ 9. Novelty in Mathematics.

A case, however, can often be made out for innovation, owing to a peculiarity of mathematical deduction. We find that after we have worked out a certain number of exemplifications of a principle or rule sufficient to familiarise us with its nature, we can learn nothing further from more examples. Once we have done sums enough to grasp the principle of addition fully, the infinity of possible sums teaches us nothing new. We come, therefore, to a stop; if we desire to go on, we must invent a new operation, say, subtraction. This involves the adoption of a *new* principle, viz. that + and − numbers cancel out, and an *extension* of the old ones, which more or less *modifies* their original meaning, whether their verbal integrity is respected or contradicted.

The same thing happens, not infrequently, to the rules of a game, to which we have already likened mathematics (Chap. XVII, § 4). After a time the possibilities under the rules are exhausted and become too well known: the game then loses in interest, and proposals are made to extend and complicate its rules. This danger-point is speedily reached in 'noughts and crosses,' later in draughts, and has recently been arrived at by the masters even in chess. There is nothing for it, then, but to relax or extend the rules.

The history of mathematics is the history of such breaches of too inelastic rules. Thus, when fractions were invented they were infractions of the unit's indivisibility, a sacred principle which conservative mathematicians could hardly bear to part with, even in Plato's time; [1] when parallels were defined as 'meeting at infinity,' the extension flatly (though verbally) contradicted the earlier Euclidean definition of them as 'straight lines which *never* meet.' Novelties in mathematics, therefore, arise through the extension by analogy of old conceptions, and in no other science are analogies pursued more recklessly and triumphantly.

It is always a question, however, at first, whether these extensions are 'legitimate.' Not, that is, whether they can, in fact, be made; nor whether they fit into the old system: for that they can be made if we choose, and that they will *not* fit in, is certain *a priori*. What is disputable is whether the modifications they demand in the old system are such *improvements* as to be worth having. Real novelties in mathematics, therefore, are as disputable as anywhere else.

What, however, is ordinarily called mathematical novelty is only psychological. It would not exist for a mind that could grasp the whole meaning and consequences of its assumptions

[1] Cp. *Republic*, 525 E.

at the time when it makes them. When we have defined the unit, and conceived the operation of adding, we have, implicitly and *in logic*, committed ourselves to all the truths of Number. That is, we have gained the power of forming them all. The fact that we do not at once grasp them all, but have to work them out when we need them, only shows that we do not grasp the whole beauty of our postulates, nor foresee all their consequences. But neither do we foresee all the moves of a game when we enact its rules. Yet they are determined in principle, and there is as little reason to doubt that mathematics is a human invention as chess.

§ 10. The Importance of System in Mathematics.

Nevertheless, mathematical truth has a peculiarity which constitutes a real difference between truths of mathematics and, say, of perception. System is much more important in mathematics than in perception. In the former systematic dependence is decisive, and the individual truth-claim negligible, while in perceptions each perception normally attests itself and is accepted at face value. We know from experience that our senses can as a rule be trusted.

Yet even this difference is rather one in degree than in kind. If our perceptions frequently yielded us marked discrepancies from reasonable expectation, they would be discounted. If a heavy drinker began to see red rats, he would do well to judge them unreal as rats; but they would be real enough as warnings of impending *delirium tremens*. Conversely, though ordinarily experience would not be allowed to correct our mathematics, we can yet imagine experiences that would induce a disuse of Euclidean (or even of all) geometry. In 1919 the astronomers encountered some, which were taken as valuable verifications of Einstein's theory of Relativity.

Still, roughly, truth in perception may be said to be based on the experience itself, in mathematics on the nature of the system. $2+2=4$ seems so independent of us precisely because it is *not* absolute truth in its own right. It depends primarily on the truth of the system known as common arithmetic, and we forget

who selected and made this system. Having once adopted our
number-system, we cannot, of course, make 2+2 anything but
4, without stultifying ourselves. For to deny it would mean
to give up, or to hang up, the system which carries all the
'necessary' truths of arithmetic in its bosom.

§ 11. Mathematical Systems Man-made Games.

But what about the system itself? Is that independent of
us? Not if 'independent' means unrelated to man (Chap. VII,
§ 11), for mathematics depend less than any science on experience, and more than any attest his ideals and constructive powers.
They yield only to lies, which are wholly man-made truths
(claims) (Chap. VIII, § 19). As (almost) free creations of
our mind they rank with our games, say chess. We make the
rules of the one and the assumptions of the other. Both have, no
doubt, departed widely from the experience which prompted
them. Chess was originally a war-game: mathematics rest on
the experiences of motion, duration, and succession, and the
need of regulating them. These yielded the stuff about which
our ideal rules were made. But once the rules were made, they
engendered necessary truths in both. By the (present) rules of
chess a castle cannot move obliquely, nor a bishop straight. So
by Euclid's rule two 'straight' lines cannot enclose a space.
Both impossibilities follow from the rules.

Why did we make these rules? Because they make chess a
good game; because they make geometry a good way of simplifying and calculating space-experiences. Some mathematicians,
indeed, believe that mathematics are *exactly* like chess—merely
intellectual games whose sole function is to entertain them.
The mathematician's sense of humour is sometimes peculiar.

Still, if they were right, the good and value and use of mathematics, as of chess, would be amusement merely, and the
'truth' of such a system would lie in its power to amuse.

§ 12. The Serious Application of Mathematical Games.

But it seems better to value mathematics *also* as an aid to
the control of experience. If so, we shall take the meaning of

pure mathematics as relative to the use of *applied* mathematics. We shall then be able to understand why, out of numbers of mathematical systems which are conceivable, so few are studied —viz. those selected because we find that they can be profitably applied to our experience.[1]

It is superiority in this point alone which renders Euclidean 'truer' than non-Euclidean geometry. The metageometries are just as *thinkable*, but not as *convenient* for manipulating perceptual spaces. The first and chief reason, then, for the exceptional position ascribed to mathematics is that, though *pure* mathematics are just games, *applied* mathematics are of the utmost practical importance, and that the essential *connexion* between the two is easily overlooked.

§ 13. The Antiquity of Mathematics.

The fundamental postulates on which mathematics rest are of great antiquity. They are made so early in the history both of the race and of the individual that little memory persists of the gropings which preceded their adoption. Still, so long as the word 'geometry' remains in use, it can never wholly be forgotten that this 'pure' science once had the impure purpose of measuring out the lands that were yearly inundated by the waters of the Euphrates and the Nile.

§ 14. The Limited Application of Mathematics.

The parts of our experience which admit of mathematical treatment are very distinctive, and by now well known. So there is no longer much dispute about their sphere of application, and little temptation to reason mathematically about subjects unsuited for such treatment. Nowadays, the misapplication of mathematics is a temptation only for pseudo-scientific pedants, though in former ages the 'mystic' properties of numbers and figures long made mathematics a hunting-ground of the mystic and one of the most popular branches of magic.

[1] Cp. Bertrand Russell, *Scientific Method in Philosophy*, pp. 20–26.

§ 15. The Alternative Systems a Recent Discovery.

Within the limits of their application, which as we saw are usually definite, mathematical reasonings are extremely useful and successful. For many centuries, therefore, there seemed to be no motive to experiment with varying their assumptions. They worked so well that it seemed a waste of time to try to alter them, except by extensions on the same lines (cp. § 9).

It was only in the nineteenth century that mathematicians, perplexed by their inability to account for Euclid's twelfth 'axiom,' began to explore the foundations of geometry and to discover the alternatives to Euclid's assumptions. Thanks to Gauss, Lobachevsky, Riemann, Poincaré, and others, the motives, the value, and the verification of the geometrical postulates can now be fully traced. In all cases they have turned out to be pragmatic.

This result puts, of course, a new complexion on the question of mathematical truth. Henri Poincaré concludes that "to ask whether Euclidean geometry is true is as void of sense as to ask whether the decimal system is true and older systems are false."[1] The function of all geometries is to enable us to calculate the movements and shapes of bodies in physical space, and which of them can do this best is an empirical question.

§ 16. Rationalism's Appeal to Arithmetic.

Rationalism, therefore, no longer gets any mathematical support when it tries to use geometry as an undisputed example of the sort of truth it craves. It clings the closer to arithmetic. Indeed, Prof. A. E. Taylor, in the early days of the pragmatic controversy, once was rash enough to stake his philosophic all on the rationalistic interpretation of arithmetical truth. He declared that "$2+2=4$ is at least one truth which does not depend upon, and cannot be in any way affected by, our will or heart or passional nature." It is a crucial case where "will has nothing to do but recognise a truth which it cannot alter," and which is absolute and *a priori*.[2]

---

[1] *La Science et l'Hypothèse*, p. 66.

[2] In the *MacGill University Magazine* for April 1904, p. 55.

In response to this challenge it will be shown (*a*) that mental activity constructs, and volitional interest sustains, the number-system in *eight* distinct ways, while (*b*) in four ways its validity and value rest on experience.

§ 17. Arithmetic and Volition.

We may first inquire how we came by our number-system. It springs, ultimately, from our power or art of counting. But what enables us to count? Nothing in nature accounts for counting—not, certainly, as J. S. Mill supposed, the existence of countable things. For things that *can* be counted need not be counted, and how they are counted depends on how they are *taken*.

The root of counting lies deeper. It lies in the most general feature of our life—the experience of *succession*. Anything experienced as successive, anything whereby we apprehend the lapse of time, can be counted. Breathings, heart-beats, pulses of attention, throbs of pain, sequences of ideas, can be counted. The stuff out of which arithmetic is made thus pervades our whole experience, and is the most universal fact in life.

But the stuff must be operated on. To get an arithmetic we must form the conception of the *unit*, and perform the ideal operation of addition. Kant, therefore, was right in holding that arithmetical truth is 'synthetic'; it does not follow from the mere definition of Number.

Now the unit is any object of thought selected, taken out of its context, and attended to abstractly, as just an object of attention. To add is to combine such units into new wholes, out of which they can be recovered at will, unaltered and undamaged. 'Two,' therefore, *means* the result of so adding 'one' to 'one,' and so forth.

Now this operation which generates 'two' depends wholly on ourselves; we can, therefore, repeat it as often as we please, and form any number, however large. We have laid down the 'law' for all numbers, once for all: all the truths of Number are logically implicit in the first addition, though psychologically they may take a deal of working out, and strike us as new when we get them. Still, we have the rule for 'discovering' any truth about Number that we need.

This, too, is why the number-system is infinite. We can form numbers large enough for any purpose. The 'unit' is one fundamental postulate: that all units are the same in quality, countable in any order, and unaffected by being counted, are others.

Now, if such is the nature of our arithmetical procedure, it is clear that much arbitrary construction comes into it. Choices intervene at every step. We can abstain (1) from selecting and attending to objects, (2) from counting, (3) from postulating the unit, (4) from postulating the sort of unit we have adopted. If (5) we had refrained from *applying* our arithmetic and regarding things as units in spite of their differences, arithmetic would never have attained full truth. It would have remained a game— a coherent play of fancy, with no grip on reality.

The application, therefore, of arithmetic to life is wholly in our power. It is voluntary, and even arbitrary. For its sphere of application has to be determined by selection. Things can be (and are) counted variously for various purposes. A glass of water may figure as 'one,' or as so many drops. We can say 'five fingers' or 'one hand,' 'twenty shillings' or 'one pound.' The preacher arguing for the unity of God could appeal to "one earth, one sun, one moon—one great multitude of stars!"

Prof. Taylor's specimen, therefore, of a truth unaffected by volition, $2+2=4$ is easily put out of action. It rests (1) on the will to make objects of attention and to count them. For $2+2$ are not 4 from all eternity: to make 4 they must be counted as such.

(2) It rests also on the various postulates about the unit which common arithmetic assumed, and which have since been extended by analogy and modified in more complicated forms of calculus. Thus, as the number-system grows and the functions of number develop, their context is constantly altering the properties of units and the meaning of '$2+2=4$.' Originally units could only be added. Then subtraction came in, with

the notion of negative quantity. Then multiplication and division, etc. Each extension of arithmetic leads to problems which the older rules considered insoluble or illegitimate (cp. § 9).

It rests (3) on our willingness to *add together* the sums we have formed separately. This we are not bound to do. Forming two wholes does not pledge us to combine them into a larger sum. We can stop counting wherever we choose: number grows infinite only if an unlimited *will to count* is assumed. There is no addition, in short, without volition. Two and two do not make four: they are *made* four, and if, in a context, it does not suit us, we can simply refuse to add. Incidentally, this is why it is so hard to convict anyone of self-contradiction so long as he retains the power of refusing to put together his contradictory beliefs.

(4) The abstract necessity of arithmetic remains an empty threat so long as it is not applied to concrete objects. But, so soon as it is so applied, it can be disputed. As Prof. Hoernle says,[1] "It is only by an enormous amount of abstraction that numbers are applicable at all. We have to disregard all the character and content of things if we want to number them." We need never grant that the '2' which compose the first sum and the '2' which make up the second can validly be united into a '4.' We can doubt whether their constituents are sufficiently akin to behave as homogeneous units in the same sum. Four gloves need not be two pairs; they may all be left-handed. In what reasonable context would 2 virtues and 2 caterpillars make 4? As nothing which we count is strictly a mere unit, and everything has an individual character, its inclusion with others in a sum can always be contested as false abstraction. The abstract necessity, therefore, that 2+2 *must* make 4 need never be conceded in a concrete case, and has no practical consequences.

(5) The *way* we count things is arbitrary, as we saw above. Anything, even 'the universe,' full as it is of a number of things, may be regarded as a whole; anything, even a soul,

[1] *Mind*, N.S., xiv, p. 459.

as a plurality of 'parts,' a heap of 'ideas,' or a number of 'faculties.'

(6) A dialectical victory over the rash assertion that $2+2=4$ *absolutely and unconditionally*, is easy to gain. For what the sum works out at depends on the *scale of notation* we choose to adopt. Ordinarily we use 10. But in the scale of 4, $2+2$ would $=10$, which would also be the sum of $7+5$, in the scale of 12. Moreover, each of these results is as true and necessary in its context as that $7+5=12$ in decimal notation. Not only, therefore, is our scale arbitrary, but we shall see in § 18 that its selection was due to an accident of evolution.

Clearly the facts of arithmetic itself here protest against those who would insist on its *unconditional* validity. As usual there are unexpressed conditions, which our phraseology ignores. But quibbles based on these will hardly be admitted by rationalism to subvert its conception of arithmetic. It will reply that common arithmetic remains our sole and inevitable method of counting, if to count we have agreed.

At this point it may be summoned to consider two further possibilities which, though not actual, are conceivable.

(7) Counting was possible, we saw, because of the empirical fact that experience is a succession or flow. Now this flow is either (roughly) equable or irregularly accentuated. It can, therefore, be conveniently represented by numbers which stand in a regular succession. But what if our experience flowed *differently*? It might then be more convenient to construct a *different* number-system to deal with it. If, e.g., it flowed in regular pulses our number-system might be required to reflect its rhythm. Suppose that every third event were accentuated, and, as it were, summed up the two before. Might not this justify us in inventing a system that recognised *two* sorts of units with different values? Such a system would be more complex than common arithmetic, but under the circumstances more natural, and in it it might become false or unmeaning that $2+2=4$. For twice two beats of a pulse would not be one pulse $+$ one beat on to the next. It would even be true that even now relations might be found to which such a hypothetical

calculus would be applicable. Thus Oxford University, until a few years ago, used to divide the academic year into four terms. But the terms were not all of equal value. For many purposes the Summer term counted as two, the Easter and the Trinity term. Hence by residing in this term it was possible to keep *two* terms.

(8) The radical changes in the flow of experience suggested above are no doubt unlikely. But a somewhat smaller alteration in arithmetical assumptions might be both practicable and, in many cases, advantageous. We could, for example, give up the assumption that a unit can only belong to one whole. Let it belong simultaneously to two: then $2+2$ may $=3$. Or consider this problem: 'There were in Chapel four Fellows, the Vice-President, and two Chaplains. How many dons were present— 4, 5, 6, or 7?' A philosophic example of similar counting may be found in Plato's proof, that the pleasure of the philosopher-king is 729 times greater than the tyrant's: here 5 are counted as 9.[1]

Common arithmetic no doubt objects to counting any number of a sum more than once. But why is that wrong? It is only a convention to count it once, and conventions may be varied. By systematically varying them we might form new arithmetics, which may even have an extensive use. For many countable things do, in fact, belong to several wholes. A man e.g. normally belongs to a family, a church, a state, a club, etc., all of which have influence on his actions. He can be counted, therefore, as a member of them all, and it would be a great convenience to have a calculus which would express these manifold relations simultaneously. Nay, is not the reason why social science is so unamenable to mathematical exactness precisely that we have not yet a calculus capable of dealing arithmetically with units that belong to more than one whole?

Metarithmetics, then, analogous to the metageometries, are conceivable. They would be generated similarly, viz. by varying systematically the simpler assumptions of Euclidean geometry and common arithmetic.

---

[1] *Republic*, 587 D.

We see, then, why $2+2=4$ seems so independent of our will, and $2+2=5$ so impossible. The reason is not that human agency has nothing to do with the making of arithmetical truth, but that we have made it nearly all ourselves. We are so proud of it, and value it so highly, that we always prefer to sacrifice a 'false' calculation to the arithmetical system, however handy it may seem at the moment. To maintain that $2+2=5$ would cost too much: it would cost us the construction of a new arithmetic.

§ 18. Arithmetic and Experience.

The dependence of arithmetic on experience may be shown quite briefly.

(1) If our experience were not successive, it would, of course, afford us no basis for constructing any number-system (§ 17, *init.*). A changeless consciousness, therefore, could have no arithmetic. In heaven, therefore, there is no counting; or, as Aristotle would have put it, 'the gods have no arithmetic.'

(2) Even though we might subjectively experience succession, and so could count, it need not follow that objectively counting had application to reality.

For why is arithmetic so useful? Because we encounter many things which are (*a*) distinguishable, and yet (*b*) so like that they can be treated as mere units of a kind. If either of these conditions failed us, as is quite conceivable, arithmetic would become inapplicable.

Thus (*a*) in a world which was a perfect continuum there would be nothing to count. A solitary cell floating in a sea of nutriment, for example, could apply arithmetic to nothing.

Nor (*b*) could it be used in a world in which all things were so disparate that it conduced to no purpose to count them together, because everything simultaneous seemed wholly different and everything successive wholly new. Yet both of these worlds might be quite as good to live in as ours (which avoids these extremes)—for all except mathematicians!

(3) What would happen to arithmetical truth if experience should so change as to render it inapplicable to our life? If

$2+2=4$ *ceased* to be useful, how long would it remain 'true'? At first, no doubt, it would be held to remain true hypothetically, even though twos and fours could no longer be found in nature. But, gradually, such imaginary 'truth' would seem futile, and ultimately we should cease to honour as 'true' what had ceased to refer to actual experience. Arithmetical truth would survive only in proverbs, which are usually truths out of date accepted without thought. '$2+2=4$' would become a traditional 'truth' like 'You cannot pour new wine into old bottles,' nor 'make bricks without straw.' But this result would really mean that in its fullest sense the truth of arithmetic depends on experience.

(4) Lastly, arithmetic is dependent on experience in a very special way. It idealises the work of man's hands in piling together such objects as fruits and stones, and his experience of finding them tolerant of such handling and willing to stay put.

Nay, more, it is literally the work of man's *hands* and dependent on their anatomical structure. For if man had not retained the pentadactylism of the primitive amphibian stock, he would certainly not have adopted a *decimal* system of arithmetic. Now, most of the other mammals have *reduced* the number of their fingers and toes, the pig to two, the ass to one. Had, therefore, a learned pig invented arithmetic his scale would presumably have been 4 or 8—just as in man the 'score' and '*quatrevingts*' still bear witness to a scale of 20, which was probably voted down on account of the inconvenience of sitting down to count one's toes as well as one's fingers. But it was a disaster for arithmetic (as for piano-playing) that a six-fingered race did not prevail. For 12 would have been a much better scale than 10, as the inventors of the 'dozen' and the 'gross' perceived. The empirical and accidental origin, then, of our scale of notation is too clear for further words.

CHAPTER XX

CONCLUSION

1. A new logic ? ; 2. Essentially a logic for use ; 3. How it becomes normative ; 4. A logic, not a metaphysic ; 5. The making of reality not metaphysical ; 6. The nature of metaphysics ; 7. The personal aspect of metaphysics ; 8. The nature of voluntarism.

§ 1. A New Logic?

May we claim to have succeeded in sketching the outlines of a new logic? This is not a claim which will be easily allowed. For despite its complete effeteness the devotees of Formal Logic are apt to argue, in the same breath, that as nothing novel can be true and nothing true can be novel, innovations in logic are either not true or not novel. So they make believe that nothing has happened—since Aristotle's day, or Hegel's.[1] Or, when reluctantly forced to face the facts by some glaring innovation like Darwinism or Pragmatism, they still contend that any particular set of innovations is not true in so far as it is novel, and is not novel in so far as it is true, but has been anticipated long ago. And in as much as in the course of a career extending over some 2000 years Formal Logic has caught occasional glimpses even of quite obvious truths, something like a dialectical case may sometimes be made out on its behalf.

Nevertheless, we should not withdraw the claim to have shown the possibility of a new logic. It is new because it is constructed on voluntarist lines, whereas all other logics hitherto have been more or less deeply, even if never quite consistently, committed to intellectualism. It is new because it is based, in principle, on a description of the concrete procedure of actual knowing, and expressly repudiates the abstraction from personality which Formal Logic has always practised and prescribed to all science. It openly rests on personal meaning, purposive thought, freedom of choice between alternatives, desires, postulates and

[1] Not that they really accept Hegel's innovations or understand them, as H. V. Knox has very neatly shown in *The Will to be Free*, chap. xxiv.

interests, hazardous selection, probable reasoning, and unending verification—all of them procedures which Formal Logic declared nefarious or impossible. It eschews as illusory the notions of verbal meaning, purity, certainty, necessity, validity, and coercion.

Yet it contrives to give quite a straightforward and intelligible account of how we carry on the business of thinking, and actually start and conclude our trains of thought. This account is fully as systematic and coherent as any sort of Formal Logic, while it is a great deal more useful, and even develops normative corollaries as definite as any which could be extracted from the old logic, and far more applicable.

§ 2. Essentially a Logic for Use.

Moreover, this relation to use is not merely accidental but essential. Voluntarist logic is systematic and coherent and normative, *because* it is useful. It repudiates the false abstractions of intellectualism, which takes meaning, truth, and use to be three quite different conceptions, simply because they are verbally distinct, and is at a loss to understand how any *connexion* can be traced between them. Because it fails to see that meaning, truth, and use are bound up together, and function together in our knowing, it separates meaning from truth and from application (use), formal truth from real, 'pure' science from applied, and commits itself to meaningless 'truth' (truism), useless 'knowledge,' worthless 'science,' and purposeless (blind) necessity (Chap. I, § 2).

But the genuine, whole, unmutilated truth is useful, because it is true to life and faithful to fact. Its usefulness for human purposes, moreover, is what confers on it the systematic coherence which Formalism professes to value to the exclusion of all other functions. For life tends to be a system of purposes which is the more unified the higher is the living intelligence that moulds the system, not because formal coherence has any intrinsic value, but because its coherence is the formal aspect of a vital harmony.

Use, similarly, determines meaning; our mental operations,

beliefs, words, and symbols all get their significance from the uses to which they are put.

Lastly, use determines value ('truth'); for it is their applications ('working') which *sift* the valuable ('true') from the worthless ('false'), discriminate the real from the formal, and continuously improve our truths.

Voluntarist logic renders itself further useful by giving up the traditional restriction to valid reasoning and the claim to absolute proof. As valid reasoning and absolute proof do not actually occur at all, this restriction was enough to render a logic useless. But a logic which admits probable reasoning thereby becomes relevant to the great masses of scientific inquiry which Formalism ignored or condemned, because they made no pretence of 'validity' (Chap. III, § 12).

§ 3. How Logic becomes Normative.

The logician, then, should not scorn actual reasoning but observe it, alike in the sciences and in practical life. He should study it, without arrogance, in the spirit of a learner, observing alike its successes and its failures, and trying to discover the reasons for them. He should not attempt to sit in judgment on life and the sciences, to lay down the law, and to prescribe rigid canons of right reasoning which he has excogitated irrespective of what is practically possible. For the facts of actual reasoning are the only source from which the principles of right reasoning can safely be derived. They are not known prior to experience, and must be verified by their applications to experience.

Initially, then, the logician is an observer of actual knowing. But he soon becomes more than this. For if he is unbiased and intelligent, he is the sort of observer who sees points in the game which escape those actually engaged upon it. He is not so completely absorbed by it that he cannot be critical, not so completely immersed in it that he can see nothing further. He can, therefore, make comparisons and generalisations, and evaluate processes and results.

Thereupon he naturally develops *preferences* for some of the actually observed procedures as against others, and is able to give reasons for his preferences. Thus his 'theory' of actual knowing does not remain merely descriptive: it begins to discriminate between *better* methods and *worse*, and in various ways to *value*.

He also becomes able to give *advice* to those engaged in actual knowing. His advice will be tentative and deferential, rather than imperative, and couched in terms like: 'Of course, you know all the facts, and may therefore have good reasons, whose weight I cannot estimate, for doing as you do; but don't you think that your methods here might be simplified, and there might take account of such and such alternative possibilities, and there again might try such and such analogies and hypotheses which have proved successful elsewhere?' Thus the logician, not being, like the specialist, restricted to a single science in his outlook, may be able to proffer *good* advice, worth taking, and even the expert may find it useful.

Up to a point, therefore, Logic will be normative, and able to prescribe improvements in cognitive procedure, even though it will not attempt to *enforce* them. For it will admit that the final judgment on their value must be delivered, not by the logician, but by the expert whose function it is to apply them, and to test them by their working. Thus the logician will be precisely in the position of the moralist who advises the moral agent as to what considerations are relevant to his case, without presuming to decide his case for him, or to assume the responsibility for his act. The Formal logician, on the other hand, will resemble the casuist who falsely claimed to have devised an authoritative code mechanically able to decide on every moral problem (Chap. XIX, § 1). In this way, then, voluntarist logic is, very genuinely, a normative science (Chap. III, § 11).

§ 4. A Logic not a Metaphysic.

It is a genuine logic also in that it is *not* a metaphysic. That is, it does not require to take refuge in metaphysics to extricate itself from logical embarrassments, and to render its doctrines intelligible, tenable, and valuable. Neither is it inwardly devoured by any hidden ambition covertly to establish some metaphysical creed about ultimate reality. All it aims at is to expound how we know and how we might improve the operations we call knowing. It does not profess to reveal the innermost secret of existence; but neither does it confess to dependence upon anterior knowledge of this secret. Its account of cognitive operation is free to all the world: anyone may use it, whether a philosopher, scientist, or practical man, provided he is willing to respect the procedure of actual knowing. It is essentially a simple common-sense doctrine.

Our 'voluntarism,' therefore, means nothing more than a willingness to abstain from the vicious abstractions of intellectualism, and to adopt a description of the knowing process which does not ignore its active, purposive, and personal character. These abstractions it regards as wanton and quite unnecessary, while the appeal of intellectualist logic to metaphysics is mere superfluity of naughtiness.

Yet a mind corrupted by metaphysics is apt to see metaphysics everywhere, and therefore takes as metaphysical the logical implication of Pragmatic, that is Scientific, Method which is known as the Making of Reality.

§ 5. The Making of Reality not Metaphysical.

It was admitted in Chap. VII, § 11, that a twofold relation was implicit in truth. It was not only truth *for* some one, but also truth *about* something. It implies both a knower and an object known, and the latter is revealed, while the former is instructed, by the knowing process. Thus *the Real-we-know* grows *pari passu* with the 'truth,' that is the 'right' and valuable relation to it, which 'apprehends' it.

But at first sight it would seem as though the changes thus induced in the object were merely subjective. The Real-for-us is clearly altered as our knowledge grows, and it is important that we should note how great may be the changes thus effected, but the real-as-it-is-in-itself is not, surely, altered by this process. Common sense at any rate seems to believe in objects that are utterly unaffected by our knowing, and do not alter as our knowledge of them grows.

These considerations form the most plausible objection to the humanist 'making of reality,' and to meet them we shall have to inquire carefully what is meant both by 'the real as it is in itself,' and by 'the making of reality.'

Now, it need not be disputed that for common sense the former phrase has a metaphysical flavour. Common sense is attached to a realist metaphysic, and is not easily persuaded that the facts it appeals to do not require, or even warrant, a metaphysical interpretation. But, if we dissent from common sense on this point, it is at least incumbent on us to explain what other meaning may be given to the distinction between a change in the real-as-known and in the real-in-itself, and how the reference to 'reality' is to be understood if it is not to be metaphysical. Moreover, it will first be necessary to explore the many meanings of the very ambiguous phrase 'the making of reality.'

(1) Commencing with the clearest and most indisputable case, we may point out that in all cognitive process we make the objects of interest and of inquiry. This is, indeed, the first and most indispensable condition of all knowing. For without it there would be no analysing of the flux, and therefore no finding (discovering) of truth or reality. In itself it hardly means more than 'if you will not look you will not see,' but it largely accounts for the persistence of differences of opinion among men. For what is real and true for us depends on our selecting interests: the answers we get follow from the questions we put.

(2) Even, therefore, where we say we have 'discovered' the real, meaning the real-as-it-is-for-us, we have made it real by directing our attention upon it selectively. For it has become real for us only when we have taken it in. It is no use objecting that it only *seems* different then, for if it seems different it really is different: the change in the appearance to us is a real one. This holds even in cases where, after discovery, we antedate the reality and declare that it existed before. For we may feel the effects before we know the cause. Radium, for example, heated up the rocks for ages before it was discovered, and miners felt the effect without knowing the cause. That is, man's 'real

world' contained an X, which the discovery *really* altered into 'radium.'

(3) Thereby the discovery changed us and altered our attitude. New truth always makes a difference to us. It enlightens us. And in altering us it alters reality. The world is not what it was now we know that radium exists. Our new knowledge is a new fact which may initiate important changes in the real.

(4) For when we change our psychic attitude we are apt to change our acts. Real knowledge does not lie idle—it colours our life. We act on it, and act differently. So reality is altered, not only *in* us but *through* us.

(5) For we have real, though limited, power over the real world, and can alter it. We have, in fact, brought about great changes in those parts of it which directly concern us in the last 10,000 years, and these changes are man-made and a fruit of human knowledge. For real knowledge is power over reality, and means control of events. Though our power is limited, intelligent use of it enables us to get what we want to a greater extent than is usually recognised. Thus we cannot, in general, change the weather (except in so far as deforesting and draining affect the climate), but we can largely avoid its effects on us. If we object to getting wet when it rains, we can stay at home under a rain-proof roof, or take out an umbrella. If we dislike the winter's cold or the summer's heat we can go south, or go up into the mountains. And it seems unwise to discourage human enterprise by asserting *a priori* that certain desirable ends can never be attained.

(6) The next sense of making reality springs from our ability to operate variously and to elicit variable responses from the real. We find that there are in the world beings which are spiritually responsive to our acts and purposes. Hence in our dealings with them we can make reality by treating them variously, or even by making them aware of our existence. A mere expression of our feeling will often change their actions. A declaration of love or hate or war will modify their reactions and perhaps their nature. Nay, social beings are so sensitive that mere suspicions and anticipations of our knowledge will

modify them. Many, for example, grow 'shy' in the presence of strangers, others 'show off.' Both behave differently in public and in private, even though they may be mistaken in thinking that they are (or are not) observed. Generalising, then, in dealing with social beings which recognise us as friends or foes, what we think and know about them really alters their behaviour, and, so far, reality.

The reason is, of course, that they assume that our knowledge is *not inactive*. If it were mere 'contemplation' no one would care. A spectator of events who never intervened would be a negligible quantity, like the 'gods' of Epicurus or the philosophic 'Absolutes.'

How far down the scale of being does this sensitiveness extend? Certainly far into the animal world. The higher animals all normally behave as hunters or as prey, and they change at once when they either perceive or are perceived. Even a beetle has been observed to 'sham dead' twice, within three minutes, in two quite different ways. When taken up by hand it curled itself up, when seized by a toad it spread out all its legs stiffly, so that the toad dropped it as an unpalatable object.[1]

(7) By extending this conception of a sensitiveness to knowledge a little further, we can say that inanimate objects also are responsive to each other, and modify their behaviour accordingly. A stone is not indifferent to other stones. On the contrary, it is attracted by every material body in the physical world. By our bodies among the rest. Of course, we are only recognised on our physical side, as bodies like the stone, and not in our whole nature. But the stone responds, after its fashion, to our manipulation. Treat them differently, and they behave differently: that is as true of stones as of men.

This sense of making reality is important, because it enables us to project the process indefinitely into the cosmic past. We can conceive the past interactions of the world's constituents to have been similar to the present, and so to have gradually shaped the reals we now acknowledge, as they settled down into the

[1] *Nature*, No. 2200, p. 191.

habits of action we now call the 'laws of nature' (Chap. XVIII, § 17). The recognition of the world's past history and still continuing evolution, which we thus achieve, is certainly realistic; perhaps as realistic as any which common sense requires. But it need not be taken as an ultimate metaphysic, for two reasons. In the first place, it does not refer to any real which transcends the knowing process, and makes no attempt to determine what the real may be 'in itself.' Secondly, the real it refers to remains epistemological and subject to the pragmatic proviso that it is, and must remain, a factor in the most satisfactory account we can give of our experience.

Now, as an item in such an account this real is not quite satisfactory. For if we regard all the determinate qualities and laws of nature now acknowledged as acquired by the past interactions of the real and as acquired in consequence of acts, experiments, and interests which have rendered determinate its initial indetermination, are we not finally referred to an original chaos, out of which our present world-order has evolved? And are we not driven to ask unanswerable questions about the original chaos from which our reality is descended?

(8) This, however, brings us up against an eighth sense of making reality, in which 'make'='create' or 'make out of nothing,' and a sense which it seems too presumptuous for any human philosophy or logic to expound. But, though it cannot be expounded, it can be disavowed, and declared irrelevant to human knowing and the seven sorts of 'making reality' which can be traced in it. *No* philosophy or science can really explain how everything arose out of nothing, and none should be required to do so. We may, indeed, have to admit the reality of 'creation,' in the shape of 'novelty,' which, *qua* new, arises out of nothing (Chap. XVI, § 6). But this sort of creation is never absolute, and obviously remains immanent in the knowing process.

So, clearly, do the real-objects-we-know, even when we conceive them as having existed æons before ever we were born. The seventh way of 'making reality' entitles us to say so. If common sense demurs, it must respectfully be asked what it can mean by a 'real as it is in itself,' and how it can conceivably be known, or known to correspond to the known reals it deals with? Until an answer is forthcoming (as it has never been), the 'real as it is in itself' must be pronounced void and meaningless.

Even though we can thus dismiss the real in itself, we have still to explain the difference between 'making' and 'finding' the real-objects-we-know. It may be pointed out that this distinction is (a) not absolute, and (b) pragmatic.

(a) 'Finding' real does not exclude 'making' real. The most real object we acknowledge had first to be made an object of thought by our selection. No 'fact' is a fact till it is taken as fact. It is only after this that it can so behave that we repudiate responsibility for it and prefer to say we did not make it but 'discovered' what was there all along. Our reasons for this distinction are pragmatic. A real that is 'found' behaves differently from one that is 'made' (Chap. XIX, § 3).

(b) Pragmatic also are our reasons for attributing reality to any object, alike whether we antedate it when found or not. 'Reality,' which is in the last resort a value (Chap. III, § 2), is attributed to objects because, and so far as, and so long as, they yield satisfactory methods for handling our experience. This is true of every sort of reality and of all our knowing; but of the changes we effect in our knowledge some only are credited to a contributory (often called 'independent') activity of the objects known. If they are such that they can object to our manipulations,[1] they are likely to be accorded this rank. But only because it works better to rank them thus; in ultimate analysis our reasons all remain pragmatic, and do not rise to a metaphysical level.

§ 6. The Nature of Metaphysics.

Even if they did, this would hardly be conducive to final agreement. For there is a dispute of long standing about the nature of metaphysics. Philosophers have never been able to decide whether metaphysics was to be the name for the *first* or for the *last* of the sciences. Is it, (1) as Plato thought, the supreme

[1] Cp. J. Dewey, *Human Nature and Conduct*, p. 91.

science of the Good from which all the rest depend, like the gods of the Homeric pantheon all dangling from the hands of Zeus, the ultimate source from which they derive their certainty and value? Or (2) is it the science of the *final synthesis* of the sciences which moulds them into a concordant whole? In view of its actual achievements both claims had to be toned down. So the first was moderated into the belief that metaphysics is at any rate an independent science with methods and standards of its own; while the second was reduced to the science of *ultimate problems* which remain over to be considered when the other sciences have done their work.

It is clear that these views indicate three conceptions of the relation of metaphysics to the sciences. The Platonic makes the sciences dependent on metaphysics; the second makes each independent of the other; the third makes metaphysics dependent on the sciences—at any rate in the sense that it has to accept and utilise the knowledge which they provide.

In point of value it is quite clear that the Platonic theory is wrong: it is refuted by the history of the sciences. Their progress would have been impossible if they had really been dependent on metaphysics for their principles.

The second theory has the drawback that if it were true it would introduce an ultimate dualism into the nature of knowledge: metaphysical truth and scientific truth would have nothing to do with each other. Moreover, the history of metaphysics hardly seems to warrant the belief that metaphysics has, in fact, an independent method: at all events, its adepts have never been able to discover it or to agree about it.

The third theory, on the other hand, which has been hinted at already (Chap. I, § 16), fits in well with all the empirical facts. It puts metaphysics into vital relation with all the sciences, and awards to it a definite and imperishable task, at which it may continue to labour, however imperfectly it is achieved. It is a conception which must strongly commend itself to any empirical and scientific philosophy.

Its only drawback, if such it be, is that upon this theory there cannot be a *final* metaphysic until knowing ends, because until

then the sciences may continue to elaborate new truths which
cry out to be included in our final synthesis. But this drawback
only attests the homogeneity of knowledge: metaphysics shares
it with all other knowledge. There is no final truth, because
there is no absolute truth, and all truth continues to progress.

All our ultimate syntheses, therefore, must be provisional and
temporary. But this should really be an encouragement to
metaphysicians; it should stimulate them to go on trying to
perfect their syntheses and to keep their metaphysics up to date.
Their position really resembles that of the historians, who can
never run short of materials for new histories, because the
course of events is ever flowing on, and providing them with
new *data* and new points of view.

It should further be emphasised that it is only by adopting
this conception of the function of metaphysics that we can hope
either to render philosophy effectively all-inclusive or to give
it the necessary authority to harmonise the sciences.

We have seen repeatedly [1] that the professions of all-inclusiveness made by the various intellectualistic absolutisms were,
in fact, illusory, because they had to select, despite themselves,
and to exclude great sections of the real on some pretext or
other, lest they should make their Absolute a rag-bag. If, on
the other hand, we assign to metaphysics the task of co-ordina-
ting and harmonising the results of the sciences, it is clear that
no scientific knowledge can be left out of its synthesis. Nor is
there anything to prevent our assigning to it also the duty of
including and accounting for everything else that has a claim
to be part of experience or reality.

For upon this conception, and this alone, it will have the
authority to co-ordinate and subordinate all knowledge in whatever way seems to it most expedient and best. So long as metaphysics professed to be a higher sort of knowledge and claimed
superiority over the sciences, or insisted on a futile 'independence,' it could be granted no authority over scientific truth.
But now that it is willing to acknowledge the use and value of
such truth and to subscribe to the unity of knowledge, it may

[1] Cp. Chap. XV, § 15 ; II, § 11 *n.* ; V, § 7 ; XI, § 15 *n.*

do science an essential service. It may be used to extricate the sciences from an apparently serious predicament in which their method has involved them. The sciences have grown up in virtue of the right they have successfully asserted of making whatever selections from the real they found most interesting and whatever assumptions they found most serviceable: this freedom has been most conducive to their prosperity and progress. But it is evident that this procedure will not offer any guarantee that their results will be *concordant*; on the contrary, it would border upon the miraculous if, as the result of each going on its own way heedless of the rest, they should all be found spontaneously to meet together in the end.

The final synthesis of their results, therefore, becomes a necessary task: but it is a task which no special science can rightly undertake, although, in point of fact, attempts have often been made to expand the conceptions of the dominant science of an age, now mathematics, now physics, now biology, etc., into an explanation of all reality. But if we assign to metaphysics the task of drawing the conclusions from all knowledge, this harmonising of the sciences may properly be left to it: just because it is dependent on all, it may be trusted to do justice to all. And just because the sciences are so independent of each other, metaphysics must be granted extensive rights of reinterpretation, in order that a final synthesis may be feasible. Thus its initial dependence on the sciences paves the way to its final superiority.

§ 7. The Personal Aspect of Metaphysics.

Metaphysics, therefore, rightly understood, must be given the power to reconsider, tamper with, and modify even the most fundamental abstractions and assumptions of the sciences.

Among these the abstraction from personality ranks very high. We have repeatedly referred to it,[1] and contended that it should be understood methodologically, i.e. interpreted as meaning, not that science has no use for the individual, but that it is precisely in order that one individual case may not exercise a disturbing effect upon the calculation of another that its indi-

[1] Cp. Chap. IV, §§ 15, 17 ; VI, § 6 ; XVIII, §§ 13, 18.

viduality is seemingly abstracted from, and that scientific 'law' is based upon such abstraction or upon a statistical average. We argued, also, that philosophers were mistaken in understanding this procedure as a *denial* that science dealt with individual cases. The intellectualists among them, however, had a personal interest in making this mistake. It chimed in with the divorce they had proclaimed between 'pure' science and applied. If this could be maintained, there would be no reference to cases involved in a pure science at all. And, conversely, the logical contemplation of a pure science would justify their doctrine that science had no use for the individual.

But it was foolish for scientists to assent to this philosophic dogma, than which nothing has done more deadly harm to science. The meaning of a science is *not* to be divorced from its applications, but to be illustrated by them, and the meaning of Scientific Method is destroyed when these are abstracted from. Hence a revision or reinterpretation of the abstraction from personality is really the salvation of science. It is essential to its *use*.

Science, however, cannot undertake it, because it cannot stultify its method. But just because it cannot, metaphysics must. Metaphysics, moreover, has more than one reason for restoring personality. (1) In the first place, it has the duty of making its synthesis all-inclusive. Now personality is a fact, and a fact of the utmost importance. For it pervades all knowing, and affects the results of knowing very subtly and to a far greater extent than either scientists or philosophers have usually realised. Even, therefore, if we regard its influence as dangerous (as it may be), it is important that it should be recognised.

(2) Metaphysics has a special interest in recognising the function of personality. Not only has it to include the personal *data* in its total synthesis, but it has to draw the principles on which its syntheses proceed, the skeleton which holds together every metaphysical system, from the personality of individual metaphysicians. The truth is, that metaphysics are far more than logical systems. In the last resort every genuine and heart-felt metaphysic is a *poem*, and derives its unity and æsthetic

appeal from the personal vision and imagination of its 'maker'
or poet.

(3) A perception of this fact is the vindication also of the
history of philosophy. It renders comprehensible *and rational*
the endless succession of systems and the lack of agreement
and finality about them. Every metaphysic differs from every
other, because it presupposes different *data*. To the common
stock of knowledge each adds, as in duty bound, the personal
data derived from its maker's personal experience. It is these
which bind together and transfigure the scientific *data* and effect
the final synthesis.

Thus, to the end of time, it will be the true philosopher's
duty and privilege to add up the sum of knowledge and to
launch upon a wondering world his individual guess at total
truth. His verdict must be personal, as now; but none the less
it will reverberate in other heads, and perpetually incite to
further efforts. Could a nobler function be ascribed to metaphysical philosophy?

§ 8. The Nature of Voluntarism.

It is imperative, however, to arm oneself with a philosophy
that will sanction such ambitions, and this is why a voluntarist
logic is a presupposition not only of every sane theory of knowledge but of every enterprising metaphysic. It begins as a sober
proposal to recognise at last the cognitive activities of man as a
whole in their unmutilated integrity, and as a protest, far too
long delayed, against the verbalisms, vicious abstractions, futile
fictions, and conventions which have long lost what meaning
they ever had, and have made of 'logic' a bugbear or a laughing-
stock. Its aim is to bring back logic from its long captivity in
Cloud-Cuckoodom into touch with human life and human
science and the interest we take in knowing. It is a logic for
everyday use, and not merely for the obscene initiation rites of
the philosopher who is 'no philosopher,' until he has been
mutilated and defecated into a 'pure intellect.'

But it has a message even for the aspirant to philosophy. For
it is a charter of freedom for the philosophic imagination,

emancipating it from its long thraldom to a sterilising intellectualism. It gives him the right to try alternatives, to experiment freely, to run risks, and, if he has it in him, to win the inestimable prize of a philosophy that satisfies to the full the demands of his whole soul. At present most of our philosophies are spiritual misfits, just because their authors in constructing them either do not dare to draw on their personal experience or disguise and distort the contributions they obtain from this most copious source.

INDEX

Absolute, The, 14, 25, 84, 144, 183, 237, 238, 378, 447.
  a chaos, 18, 183.
  a rag-bag, 86, 233, 316, 451.
  as protection against error, 15, 17.
  as referred to by Judgment, 231 f.
  error in, 181-2.
  fails to unify, 309.
Absolute Thought, 133, 240.
Absolutism, *Ch. I*, §*15*, 59 *n.*, 451.
  discredits Judgment, 231 f.
Abstraction, *Ch. XVIII*, §*12*, 408.
  from individuality, 404.
  from personality, 2, 14, 374, 440, 452.
  of Formal Logic, *Ch. II*, §*17*.
  of intellectualism, 444.
  true and false, 407.
Accident fallacies, 276-7.
Act, 38, 191, 214.
  of faith, 130, 135.
Action, 3, 51, 131 *n.*, 198, 218, 241, 242, 246, 248, 338, 346, 396-7.
  as test of belief, 171, 173.
  as test of truth, *Ch. XIX*, §*6*.
  impulsive, 195, 198, 205.
  rational, 197-8.
  reflective, 204.
  reflex, 194-5.
Activity, 94, 102, 320, 345, 354, 389, 433.
Actual Knowing, Actual Thinking, 27, 30, *Ch. II*, §§*18, 19*, *Ch. III*, §*11*, 50, 192, 193, 238, 243, 261, 263, 284, 314, 442, 444.
  experimental, 190.
  selective, 234 f.
  teleological, 190, 240.
Adaptations, 194, 204.
Addition, 433, 435.
Advances, 267, 286, 294.
Æsthetics, 36, 40, 42, 100, 111.

All-inclusiveness, 73, 75, 182, 451.
Alternatives, 66, 82, 90, 93, 111, 138, 148, 199, 203, 244, 253, 300, 305, 306, 324, 333, 357-8, 361-3, 399, 410, 440, 443, 455.
Ambiguity, 8, 265, 399.
  of good, 103.
  of language, 32, 57.
  of Middle Term, 251, 261, 264, 273, *Ch. XIV*, §*4*, 279, 281, *Ch. XV*, §*4*.
  real and potential, 9, 58, 63, 214, 322.
  verbal, 9, 214.
Amphioxus, 206, 259.
Analogy, 199, 262, 287, 313, *Ch. XVI*, §*13*, 349, 361-2, 375, 385, 407, 414, 428.
Analysis, 199-200, 215, 220, 279, 341, 342.
Animal Faith, 157, 161.
Animism, 50, 375.
Anthropomorphism, 414.
Antisthenes, 223.
Application, 31-2, 158, 275, 278, 292, 309, *Ch. XIX*, §*14*.
A priori necessities of thought, 53.
  prediction, 113.
  truths, 194, 353, 357.
Argument in a circle, 12 *n.*, 300 f., *Ch. XV*, §*10, 11*, 307, 316.
  why fallacious, *Ch. XV*, §*10*.
Aristotle, 4, 7, 10, 19, 103 *n.*, 120, 126, 148, 215, 219, 241, 270, 272, 278, 287, 288, 295, 296, 300, 301, 322, 353, 355, 391, 420, 421, 438, 440.
Atoms, 22, 132 *n.*, 329, 382.
Attitude, 38, 50, 102, 162, 218, 388, 391.
Average, statistical, 244, 453.
Axioms, 160, *Ch. VIII*, §*14*, 163, 329, 341, 358, 432.

Bacon, F., 13, 91.

Baldwin, J. M., 76 n.

Beatific Vision, 221, 242.

Behaviourism, 38, 306.

Bergson, H., 327, 341.

Bias, 324-5, 351, 362, 365, 378, 396.

Bismarck, 196.

Bosanquet, B., 13, 14, *Ch. XI, §14*, 230, 233.

Bradley, F. H., 6, 12, 14, 17, 65, 101 n., 133 n., 154, 157 n., 181, *Ch. XI, §§15-6*, 238, 247 n., 265.

Brain-development, 196, 369.

Browning, R., 392.

Butler, J., 334.

Case, 52, 71, 91-2, 198, 209, 223-4, 270, 275, 290, 292, 298 f., 323, 326, 347, 349, 382, *Ch. XVIII, §18*.

Case Law, 417.

Cassandra, 96, 122 n.

Casuistry, 278, *Ch. XIX*.

Categorical Imperative, 416-7.

Category, 113, 364, 406, 409.

Causation, Cause, 53, 91, 163, 306, 343, 409.
mnemic, 371-2.

Certainty, 245, 287, 296-7, 332.
a false ideal, 281.
intuitive, 128.
not absolute, 31.
practical, 33, 335, 351, 397.
psychological, 350, 397.

Chamberlain, Sir A., 6.

Chance, 306, 333, 335-6.

Change, 10, 237, 326, 332.
right to, 181.
salutary, 204-5.

Choice, 70, 79, 82, 91, 92, 104, 125, 135, 138, 169, 170, 286, 293, 299, 302, 303, 308, 323, 344, 440.

Classification, 403, *Ch. XVIII, §13*.

Coercion, 120 f., 125, 271, 273, 287, 303, 441.

Cogency, 79, *Ch. XIV, §2*.

Cohen, M. R., 362.

Coherence, as proof, *Ch. XV, §8*.
discredits sciences, 310-11.
ends in scepticism, *Ch. VII, §18*.
logical and psychological, 138-9, 248.
self-contradictory, *Ch. VII, §17*.
theory of truth, *Ch. VII, §§12-4*, 132.

Commands, 117, 201, 218.

Common Sense, 276, 284, 444-5.
realism, 383-4.
world, 384.

Concepts, 215, 218, 344.

Conclusion, implies doubt, 245.
more certain than premisses, 359, 361.
must come true, 261, 280, 349.
must not lose truth, 288.

Consequences, as test of truth, *Ch. VIII, §22*, 185, 203, 232, 240, 268, 282, 423, 425-6.

Conservatives, 140-1, 310, 324, *Ch. XVI, §4*, 379.

Contemplation, 67, 110, 139, 241, 447.

Context, 8, 11, 17, 24, 28, 29, 31, 49, 63, 72, *Ch. IV, §18*, 108, 158, 177, 192, 193, 208, 223, 236, 239, 246, 249, 250, 255-6, 285, 292, 380, 419, 433, 434, 435.

Contradiction, 72, 85, 329.
in Absolute, 85.
in Plato, 179-80.
no test, 133 n.
not false, 318, 381.
self-contradiction, 29, 177, 188, 318, 382.
verbal, 177, 382.

Control, 51 f., 96, 381, 396, 409, 426.
experimental, 393.
of experience, 426, 430.

Convenience, a criterion of truth 142, 358.
classes a, 406.

Conversion, false, 157 *n.*, 169.
Copula, 10, 215, 218, 227.
Correspondence, of meaning and
    words, 213.
    theory of truth, *Ch. VIII*, *§8*,
    228, 232.
    its dangers, 131.
    its pragmatic truth, 131, 265.
Counting, 433 f., 438–9.
Courage, 397.
Criterion of truth, *Ch. VI*, *§13*,
    121, 139, 142.

Darwin, C., 412.
Darwinism, 257, 440.
Data, 31, 71, 81, 86, 96, 164, 310,
    410, 411.
    are sumpta, 135, 234, 267, 386.
Deduction, 90, 349, 354, 356–7.
Definition, 9, 12 *n.*, 34.
    of Logic, *Ch. II*.
    of truth, *Ch. VIII*, *§7*.
De Laguna, G. A., 60 *n.*
Deliberation, *Ch. X*, *§11*, 204, 217.
Democritus, 370.
Demonstration, 83, 270.
    mathematical, 299.
Descartes, R., 374, 426.
Designation, 11.
Desire, 338, 354, 409, 440.
    for truth, 146, 331.
    to know, 149, 270, 320.
Determinism, 48, 244, 344, 399.
Dewey, J., 155, 449.
Dialectic, 120, 172, 240, 269, 422.
Discovery, 152, 270, 356.
    and proof, *Ch. XVI*, *§§1, 2, 7*.
    prior to proof, 321.
Doubt, *Ch. VIII*, *§23*, 200, 202,
    245, 279, 280, 322, 392,
    400.
Dream, 132, 226, 297, 374, 384,
    411.

Einstein, 16, 142, 347, 359, 412.
Eleatics, 327.
Elijah, 423.
Emotion, *Ch. XVIII*, *§4*.
Empiricism, 71, 128, 356.

Epicurus, 447.
Epimenides, 63.
Equivocations, 213–4.
Error, 15, 23, 25, 28, 42, 54, 78,
    79, 85, 110, 111, 114, 146,
    160, 166–7, 173, *Ch. IX*,
    224, 233, 266, 285, 362,
    370–1, 401, 417.
    as approximation to truth, 187.
    as coherent, 138, 139, 304.
    as demanding self-correction,
    180.
    as relative to purpose and use,
    177, 184.
    as relative to truth, 175.
    as requiring distinction of
    persons, 180.
    degrees of, 231.
    how distinguished from truth,
    Ch. IX, *§1*.
    necessary, 187.
    suppressed in idealism, 182–3.
Essence, *Ch. II*, *§§2, 3*, 77, 80,
    156–7, 203, 274.
Essential, as indispensable, 23.
    as verbal, 22.
Ethics, 36, 42, 100, 101, 278,
    416–7.
Euclid, 142, 177, 356, 357, 358,
    363, 367, 407, 412, 430.
Evaluation, 34–5.
    of data, 104.
Evidence, 401–2, 411.
Evil, 85, 182.
Experience, 218, 321, 338, 357,
    384, 409, 431, 433, 436–7,
    Ch. XIX, *§18*.
Experiment, 149, 282, 293, 295,
    317, 321, 363, 365, *Ch.
    XVIII*, *§§2, 7*, 401.
    in thought, 190.
External World, 194.

Fact, 36, 80–1, 82, 90, 92, 98, 299,
    326, 363, *Ch. XVII*, *§7*,
    Ch. XVIII, *§1*, 400–1.
    as basis for induction, 272, 299.
    as elastic, 399.
    as faked, 299, 354, 364.

Fact, as initial and terminal, 135.
  as relative to us, 136, *Ch. XVII*, *§7*.
  as selected, 354, 392, 395.
  as statistical, 404.
  as suspect, 362.
  crude, 410.
  for a purpose, 91.
  isolated, 140, 310.
  not absolute, 134 f., 272, 354.
  real, 135, 332, 411.
  real fact a value, *Ch. III*, *§3*, 154, 449.
Failure, in error and lie, 166, 184, 188.
  in falsity, 117, 147.
Fallacy of Division, 180.
Fichte, J., 376.
Fiction, 27, 56, 102, 160, 164, *Ch. VIII*, *§17*, 168, 173, 214, 220, 241, 251, *Ch. XIII*, *§4*, 258, *Ch. XVII*, *§7*, 275, 279, 345, 354, 374, 381, *Ch. XVIII*, *§14*, 426.
Fixity of Terms, 26, 28, 56, 281, 382.
Flewelling, R. T., v.
Formal Logic, Formalism, 12, 13, 26, 29, 30, 53, 64, 65, 80, 83, 97, 105, 120, 139, 158, 165, 167, 176, 177, 250, 251, 259 f., 269, 273, 275, 281–3, 303, 322, 350, 380, 440–2.
  abstracts from personality, 167, 180, 266.
  abstracts from time, 419–20.
  a game, 24, *Ch. II*, *§§11, 17*, 282.
  ambiguous, 27.
  a pseudo-science, 344.
  assumptions of, 26, 28.
  confuses truth and truth-claim, 27, 208.
  defined, 29.
  fails to coerce, 73.
  felo de se, 86.
  ignores relevance, 82.
  is meaningless, 50, 209, 293.
  is verbal, 118, 382.

Formal Logic, its *lacunæ*, *Ch. IV*, *§1*.
  misinterprets novelty, 326.
  obstructs research, 402.
Flux, 96, 343.
France, Anatole, 197.

Galileo, 141.
Gambetta, L., 196.
Gauss, 432.
Geometry, 127, 142, 310, 357–8, 429, 430, 431, 432, 437.
Ghosts, 394.
Good, 148, 154, 159, 355–6.
Grammar, vi, 36, 42, 237, 419.

Habit, 194, 195, 197–8, 328, 344 n., *Ch. XVIII*, *§17*.
Hegel, G. W. F., 14, 25 n., 405, 440.
History, *Ch. XIX*, *§7*, 428.
  of mathematics, 428.
  of physics, 311.
Hobbes, T., 426.
Hoernle, R. F. A., 435.
Humanism, vi, 59 n., 157, 160, 167, 169, 171.
Hume, D., 272, 298, 341, 376, 377.
Huygens, C., 313.
Hypothesis, 110, 131, 173, 262, 279, *Ch. XIV*, *§5*, 285, 287, 290, 295, 300, 309, 319, 322, 331, *Ch. XVI*, *§12*, 349, 351, 354, 358 f., 363, 383, *Ch. XVIII*, *§1*, 390, *Ch. XVIII*, *§§8–10*, 404, 407, 408.

Idea, 215–7, 223, 232.
Ideal Theory, 9, *Ch. VII*, *§10*, 156, 225.
Idealisation, *Ch. XVIII*, *§14*.
Idealism, 371.
Identification, 190, 229–30.
  a fiction, 164.
  a risk, 230.
Identity, 168.
  based on irrelevance of differences, 210, 273, 348.
  in difference, *Ch. XI*, *§11*.

Identity, Law of, 251, 254, 255, 257-8, 292, 380-1.
    made by judgment, 229.
    not absolute, 222-3.
    not fact, 110.
    of indiscernibles, 223.
    of terms, 255, 271.
    relative to purpose, 109-10.
    verbal, 28, 81, 273, 285, 291-2.
Imagination, 164, 345, 373, 454.
Imperatives, 208; and see Commands.
Independence, ambiguity of, 136-7.
    a valuation, 137.
    of objects, 131.
    of truth, *Ch. VII*, §*10*, 156.
Indetermination, 425.
Individuality, not unknowable, 405-6.
Induction, 90, 262, 282, 287, *Ch. XV*, §*7*, 319, 323, 330, 349, 354.
    invalid, 297-300.
Inference, 226, 239, *Ch. XII, XIII*.
    as necessary truth, 247.
    immediate, 138.
    logical, 248.
    not good, 262.
    psychological, 247-8.
    'valid,' 48, 247-8, 252, 262, 268, 298.
Infinite, progress, 115, 295, 296.
    regress, 112, 114, 126, 260, 271-2, 296.
    in proof, *Ch. XV*, §*5*.
Inquiry, 123, 139, 147, 172, 187, 191, 193, 200, 242, 342, 361, 364-5, 387, 392, 442.
    'Dispassionate,' 355.
    purposive, 147, 184; see also Question.
Instinct, 194, 412.
Intellect, 103 *n.*, 156.
    pure, 189, 200, 454.
Intellectualism, v, 78, 94, 157, 166, 190, 267, 421, 441, 444, 455.

Intelligence, 51, 57, 190, 197, 360.
Interest, 49, 80, 139, 152, 158, 200-1, 248, 252, 389-90, 441.
Interpretation, 199, 325, 384, 385, 411, 412, 414.
Interrogatives, 208.
Intuition, 112, *Ch. VII*, §*7*, 272, 330, 353, 361.
    a claim, 128.
    false and true, 127.
    psychic fact, 128.
    to save syllogism ?, *Ch. XV*, §*6*.
Intuitionism, 126, 128, 260, 272.
Irrelevance, 25, 78, 80, 87, 90, 403.
    a postulate, 342.

James, W., 158 *n.*, 212, 339, 340, 377, 421.
Jervis-Smith, F., 152.
Jevons, W. S., 346.
Joachim, H. H., 157 *n.*, 181.
Joke, 29, 160, *Ch. VIII*, §*18*, 317.
    its truth-claim, 166.
Jones, E. E. C., 284.
Judgment, Biologic of, *Ch. X*.
    Formal Theories of, *Ch. XI*.
    relation to Inference, *Ch. XII*.
    aims at object, 119.
    answers question, 111, 155.
    as about Absolute, 15, 17.
    as act, 191, 214, 215.
    as 'ambiguous,' 213.
    as best available, 202.
    as categorical, 245.
    as decision, 201-2.
    as experimental, 244, 268, 285.
    as failure, 248.
    as hypothetical, 244, 268, 285.
    as identity in difference, *Ch. XI*, §*11*.
    as 'infallible,' 178, *Ch. XI*, §*12*.
    as instrument, 217, 221.
    as necessary, 246.
    as particular in application, 243.
    as personal, 180, *Ch. X*, §*12*, 214, 216.
    as potential, 244.

Judgment, as primary, *Ch. XI, §9.*
  as reference to reality, *Ch. XI,*
    §§13–16.
  as related to inference, *Ch. XII,*
    §6.
  as related to perception, *Ch. XI,*
    §10.
  as related to proposition, 177,
    215.
  as selective, 233.
  as success, 248.
  as synthetic, 325.
  as thought-experiment, 217,
    224, 285.
  as value-claim, 202.
  changes meaning of terms, 205.
  error in, 186, 189.
  forerunners of, *Ch. X, §2.*
  has alternatives, 218.
  has central position, *Ch. X, §1.*
  has formal truth-claim, 217,
    219.
  has no universal truth, 17.
  has real meaning and truth, 118.
  has truth as property, *Ch. VII,*
    §2.
  what its universality means,
    243.

Kant, I., 14, 112, 325, 342, 376,
    377, 402, 409, 416, 426,
    433.
Keynes, J. M., 5 *n.,* 46 *n.,* 333.
Knowing, has one method, *Ch.*
    XVI, §1.
  implies truth and error, 191.
  is personal, 146, 185, 379.
  is purposive, 146.
  real, 319, 320.
Knowledge, actual, 421.
  implies sensitive beings, 447.
  ' infallible,' 178–9, 224–5.
  is activity, 320.
  is not ' eternal,' 185.
  is not impersonal, 203.
  is of objects, 227, 237.
  is power, 446.
  is progressive, 169, 185, 206–7,
    261, 294, 381.

Knowledge, is salutary, 205.
  potential, 421.
  pure theoretic, 369.
Knox, H. V., vii, 26 *n.,* 82 *n.,* 388 *n.,*
    440 *n.*

Ladd-Franklin, Mrs, 5.
Language, 379, 382–3.
  accepted by Greeks, *Ch. I,*
    §§8–9.
  as vehicle of meaning, 7, 214.
Law, 51–2, 149, 300, 323–4, 326,
    329, 343–4, 347, 349, 367,
    371, 433.
  of Contradiction, 73, 254, 381.
  of Excluded Middle, 254.
  of Identity, 251, 254, 380–1.
  of Nature, 91, 92, 96, 243, 274,
    330, *Ch. XVIII, §§15–8,*
    420, 448.
  of Thought, 13, 26, 100, 251,
    344, 381, 382.
Lead, 258, 277, 393.
Learning, 258.
Leibniz, 196.
Liar, 64.
Lie, 29, 97, 119, 160, *Ch. VIII,*
    §19, 173, 188.
  is failure, 166.
  is man-made truth, 167, 430.
  is volitional, 166.
Light, 313, 399.
Lobachevsky, 172, 432.
Locke, 130.
Lodge, Sir O., 407.
Logic, of adventure, 83, 86.
  of desire, 338.
  of discovery, *Ch. XVI, §2,* 362.
  of real knowing, 293.
  of science, 361.
  of tradition, 83, 86.
  of values, 78.
  of voluntarism, 94, 267, 339,
    345, 379, *Ch. XX, §§2, 4.*
  a bugbear, *Ch. I, §5,* 454.
  a handmaid of metaphysics,
    Ch. I, §13.
  a word-game, *Ch. I, §6.*
  or many, *§12,* 264.

Logic, as deductive, 82.
  as examinable nonsense, v, vi,
    Ch. I, §*4*, 11.
  as inductive, 82, *Ch. V*, §*9*, 364,
    392, 408.
  as normative science, *Ch. III*,
    §*1*, 98, 100, *Ch. XX*, §*3*.
  as science of thought, 2.
  as symbolic, 56, 206.
  recognises novelty, *Ch. XVI*,
    §*5*.

Mackenzie, J. S., 59 *n*.
Making of Reality, *Ch. XV*, §*5*.
Malthus, 412.
Marshall, H. Rutgers, 378.
Materialism, 414.
Mathematics, 46, 127, 149, 170,
    333–4, 362, 363, *Ch. XVII*,
    §§*2, 3*, *Ch. XIX*, §§*8–15*.
  a game, 428–9, *Ch. XIX*, §§*11–2*.
  applied, 164, 431.
  pure, 164, 337, 357, 408, 431.
Matter, 93, 312, 329, 370.
Meaning, *Ch. IV*.
  abstracted from by Formalism,
    v, 25, 74, 177, 209, 293.
  an attitude, 65, 67, 68.
  a postulate, 53.
  dictionary, 61–2.
  its fixity, 26, 28, 55–7, 213–4,
    255, 258–9, 281, 380.
  its growth, 258–9.
  its plasticity, 56, 216.
  its relation to context, 177,
    255.
  its relation to use, 23, 415, 417,
    441.
  novel, 28, 55–7.
  personal, *Ch. I*, §§*10, 11*, 14, 28,
    53, 54, 60–2, *Ch. IV*, §*11*,
    68, 72, 158, 177, 192, 210,
    266, 277, 280, 282, 379,
    440.
  potential, 216, 414.
  real, 118, 165, 211, 224, 232,
    250, 277, 279, 441.
  ' the,' 11.
  universality of, 67.

Meaning, verbal, 8, 11, 14, 23,
    26–7, 28, 53, 54, *Ch. IV*,
    §*9*, 67, 68, 192, 214.
  does logician mean what he
    says ?, 11–2.
Measurement, never absolute,
    109, 151, 370.
Memory, 131, 188, *Ch. XVII*,
    §*11*.
Metageometry, 142, 431, 437.
Metaphysics, 13 f., 25, 84, 86, 87,
    101, 132, 200, 231, 308,
    313 *n*., 327, 356–7, 383,
    414, *Ch. XX*, §§*4–7*, 454.
  as a final synthesis, 18.
  as a pseudo-science, 18.
Methodological Assumptions, 160,
    Ch. VIII, §*15*, 163, 173,
    292, 349, 381, 414.
Methodological Fictions, 160,
    Ch. VIII, §*16*; and see
    ' Fiction.'
Michelson - Morley, experiment,
    400.
Middle Term, 251, 261, 264, 274,
    279, 281, 282, *Ch. XV*, §*4*.
Mill, J. S., 217, 376, 433.
Mind, 68, 377–8.
  ' contemplative,' 398.
  continuum, 377.
  fusion, 309.
  purposive, 1, 34.
  unit, 138, 154.
  universal, 156.
Monism, selective, 232.
Moore, G. E., 157 *n*.
Moralists, 416, 443.
Murchison, C., 395.

Natural selection, 52, 196, 197,
    340.
Necessity, 48, 54, 139, 441.
  ambiguous, 123, 253.
  as dependence, 246, 337.
  for experiment, 126.
  impersonal, 253.
  logical, 125, 138–9, 247, 250,
    252–4, 254, 255, 257, 262,
    263, 271.

Necessity of thought, 67, 84, 122,
      Ch. VII, §§*4–6*.
   teleological, 253, 271.
Newton, 313.
Nonce Words, 214.
Novelty, 40, 55, 190, 198–9,
      Ch. XIV, §*7*, 284, 306, 310,
      320, 322, *Ch. XVI*, §§*3–6*,
      330, 331, 314, *Ch. XIX*, §*9*.
   creative, 328, 445.
   incalculable, 298.
   psychological, 325.
   ultimate, 327.

Object, 374–5, 433–4, 445.
   as aim of judgment, 119, 188,
      217, 227.
   as claim, 120.
   as formal, 227.
   as unreal, 120, 131.
Objectivism, 77, 183.
Observation, 371, 374, *Ch. XVIII*,
      §*2*, 389, *Ch. XVIII*, §§*5, 7*,
      410.
Omniscience a postulate, 144.
Ontological proof, 84, 380.
Opinion, 99, 178–9, 186, 224–6.
Organic Apparatus, *Ch. XVII*, §*9*.
Organism, selective, 194.

Particularity, 25 *n.*
   correlative of universality, 71.
   unknowable, 69.
Past, 131, 373, 425, 447–8.
Pear, T. H., 372.
Perception, 117, 132, 140, 193,
      215, 218, *Ch. XI*, §*10*, 228,
      246, 348, 372, 384, 403.
   error in, 188.
   selective, 403.
Personal Equation, 371, *Ch.
      XVII*, §*12*.
Personality, 24, 38, 44, 48, 87,
      101, 167, 180–1, 184–5,
      240, 249, 340, 351, 376,
      440, 452–3, *Ch. XX*, §*7*.
Pessimism, 124, 306, 399, 413.
Petitio, 261, 262, 264, 274, 280,
      295, 307, 322, 329.

Plato, 9, 19 *n.*, 69, 133–4, 159, 179,
      180, 183, 225, 227, 272,
      345 *n.*, 353, 355, 357, 359,
      360, 370, 393, 405, 420,
      426, 428, 437, 449.
Plurality, of causes, 399.
   of meaning, 8.
   of senses, 9, 58, 214.
Poetry, 345–6.
Poincaré, H., 432.
Pontius Pilate, 95.
Postulate, 161, 173, 208, 282,
      287, 320, 337, 339, *Ch.
      XVI*, §§*10–11*, 346, 348,
      349, 353, 356, 362, 373,
      381, 385, 399, 408, 409,
      432, 446.
   of meaning, 67, 348.
   of rationality, 124, 201, 265.
Postulation, 31, 50, 117, 138, 160.
Pragmatic test of truth, 2, 243, 423
Pragmatism, 157, 173, 440.
Predicate, *Ch. XI*, §*8*, 218, 231.
Predication, 403.
   a classification, 406.
   an experiment, 200.
Prediction, 52, 96–7, 199, 243,
      255–6, 272, 273, 344, 381,
      395, 409.
Premisses, 33, 83, 233, 245.
   hypothetical, 295, 322, 361.
   true, 271, 279, 281, 288, 330.
Priest of Diana, 187, 352.
Principles of rationality, 201.
   of science, 128, 355–6, 361.
      methodological, 329–30, 363,
      408.
Probability, 31, 46, 82, 114, 121,
      139, 207, 260, 262, 274,
      287, 332, *Ch. XVI*, §§*8–9*,
      351, 401, 441.
Problem, 3, 18, 77, 87, *Ch. VI*,
      §*11*, 117, 135, 147, 175,
      183, 185, 186, 189, 190,
      200, 209, 226, 239, 243,
      258, 270, 282, 320, 337,
      359–62, 364, 405, 418,
      450.
   bad, 187.

Proof, *Ch. XV.*
  its demands, 287–8.
  cumulative, 350–1, *Ch. XVIII,*
    §11.
  as Induction, *Ch. XV, §7.*
  as Intuition, *Ch. XV, §6.*
  as *petitio, Ch. XV, §3.*
  as syllogism, *Ch. XV, §2.*
  as system, *Ch. XV, §§14–6.*
  fool-proof, 321.
  formal, 320–1.
  infinite regress in, *Ch. XV,*
    §5.
  liable to ambiguous middle,
    Ch. XV, §4.
Proposition, 72, 97, 118, 190, 191,
    218, 224, 263, 285, 288,
    289, 303.
  essentially ambiguous, 211.
  form for judging, 210.
  has no absolute truth, 108.
  has only potential meaning,
    118, 209–10, 279.
  has ' terms,' 26.
  has truth in context, 17, 118.
  has truth-claim, *Ch. VII, §2.*
  identity of, 210.
  is not always true, *Ch. XII, §1.*
  is not universally true, 118.
  is self-evident, 272.
  is substituted for judgment, 10,
    12, 17, 23, 54, 177, 192,
    Ch. XI, §2, 215, 232, 237,
    238, 250, 255, 322.
  is vehicle of meaning, 108, 209.
Propositional Function, 118, 414.
Protagoras, 155, 167, 270, 343,
    371.
Proverbs, 439.
Pseudo-science, 18, 31, 90, 344,
    386.
Psychical Research, 362, 395 *n.,*
    402.
Psychology, vi, 11, 23, 121, 170,
    247, 366–7, 405.
  activist, 38.
  descriptive, 33, 98.
  in relation to logic, 23, 24, 250,
    263, 281, 282, 296, 362.

Psychology, novelty in, 282, 325.
  personal, 31, 101.
  varieties of, 34.
  voluntarist, 38.
Purpose, 19, 21, 34, 48, 49, 54, 72,
    77, 80, *Ch. VI, §10,* 139,
    146, 152, 153, 158, 159,
    160, 176, 177, 185, 186,
    188, 189, 199, 216, 223,
    240, 248–9, 251, 252, 273,
    275, 282, 292, 314, 331,
    333, 342, 357, 361, 364,
    384, 390, 392, 407, 434,
    438, 441.
  determines truth and error, 184.
  infirmity of, 187.
  its satisfaction ' truth,' *Ch.*
    VIII, §8, 404, 417.
Pythagoras, 426.

Questions, 111, 117, 138, 155,
    192, 208, 213, 218, 224,
    244, 354–5, 362, 425.

Radio-activity, 199, 329.
Rationalism, 124, 413, 426, *Ch.*
    XIX, §16.
Read, Carveth, 346.
Realism, 130, 133, 413.
Reality, aim of truth, 119.
  ambiguous, *Ch. VII, §9.*
  apparent, 132.
  as claim, 132, 228.
  as formal, 226–7.
  as immanent, 130, 228–9.
  as transcendent, 129, 228–9.
  as unreal, 227.
  as value, 449.
  changes, 205, 207.
  confused with truth, 119.
  one ?, *Ch. XV, §13.*
  physical, 227, 311, 330, 359.
  psychical, 330.
  real, 132, 227.
  real for us, 226, 232, 444–8.
  ultimate, 232, 444.
Reason, 369, 412.
Recoils, 267, 286, 294.
Reflection, 54, 87, 196, 204, 321.

Reflex, 196–7.
Relativity, 149, 343, 367, 400, 412, 429.
   of truths, *Ch. VIII*, §5.
Relevance, *Ch. V*, 49, 139, 236, 273, 318, 348, 349, 392, 403.
   of consequences, 171, 174.
   of parts, 234, 315.
Religion, 170, 173, 174, 189.
Revaluation, 186, *Ch. XIX*, §2.
Riemann, 177, 432.
Risk, 47–8, 49, 71, *Ch. V*, §4, 82, 86, 149, 190, 203, 204, 207, 223, 230, 233, 285, 292–3, 299, 315, 317, 322, 336, 339–40, 348, 350, 354, 362, 375, *Ch. XVIII*, §6, 455.
Röntgen, W., 152.
Russell, B. A. W., 6, 118, 157, 372, 376, 414, 431 *n.*

Santayana, G., vi.
Scales of Notation, 436, 439.
Scepticism, 15, 17, 84, 144, 157, 169, 181, 231, 267, 288, 350.
Schiller, F. C. S., Axioms as Postulates, 160.
   Case for Psychical Belief, 395 *n.*
   Formal Logic, v, 3 *n.*, 5, 9 *n.*, 26 *n.*, 58 *n.*, 91 *n.*, 105 *n.*, 128 *n.*, 216 *n.*, 222 *n.*, 226 *n.*, 230 *n.*, 257 *n.*, 260 *n.*, 261 *n.*, 262 *n.*, 269 *n.*, 275 *n.*, 279 *n.*, 282, 283, 344 *n.*, 347 *n.*, 348 *n.*, 349 *n.*, 394 *n.*, 399 *n.*, 408 *n.*, 409 *n.*, 419 *n.*, 420 *n.*
   Humanism, 158 *n.*, 378 *n.*
   Hypothesis, 344 *n.*, 346.
   Origin of Bradley's Scepticism, 237 *n.*
   Personal Idealism, 123 *n.*, 230 *n.*, 253 *n.*
   Problems of Belief, 104 *n.*, 154 *n.*, 170 *n.*, 172 *n.*, 205 *n.*, 386 *n.*
   Studies in Humanism, 133 *n.*, 230 *n.*
   Tantalus, 2 *n.*, 105 *n.*

Schliemann, 422.
Science, 140, 170, 287, 296, 347, 441.
   ancient and modern, 370, 422.
   as method, 187.
   each has its world, 383.
   incipient, *Ch. XVII*, §6.
   individual and, 405, 453.
   not absolute, 387.
   not perfect, 140, 309–10.
   philosophy and, 360.
   progressive, 140, 151, 168, 187, 281, 316, 352.
   selective, 315–6.
   systems of, 146, 309, 317.
Scientific Method, 269, *Ch. XVII, XVIII*, 444, 453.
Selection, 19, 20, 25, 49, 52, 60, 66, 71–2, 75, 79, 80, 81, 82, 86, 87, 88, 91, 94, 185, 202, 217, 223, 225, 233 f., 299, 314, 315, 318, 321, 323, 349, 354, 360, 384, 387, 392, 403, 410, 434, 436, 452.
Self, 342, *Ch. XVII*, §12.
Self-development of thought, 266–7.
Self-evidence, 112, 115, 295–7.
   a claim, 128.
   logical and psychological, 112, 127.
Sensation, 219.
   erroneous, 188, 234.
   ' pure,' 195, 220.
   and hallucination, 220.
Senses, *Ch. XVII*, §§9–10, 429.
   fallible, 370.
   selective, 369.
Shaw, G. B., 290.
Sidgwick, A., vii, 21, 155.
Sidgwick's Ambiguity of the Middle, 126 *n.*, 261, 275, *Ch. XIV*, §4, 279, 291.
Singer, C., 344.
Situation, 81, 88, 92, 176, 190, 193, 201, 205, 206, 218, 226, 239, 242, 243, 248 f.
   thought, 198–9.

Socrates, 4, 19, 197, 289.
Solipsism, 132 *n.*, 170.
Sophists, 4.
Soul, 19, 374–5, 378, 435.
Species, 199, 257, 382.
Spinoza, 426.
Stebbing, Miss L. S., 158 *n.*
Stopping to think, 3, 51, Ch. X, §6.
Stout, G. F., 212, 284.
Subject, *Ch. XI*, §8, 218, 223, 231, 374–5, 403.
  of inquiry, 217, 342.
Survival-value, 129, 169–70.
Syllogism, 4, 32, 120–1, 123, 260.
  as coercive, 125, 138.
  as experiment, 290.
  as hypothesis, *Ch. XIV*, §5, 290.
  as liable to fallacy of Accident, 277.
  as not formally valid, 126 *n.*, *Ch. XIV*, §§3–5, *Ch. XV*, §4, 289.
  as *petitio*, 261, 262, 264, 274, 280, *Ch. XV*, §2.
  as proof, *Ch. XV*, §2.
  can it predict ?, 256, 273–4.
  premisses involve infinite regress, 126, 260.
  premisses not absolutely true, 125, 261.
  premisses selected, 138.
Syllogistic Reasoning, *Ch. XIV*.
  claims absolutely certainty, 269, 281.
  claims it cannot lose truth, 269, 281–2, 288.
  claims cogency, 269, *Ch. XV*, §2.
  claims formal validity, 269, 273, *Ch. XIV*, §§3–5.
  claims prediction, 273.
  claims truth, 269.
  claims value, *Ch. XIV*, §8.
  is hypothetical, 287, 295, 319.
System, 18, 101, 132, 140–1, 143, 174, 319, 330, 427, 428, *Ch. XIX*, §§10, 11, 15, 433, 434, 436–8.

System, as all-inclusive, 143, 301 f., *Ch. XV*, §12.
  as chaotic, 316.
  as ideal, 142–3.
  as not selective, 316.
  as one ?, *Ch. XV*, §13.
  as open or closed, 307, 317.
  as proof, *Ch. XV*, §8.
  as related to sciences, 309 f.
  as self-contradictory, 307, *Ch. XV*, §16.

Taylor, A. E., 432, 434.
Teleology, 67, 389.
Telepathy, 334.
Thackeray, W. M., 1.
Thinking, an abnormality, 195.
  an adaptation, 196–8, 205, 285.
  experimental, 285.
  not an end in itself, 242.
  perpetual, 241.
Thought, experimental, 362.
  instrumental to life, 122, 196.
  ' pure,' 239.
Totality of Reality; see Absolute and Whole.
Trains of thought, 72–3, 82, 101, 117, 125, 177, 180, 203, 240–1, *Ch. XII*, §4, 245, 247 f., 252, 263, 267, 441.
Transcendence in knowing, 131.
Translation, 61–2.
Truism, 254, 304.
Truth, *Ch. VI, VII, VIII*, 49.
  absolute, 23, 28, 29, 31, 84, 86, 97, 105, 107, 112, 115, 134, 146, 150, 157, 188, 191, 238, 260, 279, 293 f., 310–1, 350, 353, 354, 429, 451.
  abstracted from, 25.
  antedated, 186, *Ch. XIX*, §3.
  attractive, 123.
  claim, 23, 27, 28–9, 32, 43, 81, 97, *Ch. VI*, §9, 131, 139, 165, 169, 171, 245.
  coherent, 138.
  correspondence, *Ch. VII*, §8.
  debatable, 172, 185.

Truth, degrees of, 231, 311.
  dependent on meaning, 441.
  desirable, 123, 155.
  essentially dated, 420.
  eternal, 31–2, 352, 419, *Ch. XIX, §4.*
  formal, 24, 27, 29, 31, 97, 105, 177.
  general, 31–2.
  good of knowing, 148.
  growing, 207.
  has day, 169.
  historical, *Ch. XIX, §7,* 451.
  humanised, 136.
  humanist, *Ch. VIII,* 94, 174.
  incorrigible, 394 *n.*
  independent of man, *Ch. VII, §10.*
  irrelevant, 88, 187.
  isolated, 142.
  logical value, 32, 42, *Ch. VI, §3,* 114, *Ch. VIII, §3,* 151, 153, 154, 396.
  making of, 31, 164, 426.
  material, 30–1, 46, 260, 264.
  mathematical, 297, *Ch. XIX, §§8–12, 15.*
  necessary, *Ch. VII, §4,* 247, 287–8, 296, 337, 430.
  new, 140, 142, *Ch. XIV, §7.*
  not coherent, 313.
  not final, 281, 394 *n.,* 451.
  not impersonal, 207.
  partial, 37, 43–4.
  potential, *Ch. XIX, §5.*
  practical, 95.
  probable, 45, 260, 338, 401.
  real, 28, 29, 30, 102, 118.
  relative to evidence, 400–1.
  relative to good, 154.
  relative to man, 145.
  relative to place and time, 149.
  relevant, 135.
  revalued, *Ch. XIX, §2,* 418.
  seeking, 101, 111, 123, 126, 146, 158, 185, 203, 321.
  =success, 117, 147, 186.
  to be tested, 99, 110, 116, 130, 145, 168, 350, 421, 424.

Truth, total, 17.
  truest=best, 90, 107, 135, 154, 155, 169, 174, 191, 417.
  unknowable, 131, 157.
  unpleasant, 123–5.
  useful, 157, 421, 439, 441.

Understanding, *Ch. I, §1,* 49.
Uniformity of Nature, 408–9.
Unit, 357–8, 433–4, 437–8.
Universals, *Ch. IV, §§15–17,* 93, 149, 215–6, 274–5, 325, 344, 347, 406.
  abstract, 404.
  concrete, 20, 405–6.
  verbal meanings, 2, 6.
Universe, 84–5, 235, 309, 380, 384, 435.
Universe of Diction, 89, 165, 227.
Use, 32, 158, *Ch. VIII, §10,* 177, 250, 359, 414–5, *Ch. XX, §2.*
  and meaning, 421.
  of mathematics, *Ch. XIX, §12.*
  of verbal identity, 210, 292, 295.
Useful means, *Ch. VIII, §11.*
Usefulness, 421.

Vaihinger, 164.
Valid forms, 12.
Validity, 441.
  excluded by verification, 280.
  formal, 23, 27, 30, 32, 48, 79, 83, 92, 251, *Ch. XIII, §6, Ch. XIV, §5,* 284, 288, 317, 318–9, 348.
  illusory, 263, 284, 287, 299, 320, 395.
  a false ideal, 333.
  a substitute for truth, 54, 259.
  is 'good practically,' 266.
  is less than value, 45.
  is value, 265.
  of induction, 91.
  of Inference, *Ch. XIII, §9.*
  of Laws of Thought, 251.
  of proof, 14, 44.
  real, 216.

Validity, verbal, 14, *Ch. III*, §*13*.
  was strength, 120, 259.
Valuable Reasoning, *Ch. XVI*.
Valuable *versus* Valid, 44–5, 82,
  263, 319, 322.
Valuation, 34, 39, 91, *Ch. VIII*,
  §*4*, 426.
  an act, *Ch. III*, §*4*.
  implies valuer, 147.
  true and false, 98, 103, 147, 417.
  vicariousness of, 153.
Value, 34, 186, 348, 449.
  as claim, 32, 34, 43, 99, 153,
    249.
  as commensurable, 41, 155.
  as dependent on use, 442.
  as individual, 101.
  as logical, *Ch. III*.
  as negative, 40–1.
  as objective, 39.
  as psychic fact, *Ch. VI*, §*7*.
  as purposive, 77, *Ch. VI*, §*10*.
  as social, 41.
  as subjective, 101, 102.
  as true and false, *Ch. VIII*,
    §§*2–3*, 154.
  as validity, 26, 200, 259, 265,
    320.
  judgments, 66, 136, 305.
  species of, 102, *Ch. VI*, §*8*.
  'truer' is 'better,' 168.
  vocabulary of, 36.
Verbalism, 322.
  of Formal Logic, 118.
  of Greeks, *Ch. I*, §§*8–9*.

Verification, 31, 105 f., 132, 150,
  Ch. VIII, §*20*, 170, 171,
  240, 279, 280, 281, 282,
  287, 291, 295, 309, 320,
  322, 331, 346, *Ch. XVI*,
  §*14*, 358, 371, 421, 422,
  429, 441.
  not formally valid, 261.
Verner's Law, 411.
Vibrations, 368.
Volition, *Ch. XIX*, §*17*.
Voluntarism, vi, 78, 94, 267, 413,
  426, 444, *Ch. XX*, §*8*.

Whole, 25 *n.*, 86.
  chaotic, 79.
  infinite, 308.
  logical, 314.
  not all-inclusive, 182.
  opposed to relevance, 78.
  psychological, 314.
  selective, 232 *n.*, 314.
  of reality, 232.
  of truth, 84, 182–3.
Whymper, E., 150.
Will to believe, 173, 272, *Ch.
  XVI*, §*10*.
  to watch, 388.
Wilson, J. C., 178, 212.
Wilson, President W., 5.
Wishes, 117, 201, 208.
Working, 110, 115, 123, *Ch. VIII*,
  §§*9, 10*, 168, *Ch. VIII*, §*21*,
  239, 266, 268, 331, 363,
  424.